TURTLES ALL THE WAY DOWN

Prerequisites To Personal Genius

John Grinder
Judith DeLozier

Grinder & Associates

Published by
Grinder & Associates
P.O. Box 67295
Scotts Valley, CA 95067

Master Distributor
Metamorphous Advanced Product Services
P.O. Box 10616
Portland, OR 97210-0616

Editorial and Art Direction by Lori Stephens
Printed in the United States of America

Grinder, John.
Turtles all the way down : prerequisites to personal genius / John Grinder, Judith DeLozier.
p. cm.
Includes bibliographical references.
ISBN 1-55552-022-7 : $22.95
1. Neurolinguistic programming. I. DeLozier, Judith. II. Title.
BF637.N46G75 1994
158'.9—dc20 94-32322

ACKNOWLEDGMENTS

We wish to acknowledge to following people: the participants—
the other end of the loop:

C.E. Asherbranner
Suzanne Bailey
Nancy Beplat
Jean Blair
Larry Burnett
Georgene Burton
Britt Burton
Cosette Carter
Consuelo Casula
Susan Connors
Peggy Dean
Carmel Decroos
Skip Ellis
Carole Ellison
Rosalie Fedoruk
Judy Francis
Francis Friedman
Sherrie Funk
John Funk
Amber Goldstein
George Greenberg
Sharon Grimm
Thomas Grinder
Allan Harris
Christian Hart
Poppy Hawkins
Jack Hawley
Phil Herman
Kirk Hughes
Murray Johannsen
Janece Kline
Bob Kurtz
Phyllis Murray Linhart
Catherine Long
Kari Lyn
Jerry Mader
Stephanie Mader
Thomas Malloy
Susan Marcus
Diane Marshall
Robert McDonald
Philip Milroy
Pauline Monson
Jane Monteleone
Patricia Moore
Marshall Nechtow
David Pounds
Del Powell
Alan Power
Vera Reichenfeld-Tay
Jose Rodriguez
Marne Ryan
Antonio Santos
Steven Silverman

John Simmonds
Steve Smolinsky
Jane St. Sauveur
John Stone
James Taylor
Joel Teague
Sylvia Topel
Maureen Toth
Mumtaz Vishal
Karen Weihs
Richard Zarro
Marilyn Zatkin
Deborah Zeigler

Matundu Mamingi to our African and American drummer and dancer friends

TaTitos Sompa
TaMbemba
TaMalonga
Fred Simpson

Thanks to Gary-Michael Bean for his suggestions and work.

Thanks to our staff

Laura Grinder   Stephanie Mader

Mark Carroll   Jerry Mader

Thanks to our friends who played such an important role in commenting.

Bob Dilts
Don Steiny
Susan Marcus

TABLE OF CONTENTS

Reasonable men adapt themselves to the world, unreasonable men attempt to adapt the world to themselves. That's why all progress depends on unreasonable men.

George Bernard Shaw

To our former teacher

Gregory Bateson

We hope he would be, at least, amused.

John Grinder

Judith DeLozier

WARNING TO THE READER

Neuro Linguistic Programming (NLP) represents a significant advance in the development of human choice. It places at the discretion of the skilled and balanced practitioner options for living with quality which were previously assigned variously to fate, chance, genetics, accidents and divine influence. It is important to me to explicate at least partially what I intend by the descriptive phrase, *skilled and balanced.*

The *skill* issue points to the requirement in the mastery of any interesting human skill set for a commitment to practice, the personal discipline on the part of the would-be NLP practitioner to arrange his or her own context for exploring, learning and ultimately mastering of the actual body of patterning called NLP. Success at this task identifies a learner, and the result a technician.

The *balanced* issue refers to two requirements, first, the learner's ability to integrate the skill set (mastered by the technician) into each and every area of their life, personal as well as professional. Secondly, once this integration of the technical skill set has occurred, the individual is faced with the awesome responsibility of exercising these choices with some wisdom. At this point, the caterpillar bursts the confinement of the cocoon, the technician transforms herself/himself into an artist.

All the above is a somewhat circuitous way of cautioning the would-be NLP practitioner. The world at the moment seems rather overflowing with people purporting to offer training in NLP. It is here in selecting a mentor that you, the reader, may begin to exercise one of the most crucial abilities associated with artistry in the practice of NLP—namely, that of assessing the congruency of the purported trainer. If your intuitions caution you, if you detect a discrepancy between the verbal presentation of such a person and their actual behavior and performance, keep moving and looking for an appropriate model.

If you are seriously interested in having access to quality training or business consulting applications which rest firmly on the foundation of NLP which I intended when I co-created the discipline, I invite you to contact me at:

John Grinder
QUANTUM LEAP
P.O. Box 67359
Scotts Valley, CA 95067-7359
TEL) 408-457-0529
FAX) 408-457-2834

A BEGINNING

William James is usually considered the father of American psychology.[1] He was once invited to deliver a series of lectures at Harvard on a topic of his choosing. These lectures were presented on the green and were special in that they were open to the public. After some deliberation, he chose boldly and the title for his first presentation was *Can One Prove The Existence of God?*, a topic sure to raise eyebrows in the early part of this century in New England.

Thus, it was with some trepidation that he watched the audience file into the lecture hall and, sure enough, at the very last moment, a little old lady rushed down the center aisle and deposited herself from row center.

Professor James presented his topic with his usual wit and charm. He noted as he worked his way through his lecture that the little old lady was very attentive and seemed to be enjoying herself—he did mark the fact that she seemed to laugh when no one else did. Nevertheless, all seemed quite in order.

At the end of the presentation, which was very well received, the inevitable queue formed. And, of course, at the end of the queue was the little old lady. When her turn came, she looked up brightly at James and said:

"Dr. James, I very much enjoyed your lecture. But I do still have one question."

"Please, madame, ask your question!" returned William James courteously.

"Well, Dr. James," she replied with a glint in her eye, "If there's no God, what keeps the earth from falling down?"

James quickly reviewed his options—he considered such explanatory notions as centripetal force, gravitational systems . . . but wisely chose to respond in a way as to learn something from this woman. Turning his attention back to her, he said, "Madame, I would be happy to answer your question, but tell me what it is that you believe keeps the earth from falling down?"

"Why, that's very simple, Dr. James, the earth is resting on the back of a gigantic turtle!"

James mused to himself over her extraordinary response for a moment and then with a hint of triumph in his voice asked the obvious question. "The, pray tell me, Madame, what keeps this gigantic turtle from falling down?"

"No! No! No! Dr. James," replied the little old lady, "You can't get me there—it's turtles all the way down!"

PREFACE

Immediate Context

In March of 1986, the two of us, John Grinder and Judith DeLozier, conducted a seminar called *Prerequisites To Personal Genius* in San Francisco, California with people from North and South America, Europe and Africa.

For over twenty-five cumulative years, we have developed models of people who were considered geniuses by our society. In this modeling, certain simple personal competencies were again and again uncovered—independent of substance—whether the genius was a master hypnotist, strategic corporate planner, dancer, or negotiator. These formal principles, while simple, are not easy. The task facing us was to assist the seminar participant in making the arrangements for the development and integration of these competencies—these prerequisites to personal genius. This document is the consequence of that San Francisco seminar and has the same purpose. It is, however, important to understand that there are profound differences between a seminar with face-to-face communication and a written document. The major difference revolves around the fact that the bulk of the communication in a face-to-face seminar is nonverbal and, of course, a written document relies exclusively on language.

Thus, we were challenged with the task of developing a balanced document which somehow was faithful to the experiences of the seminar and at the same time coded exclusively in a linear verbal code. In order to accomplish this, inserts were added to promote universality and participation on the part of the reader and to fill in gaps which were covered by nonverbal communication in the face-to-face experience of the seminar. Thus the document you are about to read is partially a verbal transcript from the seminar and partially a translation of portions of the nonverbal communication from that seminar into the verbal code. Further, while the seminar was completed in five days, it was, in a deeper sense, and is truly unfinished both for us and the participants—the process had been put into movement. Similarly, this written document is unfinished. May it reverberate at length throughout your neurology.

Historical Context

Now just what's this business about turtles?

The twentieth century Westerner prides himself or herself on the plethora of choices he or she may exercise. With the proper amount of capital, a Westerner can, for example, choose to buy a Chevrolet Blazer or a Toyota four wheel drive pickup, or possibly a Ford Mustang—more importantly, he can even choose not to have an automobile.

Similarly, modern Westerners can choose an empirically-based epistemology or a spiritually-based epistemology, even a nihilistic epistemology—but most importantly, they cannot not have an epistemology. They may not want one—they may even resist with all their resources some particular epistemology, but resistance itself in such a case would be an epistemological act.

A quarter of a century or so ago, Gregory Bateson recognized and coded in his writings a profound fact about human communication so obvious that it had literally escaped the work of quite able researchers in the field of human behavior for centuries. When two members of our species are face-to-face and one offers a communication to the other, all other aspects of the situation being conventional (e.g., the communication offered falls within sensory channels of the other person, etc.), then the second person cannot *not* communicate. There is, of course, plenty of latitude and many choices about how the second person may communicate in responding—words, gestures, sound, movement, all of which will be properly perceived by the first person as responses to their first communication. Notice even the limiting case—the refusal to respond—is itself a communication. When someone says to you that they cannot communicate with so-and-so, their position is epistemologically unsound. What they mean is that they are as yet unable to elicit from this particular so-and-so the responses they want.

Communication and epistemology are similar in this respect—

they are ubiquitous. One cannot *not* communicate and further one cannot *not* have an epistemology—it may be unconscious, unwanted, entirely unaccessible to its owner, but it is revealed with precision by that person's behavior.

Epistemology is the human discipline which systematically explores the possibility of human knowledge. Beginning with questions of what we can know and how we come to know what we think we know, epistemology moves to the question—can we know anything at all? The fact that epistemology is considered esoteric by Westerners is a telling indicator of how unexamined the foundation of our own beliefs, values, and perceptions is and, critically, therefore, how unexamined is the foundation of those behaviors which flow from our beliefs, values, and perceptions.

Westerners are usually amused the first few times they encounter the tongue-in-cheek definitions of a pessimist and an optimist. A pessimist is a person who perceives, values, and acts upon a container which has 50% of its volume as half-empty, while an optimist, we are assured, perceives, values, and acts upon the container as if it were half-full.

Somewhat less amusing are anecdotes such as the putative Head Start experiment done in New York some decades ago. A group of children of the same age group were randomly sorted into two groups, A and B. These groups then took a battery of I.Q. and achievement tests, and the differences in the test scores between the two groups were negligible. Next, the teachers who would in the approaching school year be responsible for instructing—for educating—these young people were told that the test results indicated that Group A was educationally gifted while Group B was educationally handicapped. When the two groups were re-tested on the same battery of tests six months later—the scores revealed that the children and the teachers had managed to make it work out just right. Group A tested gifted and Group B, handicapped.

Finally, entirely unamusing are the stories (which filter anemically through the reducing value we call our national press) which chronicle the inability of our political leaders to find equitable resolutions to the differences which are daily in Central America, Afghanistan, the Middle East . . . killing men, women and children who simply want to live in peace. Each of these are quickly and easily traceable to epistemological differences which remain unexplored.

So much of this document was inspired by the work of Gregory Bateson that we believe it is useful for the reader to have some appreciation of the context to which he was responding. Bateson was a highly creative, synthetic thinker. By synthetic, we refer to his ability to discern pattern independent of substance or context, and with breathtaking moves, he brought together in a convincing way materials which had previously been completely unassociated—thereby revealing a deeper and more satisfying patterning. So what were the salient epistemological positions to which he was responding?

The two classic epistemological polar positions in the 18th century can be usefully represented by Hume, in the British empiricist tradition, and Kant in the German idealist tradition. We will crudely sketch these positions.

The basic organizing principle in the empiricist tradition was alarmingly simple.

There is nothing in the mind which
did not come from the senses.

A position like this, when baldly presented as we have articulated it here, seems disturbingly incomplete, and this is correct—the context in which it was formulated is missing. If you had been raised in an environment where learned men were hotly debating the number of angels who could dance on the head of a pin, the above empiricist doctrine would have been a breath of fresh air. The difficulty with the position is that it rejects human beings as active agents in creating experience. More fundamentally, it cannot account for one of the most elementary experiences of the human condition—two human beings witnessing the same real world event will subsequently provide differences in their individual accounts of what occurred—differences which become more numerous as one demands more and more detail in their accounts.

On the other pole in this controversy was Kant, who bit off a lot more than was either chewable or digestible. The famous Kantian solution was to assign to each human being a set of innate, genetically specified categories through which we experience the world—what we call in the following document, perceptual filters. Kant certainly recognizes with his innate categories of perception a tremendous contribution to experience on the part of the human beings involved. Unfortunately, however, the cost is exorbitant; if our experiences are the result of deeply set filters, independent of the real world, then our ability to know the world starts to deteriorate rapidly and the world begins to get rather slippery.

It is amusing to note that Kant's position settles into an equally unattractive consequence at the individual level with respect to the same difference of perception issue on which Hume failed. Either Kant similarly cannot account for differences in perception or must assign them to faulty neurological developments of the innate categories. In either case, we believe Bateson would have commented, "Shoddy epistemology!"

There are two points on which both of these epistemological positions are quite unsatisfactory. First, note that in both cases, there is little room for individual responsibility. If the real world impresses certain sensations on the individual neurology as a function of the physical properties of the stimulus, or if we experience the stimulus sensations solely as a function of innate perceptual categories, the question of personal responsibility is moot.

The second point is the way these positions fall out with respect to the mind/body split. Hume and his troop are condemned to wander about, entertaining all and only experiences which are sensory-based, while Kant and his band sit immobilized, locked into their (individual) neurologies. Hume and the empiricist have the task of freeing themselves from the tyranny of an exclusively sensory world, while Kant and his idealists, trapped in mental categories, try to find a way back out to the real world. Those readers who have had experience working professionally with mental patients will recognize these two positions as characteristic syndromes of patient populations. Thus with respect to the mind/body issue, the empiricists have to make do with patterning exclusively in the physical world—psychology collapses into physics—while the idealists must fight for and justify each and every link from their starting position (the mind) to the world, if any such connections can be demonstrated. How would we know? In fact, the mentalist position, unburdened with any anchor to the physical world, historically tends to float off in the direction of spiritualism.

Thus, we have the general intellectual climate which Bateson was addressing. The trick was to synthesize the two polar and obviously overdrawn positions of empiricist and idealist. By accident of his birth, he tended to start with the empiricist tradition and find ways of rebalancing it. He knew in a very deep way that the 19th and 20th century methodological seduction of psychology by the pre-eminently successful physical sciences was an historical tragedy—a muddledness of astonishing proportions, an error of both logical typing and logical level. Yet, his task was to demonstrate that there are fundamental differences between the patterns of the physical, sensible world and the patterns of the world in the mind without falling into mysticism. He argued this point in a number of ways. He was, for example, quite intolerant of the fuzzy kind of thinking characteristic of the uncritical importation into discussions of mind of the physical phenomenon of *energy*. If billiard ball A strikes billiard ball B with a certain velocity, mass, and angle of impact, and the frictional characteristics of the surface they are both supported by are specified, then certain things are knowable:

1. The final resting places of A and B.
2. Independent of the particular values of A and B with respect to mass, speed, and angle of impact, one may state with confidence that the second law of thermodynamics will be respected, i.e., the physical energy embodied in the original moving billiard ball, prior to impact, will be preserved (accounted for) in the ensuing collision.

In other words, in non-living systems, there is a conservation of energy—a pattern apparently universally present. Contrast this with an analogous interaction in living systems. If I specify for you the starting position, velocity, mass, and angle and point of contact of my foot and my dog, Spirit, you will not be able to predict much. It's not even obvious that my foot will end up on the end of my leg as opposed to ending up in Spirit's mouth some distance away from the rest of my leg. To distinguish this non-conservative interaction—the typical one in living systems—from its counterpart in the physical world, Bateson referred to this as collateral energy.

Or again, his brilliant insight that both Darwin and Lamark were correct—Darwin's evolutionary contracts fit adequately the presently known world of biological forms and Lamark's evolutionary constructs are the drivers in the cultural world of ideas—is another example of his steadfast insistence that different patterns were operating in the physical world and the world of mind. While Bateson was unwavering in his perception that the patterns and laws which specify the structure of the world of mind and the physical were distinct, he never proposed a mechanism to explain how this difference came about. Bateson's thesis itself is strongly supported by a contemporary of his—the man usually considered the leading physicist of the 20th century.

> I see on the one side the totality of sense-experiences, and, on the other, the totality of the concepts and propositions. The relations between the concepts and propositions among themselves and each other are of a logical nature, the business of logical thinking is strictly limited to the achievement of the connections between concepts and propositions among each other according to firmly laid down rules, which are the concern of logic. The concepts and propositions get "meaning," viz., "content," only through their connection with sense-experiences. The connection of the latter with the former is purely intuitive, not itself of a logical nature. The degree of uncertainty which this connection, viz., intuitive combination, can be undertaken, and nothing else, differentiates empty fantasy from scientific "truth." The system of concepts is a creation of man together with the rules of syntax, which constitute the structure of the conceptual systems.
>
> Albert Einstein, *Autobiographical Notes,* p. 13

Einstein is explicit in identifying logic and syntax with operations of the world of mind which are by no means reflections of events in the physical world, nor are they justified by events in the physical world. Indeed, he is precise about the justification for such mental activity.

> The production of some sort of order among sense impressions, this order being produced by the creation of general concepts, relations between these concepts, and by definite relations of some kind between the concepts and sense experience . . . In guiding us in the creation of such an order of sense experiences, success alone is the determining factor.
>
> Albert Einstein, *Physics and Reality,* p. 292

Or again:

> All our thinking is of this nature of free play with concepts; the justification for this play lies in the measure of survey over the experience of the senses which we are able to achieve with its aid. The concept of "truth" cannot yet be applied to such a structure.
>
> Albert Einstein, *Autobiographical Notes,* p. 7

Turtles is in part a record of our effort in extending and making more explicit some of the splendid work of Gregory Bateson. In particular, we propose a very precise mechanism which accounts for this profoundly important distinction without an appeal to mysticism. This mechanism, tied tightly to the syntax of natural language systems, is presented and discussed in a humorous anecdote in Day Five.

Like Bateson, Einstein recognized the danger of the power of a syntactic system when detached from its context.

> In an early stage, the words may correspond directly to impressions. At a later stage, this direct connection is lost insofar as some words convey relations to perceptions only if used in "or," "thing." Then word-groups rather than single words refer to perceptions. When language becomes thus partially independent from the background of impressions, a greater coherence is gained.
>
> Only at this further development where frequent use is made of so-called abstract concepts, language becomes an instrument of reasoning in the true sense of the word. But it is also this development which turns language into a dangerous source of error and deception. Everything depends on the degree to which words and word-combinations correspond to the world of impression.
>
> Albert Einstein, *The Common Language of Science*

This theme constantly reoccurs in this document. Bateson was elegant in his discussion of the consequences of the use of a highly distortive, linear verbal code to represent the complex, recursive cybernetic natural world in, for example, his presentation of sentences like:

The man cut the tree down with an axe.

This sentence is presumed to represent a complex interaction among three reasonably stable elements—a man, a tree, and an axe. The syntax of English codes into a certain class of verbs a notion of agency or causality—imputing to whatever noun occupies the subject position (if the verb is in active voice) a sense of agency. Notice, however, that there are other verbal codings of this interaction which are equally interesting from an epistemologist's position. Suppose we roughly paraphrase the linguistic representation, unpacking the verb so as to make it more obvious:

The man caused the tree to be cut down
using the instrument of an axe.

Another way to appreciate what Bateson was warning us about is to consider the interaction functionally.

$f(x) \rightarrow y$
where
x is the man mentioned in the original sentence
and
y is the axe and tree.

The implicit claim revealed by this notation is that if you know (by observation or by assignment) the movements and actions of x (the man), then the consequences for the tree and the axe are predictable. As Bateson pointed out, it's also true that if I know the movements of the axe, I can predict the movements and behavior of the man and the tree (at least in the tightly circumscribed context identified by the original sentence). In other words, the axe can be perceived as the independent variable (x), and the man and tree as dependent variables (y).

Or as an epistemological flexibility drill, note that if I make the notch cut in the tree after the first swing of the axe the independent variable (x), the actions and movements of the man and the axe become similarly predictable.

We have appreciated R. D. Laing's fine coding of repression as forgetting that you forgot. And this insidious, covert quality of our verbal code has something of this same character. Note, here, we are not saying that the original sentence is wrong—only that the syntax of natural language removes certain important perceptual choices, resulting in what we called a Jackdaw epistemology (a belief system built on a single unchanging perceptual position). It seems clear to us that at least some of the major practices which have created local environmental crises would be impossible if we were to routinely occupy multiple perceptual positions in our decision-making (the triple description condition developed in the following text). Most important, we think, is the observation that the structure of the code we most commonly use in mediating our experience among ourselves and in our instructions with the world has built-in decisions

.. are deeply epistemological and of which we are unaware. As Bateson warns, unless there is some corrective rebalancing of these distortions which are part of the structure of language, we as a species may well soon be, as they say in the major leagues, out of here.

With hindsight, looking back from the 20th century to the classic 18th century, empiricist position, it is relatively easy to understand the error in both logical typing and logical level committed by the empiricists. They confused the rules which govern the operations of the physical world with the rules which govern the operations of the act of representing the physical world. The rules that apply in the physical world do not necessarily apply in the representation of the physical world.

To us, a central issue in examining epistemologies is how they account for the common situation that, given the same real world experiences, two people will honestly report profound differences in what occurred. How this issue is addressed will strongly determine the questions of personal responsibility and the so-called mind/body split. We call your attention back to a portion of one of the statements by Einstein:

> The concepts and propositions get "meaning," viz., "content," only through their connection with sense-experiences. The connection of the latter with the former is purely intuitive, not itself of a logical nature. The degree of uncertainty which this connection, viz., intuitive combination, can be undertaken, and nothing else, differentiates empty fantasy from scientific "truth."
>
> Albert Einstein, *Autobiographical Notes,* p. 13

In effect, Einstein is warning that until this "intuitive combination"—this connecting of concepts and sense impressions—is explicated, we cannot discriminate fantasy from fact in a deep sense. Our epistemologies are very shaky. Perhaps Bateson's finest contribution to this endeavor comes from his surprisingly simple notion of the *transform.* The human neurology receiving certain signals at the peripheral sense organ transforms that information from the physical world in a series of transforms, deleting and distorting it at each step until it reaches the central nervous system and is accepted as reality. Epistemology thereby becomes a well-defined task: to map the specific rules of transformation that information is subjected to in its long journey from the world to consciousness. And this was his hope—this is what he warns us we ought to be about. Bateson's transforms—fully explicated sometime in the future—will be the link which heals the Western mind/body split. The technology called Neurolinguistic Programming has begun an explication of this "intuitive combination" of Einstein. These transforms of Bateson; the process tools of the 4-tuple; representational systems; synesthesia patterns; Meta-models of language: all are cornerstones in the exploration of this mapping between sense impressions and concepts. And until this work is developed, the decisions which we inevitably must make to resolve differences will drift toward violence. This document makes a first step in this endeavor toward understanding.

Counsel To The Reader

We wish to offer some counsel as to how the reader might best use this document. The people who participated in the seminar found this format worked well, and we hope it has a similar effect for the reader. Each day we cycled on the same themes, so that one day we might be verbally explicit and on another day, the same theme would appear metaphorically. We drew from a wide range of metaphors both personal and cultural. If the reader encounters an example or metaphor which does not seem relevant to the point under discussion, we urge you to carry on with the confidence that the point is made repeatedly either explicitly or implicitly each day. So keep moving.

The reader might note that movement as a form of integration was an extremely important aspect of this seminar, as each day we danced, played music, and sang with TaTitos Sompa, TaMbemba, TaMalonga of the Kongo and Fred Simpson of California.

PREREQUISITE FOR PERSONAL GENIUS

Presented
by
John Grinder & Judith DeLozier

DAY ONE

John: Good morning, greetings and welcome. It would be consistent with the kind of wisdom, the kind of consideration of context that we want to make the focus of the next five days, from the very beginning to request full attention on your part. And I have at least two attentions in mind when I say full attention. There's what we usually call consciousness, that dynamic process of picking what parts of the world you're going to sample in awareness. In Castaneda's work that's called first attention. Then there's a second, less accessible part of us that contains, at least potentially, the kind of wisdom that I wish to develop as part of what we do here together called second attention.

Judy: . . . or the unconscious . . .

John: . . . and we need the commitment of both of those attentions to do what we have in mind for these next five days. This seminar will be unlike any other seminar you've done with us —this is not a technically oriented seminar.

It's like a feast. We've all come to a banquet and Judith and I are responsible for setting the table and I will reassure you that all the major food groups are represented. (Laughter) Now, your task in participating in this banquet is to make choices; you don't have to eat everything. There are some things you already know about and some things that you want to eat because you do know about them and they're lovely. There are other things you've never tried. You can try little bits and see how you like them. So your responsibility is that of the responsibility of an engaged guest at a feast. You're not to overeat. Certainly I would want you to sample widely.

The purpose of this seminar altogether is to make the arrangements, both structural and dynamic, in ourselves and in you as the participants here in the seminar which are prerequisite for a blossoming of personal genius in each and every one of us.

Judy: We're going to address the issue of artistry. Every artistic act presupposes a certain level of skill that a person has to attain. Once you've acquired the skills, the techniques, then you know the rules. And when you know the rules then you can bend them in a well formed way and that's artistry. So as you move through technique you move towards art—you move towards ecology. You move towards deeper and multilevel representation and that's what we are here to do.

John: Children, especially around the time of the acquisition of language, will often offer us verbal representations which seem poetic to us. They bring together in the syntactic structure of a sentence things which we've never run across at least in our adult experience. They'll attribute to the world an animacy which seems to be missing from adult consciousness. There is a sense of full participation, of identification with the world, which reminds us of possibilities which we have perhaps left behind us as adults. And the child, in bringing together sequences of words in syntactic constructions that we would never have considered associated ourselves as adults, is being a funny kind of poet. Many times what they say comes from a difference in perception which is deeper than just the linguistic competency that they're still acquiring. And sometimes by accident the juxtaposition of words trigger representations in the adult listener which are not available in states of normal perception.

Judy: It's important to give full consideration to both attentions in what we do. We're going to develop a discussion, a series of experiences with you, which proposes certain kinds of relationships between first and second attention. Relationships of respect, communication, a recognition of what functions are appropriate for first attention and what functions could best be done by second attention. In the second attention are riches which we don't normally consider in first attention—worlds of possibility which are only hinted at in states of normal consciousness. First attention tends to be very purposive, rather single-minded, very outcome-oriented, and not particularly wise. We are seeking models that will serve for this complex relationship between first and second attention. One area rich in suggestions is traditional cultures.

John: Consider what occurs when contact is made between two cultures, one technical and one traditional. Typically, the technosociety has as its representatives people who are very very purposive in their behavior, very first-attention oriented. And in the short run in a clash between first and second attentions at a cultural level the first attention will tend to dominate, will tend to succeed. And the sense of loss, the anguish at the destruction of the difference available in the traditional peoples is a demonstration of the recognition at second attention of lack of wisdom in first attention. Those of you who work in psychotherapy or education or who do consulting in the business context can appreciate how a balance between first and second attentions is essential for personal health and well-being in yourself and others. Both at the group and the individual level there are grave repercussions of how the first-attention/second-attention interface is designed.

We had the good fortune some years back to live on a plot of land for a couple of years, Judy and I both, with a couple of amazing characters. Actually quite a few of them. One of the amazing characters who we've crossed paths with was a tall, sloped-shouldered Englishman by the name of Gregory Bateson. And he used to wander about the property carefully inspecting the world, making his own observations, one of the geniuses that I really treasure having contact with. While content of this seminar really is the responsibility of Judith DeLozier and myself, we have drawn very very heavily on Gregory's work...

Judy: ... in order to expand it. ... in order to fill in some gaps. I have something I would like to read from an article called

"Style, Grace, and Information in Primitive Art" by Gregory Bateson.[1]

Aldous Huxley used to say that the central problem for humanity is the quest for *grace*. This word he used in what he thought was the sense in which it is used in the New Testament. He explained the word, however, in his own terms. He argued—like Walt Whitman—that the communication and behavior of animals has a naiveté, a simplicity, which man has lost. Man's behavior is corrupted by deceit —even self-deceit—by purpose, and by self-consciousness. As Aldous saw the matter, man has lost the "grace" which animals still have.

In terms of this contrast, Aldous argued that God resembles the animals rather than man: He is ideally unable to deceive and incapable of internal confusions.

In the total scale of beings, therefore, man is as if displaced sideways and lacks that grace which the animals have and which God has.

I argue that art is a part of man's quest for grace; sometimes his ecstasy in partial success, sometimes his rage and agony at failure.

I argue also that there are many species of grace within the major genus; and also that there are many kinds of failure and frustration and departure from grace. No doubt each culture has its characteristic species of grace toward which its artists strive, and its own species of failure.

Some cultures may foster a negative approach to this difficult integration, an avoidance of complexity by crass preference either for total consciousness or total unconsciousness. Their art is unlikely to be "great."

I shall argue that the problem of grace is fundamentally a problem of integration and that what is to be integrated is the diverse parts of the mind—especially those multiple levels of which one extreme is called "consciousness" and the other the "unconscious." For the attainment of grace, the reasons of the heart must be integrated with the reasons of the reason.

John: In particular we're proposing that health on the positive side is a state which indicates that the organism who's involved has been very very careful not to cut through circuits internal to him or herself. The issue here is integrity. Alcoholics, for example, are individuals who have drawn a line inside of their own circuitry where they have disassociated a part, the so-called alcoholic part. From first attention they do not recognize themselves in that part. And the line that they've drawn crosses circuits they have to have intact for their own integrity—in order for an integrated, ecological solution to the addiction to occur. If we draw the lines that define ourselves without respect for the integrity of the circuits that we need for feedback, for example, we've placed ourselves formally in the same position as the alcoholic has. We wish to give some rigor to the theme of chunking so as to respect the integrity of your own circuits and the circuits of the people who you merge with at various times for purposes of joint action and experience.

John: Bateson has a really enlightening description of where the self is for a blind man. The blind man moving through the world typically uses a cane. And Gregory's question is: Where does the blind man define the boundaries of self? Where do you draw those lines? Does it stop at the point of interface between the hand and the cane?

Judy: Is it halfway down the cane? Is it all the way to the end of the cane?

John: Those of you who've raced motorcycles or cars or flown airplanes know perfectly well that in a race car your self goes down to and includes the contact with the medium that you're driving over or moving through all the way to where the tires make contact with the road.

Judy: And the boundaries of self have changed. For example, riding a horse. There's Judy, there's the horse, and then there's Judy plus the horse and each of these units have different boundaries. We're calling your second attention to wake up and to serve as a guide for us and for yourselves in what happens over these next five days. Each of us has a personal ecology and a wisdom to ourselves which, if it's respected, will provide the foundation for, or, as the title of the workshop proposes, will take care of the prerequisites for personal genius. . . . What would be an example of shrinking your self-definition? In what context might that be useful?

Man: Pain.

John: Pain, absolutely. There is within us a natural predilection toward identification with other organisms and species. So when I look at Larry it is not difficult for me to identify with him as another man operating in a similar situation to the one I'm in. I can easily identify with him—even extend my sense of self to include him. Now if something catastrophic were to happen to Larry and I were the individual available to assist him—for example, there's a car accident and he's injured in some way, it's extremely important for me to be able to withdraw that identification on a temporary basis so as not to be drawn into the same state of reduced resourcefulness that he's in because of direct physical trauma. Were I to do that, I would not be able typically to act with the effectiveness required for me to reach out and do the best I know how for this brother by taking care of his injury. It's a professional requirement of people who work in emergency rooms that they both be able to extend themselves to demonstrate to the person that they're in good hands. And at the same time they must be able to withdraw the self so that the identification process is not so strong that it removes the resourcefulness they need to make the appropriate medical response.

Judy: The phrase "the definition of self" is dangerously misleading—the self is not a fixed thing, it's constantly changing. Thus we will be talking about self as a function as opposed to an identity.

John: I have been visited over the last six months by a succession of close friends and acquaintances, highly trained, highly skilled, creative individuals, who are masters, literally, of the technology which Judith and myself and a couple of other people were instrumental in formulating, in making explicit. They were, as one of them so aptly put it, bumping into the world every time they turned around. They were successful and capable at any short term objective in achieving exactly what they went after. But it was as if there was a lack of wisdom over the longer run in the class of choices that they did make. In a sense, the technology gave them the ability to succeed where in some way, without the technology, they might not have been so quick to pick that objective, to take that particular pathway. What struck me as I worked with these talented people was there was an overall lack of aesthetics, lack of artistry, to what they were doing and especially an overemphasis on first attention. A great deal of what we have to propose here involves a rebalancing as well as placing an aesthetic frame around the tools that you've been exposed to, the technology, Neuro-Linguistic Programming (NLP).

Judy: This workshop is designed to place this technology called NLP in a larger historical context—the history of epistemology. Where does NLP really fit in terms of history of thinking and other work that's been done in the same area and how is NLP an extention of that knowledge? For me it wasn't going out and doing experiments—"Do successful people really look up and right every time they're successful?" I don't know. Maybe they do, maybe they don't, but that wasn't the kind of wisdom that I personally was interested in.

John: What justifications does a man or woman typically have for selecting anthropology as a profession? From the time I was a small child with the very strong culture that my family of origin created for me, it seemed to me obvious what the justification is. Each time that I went to school or went home with a new friend from school my nervous system would have a celebration in discovering differences perceptually from what it had anticipated—what it had expected.

Judy: So *difference* is the difference that makes the difference according to Gregory Bateson. When I say nothing comes of nothing . . . What is that wonderful thing that happens when you meet people from different cultures or you read books about different cultures?—it's difference. Gregory talks about nothing coming of nothing. Just consider our neurology—we're really talking about double descriptions; we're asking, "Where does the new information come from?" Take binocular vision as an example: The difference between information provided by one retina and that provided by the other retina produces new information—information about depth is created. So even at the basis of neurology, nothing comes of nothing. Double description is the vehicle for new information.

John: Can you do this? Can you close one eye and see a flat world in front of you? Do it! I'm curious. Do each eye in turn because you'll get a different effect typically with one eye as opposed to the other. So from where I'm sitting, of course, when I close one eye, I can make you all equidistant from me. How many people can do that? How many have that perceptual shift available to them? Do you understand the sense in which those people who can recover that perceptual experience are seeing "more truly" than the rest of us?

Judy: As some of you know, we often suggest as a flexibility drill in exploring reality strategies, that you develop your choices to the point where you can hallucinate, say, your dog or cat sitting right here with the same visual reality value that you see me with. Once you've mastered your own representational ability to that degree, the question of being able to discriminate between shared reality and personally generated reality comes up. Typically, the person involved instinctively turns to double description as the way out—in this case, the person will reach out and differentiate the hallucinated from the actual objects by touch, thereby reassuring themselves by comparison using the information from a second representation. Shakespeare adequately describes the situation in *Macbeth:*[2]

> Is this a dagger I see before me,
> The handle toward my hand, come let me clutch thee
> I have thee not and yet I see thee still
> Art thou not, fatal vision, sensible
> To feeling as to sight, or art thou but
> a dagger of the mind, a false creation
> Proceeding from the heat-oppressed brain?
> I see thee yet, in form as palpable
> as this which I now draw
> Thou marshallest me the way I was going;
> and such an instrument I was to use.
> Mine eyes are made the fools o' the other senses,
> Or else worth all the rest: I see thee still,

John: You know what happened in thirteenth-century Italy. A lot of things happened in thirteenth-century . . . (laughter) One of the things that happened in thirteenth-century Italy that I'm interested in is that if you look at the visual art available before . . .

Marne: (interrupting) I'm not real good with timelines and that sort of thing but I think that's when they discovered depth perception in their paintings.

John: Perspective. They found a way, and listen to this very carefully, of mechanically distorting the relationships they knew to be true by measuring them in the world in three dimensions onto a two-dimensional surface. The purpose of this mechanical distortion is to fit the distortions in the human visual nervous system in such a way that the end two-dimensional result would appear to be three-dimensional. Mapping from three dimensions onto two dimensions is a good example of how first-attention reduction occurs when first attention tries to appreciate second-attention process. What is it that they did? Did you hear what I said? Both attentions.

I once stood on a small hill in the city of Athens, Philopappus, and looked across a distance at a larger hill, the two main hills in the area, and the second hill was called the Acropolis, and there's one structure from Philopappus that drew my eye as I looked across at the Acropolis. It was the Parthenon, now largely a series of columns with a partial roof and a foundation because the Greeks were foolish enough to put munitions inside of it during one of the wars with the Turks who then blew it up. When I climbed to the top of the Philopappus and looked across that intervening kilometer or so at the Parthenon . . . it was as if my body sang at that point. There was something so congruent about my visual experience that see-feel circuits in me were triggered. It was as if my body had found a deep natural song that it could sing that belonged there at that time. Now the startling thing is that if you now make that journey, if you walk down off Philopappus and walk over and up to the top of the Acropolis and take a tape measure and begin to measure the distance between the columns and the actual circumference of the columns—they are tapering as they move upward (until the guards come along and throw you out)—as you make those measurements you'll discover, as in the case of thirteenth-century Italy, the Greeks had a wisdom that somewhere got lost. They distorted the objective reality of the Parthenon in such a way that it fits the visual distortions of the human nervous system.

Judy: Those columns are not the same size nor are the distances between them the same. And yet as you look at it your body tells you that this objective information is false. There's something so very right about what the Greeks did with the Parthenon. Those guys had done their epistemological homework. Bateson emphasizes again and again the importance of thinking cybernetically, that is, chunking in a way that respects the entire circuit, the relationships, and not just arcs of circuits. The way in which we chunk experience can lead to epistemological errors in our thinking that are formidable. Gregory says that unless we learn to think cybernetically the entire planet could be forfeit.

John: This same phenomena of epistemologically unsound thinking occurs both at the individual levels and the societal level. We will develop and propose a well-formedness condition which allows us as individuals and societies to correct certain epistemological errors in our thinking, namely, that when decomposing experience of the world—phenomena which we wish to examine and understand—the component we wish to study must itself be an operating circuit, not simply an arc in some circuit. Science in general and psychology in particular have made monumental errors in the decomposition of experience for purposes of study. Typically, a fascinating part of the world is identified and a study is designed. The designers altogether too frequently act as if the complex phenomenon, the circuit, may be decomposed into logical variables, arcs, each of which may be studied in isolation, patterns discerned and then the logical variables reassembled as if the generalizations which define the patterning of the arcs additively define the patterning of the entire circuit.

For example, the complex phenomenon of addiction cannot, as Bateson points out, be usefully decomposed into the study of the addict, or worse, the addictive personality alone; nor can it be chunked down into a study of the chemicals involved independent of the user.

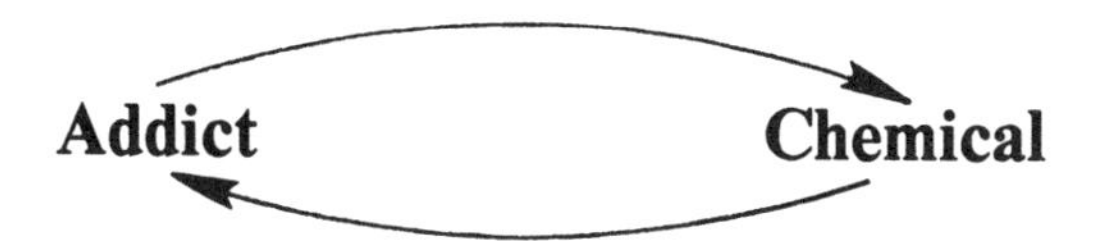

Such a decomposition of the phenomenon of addiction will guarantee a failure to discover interesting and useful patterning. Such programs are doomed to irrelevance, at best. At worst the researchers who find widely varying "patterns"—as a result of the study of only part of a relationship—will engage in polemics at the next higher logical level, arguing about whose sets of words are better to the dismay of people who have to deal with the loop of addiction in the real world and to the anguish of those who recognize the waste of human and financial resources. The results of such activity, at best, is the study of the pathological side of our species' ability to disassociate—to decompose experience without any sensibility to naturally operating circuits, . . . , and then to believe the decomposed arcs have anything to do with the world. Consider a parallel example from biology.

The concept of adaptation implies a preexisting world that poses a problem to which an adaptation is the solution. A key is adapted to a lock by cutting and filing it: an electrical appliance is adapted to a different voltage by a transformer. Although the physical world certainly predated the biological one, there are certain grave difficulties for evolutionary theory in defining that world for the process of adaptation. It is the difficulty of defining the "ecological niche." The description of the total environment and way of life of an organism. Its description includes physical factors, such as temperature and moisture; biological factors, such as the nature and quantity of food sources and of predators, and factors of the behavior of the organism itself, such as its social organization, its pattern of movement and its daily and seasonal activity cycles.

The first difficulty is that if evolution is described as the process of adaptation of organisms to niches, then the niches must exist before the species that are to fit them. That is, there must be empty niches waiting to be filled by the evolution of new species. In the absence of organisms in actual relation to the environment, however, there is an infinity of ways the world can be broken up into arbitrary niches. It is trivially easy to describe "niches" that are unoccupied. For example, no organism makes a living by laying eggs, crawling along the surface of the ground, eating grass and living for several years. That is, there are no grass-eating snakes, even though snakes live in the grass. Nor are there any warm-blooded, egg-laying animals that eat the mature leaves of trees, even though birds inhabit trees. Given any description of an ecological niche occupied by an actual organism, one can create an infinity of descriptions of unoccupied niches simply by adding another arbitrary specification. Unless there is some preferred or natural way to subdivide the world into niches the concept loses all predictive and explanatory value.

A second difficulty with the specification of empty niches to which organisms adapt is that it leaves out of account the role of the organism itself in creating the niche. Organisms do not experience environments passively; they create and define the environment in which they live. Trees remake the soil in which they grow by dropping leaves and putting down roots. Grazing animals change the species composition of herbs on which they feed by cropping, by dropping manure and by physically disturbing the ground, there is a constant interplay of the organism and the environment, so that although natural selection may be adapting the organism to a particular set of environmental circumstances, the evolution of the organism itself changes those circumstances. Finally, organisms themselves determine which external factors will be part of their niche by their own activities. By building a nest the phoebe makes the availability of dried grass an important part of its niche, at the same time making the nest itself a component of the niche.[3]

Judy: Now consider a different type of epistemological error, one where a perceptual unit, the human chin, is selected as an appropriate unit of study in evolutionary biology but turns out to have no underlying circuitry to support it as a unit of experiment coherent in itself.

. . . problems that arose in deciding on a proper description of the ecological niche without the organism arise when one tries to describe the organism itself. Is the leg a unit in evolution, so that the adaptive function of the leg can be inferred? If so, what about a part of the leg, say the foot, or a single toe, or one bone of a toe? The evolution of the human chin is an instructive example, human morphological evolution can be generally described as a "neotenic" progression. That is, human infants and adults resemble the fetal and young forms of apes more than they resemble adult apes; it is as if human beings are born at an earlier stage of physical development than apes and do not mature as far along the apes' development path. For example, the relative proportion of skull size to body size is about the same in newborn apes and human beings, whereas adult apes have much larger bodies in relation to their heads than we do; in effect their bodies "go further."

The exception to the rule of human neoteny is the chin, which grows relatively larger in human beings, whereas both infant and adult apes are chinless. Attempts to explain the human chin as a specific adaptation selected to grow larger failed to be convincing, finally it was realized that in an evolutionary sense the chin does not exist! There are two growth fields in the lower jaw: the dentary field, which is the bony structure of the jaw, and the alveolar field, in which the teeth are set. Both the dentary and the alveolar fields do show noeteny. They have both become smaller in the human evolutionary line. The alveolar field has shrunk somewhat faster than the dentary one, however, with the result that a "chin" appears as a pure consequence of the relative regression rates of the growth fields. With the recognition that the chin is a mental construct rather than a unit in evolution the problem of its adaptive explanation disappears.[4]

John: Well, at least such errors demonstrate the flexibility of our species: Who else could both break up natural circuits—natural patterning—into awkward and incoherent enough components that we confuse ourselves thoroughly and assemble unrelated parts of experience acting as if there were some natural basis for such an assemblage? By the way, if you, as children of the era of science, want something to think about, consider the wisdom of multiple descriptions of the world on the one hand, and the insistence of scientific researchers on a single representation referred to as Science. Does this mean that scientific endeavor is a fundamentally flawed human activity in that it presupposes that there is a single description that it is working towards?

NLP was designed from the very beginning to be an epistemology. And as Judy said the statements we're going to make over these five days and the class of experiences we'd like you to engage in with us are long overdue in connecting NLP with the epistemological traditions available in Western civilization.

Judy: I want to mention the range of personal alternatives and the range of human possibilities. Well, genetically, I suppose there's lots of things that are specified. I'm not sure that I know what all those things are and to what logical level they are specified and just how tightly they do hold us. But let's say we do have some limitations in what we can do.

John: We're going to talk as if the genetic structure, the genetic code, sets an absolute limit on the range of variation that any organism with such a genetic code can actually operate within. I don't know that's true. In justification for this simplifying assumption I'd say that we have not yet begun to explore either the range of personal alternatives nor the range of human possibility within those genetic constraints. My response to the notion of restrictions imposed by the genetic code and it specifying the range within which I can vary my own somatic commitments is very much like my response to the notion of so-called psychic powers. I wouldn't bloody know because I have not yet fully refined my own sensory apparatus the five channels that I already know about. I have worlds upon worlds yet to discover within what I know to be available to me as part of my heritage as a human being.

I was once out riding with some acquaintances—there were four of us on horseback riding abreast at a walk. One of the women dropped her reins across her horse's neck. Her horse, sandwiched between two other horses continued to move at the same pace in the same direction as the rest of us. After some distance, the young woman exclaimed, "Oh! What a smart and sensitive horse I have!" informing us of her belief that she had been controlling her horse with her mind alone. At the time I was preoccupied watching a marsh hawk making a hunting sweep on the next ridgeline and so didn't mention that I agreed that her mind was alone, wholly disconnected from her body and from her horse and from the context of three other riders with three other horses moving in the same direction at the same pace. Now if there happen to be genetic constraints, I have many many worlds to dance through before I come up against those possible constraints. That's the only sense in which we're accepting the notion of genetic constraints in our discussions.

Judy: When I think about other cultures I think about what they represent in terms of human possibilities: a whole set of ways to see and hear and feel about the world that could potentially resonate with my neurology, a place where news of difference is waiting to be discovered. There's a whole range of possibilities out there. How can I learn to move through them and know them better as well as to find out what my potential as a human being is? What are the personal alternatives that I can develop and how do I respect all of them in terms of circuitry, in terms of ecology, not to cut across circuits?

John: If you take a child born of any genetic background, born of any parents anywhere in the world and you put that child in the context of any culture and language, that child will master the culture and language that it's placed in at the same speed the children born of parents who are in that culture and language and have for centuries, an uninterrupted bloodline within that culture and linguistic tradition. Not only will the child learn with the same speed the language and the cultural ways of those people but the child will make the same class of "mistakes" in acquiring the language, will make the same set of "mistakes" in acquiring the cultural moves that the children born of the uninterrupted bloodline within that culture and language make. Contrary to the venerable British empiricist traditions, we humans are not blank slates *(tabula rasa).*

For example, some of you may have run across the information about Creoles and pidgin. A startling example to me of an actual relevant piece of linguistic research. (Laughter) I think that was as startling for me as the information itself. Several years ago a man named Blickerton working in the area of pidgins and Creoles offered in a *Scientific American*[5] article a report of his research. A couple of definitions: Pidgin is not a language, it's a verbal communication code which is developed when two different linguistic and ethnic groups in contact typically under forced labor conditions where they have to cooperate in order to get certain jobs done —to achieve the kind of production that gets them the food and shelter that they need for continued survival. There are lots of places in the world where such situations have occurred. Hawaii is one, Louisianna, Haiti. This is what happens when you take adult speakers of language *A* and adult speakers of language *B* and you place them in forced labor conditions, they develop a linguistic code which is not a language because it doesn't have tense or aspect—it doesn't have syntax. It's simply a verbal code to get the work done. Now, what verbal code do the children of pidgin speakers use? The technical answer is that they speak Creole. And what is Creole? Well, it turns out to be a full spoken language, syntax, tense, aspect . . . And finally and most fascinating is the question—where does this Creole spoken by the children of pidgin speakers come from? Since we're about epistemology here, let's be specific about how we would know where the Creole came from. How will we decide? What evidence will we use? Now one choice is the syntax. That is, if we examine the syntactic structure of Creole and compare it to the syntactic structure of the candidates—the language codes which could have served as a model for the Creole—we can arrive at a reasonable assessment of its origins. Well, what are the candidates? We can immediately disqualify pidgin since pidgin is not a full language while Creole is. There are the full languages of the parents' generation—whatever they were and, of course, there's the language of the dominant class who's exploiting the labor of the pidgin speakers. It turns out, according to Blickerton, that in the cases he analyzed the syntax of Creole was unrelated to the syntax of either the languages of the parents' generation or to the language of the exploiting group. So where does this language system—a system so complex that no linguist or team of linguists has ever been able to describe its rule driven structure—where does it come from? There are no suitable models externally, so where else but out of that astonishing part of our human heritage, the human nervous system. For some decades a linguist at M.I.T. named Chomsky has been arguing for an appreciation of humans as organisms who arrive with lots of decisions about what classes of experience they will have in the world already made. And further that when you consider the set of syntactic forms that human languages so far studied exhibit, especially cybernetically—that is, out of all the logical possibilities that human language and in particular, syntax, could utilize how is it that so few are selected?—you come to the conclusion that there is some very powerful filtering going on. And the filtering is occurring at the same place that Creole comes from. Specifically Chomsky proposes a set of circuits, the Language Acquisition Device or LAD, which are part of the definition of what it means to be a member of our species. Blickerton argues that Creole is the fullest overt representation of the consequences of the set of circuits called LAD. In the absence of an appropriate stable model of language in their environment the children of pidgin speakers externalize the prespecified circuits which define the linguistic part of our human heritage—syntactically they are speaking something close to deep structure.

John: By the way, if in listening to what we're doing here there's any question about what we're talking about it would be quite appropriate to make some minimal cue to request information about . . .

Woman: What's the definition of syntax?

John: *(writing on the chalkboard)*

The cat chased the rat.

is a sentence of English which is well formed.

The rat chased the cat.

is another sentence of English—also well formed. You as a fluent speaker of English know that those two sentences are representations of profoundly different events in the world if you assume they're both true descriptions. I've written these two sentences on the board and I ask you now to point to the difference. Everybody indeed agrees as native or fluent speakers of English that the meanings of the two sentences are profoundly different. And I ask you to point to the difference. You're at a loss. There is no specific place that you can point to in either one of those sentences to which you can attribute the difference *in* meaning between the two sentences. Yeah, Marne.

Marne: The order is different.

John: And the order indeed is the only thing that distinguishes the two sentences. That is, if sentences of the language were unordered sets of concepts, those two sentences would mean the same thing. But they're not unordered sets of concepts. Not only does the meaning of the words used in the sentence contribute to the entire meaning; the sequence in which those words occur also contributes. It's obviously not a simple situation because

The cat chased the rat.
and
The rat was chased by the cat.

have the same ordering in the sequences of the nouns but those two happen to mean roughly the same thing whereas the sentences I originally started with mean something quite different. So syntax is in part the study of the contribution of sequence to meaning. We are the only species known to have a syntactically based communication code. Incidentally, there are huge caveats that have to go around that like: How the hell would we know? When is the last time you successfully communicated with an ant, right? It's important to understand the caveats in terms of the tremendous perceptual filters which we have. When I was a child they had these little decks of cards where on each card, usually on the right bottom corner if you held them properly, were little scratchings. And if you looked at card *a,* you'd look there and think, "I don't know what the hell that is," you'd look at card *n,* you'd look at card *p,* you'd look at card *s;* however if you rifled the cards quickly you saw something that hadn't been there before. Because the exposure of the various scratchings to your central nervous system, to your visual system, had to occur within a certain time frame in order for you to assimilate on your occipital cortex the appropriate class of images which were being reported. If we just take time as a quantifier there are events that have occurred within the space between the last two letters in the last word that I just said which are momentous events in the physical world which we will never know about. They occur at nanosecond intervals. Doesn't mean they don't affect our experience. It means we simply don't know about those things.

Man: An example of speed of communication would be the laws that were made in the 1950s outlawing subliminal persuasion using pictures underneath the twenty-four frames a second that a person sees.

John: If you look at the electromagnetic spectrum, lay it out there right in front of you (gesturing with arm) . . .

John: . . . your eyes are tuned to one portion of the spectrum, your ears to another portion of it, your skin to another portion—who knows what other parts of your anatomy are responding to . . . But at least those three. And if you look at it you will see huge gaps where there are no sensory apparatus which can report the events that occur there.

Woman: How come NLP never dealt with those gaps?

John: Ah, I don't know if NLP did, but we did. Do you remember the 4-tuple? Did you ever run across that?

Judy: You remember the 4-tuple? Who said, "Yeah"?

John: Yeah, oh good.

Judy: Yeah, I think I remember that, yeah.

John: Ok, Vern.

Judy: Ok, Vern.

John: (writing on chalkboard) There it is right up there.

4-Tuple

$$A_d \ll A_t, K, V, O \gg$$

Judy: Ta-daa!

John: "O" for olfactory.

Woman: It wasn't there at the time I learned it.

Judy: (with mock disgust) Oh, man.

Woman: But my nose was.

Judy: But your nose was.

John: So you knew better all along. There was a wisdom to your response to NLP there.

In a book called *The Worlds of a Masai Warrior* by Tepilit Ole Saitoti[6] there is a description by a tribesman of his first experience of riding in a motor vehicle. The warrior became nauseated and had to get out of the truck and walk. What's going on here? Consider the context—from an early age he was trained to hunt, his observational powers were constantly refined. He learned to detect a bent blade of grass, the absence of the sound in a thicket, the odor of a fresh kill. And these skills were honed and automated as part of his patterns of sensing and inventorying his world. Suddenly you move this highly trained, sensorially alert organism through the environment at a speed at least twice that which he had previously experienced. And the result is predictable—the organism is overwhelmed by the information racing in through his sensory channels—he hasn't learned how to filter at that speed.

Judy: In the European tradition, juggling was classified as magic. Until approximately one hundred years ago, people had not developed visual scanning patterns which were quick and refined enough to literally see what the juggler was doing

John: Notice how fast our world is moving—something that was unequivocally magic a hundred years ago is something you're going to learn to do yourself within the next five days.

Woman: We're going to learn how to juggle?

John: Of course.

John: If you take the BaMbuti, pygmies from the Ituri rain forests of central Africa, out of that forest they become nauseous. What is it that occurs when the BaMbuti leave the rain forest? The rain forest is a vertical world. And when the BaMbuti—who have been raised and have lived their entire life in this womb (their word for womb is also their word for the forest) that covers them, that provides them with protection and is so characteristically marked by verticality—leave that vertical world, they become nauseous and some of them will collapse and fall very ill over a period of time if they are not returned to the rain forest.

John: Their sense of security is very strongly connected with the stimulation of that class of vertical line receptors in the visual perceptual system—with being in a place where they know how to perceive. Colin Turnbull gives a lovely description of his friend Kenge trying to understand the unfamiliar landscape of the savanna.[7]

Kenge could not believe they were the same mountains that we had seen from the forest; there they had seemed just like large hills to him. I tried to explain what the snow was—he thought it was some kind of white rock. Henri said it was water that turned color when it was high up, but Kenge wanted to know why it didn't run down the mountainside like any other water. When Henri told him it also turned solid at that height, Kenge gave him a long steady look and said, . . . "Bongo yako!"

(speaking with an Oklahoma accent)

"You liar!"

John: Was he from Oklahoma?

With typical Pygmy philosophy, he accepted what he could not understand and turned his back on the mountains to look more closely at what lay all around him. He picked up a handful of grass, tasted it and smelled it. He said that it was bad grass and that the mud was also bad mud. He sniffed at the air and said it was bad air. In fact, as he had stated at the onset, it was altogether a very bad country. The guide pointed out the elephants, hoping to make him feel more at home. But Kenge was not impressed. He asked what good they were if we were not allowed to go and hunt them. Henri pointed out the antelopes, which had moved closer and were staring at us as curiously as ever. Kenge clapped his hands together and said that they would provide food for a whole camp for months and months. Then he saw the buffalo, still grazing lazily several miles away, far down below. He turned to me and said, "What insects are those?"

At first I hardly understood; then I realized that in the forest the range of vision is so limited that there is no great need to make an automatic allowance for distance when judging size. Out here in the plains, however, Kenge was looking for the first time over apparently unending miles of unfamiliar grasslands, with not a tree worth the name to give him any basis for comparison. The same thing happened later on when I pointed out a boat in the middle of the lake. It was a large fishing boat with a number of people in it but Kenge at first refused to believe this. He thought it was a floating piece of wood.

When I told Kenge that the insects were buffalo, he roared with laughter and told me not to tell such stupid lies. When Henri, who was thoroughly puzzled, told him the same thing and explained that visitors to the park had to have a guide with them at all times because there were so many dangerous animals, Kenge still did not believe, but he strained his eyes to see more clearly and asked what kind of buffalo were so small. I told him they were sometimes nearly twice the size of a forest buffalo, and he shrugged his shoulders and said we would not be standing out there in the open if they were. I tried telling him they were possibly as far away as from Epulu to the village of Kopu, beyond Eboyo. He began scraping the mud off his arms and legs, no longer interested in such fantasies.

The road led on down to within about half a mile of where the herd was grazing, and as we got closer, the "insects" must have seemed to get bigger and bigger. Kenge, who was now sitting on the outside, kept his face glued to the window, which nothing would make him lower. I even had to raise mine to keep him happy. I was never able to discover just what he thought was happening—whether he thought that the insects were changing into buffalo, or that they were miniature buffalo growing rapidly as we approached. His only comment was that they were not real buffalo, and he was not going to get out of the car again until we left the park.

Judy: There's one more story that I'd like to bring up from *The Forest People.*[8] There's a young man and a young woman and they've just been married a short time and they got into a tiff over something, I don't remember if Turnbull even mentions what it is, but there is a culturally regulated way of getting married and then there's a culturally regulated way of breaking that up and the way that is done in the BaMbuti is if the woman begins to take down the hut, leaf by leaf, when she gets to the last leaf and packs up her cooking equipment, it's done. It's irreversible. So they've had a fight, they've had an argument, and you have to remember that for the BaMbuti the most important thing is the maintenance of the hunting group; they can't have people just causing a lot of unwarranted conflict in the group because it could put the entire hunting group on the line. So the woman is taking down the hut leaf by leaf and she's in tears and her husband is sitting by the fire going, "What can I do—how can I stop this?" He can't think of anything to do and she's taking off the leaves, leaf by leaf, and he's wringing his hands and pacing and all of a sudden he walks over to the hut and takes a leaf off and he says, "Yeah, good idea, let's go down and wash these leaves in the creek." And she says, "What?" And he says, "Well it's a good idea, these leaves are dirty, it's a good idea to take these leaves off. Let's go wash them together." And she goes "Ah!" Now it's really interesting because Turnbull said that for the next month he noticed that in this particular encampment couples were taking leaves off and going down and washing them in the stream and that he'd never seen that behavior occuring in the group before and he never saw it after.

The !Kung San[9] or bushmen of the Kalahari are a fiercely egalitarian people, much like the BaMbuti of the Ituri rain forest, in that maintenance of a cooperative framework must occur in both cultures to insure the preservation of the hunting group. The promotion of symmetrical relationships among individuals insures that there is no concentration of power that may negatively affect the group, and insures that too much responsibility does not fall on one person for fulfilling a large and complex social role. Two very important roles among the !Kung San are the hunter and the distributor of the meat. The hunter has great responsibility for the acquisition of meat, so great in fact that when a successful hunter returns to camp he typically appears quite dejected and forlorn. When asked about the events of the day he berates himself as a hunter, claiming clumsiness and stupidity. However he will say he may have seen something—probably not much, probably not worth eating. Through this kind of exchange the people at camp elicit important information about the kind and size of the prey. Then adjustments as to the number of people and implements needed to retrieve the meat are made.

Since both the distributor of the meat and the hunter are such powerful roles in the culture we would expect some mechanisms of separating these roles to ensure the maintenance of symmetry, distribution of power, and the cooperative framework. When asked about the hunter's responsibilities the !Kung San reply that it's quite simple, "The owner of the arrow is the owner of the meat." At first consideration this proverb appears to be a paradox as it collapses as opposed to separates the roles of hunter and distributor. However, one evening sitting around a fire at one of the !Kung San sip wells in the Kalahari, a clever anthropologist who was watching the hunters prepare their arrows for tomorrow's hunt asked, "Whose arrow is this one?" "Oh, that's hers," said the hunter, pointing to one of the older women in the hunting group. In response to the anthropologist's persistent questioning, the hunter inventoried the arrows in his quiver and to the anthropologist's amazement, not a single one belonged to the hunter himself. By this inventory a whole new set of possibilities were presented. The !Kung San hunter does not necessarily use his own arrows when hunting. Now the proverb takes on a fuller meaning achieving a new depth in our appreciation of the culture. Since the hunter has such great responsibility for acquisition of meat he is not also expected to fulfill the role of distributor. Further we know from other readings that different poisoned arrows are used to kill different animals. The decisions about what animals will be hunted and therefore which poisons are appropriate are made around the campfire the evening before the hunt. This implies that important decisions about owners of arrows and owners of meat are being made well in advance of the hunt. These are deep decisions about social responsibilities, equality, and maintenance of the hunting group.

Hopefully this offers some understanding first in the area of first- and second-attention balance, as on first, conscious examination the "owner of the arrow is the owner of the meat," presents an attitude of simplicity—which in turn implies much deeper balanced and more complex relationships for the !Kung San. Secondly, we are offered a new description of developing a balance with respect to complex social relations.

•

John: So, what kind of characteristics, when you think of a culture, distinguish it and the everyday life of the participants from the situation as you understand it to be in our social system here? What sorts of things occur to you? Give some thought to what differences are important as far as you're concerned in the daily life of someone who is embedded in a culture which is still coherent, has not been disrupted by contact with technological society, and the experience on a daily basis that you have in our social system. Yes.

Woman: In many situations you are deciding what's appropriate behavior in our society, but in a culture you know . . .

John: . . . it's specified.

Judy: It's externally specified and everybody agrees.

John: Take the leaves as an example. Judy was pointing out that there is a coherency to the woman disassembling the hut leaf by leaf because a great deal of communication—both between the couple and the rest of the encampment, and between the man and the woman who constitute the couple for that hut—is done through the hut through the arrangement of those leaves, for instance without any verbal communication. For example, the woman's invitation to engage in sexual play is signalled by a certain placement of the leaves. This is never spoken but the man who is alert to such signals will recognize a certain arrangement of the leaves on the hut as an invitation for that evening. The womb of the mother, the hut, the encampment under the forest, and the forest itself, are multilevel representations of security which encloses the BaMbuti during their normal life cycle. Each one of those have the value of offering communication signals in a way that you're proposing. There are certain traditional patterns of behavior which people know they can use to accomplish their outcomes in a culture which is still coherent. It doesn't require first attention in many cases.

Woman: The other side of that is that in a society you can set your own structure.

Judy: In a society.

John & Judy: Ding, ding, ding! You may now spin the wheel in the lottery. That's what we're about.

John: It's important for you to give some thought to what it is that distinguishes a coherent culture from a society. We're going to use traditional coherent cultures as a model to suggest how we can create our own. We can appreciate what differences there are, some we will wish to discard, some we will wish to recapitulate in creating our own personal culture. There is a richness, for example, to the BaMbuti communication system which is in many cases iconic and second-attention oriented as opposed to our society's first-attention orientation; there's a predictability. Once TaTitos Sompa, who you will meet and work with this afternoon, is comfortable with the relationship he has established with you, he is like an agent of entropy. There's value placed on pattern interruption, on disruption of normal states, on disruption of perceptual filters, all within boundaries of respect, one person to the other. And there is a balancing within his culture—the ritual and the forms are specified to the degree that everyone knows what the choices are in responding to certain situations, whether they're trapped inside—the case that Judy was talking about—or in fact, they have perfectly good alternatives and the question is an aesthetic one, that is, which one will they choose that seems most appropriate, in the sense of artistry, for the situation they're faced with?

John: From a Western position, especially American, those seem to be constraints on behavior. "We can only do these things? Who says?" Remember, however, there is an entropic principle at work inside of the ritual that we're talking about. That's an important design element—at which logical levels will you insist on stability and at which entropy?

Woman: My question is, in our culture, where there are so many alternatives, where you can make your own, doesn't something of the reverse happen because security is so difficult to come by. So that person who breaks the convention which is insecure in the first place is often not valued because it brings that security up just like the flip side.

John: Sounds like a verbal coding of a lot of experiences I've had —of being the person who made what I would consider a creative act to the anguish of everyone around me who was totally disrupted by the prospect of having to consider yet another alternative. I've also been on the other side where people proposed an alternative to what was going on which I thought was outside of the boundary of respect for the human beings involved.

Judy: "I'm creative, you're flexible, he's erratic!"

John: Now whether or not that was accessing a lack of security in me I'm not sure.

Judy: You were insecure?

John: Quite. That's been one of my problems for a long time—that and modesty. So in a society such as ours you don't necessarily receive the affirmations from the outside world—but in a culture you do.

Patricia: I think that my perspective differs slightly. The idea that I keep coming back to is that we each have our own symbols, like the analogy of the woman placing the leaves in certain patterns that signal certain things. The problem is that the symbols are our own and so we're having to spend a lot of time sending them out and it's not quite gotten by the other person and we're trying to interpret what the other symbols we're receiving are.

John: Have you ever had close friends who are from different cultures who marry?—it's very instructive. For example in a high-stress situation an Englishman or an Englishwoman will tend to become extremely courteous in order to not exacerbate an already difficult, stressful situation. If you're from a Mediterranean culture, however, this is unequivocal evidence that they have just withdrawn from the relationship. And nothing could be further from the English intent when they offer you that courtesy. It's their way of saying, "The situation has become so difficult that I don't know what to do to alleviate the stress except to become courteous and hope that time and good intention on both our parts will cause a reduction in the difficulty in the situation we find ourselves in." In a Mediterranean culture, that's taken to be a lack of commitment—a signal the relationship is over.

José: I was thinking of the games that we play, especially children's games. They have a purpose.

John: Let's go to the rain forest again. Within the encampment there is a special place central to the encampment where children play. Anywhere from roughly two years old up to puberty children get together in the *bopi* as it's called and they play. And if you watch their games very carefully, as Colin Turnbull did over the two-year period he lived with these people, you'll discover some amazing things. Now in this culture the integrity of the hunting group is the highest value. It has to be because without that you die—a certain size and balance of hunting group is required for you to succeed just at the level of food and survival.

In the *bopi* there is a game where the children will begin to climb a sapling, say a thirty-foot sapling. As they climb the sapling the sapling is bent over until it's within two or three feet of the ground. So you have a half a dozen or so children who have succeeded in moving together in a cooperative frame and have brought this sapling down to a safe distance from which they can leap off. The children hanging in the sapling sing together and at a certain point in the song they all leap off at the same time.

Judy: By the way, among the BaMbuti the same word is used for lovemaking, dancing and this children's game we're describing here.

John: Now, when I first ran across this example I went, "Where in my childhood was I given reference experiences for cooperative behavior along these lines?"

Judy: How do they think about and respond to the child who goes, "Uh, well I'll just do a little razzle-dazzle, you know, and I'll stay on until the very last second so that everybody jumps off before me"? (Laughter)

John: The world, not the other children, teaches that child an important fact about cooperative behavior. That child is flung through the air, lands somewhere in the forest. Now when Judy and I were first talking about this brilliant example, our first move was, "Why don't we import it into our society?" The fact that you have to search rather hard for cooperative reference experiences in childhood tells me that we are unbalanced in this area of cooperation/competition.

Judy: Think about how many people in management have to do team-building.

Woman: I had that experience coming from a large family.

John: So do I, coming from a large family.

Woman: "Four Bags on the Mill," "Red Rover."

John: Suppose we just transplanted that children's ritual into an American playground. The adults would be the problem. Because what happens when that child hangs on just a little longer and flies through the air? Well, in the *bopi* the adults are close enough that they notice but they don't indicate that they notice. They simply make sure the child is not injured and they leave that child alone. No one runs to comfort that child. And when that child comes back to join the other children playing in the *bopi* the children do not accept that child back for a period of time.

Judy: They might even give him a nickname for a while, like "Waits-Too-Long-To-Jump" or something.

John: As some period of time passes the child is then reincorporated into the play group. And no rancor or discrimination is carried forward subsequent to that point. They've done the appropriate thing and now they are reincorporated as a full participant in the game.

Judy: That's the exact same mechanism that's used with adults to maintain the cooperative framework within the culture if they break a rule.

John: What would happen in an American playground? Well the problem would be the adults. Because if one of those children got thrown the adults would be all over that kid. The secondary gain inherent in the attention that would be offered to that child would reinforce the very behavior which the original game was designed to rebalance.

Marne: The equipment would be outlawed. The game would be eliminated.

Judy: The school would be sued; it would have to shut down.

John: "Outlawed"—Marne uses exactly the right word. In a traditional culture the internal representations that I carry to guide my behavior are constantly mirrored and echoed by the structure of the culture that I'm living in. That is not true in your everyday life.

Judy: But how do we do it? Law!

John: Legislative maneuvers and law are the faint reflection and the distant echo of coherent culture. And you can grade cultures on their coherency by noticing what forms they use to bring deviant behavior back into line. In a coherent culture, ridicule, laughter, and scorn typically handle most of the situations that occur. Why? Why do they work there but not here? Because if we are members of a coherent culture I know that the internal representations of the other members of the tribe match my representations and the cultural practices are structured so that there's a constant cycle of reinforcement of those values. And I can count on them being there as sure as he's a member of my culture. Therefore I only have to behave with laughter, ridicule, et cetera in such a way as to access in him the very representations which will cause him now to change his behavior, to bring it back into alignment within the range which is acceptable in our culture. And insofar as force, police, military, and legislative work are required to contain deviant behavior there is no internal culture which is matched by external forms. And you have a measure of loss of coherency in the social system.

Woman: In our society a value judgement has been placed on ridicule and scorn as being inappropriate behavior. You know the comment that you hear people say: Children are cruel. In fact, what they're doing is exactly what they did in your example, and yet children are then taught or told that it's inappropriate to be "cruel."

John: See your attorney instead. My lawyer can beat up your lawyer.

Man: Can I ask a question? In that ritual children's play do they teach themselves, generation to generation, or does an adult teach them how?

John: No, the children teach themselves. All of the recruitment is from within the group. Richard?

Richard: That's a big difference. I was raised in a large Italian family and interaction between my mother and father was highly structured; however, after dinner we did something which altered that structure—we played music. It seemed that Father now blended in. One son would go on a drum, another one on a harmonica, another one on a guitar, and another one on a piano. Something was taught there that wasn't taught elsewhere. It allowed access to my parents in a way that I didn't have access to before. They could go out of note, they could go out of key, just as I could. And together it sounded OK. After the music was over another set of roles went into effect. "Alright, it's bedtime." That was exactly it. And ritual, religious ritual, seemed to be able to set the frame with archetypes and the rest of it so that Father became connected to God and Mother became connected to the Blessed Virgin in the Catholic faith.

John: Which was always hard to figure. I mean my father was a carpenter but I know my mother was not a virgin, right? (Laughter)

Judy: Music was a framework within which the cybernetics of the family could temporarily change.

Richard: It was extremely different. It was like night and day. Because then when it ended that whole bubble ended and then it was back to a completely different world.

Judy: And it gave you another description.

Richard: Oh, yes.

Judy: Nothing comes of nothing.

John: In Gregory, every difference that we detect presupposes a double description. Among some of the American Plains Indians the metaphor that occurs is the medicine wheel. If we place a quiver or an arrow in the center of a circle of people and ask them to describe with the kind of careful witness descriptions which occur in Heinlein's notion of witness in *Stranger in a Strange Land*[10] so that they're being offered an opportunity to describe in sensory specific terms without evaluation what they see as they look at the arrow. Notice, just by the geometry of the situation those descriptions will differ.

Judy: They all have a different perspective.

John: Each one of them occupies a different spatial relationship with respect to the arrow. And as it says in *Seven Arrows,*[11] if we take something as intangible as honesty (which is a pretty rarefied concept) the variation in the representations increases.

Judy: The minimum unit of mind is difference. Where does new information come from? It comes out of difference just like depth perception comes out of the two convergent images. A new class of information emerges from the synthesis of two different descriptions. One of the well-formedness conditions we're going to insist on in working towards personal genius is that you need at least two descriptions before acting.

John: You mentioned music. You used that as an example of a second description of a family system. The first one was the standard practices in the family. The second one was the special situation of playing music together. A third one as you pointed out was religious practice. So there were at least three perceptions of family structure. Religious practice, I think, would tend to echo more the regular practices in the family in terms of who was God and who was not. (Laughter) In a traditional culture there is rarely music without dance and rarely dance or music without singing.

Woman: I think the differences in cultures and societies is that in cultures there seems to be a higher force that determines what's beneficial for the members of the culture. It's brought down through laws, religion, taboos, et cetera, whereas in a society it seems to be more short-lived and it lives almost as long as the members do and it's up to them individually to decide what's good for them as opposed to the culture where it's determined for you.

Judy: Well, the way I was thinking about it was that if you take an individual and you put them in the environment, they constantly have to change their behavior in response to the environment and what's going on. I mean, you do it naturally, right? And if you have a set of oral traditions that are passed on from generation to generation, the set of transforms that information goes through will match the shifts the tribe has gone through in coevolving with their environment—it will therefore be up to date. It'll make sense, it'll make coherent sense. If you place that oral tradition outside the human neurology and you write it down and it becomes static, it's got to constantly be interpreted. It will generally lag behind what's really appropriate for this time and place.

John: In an oral tradition there is no conscious editing of previous tradition because the storage system for the oral tradition is the neurology of the participants . . .

Judy: . . . somatic storage . . .

John: . . . which implies that as the environment or social organization of the tribe changes, second attention will automatically edit the old oral tradition so that it corresponds with the actual state of affairs—unless the rate of change is too rapid.

You can even be more precise about the second case where you get an extra somatic storage—when you write it down. An important thing will occur over time: fragmentation, splintering. And the basis of that will be the fact that you'll have a fundamentalist position (laughter) and you'll have an interpretation that says we need to update what was written. Now if you put on top of the whole system a frame that says this is the inspired word of whatever the highest principle you can appeal to . . . (Laughter)

Judy: . . . then you're going to have to have an institution to protect it because somebody's got to make the decision about what information is allowed in there that may potentially change it—that is, you have an institution carrying out consciously what our perceptual filters do unconsciously. Whereas in an oral tradition the neurology is going to make the update automatically. The editing is going to occur naturally. . . . (pause) . . . The West Africans often talk about "closing the circle."

John: If a group of children are denied access to their parents' parents, the circle is broken and it's broken in both directions. There are natural alliances between children and grandparents. And what is the gain on both sides? Well, for the children, by knowing the grandparents the children come to a second attention appreciation of how their parents got that way.

Judy: It develops another description of how our parents got to be who they are—by appreciating the context of their development.

John: And number two, of course equally important, the grandparents are exposed to the rejuvenating influence of those new neurologies, themselves forming their own generalizations at the second attention about the amazing and complex rich world around them. So there's that rejuvenation effect for the older generation. It keeps them alive to the new class of experiences that the children have to deal with.

Woman: The other part about culture as opposed to society is that in the sense of cultures there's a real sense of natural physical environment being included in that culture and not being outside of the culture; whereas my experience in this society is that somehow there's a separation between the natural environment and the social one.

Judy: That's a circuit that's been cut in our society. Think back to the Puritans when they first came to what is now the United States. They did not know how to survive in this environment and so they built little forts, cut everything down inside and made walls and inside these walls they were safe and outside, well, they could die out there. So if you take the literature from that time you get this whole representation of the "red devils." Well interestingly enough, those "red devils" could live out there in the wilderness and they weren't dying. So slowly by slowly you have people leaving the group inside of the forts and going and living with the Indians. You did not have the other way, though. You did not have the Indians coming and asking if they could live in compounds. (laughter) And then little by little you'd get the people like Daniel Boone who could survive in that wilderness and you'd have the whole evolution in thinking from the concept of "red devil" to "noble savage."

John: A beginning of wisdom. The quality of the relationship a people have with the context they're in is a reflection of their collective wisdom. And that context, of course, can be intellectual and artistic, and it can be environmental in the strong sense of physical surroundings. Historically, we did not always have the kind of command of technical power that we have now. Humans have always changed their contexts in a physical sense, by living in caves, by building houses and so forth. But with the industrial revolution and its subsequent centuries now there's come to be a concentration of technical power that allows us to change our environment in a strong way and thereby loose the wisdom of the interaction with the natural environment in which we originally developed. And so I take one component of wisdom to be an appreciation of the fact that the circuits that determine our own well-being must include the environment—both our internal environment and the external environment as an essential part of the circuitry.

Roger Fisher[12] once told me the following story: A bomber crew during the second World War was selected to test a new aircraft. The crew was pleased with the results as they pushed the new airplane through the various tests. Late one day they were flying at 40,000 feet and began testing to determine how well the aircraft's engines could be re-started in the air. The pilot and co-pilot skillfully and carefully shut down each of the four engines one at a time, pausing, and then re-starting it. Successful at this level of testing, the pilot and co-pilot

shut them down two at a time then restarted. Next they shut down three of the four engines successfully restarting. Finally the pilot shut down all four engines. A deafening silence ensued. At just about the same time both the co-pilot and the pilot remembered an interesting clause out of the specs manual which noted that an engine can only be started or restarted if
(a) one of the other engines is going or
(b) there is an outside power source as a booster.
It was at this point that the co-pilot turned to the pilot and said, "Boy! are you in trouble!" (laughter) . . .

However it wasn't long ago that in standard business practice, the water used to cool the plants and to take the effluents from the processing, the air into which we put the residue that we created as by-products of manufacturing process, those were literally called "externalities." They were externalities because they were not required on a balance sheet as part of the costs of doing business. There is no wisdom there—strictly first attention.

Judy: But think about it, that's what first attention is for, short-term outcomes.

Woman: You can see this in India in the taboo against killing cows. The cow's sacred status developed out of the cost /benefit relationship between eating your cow during an extended drought or else going hungry and saving the animal so that when it starts to rain again you'll be able to farm. Eventually this was brought into the cultural wisdom through the Hindu religion and now it's become a taboo to kill a cow.

John: It is important in biological systems, living systems, that the triggering mechanism for any critical response in some part of our physiology not be a deficit of the very thing that that circuit is designed to supply. The breathing cycle, which is unconscious for most purposes in us, is not triggered by a deficit of oxygen. There would be no wisdom in a circuit like that. It's triggered by an excess of CO_2. So the automatic system signal for us to take another breath is not the absence of the critical element that we need but the presence of a complementary element driven by gas exchange in the lungs. Notice that this is important because if you have as a part of your design a deficit of a critical variable as the trigger for replenishment you can have lethal values on that variable before corrective responses are triggered properly.

So here's a hard one. India has population/food imbalances. So here's a logical level puzzle: We go, "The people of India are starving and we have lots—huge storage systems for grain and corn and they're full." So number one, we have the resources and number two, we have some natural strategies, just as I was mentioning before, I can look over and see Larry and go, "There's a brother." I can identify with him—it's a natural movement. We look across the world and see the people in India starving and we go, "We have the food—those are people just like you and me. Let's demonstrate *we* care by sending food." What's the critique of that cybernetically?

Woman: The piece that's missing is how they can generate that for themselves.

John: How they can generate that for themselves. Most welfare programs, whether internal to this nation state or across nation states, do not address the relationship between the people receiving the aid and the context of the problem. You are violating a well-formedness condition by intervening at the wrong logical level.

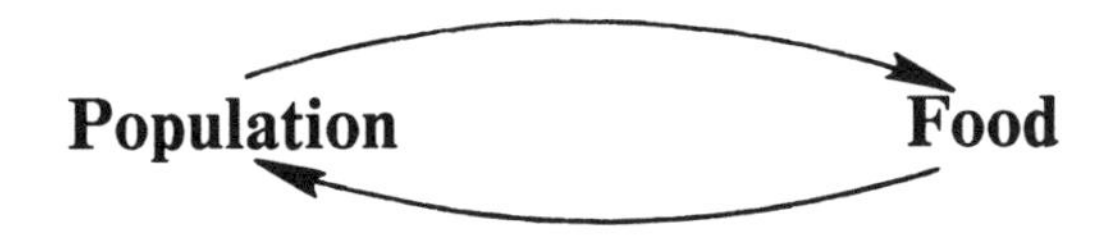

Inspect the circuit—note that in this loop, any increase in number on the population side of the loop demands (minimally) a corresponding increase on the food side. However, the converse is true as well—any increase in the food availability tends to kick the numbers on the population side of the loop up. If you supply food to a population that's already in excess of what their own production capacity can support, you create the precise conditions for an increase in population —pushing them further out of balance with their food supply —an escalating cycle.

John: To me it's hard to say what practical responsibilities we have in this area but it seems to me that we must take seriously the well-formedness condition concerning intervention at the appropriate logical level. Let me give you an example that I'm more connected with. There's a tribe that lives in the southern deserts of Ethiopia and the northern plains of Kenya. Like the Masai, these people are a proud cattle people.[13]

The cattle are also the symbolic and literal measure of personal and tribal success. This is their reservoir—their Fort Knox. And they identify strongly with their cattle. The European planners sat down and drew straight lines on a map dividing up portions of this continent called Africa where this tribe happens to live and their traditional grazing happens to fall into three different countries: Uganda, Ethiopia, and Kenya. They are now pushed by these nation states into an area which has the cattle bearing capacity of roughly one-fifth of the cattle they have at that time.

Judy: So what happens?

John: Here is a group of people who are brilliantly adapted to their environment until there's a pressure, applied at a high rate of speed, to change. Notice the rate of change that's required to adapt is beyond their flexibility at this point because of the deep cultural commitments. Is there any way out —other than accepting the destruction of that culture? Not necessarily the people. The people could be brought out. They could survive as people, but that culture is finished given the geopolitical situation that those people happen to be in.

Judy: And like Britt mentioned earlier, if that were a long-term and slow pressure, you could almost guess at how the culture would have to change and evolve to maintain their investment in their cultural practices. But if the investment is great and the time pressure enormous—it's like the whales' investment to water and the elephants' investment to land—it's great enough that they won't survive. If the water covered the world the elephants aren't going to make it and if the oceans dried up neither are the whales.

John: The tribe apparently doesn't recognize the lethal nature of the situation they're in. They know things are bad, there's no doubt about that because people are starving. But the issue here is the investment at the level of their perceptual filters. In the case of the tribe with their tremendous investment in cattle as the central core concept organizing their culture—the basis of their self-identity as a people, they will not perceive that the lethal values of overgrazing have been reached until it's too late. Their cattle will continue to gaze in the limited space they have until the land is overgrazed to the point where it can't recover. I'm talking about perceptual filters that extend to the peripheral sense organ. Erickson[14] reported on the quality of such filtering in his work with altered states—for example hypnotic deafness. Now I can ask José to pretend to be deaf and he can inhibit certain responses to surprising noises especially when they come from sources he can't see. And he might get quite good at that. A second, higher quality state of hypnotic deafness would be where he does alter his state but he alters it in such a way that he only inhibits the response. That is the actual sound signal goes through the peripheral organ and arrives at the central nervous system and there the inhibition occurs—there's no overt response to it. If I'm very acute visually I can probably see his pupils contract when somebody makes a loud sound behind him unexpectedly—but there will be no orienting response for example. The third grade of hypnotic deafness is what I'm talking about in terms of deep beliefs and cultural commitments, and what Judy's talking about in terms of investment. . . .

Judy: at the periphery. . . .

John: . . . It's where you've altered your neurology to the point where the signal never arrives at the central nervous system.

That the filter occurs out toward the interface between the world and you—the peripheral sense organ.

Judy: You can't see what you can't see. Well, you can't know what you can't know.

John: There was a woman in a seminar I did several months ago who asked me to help her make the following personal arrangements. She was married to a man who she in most ways was quite pleased with. He had some irritating habits or incongruities that she just found less than aesthetic. What she wanted to do was arrange a perceptual filter which would do two things: First of all it would screen from her awareness those particular annoying peculiarities that this man had, in terms of his thinking and the way he conducted himself in the world. Secondly, she wanted this perceptual filter to shunt that information so it never reached her central nervous system but instead put it in some safe place so that if the incongruities reached a certain cumulative value she would suddenly become aware of them.

Judy: Certain thresholds.

John: Now, I looked at her and I said, "And that's the history of your relationships with men." That is, not only does she have these idyllic relationships for short periods of time with men, but at the point the threshold value is exceeded there's a figure ground reversal and the idyllic existence she had had for six months with this man now turned out to be all a lie. Every bit of it. So you get a complete reversal. The danger here is that is if you set your thresholds too high, like the tribe, you can achieve a state of runaway, in terms of overgrazing, in terms of the accumulation of nonsense below threshold. No matter how much you may consciously want to do the right thing, the appropriate ecological thing, if the threshold values on your sensory apparatus are set too high, you can achieve a destructive or even lethal value on that variable before the threshold is crossed and you recognize it.

Bateson made a claim that unless we learn to think cybernetically we may have a very limited run on this planet. That's going to include topics such as how to sort the circuits in such a way that their integrity is respected, how to set threshold values, and how to change the definition of self as is appropriate to context. Before the industrial revolution if someone got a little bit strange the problem was local—the people and families and village dealt with it sometimes by incorporating the behavior, who knows? There was no problem with that because that person did not have at their command enough technical leverage to affect the remainder of the family, the tribe, the group they lived with. So that a lack of wisdom on the part of one or more of the organisms in a group was balanced by the group. However with the tremendous technical leverage available in our society, a mistake, a madness, a lack of contact with context, a failure of wisdom in one organism can have a tremendous impact not only on the local environment but the entire planet.

We believe that consciousness has feedback into the remainder of mind and so an effect upon action. But the effects of this feedback are almost unknown and urgently need investigation and validation.

It is surely true that the content of consciousness is no random sample of reports on events occurring in the remainder of mind. Rather, the content of the screen of consciousness is systematically selected from the enormously great plethora of mental events. But of the rules and preferences of this selection, very little is known. This matter requires investigation. Similarly the limitations of verbal language require consideration.

John: Think about where representational systems fit into that. Think where Meta-model/Milton-model work fits into that. We have available a technology which can address that class of questions with some precision.

I continue:

It appears, however, that the system of selection of information for the screen of consciousness is importantly related to "purpose," "attention," and similar phenomena which are also in need of definition and elucidation. . . .

If consciousness has feedback upon the remainder of mind, . . . and if consciousness deals only with a skewed sample of the events of the total mind, then there must exist a systematic . . . difference between the conscious views of self and the world, and the true nature of self and the world. Such a difference must distort the processes of adaptation.

In this connection, there is a profound difference between the processes of cultural change and those of phylogenetic evolution. In the latter, the Weismannian barrier between soma and germ plasma is presumed to be totally opaque.

John: There is a standard doctrine in biology which indicates an asymmetrical relationship between genetic structure and the actual form of an individual. In the age-old controversy between Lamarck and Darwin, Darwin has been selected at least at this point as the winner. Lamarck proposed that if I become a technical rock climber and develop tremendous upper body strength as part of that endeavor that if I father a child subsequent to acquiring those physical characteristics such characteristics could be passed to my offspring. There is no evidence for this proposal in fact. Lamarck was right, you know, but in the wrong domain. Lamarckian evolution is the selection process in learning and culture whereas Darwinian evolution is the model for genetics in biological systems. Weismann's barrier is a proposal that no part of the somatic investment of any phenotype, any individual organism, could ever cross back over the barrier called Weismann's barrier to the genetic structure. This precludes the adaptation being genetically coded in one generation.

There is no coupling from environment to genome. In cultural evolution and individual learning the coupling through consciousness is present, incomplete and probably distortive.

It is suggested that the specific nature of this distortion is such that *the cybernetic nature of self and the world tends to be imperceptible to consciousness,* insofar as the contents of the "screen" of consciousness are determined by considerations of purpose. The argument of purpose tends to take the form "*D* is desirable; *B* leads to *C*; *C* leads to *D*; so *D* can be achieved by way of *B* and *C*." But, if the total mind and the outer world do not . . . have this linear structure, then by forcing this structure upon them, we become blind to the cybernetic circularities of the self and the external world. Our conscious sampling of data will not disclose whole circuits but only arcs of circuits, cut off from their matrix by our selective attention. Specifically, the attempt to achieve a change in a given variable, located either in self or environment, is likely to be undertaken without comprehension of the homeostatic network surrounding that variable. . . . It may be essential for *wisdom* that the narrow purposive view be somehow corrected.

The function of consciousness in the coupling between man and the homeostatic systems around him is, of course, no new phenomenon. Three circumstances, however, make the investigation of this phenomenon an urgent matter.

First, there is man's habit of changing his environment rather than changing himself. Faced with a changing variable (*e.g.*, temperature) within itself which it should control, the organism may make changes *either* within itself *or* in the external environment. It may adapt to the environment or adapt the environment to itself. In evolutionary history, the great majority of steps have been changes within the organism itself; some steps have been of an intermediate kind in which the organisms achieved change of environment by change of locale. In a few cases organisms other than man have achieved the creation of modified microenvironments around themselves, *e.g.*, the nests birds of . . . birds, concentrated forests of conifers, fungal colonies, (coral reefs,) etc.

In all such cases, the logic of evolutionary progress is toward ecosystems which sustain *only* the dominant, environment-controlling species, and its symbionts and parasites.

Man, the outstanding modifier of environments, similarly achieves single-species ecosystems in his cities, but he goes one step further, establishing special environments for symbionts. These, likewise, become single-species ecosystems: fields of corn, cultures of bacteria, batteries of fowls, colonies of laboratory rats, and the like.

Secondly, the power ratio between purposive consciousness and the environment has changed rapidly in the last one hundred years, and the *rate* of change in this ratio is certainly rapidly increasing with technological advance. Conscious man, as changer of his environment, is now fully able to wreck himself and that environment—with the very best of conscious intentions.

Third, a peculiar sociological phenomenon has arisen in the last one hundred years which perhaps threatens to isolate conscious purpose from many corrective processes which might come out of less conscious parts of the mind. The social scene is nowadays characterized by the existence of a large number of self-maximizing entities which, in law, have something like the status of "persons"—trusts, companies, political parties, unions, commercial and financial agencies, nations, and the like. In biological fact, these entities are precisely *not* persons and are not even aggregates of whole persons. They are aggregates of *parts* of (whole) persons. When Mr. Smith enters the board room of his company, he is expected to limit his thinking narrowly to the specific purposes of the company or to those of that part of the company which he "represents." Mercifully it is not entirely possible for him to do this and some company decisions are influenced by considerations which spring from wider and wiser parts of the mind. But ideally, Mr. Smith is expected to act as a pure, uncorrected consciousness—a dehumanized creature.[15]

John: Part of our purpose here is in developing strategies which allow a corrective set of wisdoms to the purposeful consciousness which is such an important part of our operation in a fragmented society—one where we cannot count on a resonance between our internal values and those of the people we have contact with on a daily basis.

Man: If we agree that a desirable goal is for people to become aware of that symbiotic relationship between man and his environment and that the conscious mind tends to rule out that recognition because it's so purposive and narrow, the thing that occurs to me is that to become aware of that relationship is to go about something that has an unconscious purpose. When I was younger I used to go for walks in the hills and woods and I had no conscious purpose. I just felt like I wanted to do it for some reason. And when I was out in the environment, not surrounded by manmade structures, I tended to have a much clearer understanding of what it means to say I'm a part of the Earth and the wind and the trees, I felt a part of things. So maybe one answer is to have people go through things and have unconscious purposes as opposed to conscious purposes.

John: The thing that comes to my mind is rites of passage which involve the ability to identify with living systems by becoming them. If I come up with a base metaphor for what I do—I'm very good at exploring new territory. And there are several decisions I have to make each time I commit myself to a new territory. And some of the decisions involve whether I will attempt to merge with that environment or will I attempt to somehow be a self-sustaining unit and carry my own food sources, protection, shelter and so forth. And unless I venture into a part of the world where no humans now live, I always choose the first alternative. By involving myself at that participatory level I change myself in deep deep ways. Such a rite of passage among our people in this society would bring home that class of events in a way that would be useful. Take a break. During the break I'd like you to mull over two things:

Judy: First, a puzzle. What is the relationship between addiction and acclimation?

John: And secondly, begin to sort, at second attention, where in the NLP technologies some reference to context—some wisdom—is already built in. What are the technologies that have been offered in the patterning called NLP which address second attention as opposed to first attention? Which address the distortive effects of language? Which constitute questions and possible techniques regarding how you might interface first and second attention?

Judy: Questions of ecology.

Man: Personal or global?

Judy: Global *and* personal. We're talking logical levels.

John: Be back in ten minutes.

BREAK

John: Acclimation and addiction. Are there any people here who live above 8,000 feet? Any people from Colorado? Do you find a difference in your breathing here? What difference do you sense as you sit here almost at sea level?

Woman: I don't breathe as much.

John: You don't breathe as much. And your sensation as well?

2nd Woman: Slower and deeper.

John: Slower and deeper. Now I think almost all of you who didn't raise your hand have had the experience of going from a situation at sea level up to above 7,000 or 8,000—even 10,000 or 12,000 feet. There are some minimal cues. (Laughter). The physiology changes as you change your altitude.

Here's your first puzzle: What's the relationship between addiction and acclimation? In what way are the processes that a drug addict goes through and someone who moves from sea level to 12,000 feet goes through similar? What are the differences? Pose that question for yourself—we'll come back to it shortly.

We're inviting you to consider the differences between a culture and a society. What's the difference between Los Angeles and yogurt? Good, Stephanie, tell them.

Stephanie: It doesn't need a punchline does it?

John: Obviously not—'cause yogurt has culture. No problem, some of my best friends have gone through L.A.

Marshall: You could become unacclimated. I mean you could . . . addiction is something that's apparently difficult to get rid of. You can lose your muscles if you don't use them.

John: Notice what happens when you go from sea level to above 10,000 feet.

Woman: You adapt.

Man: You gain rapport with the changing environment.

John: And what's the first class of maneuvers your body goes through to "gain rapport with the environment"? Tachycardia and then later change in the hemoglobin carrying capacity of the blood but that didn't happen immediately. Tachycardia happened immediately.

Judy: The first response is a stressed response. Alert! Something different in this environment. Then over a period of time the body goes through a set of deeper changes, somatic changes . . .

John: What's the wisdom of that?

Man: The body has a position that it wants to maintain and then it doesn't get the external stimulus. It has to adjust—whatever it can do in order to get back to its equilibrium.

Judy: It wants to maintain that homeostasis—the body is a basically conservative unit.

John: It wants to maintain equilibrium. And notice the problem the human body has to solve when moving to altitude is hypoxia—a deficiency of oxygen reaching the tissues and the first class of responses is quite predictably, hyperventilation and its associated consequences—e.g., tachycardia. This is obvious to the runner, to the athlete—the body already knows that these are the first line of adjustment. However if I now turn around and there's a bear there in the mountains and I'm already at high heart rate and respiratory panting I don't have any reserve, any emergency circuits to throw into the loop to make sure that the bear and I go our separate ways with due respect to each other, . . . and part of me doesn't go with him. . . . (laughter)

Judy: . . . spread yourself all over the mountain.

John: So the wisdom of the body in this case is that it immediately makes the required adjustment and then it says, "This is a gross overexpenditure, an inefficient expenditure, of something we may very much need, in terms of survival. We have eaten up our flexibility." So then deeper somatic processes become involved. José mentioned the hemoglobin fixing capability of blood—how much oxygen the blood can carry. And so a series of deeper processes go into operation —in addition to the process of the transport of oxygen in blood bound to hemoglobin:

- pulmonary ventilation
- pulmonary diffusion of oxygen

- tissue diffusion
- increased cardiac output[16]

(pausing) . . . Now, in addiction what happens?

Woman: Isn't part of addiction adapting to one's environment?

Man: But now you have a boundary situation. You're changing something within your own boundaries. There's no connection with environment.

John: Sure there is. Isn't that exactly the difference between homeopathic medicine and traditional Western medicine? Homeopathic medicine uses substances, externally introduced originally, to stimulate natural body processes which have the ability to produce those same beneficial substances internally . . . , externally introduced substances so that the body becomes autonomous of the external stimuli. In that case, in homeopathic medicine, you have a case for arguing your point. But I'm claiming that's exactly not what's true in addiction. The addict is pushed, like the altitude pushes the person undergoing acclimation, to maintain the new homeostatic levels. A constant supply of some externally introduced element is required—in this case the drug—just as a constant environment of reduced oxygen level typical of high altitude is required to maintain the homeostatic level that is finally achieved through acclimation eighteen months after you've acclimated or become addicted to altitude.

Judy: Certain somatic changes occur which the body will try to maintain because a somatic investment has been made over time.

John: There is no autonomy to self in acclimation and there's no autonomy to self in addiction. Both of them depend on the continued presence and introduction of contextual features, in one case reduced pressure at altitude, reduced oxygen content in the air, and the other case cocaine, heroin . . . , whatever drug is involved . . .

Judy: . . . alcohol . . . once a somatic investment has occured over time, whether by altitude or by drugs, the body, being conservative, will want to maintain that homeostasis.

Pauline: I want to make a comment about the differences—with acclimation you then get choices, more choices that you had at the beginning of the process, whereas with addiction you're narrowing your choices and you can't do things . . .

John: I would argue this instead—one of the reasons that "common sense" dictates to the addict that he or she should have another fix of whatever or another drink is that the new homeostatic level that's been achieved under addiction or acclimation has to be sustained by the same or an increasing amount of the external stimuli, either the drug or the altitude. From the addict's perceptual position, the lack of the drug has profound negative repercussions in terms of reducing their choices. So that it's only "common sense" to the addict to get another shot, take another drink because if they don't they lose choices. So the argument about choice from the perceptual position of the addict is precisely the situation you have when somebody is acclimating.

The human body is a profoundly conservative organism—definitely right wing—in that each time you go through the tremendous effort and investment of finding a new homeostasis . . . I was looking at one of these silly things they put in the Sunday supplement the other day where they were awarding points for stress . . .

Judy: . . . stress points . . .

John: . . . and of equal stress to people are the experiences of entering a new relationship or ending an old one. There was that much wisdom in this thing. That is beginning a marriage or finishing one through a divorce were equally stressful because of the class of adaptations that have to be made to achieve a new homeostatic level.

Woman: But it takes two wings to fly.

Judy: I knew that . . .

John: There are profound differences between the living and nonliving systems. One of the differences is given by the fact that the second law of thermodynamics—conservation of energy—applies absolutely unequivocally, no exceptions known at this moment, in the world of mechanical nonliving systems. So the basic unit in which you can inventory a mechanical system is energy, in the physical sense of energy—not the Santa Cruzian sense of energy . . .

Judy: . . . that's cosmic energy; that's something else . . .

John: It's definitely something else. But in the case of living systems . . . So if I kick my dog two things occur. At the level of the physical body John and the physical body Spirit, my dog, when I kick my dog she will actually physically move and the first part of her movement, unless she sees me coming, will be absolutely predictable by the laws of physics. That is, there is a certain amount of energy I put into the kick, a certain amount is received, there's friction at the interface and her body moves a certain distance . . .

Judy: I have to disagree with that.

John: Oh, do you?

Judy: I'm sorry, I really have to disagree with that. If you kick a ball I would say that the law of physics would apply. But because Spirit is a living system in herself there's a degree of unpredictability.

John: . . . and where does the unpredictability come from?

Judy: From the fact that you don't know which way Spirit's going to run. And not only that, the conservation of energy is violated. Dogs always move further that the kick would move them. (Laughter)

John: Too true. If I kick the ball there's a deterministic system. If I kick another living organism the system becomes nondeterministic. Take the famous croquet game that Alice got involved in. The rules of the game of croquet are known

. . . And in so far as the humans who entered the frame of interaction called croquet agree to abide by these rules we have a deterministic system—that is, for any situation which can legitimately arise within the game there are specified procedures which determine the next move. There are different logical levels of rules. At the elementary level, certain elements of the game are identified as mobile—the croquet balls, the mallets, the players. Other elements are fixed—the stakes and hoops, the surface on which the entire game occurs . . . And, of course, more complex rules . . . If player *A*'s ball passes through hoop *n* prior to player *B*'s ball then a penalty pass is awarded to . . . But what was poor Alice to do when she found herself gripping a flamingo with which she was to strike a hedgehog? Energy in living systems has a different function and it's called collateral energy. The distance the hedgehog rolls is simply not predictable from a measurement of the direction and energy with which Alice swings the flamingo!

Judy: So how can one person make a statement that perhaps changes the world?

John: Russia went through some enormous changes in the second decade of this century. If you measure the energy transaction involved, in terms of the energy expended in the Russian revolution as opposed to the amount of energy it took Karl Marx sitting in the British Library to write the words which triggered those behaviors, then you understand that the conservation of energy is not an appropriate way of organizing in the world of mind—of living systems. The notion of collateral energy means that the interacting units of mind carry their own energy sources and conservation of energy has nothing to do with what occurs at the point of interaction between living systems.

Woman: Who says so.

John: I say so.

Woman: I don't agree with you. . . . , I agree in the sense that I carry my own energy source, but in the sense of energy not being conserved I disagree. In the sense of just being a functioning unit, to me part of balance is how energy effects . . . , how energy is . . .

John: Now let me tease out the part that I want to focus your attention on. If we could have measured the sound waves, the energy in the sound waves of my words that struck your ear, n units of energy were offered there, at the physical level. The amount of energy it took for you to go through the thought process to formulate your own thoughts, to move your body during the communication, will be greater than the energy that you received which was the "stimulus" for the responses you made.

Woman: You're not my source of energy though.

John: Exactly the point I'm making. So there's no conservation of energy across the interface between us. There may be a balancing and an elegance to the way you perceive, store, and choose to use energy within your own collateral sources. All that means is I could kick you and you wouldn't necessarily move at all. Or I could say the words, "I'm going to kick you," and get a tremendous response—but that decision is resident in you. The way you choose to expend your collateral energy, that you have at least partial control over. However, at the interface where billiard ball *A*—with a certain momentum, angular motion, and kinetic energy—strikes billiard ball *B*, the final resting positions of those two billiard balls are predictable if you know the surface upon which the collision occurs. When a foot strikes a dog there's nothing predictable about the final resting places of either the foot or the dog.

Woman: What has that got to do with conservation of energy?

John: Because you cannot predict from an examination of the energy in the stimulus how much energy, if any, will be displayed in the response in a living system.

Tom: There's another entity here. I think there's, like, matter, energy, and then pattern or information or mind or whatever you call it. We worked a long time with . . . , Newton worked with matter a lot and started to discover energy. Then Einstein said, "OK, we can interchange mass and energy by certain laws." There's another part of that triangle which is the pattern in which the energy and matter is arranged which we call information. Computers aren't interesting because of the energy going through them or the particular pieces of glass and plastic they're made out of. They're interesting because of pattern. And I think what we're talking about here is the possibility of the next Einsteinian revolution, which would address the question of how we interchange pattern or mind with energy and matter. I don't know if there's conservation or not, but since conservation has to do with matter and energy then we're talking about mind and how that translates and we know mind affects matter and energy and vice versa.

Judy: The basic unit of inventory in a nonliving physical system is energy, and the basic unit of inventory in a living system (or mind) is difference. Configurations of difference are patterns. And so the next logical level in understanding the world of mind is pattern and redundancy, which are nearly synonymous terms. There is an inherent conservativeness in the body that says if it's going to all the trouble to make the adaptation by change of altitude or change of chemical environment then it's only "common sense" to constantly seek increased or sustained stimulation from the class of variables that got you the adaptations. Yeah, James.

James: With acclimatation you can go to a high altitude and come back to sea level in comparative comfort. You can't do that with addiction. But talking about your pygmies, they could not adapt to the outside world, you know, they'd get sick and whatever, but going back to their rain forest would produce comfort.

Georgine: There is a certain amount of flexibility in all this because I know, as I go up and down in altitude—maybe I'll live at sea level for a while and then I'll go back to my mountains, . . .

John: It gets easier.

Georgine: . . . a lot easier and I would assume the same thing holds true for addiction. That once you start using a substance like that that it's easier to get into others or your body adapts or . . .

Judy: . . . that the body learns at another logical level after the circuits have been used, and the body learns how to do that more quickly. So you're learning to learn.

John: . . . as well as linseed oil, you think? If you take two samples of linseed oil, *A* and *B*, from the same source and place sample *A* in the sun, it will begin to turn gummy. Then you remove it from the light. Next, after a suitable period of time, you place both samples in the sunlight and—guess what? Sample *A* demonstrates that it has memory and has learned to learn—'cause it will become gummy significantly faster than sample *B*.

Judy: . . . tacky . . . (Laughter)

Patricia: Is the issue with conservation of energy that you were trying to predict the pattern so you would know what amount and where to put the energy to get the outcome that you wanted?

John: There were several purposes in us bringing the discussion up. One is that energy is such a ubiquitous concept in discussions of mental activities and it's wholly irrelevant. The metaphor which informs Freud's work is the Industrial Metaphor. Because of the inordinate success of the physical sciences there has been a seduction of the thinking patterns in psychology so that most of the work depends on quantification. I mean if you look at the nonsense that is published in journals . . . I will make a stronger claim: The failure to recognize this qualitative difference has made psychology the science of mediocrity. Any time you explore human performance quantitatively by averaging across subjects you have blurred the very differences which make the topic worth pursuing.

A hundred years or so ago in Austria and in Germany there were psychologists who had these great battles about "imageless" versus "imageful" thought.[17] The methodology they used to approach the study holds really important suggestions for us.

What these people in the Austrian school did was to take people who were quite good at reporting on internal representations and trained them to be the best that they could be. And when they had their trained subjects, not college sophomores, but trained subjects who had committed a serious amount of somatic flexibility to these tasks they then began to explore the patterns of internal representation, the controversy between imageful and imageless thought. By so doing they taught us the lessons we've dropped—we've failed to carry on into modern work. Rarely does anyone in psychology use trained subjects. But it's by using trained subjects that we can explore and push the limits of human performance. Not by taking a group of sophomores and deciding on the average what half-assed performance we're capable of. That's the sense in which psychology has become the science of mediocrity.

Judy: (as the rain outside becomes into a downpour) The world agrees! (laughter)

John: I rest my case. (laughter)

Judy: . . . certain emanations from the outside resonating with certain emanations from the inside . . . (laughter)

Man: Along the same line, psychology has sort of built its models on the latest machines. So Freud had steam engines and plumbing.

John: You needed Draino.

Man: And the behaviorists came along . . . So then we got the telephone, and that was the next thing . . .

Judy: They kept forgetting to ask if anyone was there.

Man: And now we've got computers so finally we have a psychology where . . . But no one has a living system model. Maybe the planet Earth should be the model, or some other kind of . . .

Karen: You used the phrase "used their common sense" when you were talking about the urge to maintain homeostasis in addiction. I'd be interested to talk a little more about what the urge to move away from homeostasis is, where that comes from.

John: Acts of the will. I used "common sense" in two ways. I used common sense in a positive way to mean the intersection of your representational systems, that is, the senses of vision, audition, olfaction, . . . the kind of common sense that we typically use as the basis for first attention. There is another meaning of common sense which I was using when I talked about addiction: if you think linearly *(i.e.,* conscious, purposive, first-attention behavior*)* and you're addicted or acclimated, when the external context or stimulus is removed, you feel bad. It's only "common sense" as I'm using it now to think linearly and go, "Ah, I know exactly what will fix me," not understanding—just as the cattle-herding tribe, because of their perceptual filters, is not understanding—the long-term escalating nature of that kind of common sense as opposed to having the wisdom to consider several steps down the line and indeed to notice that "down the line" curves right back through you. What goes around comes around. And if you can learn to think in circuits and loops . . . (John begins to dance with Pauline) If we're dancing together there is a loop. You may, because of cultural tradition, say that John is leading and Pauline is following. I doubt that you would say that if you saw the two of us dancing very long, but nevertheless you can punctuate this circuit so that I'm leading or she's leading. With the finest dancers that ambiguity becomes complete.

Judy: Now if he breaks part of the circuit . . .

John: . . . if I'm not holding her there (removing his right hand from Pauline's waist) and we're not accustomed to dancing with only this much of a circuit, the circuit's been broken. The difficulty of dancing with grace together when part of the circuit has been interrupted is very difficult. I'm saying that "common sense" would say if I'm dancing with her and I need to make another move I might go, "Oh, I know, I'll release this contact point on her side. I can make this little move over here and get back." (laughter) During that move I have lost part of the circuit I need to know where she is. Because she's signalling me by changing pressure here just as I'm signalling her with my hand where I propose we go next. And we have to find some interesting way of agreeing about that in this dance. So to me those are two ways to use common sense. In the context that I was talking about, addiction, "common sense" means one-step, first-attention, linear thinking. And that can kill you. That can kill you in the long run.

Woman: I'm glad you added the others because hopefully we can develop a . . .

John: A common sense.

Woman: . . . a wider common sense.

Judy: That's horse sense. (laughter)

John: Here's part of the second thing I asked you to think about during the break: How does the NLP material that you've already mastered fits into the historical context we've been developing here? . . . (pause) . . . For example, what does the nominalization "understanding" mean? Somebody give me that definition. What is understanding? Come on, you're all trained, come on. Jump on it, Allen.

Allen: Relating something new to what I already know.

John: No, that's how to fail to learn.

Britt: Taking experiences that you've already had and applying them to new situations to try to figure out what the new situation is. So you put it in terms that you can already "understand" or that you can relate to . . .

John: . . . interesting. Where I was going has nothing to do with where these two are going. (laughter) And there's something really important about this. Notice in a sense they are destroying their ability to learn anything new—so they may understand everything and die of boredom. How many times have you been in situations with someone who insisted on relating everything that you were proposing to something they already knew? I mean those people have now picked out a meta-strategy which will defeat their ability to change themselves based on difference. "In other words you're saying . . ." "Isn't that just like . . . ?" Well if it were just like that I'd say it was that. The fact that it's not just like that makes it interesting. I'm proposing that you disassociate from your previous experience, that you know nothing and you approach this freshly. By the way, this is part of the instructions for what you do this afternoon with TaTitos Sompa. You're going to be invited into a world that most of you have never been exposed to. My proposal is that you disassociate and build yourself an altered state in which the African experience that he's going to offer you is not related to things you already know. Because by failing to do so you'll rob yourself of some of the freshness of what's being offered.

Gloria: Well, I'd say that understanding comes from analyzing, rationalizing, interpreting things and that really understanding comes from experience.

John: OK. But let's even be more precise. How do you know . . . If I go, "I understand what you just said," as opposed to, "I don't understand what you just said," what are the internal events? Marshall, save me. (laughter)

Marshall: When you understand something you can use it as if it were your own and then generate new examples of it.

Christian: I don't know if this answers your question. Using the NLP model, it's having a clear picture, having a feeling that coalesces. Using my own experience on that kind of submodality model, I think that I understand something whenever I have the feeling that I understand it. So it basically comes down to having a clear picture initially or feeling that I understand it, feeling that I could explain it if I had to or that I could make a representation of it . . .

John: I'm going to claim that there are two dimensions to understanding. And what you're talking about is first-attention understanding. Nothing wrong with it. I'm just pointing out it's first-attention understanding because what it says is I have a clear image, I have a feeling for it, I have some sounds that are associated with it, I have some words, possibly some odors and some tastes that are associated with it. That is to say I have a 4-tuple, that is I have auditory, visual, kinesthetic, . . . representations. In each of my major representational systems I have representations which I can inspect one by one; I can bring them to first-attention consciousness, inspect them, and go, "Uh-huh! I got pictures, I got sounds, I got words, I got feelings, I got smells, I got tastes." More importantly than just that—that's a necessary condition but not a sufficient one—in addition to having representations across all the major representational systems they have to be congruent one with the other.

Some types of schizophrenia are a result of long term exposure to perfectly correlated experiences which are not congruent one with the other. This is horizontal understanding. This is first attention understanding. You know how to do that. Whether you make use of that tool is a question of your own personal competence and your own personal disciplines. This is where wisdom begins. Because I say now that at the first attention this is understanding. But at a deeper level you'd have to have vertical understanding in order to apply your skills with wisdom. And by vertical understanding I mean that you take this coordinated experience which you've achieved with first attention and you discover its depth—you do not understand it until you can relate it to context. So vertical understanding presupposes horizontal understanding and it is related to context in that you've found a loop between your horizontal understandings and the context in which it occurs. Virginia Satir says, "Follow your gut feelings!" However, unless you actually have her guts you are liable to get lost. You could be the finest card player in Las Vegas but unless you figure out, in context, when it's appropriate for you to use that class of tools you're going to end up in a back alley somewhere. We're proposing that contextualization is the beginning of wisdom.

Carol: Would that be like learning the NLP skills in practitioner training, that's the context of it but it's really learning without the context—transferring it over to the context where you need to use it ecologically is the task?

John: You can achieve this in training. And you can get hints about this because you actually form relationships with other people there, the trainers and the other members of the staff. But until you've transferred the horizontal understanding you've achieved and practiced in the class of contexts that you operate in, you don't understand.

Britt: So this is where education breeds mediocrity. It's because we learn horizontally . . .

John: At best.

Britt: At best.

Judy: At best. (laughter)

John: In the heyday of behaviorism there was a guy named Tolman[18] at Berkeley who said, "Are you kidding me? Are you going to tell me that everything can be explained by muscle twitches?" So he did some extraordinary things. He took mazes and he trained rats to run the maze to criteria. Then he filled the maze with water and noticed they could swim right to the food box. That was absolute counterevidence of the current theory of behaviorism that said they've learned it because of certain muscle tensions. And muscle tensions in swimming and running are different.

Even way back in Watson's[19] original experiments—Watson being the man who was most closely identified in our country with developing behaviorism—he noticed that when he trained rats in a maze and then reoriented the maze 90° and 180° in the room that they had been trained in, they ran into walls; they tried to turn shorter corners because of the change in their orientation to stimuli which had nothing to do with kinesthetic representation even in his original experiments.

The funniest of all of them was the work where an experimenter[20] took rats and he put them in straightjackets . . .

Judy: . . . he put them on little trains . . .

John: . . . and ran them through mazes. And when they were going through some portions of the maze, at a choice point, he would actually shock them—this was a "bad" place. And if they were taken down a little trolley to the food box where they were rewarded. He also left open a third, so-called "neutral" choice. So there were bad places, good places, and neutral places. Now if you expose a trained rat to a choice point between a bad and a good place . . .

Judy: No problem. Which would he choose?

John: The good, absolutely.

Judy: But if you exposed him to the choice between neutral and the good which do you think he chose?

John: The neutral.

Judy: Curiosity, like play, is a larger frame—a higher logical level.

John: And they couldn't understand it. Just as the politicians can't understand why we have the same problems every four years. Because the logical levels were not respected. You cannot train an animal to be curious or incurious. You can train it to know places that are associated with certain kinds of experience, food or shock, but given a choice between a certain reward and someplace they've never been before, the higher logical level variable called exploration or curiosity kicks in even in a rat. (laughter) And if you don't appreciate the difference in logical levels and you treat people that way, what the hell do you think you're going to get besides the mess we've created? It's astonishing that those logical levels are not recognized in the class of reinforcements that go on among people.

José: How much of a genius would Einstein be among the pygmies?

John: Great question. (Laughter)

Judy: You would certainly get a double description.

John: What he's pointing out is very cybernetic. Most genius has to involve a profound interaction with the environment otherwise it is not recognized. Now I mean, we've got to be careful about the notion of genius. I have watched men and women doing things like sewing and carpentry and thought, "That's brilliant—that's genius." So genius is not necessarily only the class of genius defined in terms of social recognition.

José: In other words you're talking about context and understanding. Not a recognition by the pygmies but how would Einstein think about himself as a genius among the pygmies.

John: I've got your question. Of course it's a rhetorical question so I won't answer it. But it's an important question to consider. I believe that if Milton Erickson had been in any other profession he would have excelled primarily because in his strategies he placed such an emphasis on feedback. I'm not sure that that was true in Einstein's case. Major portions of the circuitry that he used to establish himself as a genius did not involve feedback from the world. He was a self-operating, self-contained unit in many of his strategies as opposed to Erickson who used a lot of feedback from the world as a way of guiding him to certain understandings and recognitions.

I hope you come to an appreciation of the interaction—of the circuitry—of the individual with their context. One of the differences between a society and a culture is that you do not have external support for your values in a society. You cannot count on external support for the balances needed within you. In a fragmented society, where there isn't a culture that reinforces those balances, it becomes very important that well-formed design principles be used in generating the personal culture. We're proposing, as we develop this with you, a very specific structure for internal personal culture. It's going to be content-free but it's going to be structurally specified. It deals with issues such as demons . . . , I want your demons . . . Wake up! All of them out there. Because I want them available for what we're going to do. I also want those demons caged, and, in the metaphor we're working on, the cage is the context within which the demon is free to operate. Demons —every one has their demons . . . in some of us these demons are slumbering, in others they are completely awake and out of control. Not surprisingly the issue is balance—better let slumbering demons lie than arouse them without proper arrangements—the care, feeding and training of demons—where do you assign stability and where do you foster entrophy—. . . Michael Colgrass won a Pulitzer prize for musical composition some years back—he has a very well developed demon for composition. As Michael says when he has committed—becomes his demon, he can compose as easily in Times Square as in a hideaway in the Blue Ridge Mountains. And as he points out there are grave repercussions of the timing of letting loose your demons. Colgrass once received a phone call the evening before he was to leave Toronto to vacation in Florida. The caller wished to discuss with Michael the commissioning of a work. Over the years Michael has developed a facility in handling the business side of being a professional composer. Issues such as the theme of the composition, the orchestra, the soloist to be featured, the time alloted prior to first rehearsal, the money available, . . . form some of the facts he has learned to elicit in making appropriate decisions in this area. He relates that once these pieces of information are fixed it is not unusual for him to hear the opening bars of the composition at that point. To his subsequent consternation, he discovered himself deeper into the discussion than he had anticipated, . . . , and before he could interrupt the process, the demon had the information, made an affirmative decision and presented him with the beginning of the work. Well, poor Michael, acting as if everything were normal, he flew to Florida. He describes lying there on the beach pretending not to notice the wonderous productions of his demon—he said it felt very much like a child tugging on his clothing . . . and like a child, he was not to be denied. By the way, he is on excellent terms with his demon—they're old friends—be judicious in how you make arrangements with your demons . . . and make your arrangements before you wake your demons. The controller for the demon's responsibility is two fold—first to define the context for the demon and to insist on the demon respecting those boundary conditions and secondly, to make sure that the demon has absolutely no interference when operating within the context for which that demon has been given full and primary responsibility.

Woman: Part of what you'll be talking about is how to implement that structure?

John: Oh, with precision . . .

Judy: . . . down to little tiny circuits.

John: Part of your ability to express your personal genius is your ability to move in this latticework inside of you in such a way that, once arrangements have been made for balance and a lifeline is securely fixed, that you essentially go down inside your circuitry and become the demon that you're capable of being in the context.

Judy: So self becomes a dynamic function as opposed to a static definition. John and I and Richard were talking with Gregory Bateson and he looked at us and said, "This notion of nominalization is brilliant." Because, you see, he spent time and effort writing to demonstrate that the minimum unit in mind is difference and then spent more of the same arguing that difference presupposes double description. All of you who trained in the Meta-model, I hope, go, "Of course difference presupposes double description because the word 'difference' is a nominalization which comes from a two-place predicate (or a relation or a verb, however you want to talk about it) which has a subject and an object." From the linguistic structure itself you know that there were at least two relata, that is, two things that this thing called difference was the relationship between. So we're going to propose that one of the differences that makes a profound difference is the flexibility that you need to identify with subcircuits within yourself—once the balance and lifeline arrangements have been made so that during that period you know nothing outside of precisely those things which you need to know to get a particular task done—and that there's a wisdom and balance to the entire structure.

John: There are some interesting things that will occur neurologically. That's why dreaming is a critical part of what we're doing here.

Judy: . . . and that's the integration we talked about earlier in the reading from Gregory's article. If the culture produces an art that's totally conscious, or if a culture produces an art that's totally unconscious, it's not going to be great art. Because art always appeals to multilevels. Great art always appeals to multilevels and their integration . . .

John: . . . we have two tasks that we wish to deal with today which are recognizable by you. (Laughter) One is "stopping the world." The metaphor comes from Castaneda. The second one comes from an amazing woman named Viola Legere, an Acadian. Acadians are the people of French descent who were in Canada when England and France had a war in the middle 18th century and England won.

Judy: Do you all remember the poem of Evangeline?—a poem that came from one of the tragedies of the Acadians when they become British subjects as a result of France losing the war to England.

John: They were moved wholesale to the part of North America now called New England. Some time later about half of that group were moved to Louisiana and become the Cajuns and the other half went back to the province which is now called New Brunswick.

Viola Legere was an Acadian high school teacher who ran the drama club. One of her friends is a famous playwright in Canada and wrote a play called *La Segouine* . . .

Judy: . . . about a seventy-five-year-old woman. . . .

John: . . . with thirteen children . . .

Judy: . . . ten of which have died because they were born in the winter . . .

John: . . . and for two hours she's on stage all alone. The artistry and commitment the woman displays are impressive; she even does shape changing. She's never had a child herself, yet —those of you who are alert to physiological differences such as the abdominal distension that is typical of a woman who's had a lot of children can appreciate this—her body changes shape and shows that distension. When she becomes La Seguine there's no ambiguity, she is that woman. And she's talking over her back fence and by God, Larry, she's talking to you and nobody else is there. Of course, simultaneously she's talking to you, David, and you know nobody else is there either. Her presence is magnificent. Viola Legere is one of the most balanced human beings I have ever had the pleasure of meeting.

Well, a question came up the following morning when a French Canadian named André asked me, "What is the difference between Viola Legere when she is being La Segouine and someone who is treated by a psychiatrist in a mental hospital for delusions?" And my answer was, "There's a tremendous difference between the two. She's an artist. And therefore her madness is gloriously artistic. The madness of someone in an institution typically doesn't have much artistry nor does it respect context; that's La Segouine. But Viola Legere is gloriously, artistically mad when she does those things; and that's why theaters have curtains and scripts have final sentences in them and then they end . . .

Judy: . . . and directors . . .

John: . . . are present during performances.

Judy: Legere tested John with some tasks before she was willing to commit to a demonstration of her acting ability. The things that she asked John to do were her way of determining whether the contextual markers were stable enough to safely enter another world—her way of saying, "You're going to be my director and I want to make sure you can get me back 'cause I'm going to go become La Segouine . . ."

John: ". . . I'm going to become gloriously mad . . ."

Judy: ". . . inside this frame . . ."

John: ". . . and it's your job to sustain the frame so I can get back."

Woman: That is also the function of a group in shamanistic journeys.

John: This lifeline notion reminds me of John Rosen too. John Rosen was a psychiatrist who in the '30s and '40s, according to Scheflin was one of the few psychiatrists in this country who was considered successful with institutionalized patients.

Judy: He would join their reality so well that he'd spoil it for them. He would so completely occupy the patient's niche, the patient would have to move.

John: Now unfortunately Dr. Rosen was not trained in the art of acting. He was obviously a natural but he wasn't trained. So every three or four years, according to his Boswell, Scheflin, he would forget to come back and would have to himself be institutionalized and there was a struggle to bring him back. Consider the balance of this woman Viola Legere. Rosen was a brave man because he did it without safeguards. But that's crazy—and it turned out to be that way.

I make the following claim and I ask that you check in your

own heart and determine if this is true. Start with the assumption that you're capable of personal genius and the major thing that prevents most of you from exercising that personal genius is that personal genius presupposes a passionate 100% commitment to the moment and the context. Therefore, if you have a question about whether you could get back, there will be an incongruity you will experience at second attention which will defeat your attempts to achieve personal genius.

Woman: There are serious consequences.

Judy: In addition to doing La Segouine—who is a single character who may be talking to you over the fence or scrubbing the floor—Viola Legere does a one-woman show where, like Lily Tomlin, she changes personalities maybe six or seven times. She simply turns around and when she comes back around she's a different person. People ask her, "God, isn't that hard? Isn't that hard to make those turnarounds?" And she says, "No. What's hard is crossing no-man's-land from Viola Legere to any other character and once I'm there I can change characters any number of times."

John: And what was she talking about in terms of the difference in effort? Logical level. That is, within the same logical level there's a lot of freedom to move around. Moving from one logical level to another requires a lot of effort and . . .

Judy: . . . a lot of skill . . .

John: . . . and a tremendous personal commitment.

Karen: What I think you're saying is that you have a presumption that we each have a sort of core reality and a set of connections to the world that are essential. Do you think that's different from one person to another?

John: Absolutely.

Karen: Some of us don't have many of these connections or have them organized differently?

John: Yeah, those are the interesting differences between us.

Judy: Absolutely.

John: And what is the difference? The difference is knowing context.

Georgine: No . . .

John: Oh yeah it is!

Georgine: Well that may be, but that's . . .

John: See, if you took the madness that you've been able to display at various times in your life and if you had put that in the proper contexts people would acclaim you as a genius.

Georgine: They were in the proper context at the time.

John: You don't know that. And there was a lot of feedback from the world that you got indicating that it wasn't the proper context as far as other people's perceptions were concerned.

Georgine: But as far as our results were concerned . . .

John: Now you're talking about first attention. Results is like "purpose" is like "outcome." So you can achieve exactly what the whole group agrees is your purpose, but if the methods you used don't respect the context, you're not going to receive the accolades of the world.

Georgine: But do you care?

John: Some geniuses do and some don't. Gregory confesses in his work that he's not a man who could work without feedback. I take it that Einstein was. He worked on his own for decades with little or no recognition and then, *pop.* That is one of the differences that we were just talking about with Karen's proposal. I'm not saying that you have to respect context. I'm saying: understand that part of wisdom is either respecting context or accepting the consequences of not respecting context.

Georgine: But going beyond the limits, when you go for breaking the limits, OK, you're going to go into areas that are not acceptable to other people because they haven't been there. So you're going beyond their limits and that's going to put you in territory where all of a sudden you have threatened the reality of a lot of people around you.

Judy: And then they go, "Yipes!"

John: I'm willing to violate certain presuppositions of context. There can be an ecology even to the way I do that. For example, if I walk in and talk to a group of psychiatrists, I'm going to infuriate them in certain ways. If I do so because I operate with respect—that they are still organisms that can learn something new—they may not like me at the end, but I'm not in a popularity contest. If I have changed some of their circuitry by my performance then I'm perfectly happy to accept that as the compensation for my work, as opposed to their applause. So I have my own quality standards about what I'm supposed to be about and that may ruffle lots of feathers. I'm claiming that I wouldn't bother to ruffle the feathers if I didn't believe there was a responsiveness and intelligence to the organism whose feathers I was ruffling. I would walk by it like a stone. So I appreciate that you have to make another class of contextual decisions. If I go out and learn to speak KiSwahili, there are stages in my acquisition of language when I babble like an idiot. I may produce poetry accidentally, but I'm not a poet, I'm a child at that point. I become a poet when I so well master the language that when I break the rules I know the rules that I'm breaking. As Gregory says you look at a crab and notice they have one large and one small pincer. The beauty in the crab and the fact that it's a living system is contained in the pattern created —proposing symmetry and then denying it. It proposes a rule that's followed everywhere except here. And the thing that makes it interesting is that it now violates the rule that it itself has proposed to your perceptual apparatus.

Judy: By what? By size.

John: By scale.

Woman: That's the exciting part.

John: You have to master the rules and then you can break them in aesthetically interesting ways.

Judy: There's this really interesting article called "Men are Grass" written by Gregory Bateson.

John & Judy: All men are mortal. Men die.
Socrates is a man. Grass dies.
Socrates is mortal. Men are grass.

Judy: Now that's a logic of the second attention. I understand that perfectly.

John: And so does any poet.

Judy: That's the basis of poetry to me. I go. "Oh yeah, well, grass is a living thing, I'm a living thing, men are grass. No problem." That's also the basis of craziness.

John: The difference between the poet and the person who's locked up for using syllogistic second-attention forms is the difference between understanding contexts. The poet creates perceptions of the world that are not available to first attention. And when the poet succeeds everybody's second attention goes, "Bravo!" But the poet knew behaviorally what the rules were and chose to break them in a specific way even though he or she may not be conscious of the mechanisms. Whereas, someone who is now locked up has lost the context in which those syllogisms were a primary tool of their performance, that's all.

Carol: You keep mentioning logical levels and I don't have an understanding of what that means.

John: It's essential to the construction project that we're going to do. So, someone give me an example of logical levels.

Richard: Let me give an example that comes from a story about a man who's in debt in a time when people were incarcerated for being in debt. This man has a daughter. So the person to whom the money is owed comes up and proposes a very logical solution to that. He's going to put two pebbles in a little bag: if she pulls out the white pebble the debt will be erased and she is free, but if she pulls out the black she has to marry this guy. So your logical approach to that would be, well, there are three obvious logical possibilities. One, she pulls out the white; two, she pulls out the black; or three, she refuses. There is another solution that comes from being outside the problem itself and it requires a certain amount of flexibility. So she agrees, and as the man is picking up the pebbles she notices that he picks up two black pebbles and puts them in the bag. So now she's confronted agains with another set of possibilities than those which the logical mind would present. She could expose him as a cheat, so on and so forth. In any case, her solution to the problem was she goes in, makes the choice of the pebble and clumsily just drops the pebble she chose. And she goes, "Oh my! I dropped the pebble." And she says, "Oh, but we can tell which one I picked by the one remaining."

Judy: Pretty good.

John: Logical levels. One of first attention's functions is modeling second attention. In a multiple personality there are parts of the personality that know about other parts and parts that don't. An organizational hierarchical structure is an example of logical levels. In the context of talking about the human being in a society, the family, the affinity group, and finally, the tribe, are logical levels of organization. So, in conclusion, relationships define logical levels. For example, the number "one" is simply an integer, a natural integer. It's a member of a set called "the set of natural integers" which, in turn, is a set in the set of rational numbers which in turn . . . , that is, each set is defined by the inclusion of its subsets. We'll make it more specific when we begin to build the structure of the personal organizational model. For example, a demon is at a lower logical level than the controller for that demon. It has to be. Otherwise you get all sorts of strange things. OK. I think there are two tasks that need to be done.

Man: It's after one.

Judy: Yipes.

STOPPING THE WORLD WITH LIFELINES

John: The two tasks that I wish to accomplish before I put you in the most artistic, capable hands of TaTitos Sompa this afternoon at three-thirty are the task of "stopping the world" and the task of arranging and using lifelines. They go together into a single unified exercise.

Judy: You all know "stopping the world" from . . .

John: . . . Castaneda

Turning off internal dialogue . . .

There are two minimum requirements to achieving the "stopping the world" state. Remember the discussion about understanding and how you understand by relating experience to what you already know? That's one way you sustain your world. If every new input is recoded—especially before reaching the central nervous system and consciousness—into something you already know, there's no disturbance of the homeostatic levels on the one hand and on the other hand, you don't learn anything new. So ongoing verbal description of the world is one way that you sustain the world that you already know, categorize it, and recode it. The second thing is foveal vision. You know, there are 160,000,000 cones and rods in the retina. There are magnitudes less tracks in the optic nerve. And as you move back in the optic nerve to the optic chiasma and then further back, at each level, at each synapse, there's a reductionistic mechanism being employed. Transform, transform, transform, transform . . .

your two fingers up at about arm's length. Now close your left eye. Now focus on your left finger with your right eye and slowly, without shifting your gaze, so that your right eye is looking at your left finger, move your right finger away. After about four inches of separation the top of it should disappear. If you don't notice that, go past that spot and then come back. No-no, much too far. About this far is where you're going to find that.

Woman: I'm watching my left finger.

John: You're watching your left finger . . .

Judy: . . . with your right eye . . .

John: . . . with your right eye only, one eye. And as you move across there's a place where the top of your right finger disappears. And it appears again. Isn't that amazing?

Judy: Where did it go?

John: The part about it appearing again is what I'm really thankful for. (Laughter)

Judy: Yipes!

John: Now what you're discovering by a simple little demonstration is something that is part of your heritage as a human being. It's called your blind spot. Obviously where the tracks from the retina leave the retina is a blind spot. Notice that we fill this with an automaticity that can only be teased out by a careful examination of our experience using monocular, as opposed to binocular vision.

Judy: So there, new information is right at the end of your finger.

John: And so is the blind spot. Depending on which way you're moving. So foveal vision employs the class of receptors that are centralized in the eye, usually called cones. Rods, which constitute the major anatomical structure in the periphery of the eye, are the major element in your way of witnessing the world through peripheral vision.

Judy: As John mentioned earlier, if you focus on the blackboard here, where in the room do you notice movement? It will be in your peripheral vision.

John: And if you think that's where it actually is, look across the room and you'll notice suddenly it shifts. There are many examples available in the inspection of everyday experience about the class of transforms that occur between the interface of the world and us called our sense organs and what we ultimately come to appreciate as our world as constructed by those transforms in representational systems in consciousness.

Judy: As it filters down literally.

John: We're proposing that from now on, when you act in the world you use this next exercise as your prototype—to arrange for Viola Legere type contextual markers and a lifeline. Then you "stop the world." Now notice that what happend when you "stop the world" is in part a function of the methodology you use for "stopping the world." If you're using a deep, deep trance, and go in and make those requests of your second attention and get a confirmation and then come out of the trance into the altered state of having "stopped the world" you'll have one class of experiences. It will be profoundly different, typically, than what happens when you "stop the world" by finding an access point to a highly focused state where historically you did "stop the world" and you now retrieve the physiology and the experience of that state from your personal history. There will tend to be some substance, some content from the original environment, the context where you "stopped the world" before that will intrude. There will be differences using those approaches.

Judy: In Castaneda's descriptions of "stopping the world" he talks about children . . . , he uses the concept of "seeing," when you stop internal dialog and you stop foveal vision and you're seeing with just peripheral vision, the world looks amazingly different. He talks about the range of human possibilities being out there and culture resonating with a few of those possibilities—the emanations on the outside and the inside matching. And it's so liquid that in order to stabilize it children are taught language. They're constantly reinforced with language as a way of stabilizing and fixing that point. He talks about children being "seers," and then the parents start making descriptions of the world and telling them who they are—they learn language and then the world stabilizes. It's another description.

George: I'd like a reference experience for having this peripheral only vision.

John: Take your finger and put it out here and look at me. Now, how many fingers do you see? Two, right? The space in between those two fingers doesn't exist except as an artifact of your neurology, right? You can demonstrate that by looking at your finger. How many of me do you see?

George: Two.

John: Now, if you were to take an object which you wish to fix your attention on and look past it so that it becomes blurred —just as I'm looking past my finger and seeing you resolved but my finger is now indefinite, it's not as resolved—you would begin a process of learning how to look at someone and give up foveal vision, especially if you paid attention to the kinesthetics of your eyes.

George: I have a reference experience for something like what Deborah calls "full-view" vision where I can literally see out to the end. But nothing in the middle disappears unless I close my eyes.

John: So, I'm saying, stare at a blank spot to occupy your foveal vision and attend to the activity in your peripheral vision; that will accomplish the same thing. If you give your foveal vision nothing of interest, it doesn't change; it fatigues itself. Those are some of the ways of achieving that particular part of the visual experience.

Judy: Think about the little eyeball moving twenty times a second. 'Cause if it did stop, it would fatigue.

George: Yeah, but it doesn't.

Judy: Yeah, so it keeps moving.

John: In fact they took a small miniaturized projector and mounted it on a contact lens.

Judy: It was a little teeny . . . (Laughter)

John: The pictures looked big though. But they only lasted a few seconds because the contact lens was sensitive to that twenty times a second movement of the eye—your eye cannot see from a single perceptual position, it's constantly moving. We're unaware of it just as we're unaware of the blind spot. But in this case since the contact was sensitive to those eye movements the projector mounted on it remained in the same relationship to the retinal receptors even though the eye continued its movement. The pattern of light entering the eye was therefore falling continuously on the same receptors . . . after several seconds the person's perception of the image disappeared completely . . . then it reoccurred when the nerves recovered, disappeared, reoccurred, disappeared . . .

There is a wisdom here that far exceeds the subset of you which is called consciousness or first attention. There are certain disciplines and practices the conscious mind, first attention, needs to master to keep up its part of the relationship with second attention. Erickson used to liken a conscious-unconscious relationship to a rider and horse. The rider could choose a place that he or she wished to go. In proposing it to the horse there was an understanding that unless the horse agreed, they weren't going to go there together. (laughter)

Judy: That was the first thing.

John: The second thing was that once there had been an agreement between the horse and rider about where they were going it would be arrogant and foolish of the rider . . .

Judy: . . . to try to tell that horse how to . . .

John & Judy: . . . make each specific step.

John: It would be wise to leave that level of detail to the horse, trusting its strength and balance and power. And how you request assistance from second attention is one of the most important things to be learned about here. There are things called well-formedness conditions and intensive definitions which are ways of making requests without being overly specific. So if I say to my unconsciousness, "Please create a situation where I notice those things which are of relevance to the task at hand," and now I name the task, I've behaved in an appropriate fashion in terms of first-and second-attention relationships. And I'm making use of the strength and the balance and the wisdom of second attention in a respectful way by not overspecifying the substance of the experience.

The only thing we haven't discussed are what arrangements you make for your lifelines. This is critical. And if you've ever worked in this arena before you have noticed that lots of parts of you, for your own protection, will interrupt your process. Maureen gave the example, that when she goes into certain classes of altered state there's a panic response that gets triggered and she's pulled back immediately. That panic response is an important ally in second attention that says, "You have not made the proper arrangements therefore you may not safely enter or remain in this class of experiences."

Judy: Do you remember what Carlos had to do all the time?

Woman: Note-taking?

Judy: Right. Write, right, write. "You better write some more." Don Juan insisted Carlos write for his own comfort.

John: Witness responsibilities—Larry and I are a team now. And he's going to go into his particular "stopping the world" state. Now you will be working in pairs like Larry and me. So I'm his guardian angel, his witness—however you want to label this relationship. There are two ways in which I want you to comfort your associate in this exercise and they're both nonverbal.

One is this: You stand behind your partner and take your hands and place them firmly across the solar plexus here—gently but firmly, being sensitive to the breathing rhythm—and you will find, as Larry is, it's a very comforting thing to do for a human being.

We can both experience it, correct?

Larry: Yes.

John: A second way to comfort your colleague should it prove to be appropriate, is by rocking. Whether it's rocking like this or rocking back and forth this way. It would be nice if it were coordinated with the person's breathing as well, of course. Or if the person happens to be on the ground then you roll them back and forth on the ground very gently. Thanks, Larry. I limit your comforting interventions to those two. Our whole discussion this morning about the difference between culture and society means you cannot depend (as you can in this workshop) on having matching values and representations in other people. That's the difference between a society and a culture. Therefore it becomes very important that in your position as witness you are not overly active. I do not want you to rob the individual who's going through this exercise of the experience by being overly helpful. This is one arrangement which I insist be explicit between you and the other person. If I'm working with Larry, he finds himself a nice, balanced, stabilized resource state where both first and second attention are available and then I anchor it. He says, "This is the state I want you to bring me back to if you bring me back," and I'll anchor it. When we're both satisfied that that anchor works—we could break the state and I could check the efficacy of the anchor and if we both agree it works your two fingers up at about arm's length. Now close your left eye. Now focus on your left finger with your right eye and slowly, without shifting your gaze, so that your right eye is looking at your left finger, move your right finger away. After about four inches of separation the top of it should disappear. If you don't notice that, go past that spot and then come back. No-no, much too far. About this far is where you're going to find that.

Woman: I'm watching my left finger.

John: You're watching your left finger . . .

Judy: . . . with your right eye . . .

John: . . . with your right eye only, one eye. And as you move across there's a place where the top of your right finger disappears. And it appears again. Isn't that amazing?

Judy: Where did it go?

John: The part about it appearing again is what I'm really thankful for. (Laughter)

Judy: Yipes!

John: Now what you're discovering by a simple little demonstration is something that is part of your heritage as a human being. It's called your blind spot. Obviously where the tracks from the retina leave the retina is a blind spot. Notice that we fill this with an automaticity that can only be teased out by a careful examination of our experience using monocular, as opposed to binocular vision.

Judy: So there, new information is right at the end of your finger.

John: And so is the blind spot. Depending on which way you're moving. So foveal vision employs the class of receptors that are centralized in the eye, usually called cones. Rods, which constitute the major anatomical structure in the periphery of the eye, are the major element in your way of witnessing the world through peripheral vision.

Judy: As John mentioned earlier, if you focus on the blackboard here, where in the room do you notice movement? It will be in your peripheral vision.

John: And if you think that's where it actually is, look across the room and you'll notice suddenly it shifts. There are many examples available in the inspection of everyday experience about the class of transforms that occur between the interface of the world and us called our sense organs and what we ultimately come to appreciate as our world as constructed by those transforms in representational systems in consciousness.

Judy: As it filters down literally.

John: We're proposing that from now on, when you act in the world you use this next exercise as your prototype—to arrange for Viola Legere type contextual markers and a lifeline. Then you "stop the world." Now notice that what happend when you "stop the world" is in part a function of the methodology you use for "stopping the world." If you're using a deep, deep trance, and go in and make those requests of your second attention and get a confirmation and then come out of the trance into the altered state of having "stopped the world" you'll have one class of experiences. It will be profoundly different, typically, than what happens when you "stop the world" by finding an access point to a highly focused state where historically you did "stop the world" and you now retrieve the physiology and the experience of that state from your personal history. There will tend to be some substance, some content from the original environment, the context where you "stopped the world" before that will intrude. There will be differences using those approaches.

Judy: In Castaneda's descriptions of "stopping the world" he talks about children . . . , he uses the concept of "seeing," when you stop internal dialog and you stop foveal vision and to educate it as to what the specific contextual conditions are for it to hit the button.

Maureen: The most important experience that I went through—that I now feel was necessary for me to go through in order to extend my skills as a racing driver—was to lose control of the car. And when I was going through my instruction process it wasn't until I lost control of the car that the instructor walked away from me and said, "You're fine." And I looked at him and said, "You're crazy!"

John: . . . but he was right.

Maureen: After that experience it was so obvious to me.

Judy: There's a concept called "controlled folly" in Castaneda's work. You cannot make a full commitment unless you know what the worst case consequence is and are willing to accept that. Your ability to go out of control with the car and survive it was the last piece that you needed to know so that you could make a full, passionate, 100% commitment to that activity. You had done everything, that is, you achieved excellence in that form. That's a kind of personal genius and it's a really good example of extension of self too.

John: There are certain parts of me that say extension of self should include food at this point. An hour and a half, please be prompt, and bring back loose clothing to give you freedom of movement so that you can participate in the activities that will begin at three-thirty this afternoon.

Deborah: You said . . . , one of the things you said I have translated carefully but I'm not sure it quite fits and that's this description of what I call "full-view, F-U-L-L-dash-V-I-E-W," (laughter) vision and ah . . .

Judy: Foveal. (writing on board) But I like that—"full-view" However, like most first-attention translations, it's totally misleading. (Laughter) So the fovea and the periphery of the eye give rise to different classes of visual experience. Extend is under certain kinds of nicely altered states you get tunnel vision, that is, all you have is foveal vision, the peripheral vision disappears.

Judy: Don Juan says that after "stopping the world," the next step is "seeing" which he defines as "responding to the perceptual solicitations of a world outside the description we have learned to call reality."

Woman: When you talked about establishing a lifeline, do you want us to be able to do that ourselves?

John: . . . Yes, with instructions from us and a cybernetic first-/second-attention feedback loop of proposal, request, proposal, request to come to an assurance, before you make the step into "stopping the world," that you have a secure lifeline, that, in the worst case, can be tugged gently and bring you back nicely. That's the purpose of your pairing with some witness during these experiments and perhaps setting up an agreed upon signal that will let them know to bring you out.

Maureen: I think I have that already, however it's very quick to panic and pull me back.

John: Right. So the panic response is a function within you that says, "Aha! You could get lost here." You used to drive race cars? When you were driving race cars you made that complete demon commitment. You had to to be good. In that context your consciousness let go and allowed you to extend your definition of self to the tires. The basis of any aesthetic act is skill. And it's our responsibility to ensure that the proper tools are available to you so that as you do these exercises the panic function can go, "I'm sitting here ready to press the button to pull you out but I have criteria that we've agreed upon that says when—under what specific conditions—I should pop you." That'll give you the freedom of going into the state and exploring it without being yanked back immediately. That is an important positive function within you and I would never interfere with it. I would like of trance work if you are capable and have been trained in the technology of the second attention called the Ericksonian Model. You may use a device such as reframing . . .

Judy: . . . to set up a. . .

John: . . . relationship between first and second attention and propose from first attention that you have this class of experiences and confirm the acceptance of that proposal with an involuntary second-attention signal.

Judy: Or you can remember some time when you actually were so focused that you did not have internal dialogue . . .

John: . . . and then reaccess . . .

Judy: . . . that state and anchor it . . .

John: . . . fully. Let those possibilities, along with a dozen other possibilities that I hope also occur to you about how you might accomplish the task, let them sit over lunch. Understand that we will ask you not to do this exercise until you have made the appropriate lifeline contextual-marker arrangements so that you may do it with complete safety. Safety in the sense that you'll come back. I have no guarantees as to what you'll meet when you go to second attention. That's the importance of you going yourself. It's also the importance of you having a witness who will accompany you as a fallback —to pull that lifeline back just as Viola Legere insists on curtains, scripts, and directors.

Woman: When you say foveal vision, is that like phobia?

John: Possibly . . . Look over at that circle on the wall. So you can see my hand moving easily. The periphery of your eye is built to detect movement. The foveal vision is built to detect color. You see grays in your peripheral vision largely. So they are really two systems; in fact, there are pathologies of the eye where you lose either foveal or peripheral vision differentially showing that there are different tracks. Another way to do it

John: You do not see me; you see events on your occipital lobe.

Judy: I hate that. (Laughter)

John: Bateson says that the tree that I see with my eyes closed is more truly mine than the tree that I see with my eyes open. Since there's no external pattern impinging on that occipital lobe event called "seeing the tree" it's easier for me to change the tree if I have nothing out there to coordinate. The delight and the danger in human neurology is to push your perceptual filters so far out in the periphery that you don't know what you're deleting. It's taking the cognitive strategy that Allen and Britt offered, which is "common sense" in our culture, and pushing it out to the periphery so that difference is destroyed before it ever achieves any status in our central nervous system. Our neurology already does that to a degree that's unbelievable. The fact that there are 160,000,000 cones and receptors in the retina and magnitudes fewer tracks in the optic nerve tells you that what we're seeing is not what's there. It's some interesting transform of the light pattern reflected from that object on the retina.

What are expectations? Who here has the background to tell us what the connections between afferent and efferent nerves are? If my hand or my foot touches something hot outside of my visual field I will withdraw that limb before the signal reaches my central nervous system. That loop will occur at the spinal cord. And that makes a great deal of sense in terms of preventing injury to the organism. But when we take our preconceptions and push them, by the same mechanisms of use and disuse, atrophy and patterns of muscle tension, out to the peripheral organs we become a self-validating, impermeable system which can't learn because we're destroying difference at the periphery. Changing foveal to peripheral vision and changing internal dialog to silence, become extremely important as ways of establishing access to second attention in a way that will allow us to do the kinds of design aesthetically, that we wish to do in this workshop.

There are many ways to achieve the kind of focused state where you "stop the world" in Castaneda's terms—no internal dialogue, no foveal vision. You could do it through a piece cleanly—then we may begin the exercise with one more signal and that is, "What, Larry, will your second attention do to indicate to me that I am to take one of these comforting actions?" He just offered me a signal. Now notice when I asked the question he may or may not have been conscious of the signal but he did offer me one. For those of you who couldn't see it was a lifting of his hands and then a dropping. So I then confirm the signal; I get the acknowledgement, the nice unconscious head movement that he just offered me, "Yes, that indeed was the correct reading, John." When that signal has been verified then I invite Larry to "stop the world" by whatever method he chooses. If he wishes an outside resource person in terms of me helping him with an altered state or something, that's a negotiation between Larry and me. It has nothing to do with the structure of the exercise. It will be a personal negotiation between the two of you.

Now you have a safe way out. Consistent with the kind of autonomy we're trying to build, the kind of integrity to your own circuitry, I want you to make those same arrangements internally. I want you to decide in a second-attention/first-attention interaction, what will constitute a signal from the environment, internal or external, that you are to come out of the "stop the world" state. I want you have the freedom to remain there until something that falls into that category occurs. It could be the smell of smoke, it could be the fact that as you scan your peripheral vision your witness is gone, the one who is supposed to be holding your lifeline is gone—that would be a signal for me to come right out—it could be the anchor, the touch that you've arranged with your colleague. It could be times driven, "In seven minutes, by clock time, bring me back." Involuntary signal says, "Yes." You go. Contextual markers such as the curtains on the stage, the end of the script, and the director can serve as your prototypes if you wish to make more elaborate arrangements in terms of lifelines. The sequence is to set your own lifeline first, then determine the method for entering "stopping the world" states, then make your fallback arrangements with your witness so that they can get you out if necessary. Good enough? I'd like you back in a half hour—fifteen minutes for each of you. Let's go to work.

John: In structuring this seminar there are four components that I want your commitment as participants to carry through on. There's roughly four or five hours a day with Judith and me. There is an amazing event that will begin at three-thirty every day and will run for an hour and a half with TaTitos Sompa. We'll be participating, as will you. And those two elements of the workshop are essential. It's not that we're inviting you to participate in dancing, drumming, and singing. It is an essential part of the workshop that you participate.

John: Comment about how you participate: Some of you have kept your physical competencies, your personal flexibility and strength. Others of you have not. Each of us is different in that class of commitments. It would be entirely incongruent with what we're doing here for you to behave in the dancing and singing in such a way as to not use feedback and end up injuring yourself. That would be absurd. It would be a direct statement that you have not the class of sensitivity and feedback needed to participate in this workshop to begin with; that would be self-indulgence as much as people who do not maintain state in the context of stress. These are in a sense prerequisites to do the kind of evolutionary work that this workshop is designed to do. Therefore I call upon your second attention to offer you unequivocal signals during the workshop. You can participate at many different levels. The fact that you get a signal that says, "Uh-huh, lower back now needs time to relax and rest a little bit," that calves are saying, "Cool it for a while," means that you now participate in another role in the same ceremony. That is, you may find yourself standing to the side catching your breath because of signals you get, or relaxing and smoothing out certain muscles while the dance continues. Your voice and your hands (in terms of clapping) are as important a demonstration that you're participating, that your spirit is merging with the other participants to make this an example of balance and harmony which—some of the characteristics of the community and personal cultural model we think underlies personal genius.

Judy: It's like a community, if you go to a traditional community, not everybody's dancing, not everybody's singing, but everybody is participating in some way to support that activity.

John: So the first two elements of this four-part workshop are the daily work, in the sense of four or five hours with Judy and I, and an hour or two with Titos. In the evenings we'll be sending you to different places in the city. Or you can go in the morning, before the seminar, if you'd like. We'll be sending you there with instructions on how to organize your perceptions and your states as you approach these parts of the city. And fourth, and certainly not last in importance, is dreaming. We will give instructions on how to set up dreaming. You have the task of exercising your personal disciplines to insure that you either carry those instructions out or find an alternative set of instructions which are equally efficacious in setting up your dreaming. If we're going to accomplish what we consider minimal in our work we need the full cooperation of your second attention for dreaming purposes.

John: Your homework assignment for tonight is to walk the Golden Gate Bridge.

Woman: Ha.

John: You are to walk it, understanding that it is a bridge in many ways—it connects two things which otherwise would be separated—and it does so, not by being a rigid structure, but by actually moving in the wind in response to the pressures from all sides. You are to walk the bridge in one direction in any state of consciousness that you'd like to have, but in walking back across the bridge I want you to walk it in a "stop the world" state. You're to do this in pairs, just as you did this afternoon, with a baby sitter, so that you have a fallback outside of yourself to insure that you will safely make that particular journey. This gives you a freedom that you might otherwise might not have. Understand that your objective over the five days is to be able to do this solo. But for tonight I want you to walk with a baby sitter.

George: Isn't that a . . . I'm not familiar with the Golden Gate Bridge—I mean what . . .

John: It's very hard to miss, George.

George: Is that a nice place to be? Is it safe?

John: It's wonderful.

George: In New York you can't go places . . .

John: I understand. I wouldn't send you across the Brooklyn Bridge.

Man: We have a built in ecology coming from New York.

Georgine: But if my partner and I are both doing the same thing . . .

John: No, one at a time. You got it. I want you both to have both moves.

Any aesthetic act, any artistic form, requires an underlying level of skill. The person who dances ballet (or African, or jazz) makes it look easy. That's part of the art form. That doesn't mean it is easy. That means they have so mastered it so that they may release their spirit inside of the form. And what you see is their spirit, informing their body; there's a freedom of action and a relaxation. One of the signals that you've mastered something is that you use the minimum effort necessary to carry it out.

Judy: Any art requires skill, and once you learn the skill and know the rules then you can bend them . . .

John: . . . and thereby achieve a certain class of creativity. Alright. Dreaming: Let me remind you how to set up your dreaming. Obviously the substance of the dreaming is the content of today's work. Each of you have reacted differently to things that Judith Ann and myself have presented here.

You will respond differentially to TaTitos and the rest of the people who are here to assist us in this next phase. Your ability to let your second attention select is an important feature of a healthy relationship between first and second attention, conscious and unconscious performance. Therefore make yourself a quiet time, after you do your homework and before you drop off to sleep, in which you invite your second attention to propose symbols—in the form of visual images of what happened here, of a particular move you saw one of the dancers make, or something that you heard, or a feeling which emerged as a response to today's events—which can serve as a trigger—an access point in your dreaming. You are to hold that representation as the last first attention conscious representation before you drop off to sleep tonight. You can enhance it by overlapping from whatever representational system that symbol is offered in to the corresponding representations in the other systems. If I saw a picture of one of the dancers move as the symbol from my second attention then I might hear the rhythms of the drums to enhance it—entertaining all representational systems as I drop off to sleep.

Judy: A second method for doing this is similar to what we just played with in this exercise. Request that the second attention take care of dreaming in the sense that John has talked about. As long as the signal is involuntary you can't kid yourself. Thirdly, using some of the Milton skills, go into a deep trance with the request to your second attention that you go from the deep trance, having identified the appropriate symbol to set up your dreaming, into a regular physiological sleep with its appropriate dreaming phases.

Mumtaz: Do I choose the symbol, or do I . . . ?

John: No, you request that from second attention. You're not competent to choose a symbol. It's only your life, see? (laughter) Alright. When you're in the dream—and again, all of you will move at different levels—I want you to be able to do a very simple task, the one specified in Carlos's work; I want you to be able to look at and see your hands. Now there are unconscious minds out there that are already going, "It won't be the hands."

Judy: And that's OK.

John: It may be some other part of the body. The trick is to see that part of the body and then quickly glance away, and come back to it and glance away as you examine the surroundings you find yourself in in your dreams. This way of beginning to exert control in this other reality should in no way interfere with the dreaming that we've arranged. If you have succeeded at this when I want you to be able to see yourself from the outside after you've seen your hands. I want you to be able to shift to a disassociated perceptual position. These are syntactic exercises which begin to give you some idea of the possibilities in dreaming—they are to be subordinated to the substance of the dreaming.

Woman: When you're talking about "outside," are you talking about while you're dreaming—that you're watching yourself dream?

Judy: Yes, from a disassociated position.

John: Remember, you start from the integrated position, you see your hands from that position, and then you may go out.

Woman: You want us to come back in?

John: I want you to come back in.

Man: In the dissociated dream do I see myself asleep dreaming or do I see myself in the dream?

Judy: Good logical level question.

John: If you see only one of the two, the latter. See yourself in the dream. If you can see both, you've got two logical levels represented. And you're getting close to the dreamer and the dreamed.

Go get an involuntary signal system from your second attention that says that you will be able to take this experience with TaTitos and keep it separate so it can constitute for you a separate reality—a double description—in the strongest sense, one that you could draw upon for strength and resourcefulness at some point.

This thing we're about to do is a whole world in and of itself and has the well-formedness characteristics of the kind of world we're building in each one of us as a prerequisite for community. This has balance, this has movement, this has elegance, this has rhythm, it has focus, it has a focused demon states associated with it, it has all the things that we're playing with, it's dynamic, and not only that, it's externally available and could be used as a model for your internal organization. With that in mind—as you know, in learning a language one of the things is to make sure not to translate until the new reality has a stability of its own. If you attempt to translate too early you destroy the difference which makes a difference which is the point of an altered state, a different reality, and different cultures and languages. Do all that, sleep deeply tonight . . .

Judy: . . . that should be easy enough. No problem.

John: . . . and be back ready to go at nine o'clock tomorrow morning.

DAY TWO

Judy: Hello, hello.

John: Hello, hello. Well, did you all dry out? Now, those of you from the East, if I hear you complaining I know it's a simple case of self-indulgence so don't give me any of that. (laughter) It's better to be wet and warm than it is to be wet and cold. This is a benevolent dictatorship. You think this is a democracy or something? (laughter) This cybernetic stuff has gone far enough.

Judy: Do you remember the petty tyrant from Castaneda?[1] (Laughter)

Woman: My pen started writing something or other.

Judy: Petty tyrants? The usefulness of petty tyrants. (laughter)

John: It's quite easy as drummer to create the amusing illusion for myself that as I'm drumming, the bonding is so tight between me and the dancer that my drumming is making the dancer move.

Judy: No-no. The dancer is making the drummer drum. (laughter) . . .

John: . . . fortunately, I've had the good fortune to be on the other side of the loop as a dancer and be utterly convinced of what Judy said, my moving makes the drummer create those particular sounds. It's a lovely example of the kind of loops that I hope become omnipresent in your perceptual experience as a result of what we're doing here. Strive for the ambiguity; I'll guarantee if the dancers have the illusion they're making the drummer drum and the drummers know they are making the dancers move then everyone has the connection in the loop we're working for.

Judy: TaTitos was pleased at everybody's response, not only in their dancing but also in their singing. I've danced with Titos for some time and periodically we sing. We've been trying to learn one song for four months. One of the songs that you were singing yesterday, that song had spirit.

John: Where the spirits have gone.

Judy: He was very impressed.

John: Sitting where I was in the altered state I was in it was easy to perceive your bodies serving as expressive instruments for your spirit. It's easy for me to know who is still self-conscious and who has committed themselves in the Viola Legere sense —of having set up the lifelines and gone, "Let's go for it!"— where we're safe, where we may free certain parts of ourselves.

Alan: I'm still having a problem with stopping the internal dialogue. In crossing the bridge for instance—I really enjoyed it by the way—there were lots of nice things going on—I still have a guy inside who's saying, "Hey look at that vertical stuff and all that horizontal stuff" and checking out what's going on visually. There's a check-out God-damned guy and I . . . (laughter) Do you have a nice suggestion for him?

John: Sure, tell him to check out! (laughter)

Alan: I want to be able to really stop internal dialogue.

John: Let me be more sympathetic—"stopping the world" is a non-trivial task, since the everyday perceptual world is altered by stopping the flow of interpretation. The combination of foveal vision and internal dialogue robs us of news of the world. Seeing with foveal vision is responding to the perceptual solicitations of our outside world, our internal dialogue interprets these solicitations, develops a description, and we call this reality.

Judy: Yes, inventory. Inventorying these solicitations of foveal vision and developing a description is the job of the first attention.

John: You have a resource. In the context of the tasks we've given you without further instructions, you experienced it as an irritant because it was interruptive of the pure focused state that you were working out of, "stopping the world." It is an appropriate function of first attention to take inventory and that's what it was doing. So, it's important to begin with an appreciation that it has a powerful and positive function. Now the issue becomes where and when should it let you know of the inventories that it continuously takes? So it's not an issue of asking that part not to perform because that's what it does. The issue becomes, as Judy would say as a dancer, "It's all in the timing." When are those reports appropriate . . .

Judy: (interrupting) . . . timing is everything. (laughter)

John: I would like. . . . , would you like to say that again . . .

Judy: (interrupting again) . . . timing is everything. (laughter)

John: You know petty tyrants come in many forms. (laughter) This morning we have a tale to tell and we're going to wend our way toward addressing specifically the issue of the timing and function of first-attention work including inventory-taking. First I'll point out something else. Alan, when you were dancing with Titos yesterday, you were not taking inventory.

Judy: You were really dancing well. I've seen people struggle for a year to get to the some of the moves . . .

John: . . . you got yesterday.

Judy: And do you remember what you said?

Alan: I'm not sure.

Judy: Think about it because that's a really interesting . . .

James: Well, what did he say?

Judy: I'm not going to tell you. (laughter) He has to remember . . .

John: You're just listening in on the conversation, James. Relax. (laughter)

Judy: What he described to me was that he dropped into a cybernetic loop with TaTitos which was directly visual-kinesthetic, visual-kinesthetic. He said, "As soon as I let my body go into the positions as TaTitos, I flowed into it."

John: So Alan's question is most timely . . . . . . I think we both appreciate what an important task this first-attention part has and at the same time recognize that a bit of scheduling is required so that when it reports the results of its inventory it will be at a more appropriate time than interrupting committed states. Now many of you had the following experience. Perhaps it was on the Golden Gate last night or during an exercise yesterday or some practice sessions you scheduled on your own initiative during various parts of the time that were free—all eight or nine hours we've left you free. Many of you I suspect could report a situation where you achieved stopping the world and there was this absolute sense of internal quietude and alertness at the same time and then halfway through the time period you had negotiated a voice went off and went, "God, is it quiet!" or, "We're really doing it!" (laughter) As far as I can tell the most important skill you need to bring to this sort of work is a sense of humor and as long as you can maintain that I think the rest will fall out as a natural consequence.

Julie: So from what you've said as we walked across the bridge, those different . . . , for me there were different things that happened, my eyes tended to cross and then I would find myself slowing down, speeding up, those are things that the second attention is just doing.

John: (echoing) . . . that the second attention is just doing.

Julie: Right. And then first attention pops in, you know, and . . .

John: "Commentary, commentary. Commentary, commentary. Evaluation, commentary, evaluation . . ." Yes, that's what first attention does.

Julie: So I'm to trust doing whatever I find myself doing, just to trust that.

John: My response to you is the same as to Alan. We're heading exactly for the scheduling that you need. I said yesterday directly, "Second attentions, wake up!" and I said, "First attentions, wake up!" I usually teach straight to second attention and simply entertain you at first attention. We're not doing that this time. We're insisting that both attentions have their proper functions. . . . and insisting on the cybernetic nature of the relationship between the two of them. The fact that they're both alive and well is good news. The question of how we now bring them together in an alliance is the subject of the next forty-eight hours.

Judy: Consciousness or the first attention is modeling second attention, that's what it's for, to pick out what enhances our reality so that we know where we are and how to appreciate the rest of the world.

Carol: I had real problems last night . . .

Judy: Oh, not you, Carol. Anybody but you . . . (laughter)

Carol: . . . reading over my notes trying to figure out what was I supposed to experience going over the bridge. (laughter)

Judy: What did you experience?

Carol: Well, that's what I want to comment on. All the way over I had the two people I was with explain to me what I was supposed to experience.

John: There are many forms of petty tyranny.

Carol: Alright, thanks a lot. So coming back, the interesting thing was that although they tried to explain it to me in many different ways and I tried to clarify it, there were times when I experienced something I hadn't experienced before. And when we talked about it later I couldn't talk about it—which is exactly the point. Now I understand that all that set-up allowed me to be able to do that. To have a new experience that was not related to . . .

John: . . . first attention in any familiar form. Those of you who are Castaneda fans will remember, it's in one of the more recent books, he suddenly discovers that he has spent twice as much time with Juan and Genaro . . .

Judy: . . . as he consciously remembers.

John: And that's when he was living in second attention without the first attention doing any modeling.

Judy: One reason for choosing Don Juan's information as a "description," as a possible description, was because he did go right to the second attention, whereas Bateson offers a different kind of description, but there's a lot of similarities in terms of where they're going . . .

John: Definitely different paths.

Judy: Yes, different paths.

John: Double description.

Mumtaz: I walked the bridge metaphorically and it was a varied experience of being in "up-time." Just no internal dialogue until the breeze was swinging the bridge and made me feel dizzy and I couldn't do any more about it. So I think I asked my unconscious, "Could I finish this task without the breeze?" and I did! (Laughter)

John: Dizziness. As children, if you remember, that was a highly valued experience. My father would pick me up and throw me into the air so I was weightless. Or we would have games like the merry-go-round game in the park, and the faster we could go and the more disoriented we could get the more fun it was.

Woman: That's true.

John: What is it about adults that have forgotten the joy of abandonment in that sense? Now there is a way that you can have your cake, at least part of it, and eat part of it too—you have to be careful about which part. Notice the sensation of dizziness can only occur if their's a relative motion between the perceiver and the environment. So that one way you can control the rate of dizziness until you can abandon yourself to it safely—to arrange your lifelines, arrange your context so that it's appropriate—is by yourself orienting and moving with the direction and sense of spinning. And when that occurs then you have control over the sense of dizziness so that you can become slightly disoriented by spinning with the movement and then slow your own spinning down to the point where the disorientation increases and, just like gears in a car, you can have control over the motion that you experience relative to context.

Judy: In ballet we spot. Spotting doesn't make dizziness go away but it helps maintain orientation and for me it's just straight training. The more I do it, the more times I can do it, the better I can do it. But after I go one direction I have to go the other way to unwind. (laughter)

John: Balance. Balance.

John: Part of the artistry of being a well-trained athlete for example is to know what to ignore and what to pay attention to, right? Sorting. The second thing is no matter how passionate and committed any state you ever enter is there has to be a set of survival programs that have an interrupt priority. You maintain enough sensing of the environment outside of the frame of what you need specifically for the task to which you are passionately committed, that if certain signals come up that may mean your physical survival is at stake, those always interrupt your focused state. So if you are walking along Golden Gate Bridge and encounter someone who is not quite right who happens to have in their hand a piece of metal sharpened at one end—often referred to as a knife—but you wouldn't know it in the state you're in, it had better interrupt any program that you're in so that you can deal effectively with it at that point. And that's true if you're a pole vaulter and some spectator steps out into the approach path. Doesn't matter, it could happen in any environment that other living organisms are involved with. That's the sense in which I consider it inappropriate for you to seal off the world. You can create the absolute experience of a full, passionate commitment while other parts of you monitor the environment like a "baby sitter." It's a term that comes out of field intelligence work . . . if you're going to have a meeting with someone where there is a possibility of entrapment, you always take a babysitter along who watches your back. I want you to all have your own babysitters.

Man: In fact, in moving from the state that you're in walking across the bridge to having the monitor, the baby sitter, give you the information, you instantly change to a state appropriate to survival and you're 100% in that next state.

John: Yes, in the next state as passionately as the last.

Judy: You don't have reflexive consciousness there either. But the idea that you brought up about doing it and finishing and then going, "How did I do? Did I do a good job?" makes sense. While you're in that 100%-committed state just doing it, you're not making any judgements.

John: Ah-ah. Now this goes right to Alan and Julie's question. One of the appropriate functions of first attention is in taking inventory. So if it takes inventory without a diminution of the quality of the focused state, that is, there's still a 100% passionate commitment to exactly the class of variables necessary for the task and someplace out of awareness without a diminution of the quality of the state you have an inventory takes, the only question becomes: When do you get the results of the inventory?

NLP is based on the assumption that we can model our own experience and therefore accelerate our learning process in tremendous ways.

Judy: That's where it fits into epistemology—how we know what we know.

John: The issue here is that many first attentions are self-indulgent. They get out of control and out of sync with second attention. And number two, even more dangerous, is they come to believe their own models.

Judy: The difference between a model and a theory . . .

John: . . . is that a theory is not necessarily falsifiable. One of the well-formedness conditions on all first-attention work in modeling is that you must seek the counterexample to refine your model. After initial success, you learn by your mistakes not by your continued successes. The question is can you choose what class of mistakes are appropriate in terms of risk for the activity you are presently engaged in. Subsequent to a performance an athlete can improve greatly his or her compentency by reviewing the experience in a balanced way—having first attention go back over what was not available to it at the time of performance. However, with a proper relationship between first and second attention, first attention can model aspects of the second-attention performance which will improve it. And that's indeed how people bootstrap themselves up to higher and higher levels of performance.

Judy: Bateson makes a wonderful comment about science when he says science never proves anything.

John: Never.

Judy: It improves and it disproves . . .

John & Judy: . . . but it never proves anything.

Judy: And that's why he says, "Look we really do need a meta-science. We need a science called epistemology which is how we know what we know." Since everything goes through transforms in our neurology, we need to find out more about those rules of neurological transformations. What are the distortions and the deletions between what's going on out there in the world as this information goes through our eyes, as it goes through all the transformers in our nervous system to our brain, as it goes from second attention modeled by first attention. "Life is the art of drawing sufficient conclusions from insufficient evidence." We're filling in gaps all over the place and calling the end result of this gap filling "reality."

John: Can you fit this into what your question was related to?

Judy: More descriptions.

John: Let it sit for a minute. OK.

Georgine: That's fine.

Judy: What's really wonderful about it is that it's another description, and if you go back to what we said yesterday about nothing coming from nothing and double descriptions, comparing those descriptions gives you new information. News.

Robert: The difficulty I'm having with that is that I don't understand where, if I'm 100% committed to what I'm doing, the extra percentage that's discovering whether or not there's a sharp object in someone's hand can come from.

John: Do you understand how this paradox can only exist in first attention? Logical levels are of use here, Robert. Do you know about the Russellian paradoxes? Suppose I write . . . (writing on chalkboard)

The sentence below this one is true.
The sentence above this one is false.

Woman: . . . what does Russellian mean? Bertrand Russell?

John: The very one.

Judy: Mr. Whitehead's friend. (Laughter)

John: So if this top one is true then it says this bottom one is true. But if this bottom one is true than it says this top one is false. So that we're now locked into a paradox. Now notice this class of paradox characteristically involves self-reference. It's a result of first attention modeling itself, without reference to the whole first-attention/second-attention cybernetic loop.

Man: How, specifically, do you mean that, with this sentence? How is it self-referential?

John: Well, the sentence refers to itself within its own structure.

Man: Because it's talking about *this* one . . .

John: It says the sentence below *this one—the one that you're presently reading.* Now it's a fascinating study in and of itself what sort of paradoxes you can create with consciousness. First attention is always a proper subset of second attention. It is wholly contained, that is, there is nothing in first attention that didn't come through second attention—with one fascinating exception—a brilliant exception—a mistake that distinguishes us from all other species—call it one of the magic moments in human history—it'll come around.

It's interesting to note in passing one of the paradoxes associated with reflexive first attention. Let's use the following scenario to illustrate the paradox—here's Ken Kesey standing on the corner in Winslow, Arizona, hitchhiking back to California—in his nearly perpetually altered state, he is sensing his environment—entertaining representations of the cactus flowers, bright blue sky, carbon dioxide, pickup trucks slowing down, . . . After several hours, he gets tired of waiting for a ride and disassociates from the sensory environment (attending only to cars or trucks stopping at the sensory level) to metaposition. He moves up a logical level so that the representation he was formerly fully committed to becomes one of a subset of the new representations he is entertaining. For example, he may be perceiving himself from a position above and behind his actual physical location on the corner —a bird's-eye view. Notice that as soon as he does this he has enlarged the frame—the representations he was committed to prior to moving to meta-position are still present but reduced in scale and diminished in detail and enclosed in a larger set of representations—perhaps the section of town he's in or the whole of Winslow or the state of Arizona or the American southwest. Each logical level shift in representation increases the scope of what is covered in the representations at the cost of detail. Now notice that in moving to meta-position he has entered a distinguished set of states—reflexive first attention —the organism is entertaining representations which include a representation of the representer, . . . or do they? Strictly speaking when Kesey sees himself standing on the corner, the implied position of the representer is physically above and behind the image of Kesey on the corner—here is the difficulty—suppose we move Kesey up a logical level—to a position, say, where he represents a Kesey on the corner and one above and behind the one on the corner. At this point we have Kesey entertaining representations which are complete for the first meta-position move in the sense that they include a representation of the representer for meta-position move one —this is accomplished however at the cost of creating a second meta-position whose physical location is implied by the new class of representations but not represented. Thus no matter how many meta-position moves we use, this difficulty will recursively arise. Consequently, we may deduce the Incompleteness Theorem.

Incompleteness Theorem for Representation:

There exists no pure reflexive first-attention state in humans such that for any particular moment in time, t_i, all the neurological activities of the organism are represented. In particular such reflexive first-attention states will fail to include a representation of the representer of that class of representations in the representations although they may include the representation of the previous representer (the representer at time, t_{i-j}, where $j > 0$).

Some of you may recognize a similarity between the Incompleteness Theorem for Representation and several other interesting proposals relatively recent in human thinking—Bateson's representation uses the screen of consciousness metaphor—roughly, if we have a screen, $screen_1$, on which is displayed all the neurological activities of an organism, then it fails to represent the screen itself. If we enlarge the screen—call the enlarged screen, $screen_2$—to include $screen_1$, then $screen_2$ itself is not represented, . . . We're running one step behind. Gregory was inspired in this matter by Russell who, in his masterwork with Whitehead, *Principia Mathematica,* in order to avoid certain paradoxes, legislated a meta-rule for set theory which states that no set may be a member of itself. Bateson was tempted for some time to use this meta-rule as part of an approach to sorting out schizophrenia—(at least, in the clinician's mind) the double bind theory of schizophrenia. Personally, I think there are several examples reasonably well-known to us Westerners closer to this Incompleteness Theorem for Representation—Gödel's Theorem, for example. In the '30s Kurt Gödel, a meta-mathematician, proved, roughly, that any logical system rich enough to represent arithmetic is essentially incomplete—that is, one can, given any such logical system, S_i, construct a statement in arithmetic known by alternate means to be true which cannot be proved within the system. Actually he did something much more powerful—analygous to our second meta-position move with Kesey, he proved his theorem recursively—that is, if you construct a new "larger" system, S', which includes both the old system, S_i, and the statement known to be true in S_i but unprovable, one can construct a new statement for S', again known to be true but unprovable. The result is recursively true.

Neal Cassady, a traveling companion of Jack Kerouac and the driver for our friend Ken Kesey's Merry Pranksters, was perpetually frustrated by his inability to catch up with himself—his endeavor was probably flawed in design from its inception because he used language as part of the procedure. His intent was to be temporarily current; he is reported to have spent significant amounts of time uttering the word "Now" again and again at increasing speeds and varying volumes and intonations but, alas, to no avail; by the time he finished speaking he had fallen behind again. It was even rumored that he used amphetamines as a final resort, again futilely.

Don Steiny told me of an amusing example of the Incompleteness Theorem from Monty Python Flying Circus. Two of the Pythons crew are crossing a barren desert. They run out of food and water. Lying close to one another-close to their end they muse about how they came to be in such dire straits. Close to their last one suddenly observes to the other, "Wait a bit!—who's running the camera?" This leads to the discovery of the camera crew. Switch to a perspective of the camera crew responding to the two previously isolated dying men. Some time after sharing their meager resources both the original dying men and the camera crew are out of food and water stranded in the desert until, of course, someone asks again, "Who's running the camera?" . . . ad nauseum.

Rosalyn: What was it that Gregory Bateson did with his first attention that . . . Was it the kind of thinking that you do in a chess game?

John: It's like that. The problem is that the rules of this game are not specified and the rules of chess are. Gregory speaks of the double habit of mind.

As I understand it, you have asked me for an honest, introspective—personal—account of how I think about anthropological material, and if I am to be honest and personal about my thinking, then I must be impersonal about the results of that thinking. Even if I can banish both pride and shame for half an hour, honesty will still be difficult.

Let me try to build up a picture of how I think by giving you an autobiographical account of how I have acquired my kit of conceptual tools and intellectual habits. I do not mean an academic biography or a list of what subjects I have studied, but something more significant than that—a list rather of the motifs of thought in various scientific subjects which left so deep an impression on my mind that when I came to work on anthropological material, I naturally used those borrowed motifs to guide my approach to this new material.

I owe the greatest part of this kit of tools to my father, William Bateson, who was a geneticist. In schools and universities they do very little to give one an idea of the basic principles of scientific thinking, and what I learned of this came in large measure from my father's conversation and perhaps especially from the overtones of his talk. He himself was inarticulate about philosophy and mathematics and logic, and he was articulately distrustful of such subjects, but still, in spite of himself, I think, he passed on to me something of these matters.

The attitudes which I got from him were especially those which he had denied in himself. In his early—and as I think he knew—his best work he posed the problems of animal symmetry, segmentation, serial repetition of parts, patterns, etc. Later he turned away from this field into Mendelism, to which he devoted the remainder of his life. But he had always a hankering after the problems of pattern and symmetry, and it was this hankering and the mysticism that inspired it that I picked up and which, for better or worse, I called "science."

I picked up a vague mystical feeling that we must look for the same sort of processes in all fields of natural phenomena—that we might expect to find the same sort of laws at work in the structure of a crystal as in the structure of society, or that the segmentation of an earthworm might really be comparable to the process by which basalt pillars are formed.

I should not preach this mystical faith in quite those terms today but would say rather that I believe that the types of mental operation which are useful in analyzing one field may be equally useful in another—that the framework (the *eidos*) of science, rather than the framework of Nature, is the same in all fields. But the more mystical phrasing of the matter was what I vaguely learnt, and it was of paramount importance. It lent a certain dignity to any scientific investigation, implying that when I was analyzing the patterns of partridges' feathers, I might really get an answer or a bit of an answer to the whole puzzling business of pattern and regularity in nature. And further, this bit of mysticism was important because it gave me freedom to use my scientific background, the ways of thought that I had picked up in biology and elementary physics and chemistry; it encouraged me to expect these ways of thought to fit in with very different fields of observation. It enabled me to regard all my training as potentially useful rather than utterly irrelevant to anthropology.

I want to emphasize that whenever we pride ourselves upon finding a newer, stricter way of thought or exposition; whenever we start insisting too hard upon "operationalism" or symbolic logic or any other of these very essential systems of tramlines, we lose something of the ability to think new thoughts. And equally, of course, whenever we rebel against the sterile rigidity of formal thought and exposition and let our ideas run wild, we likewise lose. As I see it, the advances in scientific thought come from a *combination of loose and strict thinking,* and this combination is the most precious tool of science.

My mystical view of phenomena contributed specifically to build up this double habit of mind—it led me into wild "hunches" and, at the same time, compelled more formal thinking about those hunches. It encouraged looseness of thought and then immediately insisted that that looseness be measured up against a rigid concreteness.[2]

John: What is it that a professional linguist does? Suppose I go,

Mary took John's shirt off.

Now, how many ways ambiguous is that?

Woman: Several.

John: Several. Now that's pretty precise.

Man: What did you say?

John:

Mary took John's shirt off.

How many ways ambiguous is that sentence? OK. Part of the ambiguity revolves around who had John's shirt on. If John had John's shirt on and Mary took it off that's a profoundly different experience, at least for John (laughter) than if Mary had John's shirt on and took it off. And Mary could have taken John's shirt off of George, who we haven't mentioned at all. And now we've got a *ménage á trois* and we're in trouble, right? I don't really care how many ways ambiguous the sentence is—I'm interested in how you discovered that, the process of exploring your internal circuitry in discovering the ambiguity. What did you do to answer that question? And this is in part, Robert, what we were talking about. So Larry did it this way (mirroring Larry's gestures) and that's as elegant a communication as I've seen from linguists who do this professionally. What is going on? What were you doing yesterday when you sat here and listened and participated? You're checking circuits. Does this resonate? Or not resonate?

"Does this fit?" "Can I find the subcircuits that they are discussing now?" "Am I organized differently?" "Seems like it." And those are some of the proposals being made this morning. One of their most powerful professional tools that a linguist has to have is the ability to do internal congruity checks. If you watch professional linguists or mathematicians working with your acuity, it's quite obvious what's going on. . . . (pause) Here's something that really surprised Gregory. I hope you are not surprised by it although I do hope you're surprised by Gregory being surprised. I hope you go, "Of course." Then I'll ask you, "Of course, what?"

Judy: Gregory was delighted in his surprise; however surprised he was. What are the responsibilities of the first attention in terms of that loop, the connection between first and second attentions? You know, we talk about these responsibilities, saying, "I'll turn it over to my second attention. It can take care of it."

John: Remember what Judy read yesterday about how if a culture makes a commitment, an unbalanced commitment, to all conscious or all unconscious activity in their art, then it is unlikely their art will be great? That's true personally as well. Unless you have a dance between first and second attention —and you know how fluid you have to be in a dance—it's unlikely that you'll achieve the kind of personal genius that is the point of this seminar. . . . (pausing) . . .

OK, so here's what Gregory was surprised about. By tracking I refer to the task when there is some spot on the screen that moves in a certain pattern and you have a circle and two controls here that give you vertical and horizontal control so you can move this circle. So when the spot appears here of course, you have to move the circle down, et cetera. Now it turns out that if you give people the task of tracking spots that move in patterns that can be represented by equations that are linear as opposed to nonlinear in nature as opposed to nonlinear . . . So a linear equation would specify a pattern so that the spot always moves in a straight line. The line can be in any direction, but for the duration of its movement until it's caught again by the tracker with the circle, it always moves in a straight line as opposed to a curve. A curve is not a linear function, right?

For example $x = y + 5$. That's a linear equation. That is, if we put a grid across here so this is the zero-zero mark here . . . , it says when y is 2, let's say right here, then x is going to be . . . ?

John: So the point is going to be out here somewhere, right? On the other hand, if you have an equation such as $x = y^2$ you've moved into a nonlinear representation. You're going to get a curve.

Take $x = 2$ and $x = 4$. Do you all remember this from high school algebra?

Woman: Why are you going to get a curve?

John: Get a piece of graph paper and work it out. Now the interesting thing is that if you take one group of trackers and you give them only linear spots to track, and you take a second group and you give them only nonlinear spots to track, and then you reverse the group conditions after they've had some tracking experience, the results are very close to no transfer of learning. That is, the learning curve they have to go through seems to be unrelated to their previous experience —whether they start with the linear or nonlinear task, when they switch to the other condition they start learning all over again. This surprised Bateson. Why did it surprise Bateson? Well, he said, "How can it be that the learning performance of our species respects these symbolic representational differences—the difference between linear and nonlinear functions?" And that's my question for you. What's the connection?

Tom: The symbols describe our experience first.

John: Say that louder, Tom.

Tom: The symbols came to describe our experience and so, it's not respecting those symbols, it's respecting our experience . . .

John: . . . which is modeled . . .

Tom: . . . by those symbols.

John: So you understand how first-attention, linear thinking presents a problem if you approach the problem that way—I just gave you a problem linearly, and thereby trapped you into thinking linearly. But if you go, "Wait a minute? Where did this stuff come from? This wasn't handed down with the Ten Commandments."

Judy: They dropped a plate. (Laughter)

John: There were fifteen.

Judy: It was on the other one.

John: Gregory says that unless we learn to think in loops that respect circuit integrity we're in deep trouble. The preponderance of technical society operates in first attention and it's going to get us in deep trouble. And he confesses as he makes this remark that he himself has not been successful in consistently thinking cybernetically. And the fact that he's surprised by this tracking experiment is a dead giveaway that he has not yet fully operationalized the notion of cybernetic thinking. Because, as Tom says, these things are nothing more than a symbolic representation of our experience of the difference between straight lines and curves.

So just as the linguist, the professional syntactition, uses his or her own circuits to know whether what they're doing really does fit into the grammar which is neurologically represented, the so-called "purest" of all sciences, mathematics itself, is based upon that same cybernetic loop. We have certain filters to the world which bias the information through our sensory apparatus into second attention and then into consciousness, first attention, in such a way that our symbolic representations are always going to be an interesting integration of what we can represent and what's out there in the world. But you have to take both sides of the loop to have an appreciation of what epistemology might be.

George: I'm still puzzled by what Bateson might be puzzled by. Are you saying that all nonlinear functions are equally transferable, rather than there are classes of nonlinear functions . . .

John: No. I'm reporting that people track and learn differently when approached with a task where there is a linear as opposed to a nonlinear function to track. Now, at the metalevel, which is where you first asked the question, I'm surprised that Gregory was surprised. Gregory was surprised because he was thinking linearly. The antidote to such linear thinking was Tom's, where he said, "Well, where the hell do these symbolic representations come from?" And the answer is they came to us through our sensory apparatus and we developed an arbitrary representational system that made the distinction which is a distinction about the relationship between the world and our own neurology, not solely about the world. It's a statement about an interaction between our circuits and the world. Now, your other question is of interest to me personally too, and irrelevant to our discussion. Do you understand that? . . . Consider the implications here. Note that for information to become human knowledge it must necessarily be filtered through some human neurology and then be represented. Both the neurological filters and the bias of the representational codes used guarantee that human knowledge will always be a product of what's out there and all the distortions of our neurology. Even the physicist working down the road here at SLAC (Stanford Linear Accelerator) when using instrumentation must push the "data" through his or her own nervous system to achieve a representation which may lead to "understanding." This is the sense in which all human activity—the physicist, the dancer, the biologist, the negotiator, the musician, the pilot, et cetera—occurs within the meta-science called for by Bateson, epistemology.

Woman: I keep thinking that the experience I had this morning of walking across the bridge, that's sort of a combo of this and the eye. It's like I felt like I was learning to walk again. It's like my legs weren't functioning, they felt wobbly because of the information that I was taking in. There was a sense of . . . , like I was so programmed to operate based on the way I usually took it in versus how I was experiencing . . .

John: Nice. It's a lovely communication. Let the record show that her hands moved . . .

Georgine: I keep going back to the culture/society differences. And I also always try and relate this to my children, what they're going through at this point in time, and I relate back to what I went through as a child experiencing things. And quite often when you go through the initial learning process in anything you get to that first stage where you understand or you know that you know and then immediately somebody wants you to tell them what you know. And as soon as I would go through that experience and I couldn't tell them I would then place a value judgement on what I had done and say, "I guess I didn't learn it."

Judy: You guessed you didn't learn it because you couldn't talk about it. It's not coded into auditory-digital. The question of where along the process you make a judgment of value as opposed to just appreciating difference is an important one.

Georgine: And it continues to happen to me. My husband's family is Hungarian and speaks Hungarian as a first language. And quite often something will happen in a situation and my mother-in-law will not understand. And I'll understand what happened, I will laugh or I will respond appropriately. She will turn to me and say, "What happened?" and I'll say . . .

Judy: . . . "Uhhh . . ."

Georgine: . . . "I don't know."

Judy: That's when you have to say, "You sort of had to be there." (laughter)

Georgine: You know, she looks at me and says, "You're pretty dumb aren't you?" and then I'm lost and then I pull back again and say, "Well I guess . . ."

John: Difference without evaluation. In our society, if information cannot somehow be coded at first attention—if we cannot talk about it—it is often judged as invalid. To connect the idea with just this first-attention coding called language is a failure to respect the dance between first and second attention and to evaluate only part of a complex interaction—an arc, part of the loop. Notice that by making the filter dominant our society dismisses much of the wisdom of second attention.

It would be interesting if the definition of "civilized" was understood in terms of how we responded to difference. If you can recognize difference without making the automatic leap to an evaluation the world will open itself to you—offering you riches. Difference is what we're built to detect and to work with. Not evaluation. Evaluation is an overlay by certain kinds of social systems, certain kinds of socialization processes, certain kinds of physiological mechanisms to protect homeostatic centers.

As the governor of Texas said, when? about 1917? Remember the guy's name?

Judy: James Pa Ferguson.

John: Ferguson.

Man: Richardson.

John: Richardson?

Man: Richardson.

Judy: Ferguson.

John: Ferguson. I vote with her. Whoever the governor of Texas was in 1917, upon being presented with a bill to sign for the continuation of bilingual education in Texas (they had it back then, in 1917), upon the occasion of vetoing it . . .

Judy: . . . made the following statement . . .

John: He said, "If English was good enough for Jesus Christ . . . (laughter) . . . it's good enough for the school children of Texas."

John: Well, it's the same thing that we've talked about for a long time—the connections between language and experience. Sapir talked about it, Whorf talked about it. The language code itself creates, in the sense of first-attention inventorying, categories of perception, and if parts of the world do not fall into those categories we do not habitually experience them in first attention. Linguistic codes are obviously not so deep that we can't access and change them. In fact, the fact that some of us here are polyglots—can speak with fluency several languages—is an indication we have that kind of flexibility in our neurology if we choose to exercise it. When I lived in Europe and was learning another language I was in the appropriate context, and that's the important thing, the context. Previously, of course, I had tried to learn languages in a standard educational context—in a cardboard cubicle, with pressure on my ears from the earphones, and a voice going, "*der Tisch,* the table, *der Tisch,* the table." There weren't any tables around, there weren't any "Tisches" around either, (laughter) there was nothing except this idiot voice . . .

Judy: Which one? (laughter)

John: So if I want to learn a language in a culture I get inside of it. My body becomes a mirror, I extend self to the point that I am automatically mirroring. I extend myself so that any tonalities that I hear in the speech pattern, any tempo moves in the speech pattern, I automatically echo. Those are the primary considerations.

Part of my proposal about creating a separate reality for what we did with TaTitos yesterday is based on the principle that as you approach any new reality, whether it's culturally/linguistically defined or a reorganization of your own circuitry, there are good reasons to respect its fragility initially and to build a separate protected environment for it until it becomes robust enough that it serves as an adequate second description to your original language and culture. When it has the robustness and strength—when it's stable enough that you can map across—then you really truly are fluent in that sense. I was noticing some of the polyglots giving me "Yes," that this matches your experiences as well.

Judy: Do you still have that question, Antonio?

Antonio: Oh, yeah. . . . (pausing) . . . I was lost in what you were saying and I forgot my question. I was yesterday on the bridge and I decided to cross the bridge in that state and I let my horse go and my mind was going, you know, my first attention was going crazy. And I had a third person that comes in, "No, that's OK, you can do it, you can go." And this third person is the one that I trust, that monitors what's going on. So I went across the bridge and my first attention was all over, you know, and when I got to the end (this morning I am windburned on my face) and I was asking myself, "Can you be injured going through this thing?" And then I was on the bridge and I was thinking, "Wow, that's crazy, man. John Grinder is a crazy guy." (laughter) "How can he ask you to do this kind of thing?" But I went, you know, and I crossed it and it was OK. And now I'm thinking if I was going to be seriously injured would I have stopped because I only burned my face, you know. And then this morning I was talking to myself about it. And I guess I was going to get out of it if it was serious. So I was thinking about that.

John: It's an important thing to think about, Antonio.

Antonio: It was a question for me, you know. I'm not sure if I was going to get out of it.

John: That's the point . . .

Judy: . . . of contextual markers . . .

John: . . . of lifelines. Remember I said that I want you each to end up being your own baby sitter. The baby sitter has really important and powerful functions for you. And unless you have a trained baby sitter to watch your back, you don't, in my opinion, have the right to indulge in the altered-state experiences we're engaging in. This is only indulgent if it isn't contextualized. You can't unleash your spirit safely unless you have someone who can contextualize its behavior. There are many kinds of bridges. Castaneda reports being on the edge of a cliff and going through a powerful storm in the mountains, sitting with his back to the wall, and seeing a bridge that connected the ledge that he was on to another part of the mountains. And the bridge was so substantial in his visual perception that he was about to cross it when in fact his baby sitter for that episode, don Juan, seized him and forced him into another state. So it becomes extremely important in exploration of the class that we're involved with here, in terms of altered states and altered realities, that you have a baby sitter who is impeccable in protecting you. . . . (pausing) . . .

And that's the importance of the impeccability of the baby sitter in making that class of judgments. And by the way, how much windburn . . . , for several years I have been climbing with a world-class rock climber, Geoffrey, who has taught me amazing things. He did things I didn't think anybody could do and then I got to do them myself. Now when I started leading, which is a profoundly different experience than seconding on a climb . . . The leader on a technical climb, working on a sheer wall, has to be able to make the class of physical moves that are required and maintain state control so that there's not an excessive expenditure of energy. You were a professional soccer player and understand how we typically over-muscle every move during the learning phase.

Judy: No efficiency.

John: And there's no grace to over-muscling a move, right? It's true, you get the outcome but that's satisfying only if you believe the outcome is the point of the activity. If you are a really fine learner—and this is part of the spirit that I saw you exhibiting yesterday, Alan—you let go. That is, in that movement you were making with TaTitos, you put your body in certain positions, and as soon as you let your body go into those positions and relaxed it knew what to do.

Judy: And it facilitates the next move. And you go, "Whoa, that makes it all the easier."

John: And there was a release of effort on his part. It took him less effort to dance across the room with TaTitos than any other move he made even though his moves were at least as extravagant in terms of changes in posture and the speed at which the changes had to occur. And the issue here is not only efficiency in learning in terms of release of excess tension, but as Judy once asked me as she was working on a ballet routine, she said, "How do you keep from exhausting yourself when you're climbing?" And the answer is, "You never use any more than the set of muscles necessary to sustain the movement you're making." Because if you don't isolate the muscles you're overworking. And if African dance does not include the art of isolating parts of the body that Westerners don't normally isolate, I don't know what does. You isolate the muscles so that you only use the minimum set. Remember the basis of any art or fine piece of athletic work or the technique called NLP is skill. The point of the skill is to make it look easy. And it is easier for a professional to make the move than it is for an amateur. That's part of the difference between a professional and an amateur.

Judy: Because you've determined the most economical way to make the move—you've determined the efficiency involved.

John: Now, in technical climbing, the other thing about leading as opposed to seconding, is that when you're seconding, the moves are as impossible for you as they are for the lead climber but you're protected. As the lead climber you have to decide how much risk you're willing to take. When you're seconding, your lead climber is already on a station where he or she is locked in and sitting there so that if you fall you're going to be caught.

Judy: So you're allowed the freedom to fall.

John: And that's the point of your baby sitter last night. Now when you become a lead climber suddenly a whole new dimension to the sport occurs. You have to figure out how much risk you're willing to take. And I don't know in your world what the tradeoff is between windburn and the kind of experience you had, but it sits well on your face this morning. (laughter)

Judy: John used to tell great stories about how to do climbing has evolved. And here we're talking about development of epistemology using different descriptions to get to difference (the basic unit of mind), to make those understandings. Fifteen or twenty years ago in climbing, the metaphor was: Attack the mountain. You have tons and miles of ropes and you're pounding things into the mountain and you're climbing up and pounding more. And you just place and leave all this hardware along the way. And now rock climbing has evolved into a balance of not only how you use your body, but what the rock has to offer. And now it's like a dance with the rock. That really makes cybernetic sense to use the rock and what it has to offer, as opposed to attacking the rock.

John: My climbing partner, Geoffrey, was once asked by his mother, "Why do you go do these things?" And the standard answer is, "Because it's there," right? Geoffrey was more careful with his mother and he said, "Mom, you remember when you were a kid. You used to go to the playground and you could swing on the swing and go around on the merry-go-round? It's like the mountain gives me as an adult a playground. It's as if God created this playground for adults and he really does have the technology." (laughter) And Judy's description about the attack and now the dance is one example of considering and respecting context.

Rosalie: Years ago I was learning T'ai Chi dancing and a world-class mountain climber came along and he said, "I want to take all of you to climb rocks. Who wants to come?" And none of us had ever climbed rocks. A couple of us said, "OK, we'll go along with you." So he took us to a park in Oakland. He took us to a very high rock and nobody would go up. We were all scared. And then he took us to one very simple rock. He said, "This is a rock that all of us practice on." It wasn't very high. And he kept us there for two hours; two hours, and nobody but him could climb it. And he said, "Well, you know, why don't you dance with the rock. Why don't you do your T'ai Chi with the rock. So we all started doing T'ai Chi with the rock. Then we climbed trees, we did everything. Two hours later, you know, by that time I was barefoot—forget about shoes. I had chalk on my feet and chalk on my neck . . .

Judy: . . . on your nose . . .

Rosalie: . . . yeah, on my nose. I was going to get the hell up that rock one way or the other. But I hadn't succeeded and finally after two and a half hours my perception changed. And I was up the rock and don't ask me how I got there (applause) but I never saw a rock the same way again. It was like the rock and me were one. There was like this melding or blending and I never . . . , it was like then instead of going to museums I used to go around and I was real weird . . .

John: . . . checking rocks out. (laughter) . . .

Rosalie: . . . checking out rocks. I saw rocks in a way that I had never before. They were so beautiful that I didn't want to spend my time looking at pottery. I was looking at rocks.

Judy: There are the perceptual shifts that John goes through after, say, the second day: When he's been in the world of verticality for that long profound perceptual shifts occur, such that little tiny cracks become giant crevices because that's where his hand's got to go. It's like the world shrinks to a point and then this world expands inside of that frame.

Rosalie: I would climb blindfolded. It's much easier.

Judy: I believe that!

Rosalie: Much easier. I was going up, you know, and I got nine-tenths of the way up and my internal voice came in. And this was a big rock.

Judy: "Holy-moley!"

Rosalie: "Holy-moley!" "What the hell are you doing here?" And there I was hanging on. I couldn't move. Of course nobody could come up and get me. But it was like the voice was totally paralyzing. If I hadn't had the voice I would have made it up.

John: And I still say that voice was doing exactly what it was supposed to do at the wrong time . . .

Judy: (interrupting). . . timing . . .

John: (interrupting) It's all timing. (Laughter)

Judy: (interrupting) Timing is everything.

John: (interrupting again) That's what I mean. (Laughter)

Judy: A couple of people were mentioning going across the bridge and going into "stop the world" states, with no internal dialog and no foveal vision; and having different sensations, a shaking in the legs or a difference in the muscle tension in their body, or having the sense of walking very slowly. These different sensations make sense when we consider the processing of information that occurs in our neurology. Information comes in through our senses, goes through a set of transforms to second attention and is finally modeled by first attention. The distortions that occur between the world and what we perceive in first attention is a result of a set of rules. So the way in which the world is deleted or distorted is the question—not whether deletion and distortion will occur. There is still going to be a set of rules that apply. There's still going to be a set of transforms. And I don't know what those are but there's going to be some consistency in that . . .

John: . . . because the neurology of peripheral vision is as specified as that of foveal vision. Although it may be as unfamiliar to first attention as it is systematic.

"The first act of a teacher is to introduce the idea that the world we think we see is only a view, a description of the world. Every effort of a teacher is geared to prove this point to his apprentice. But accepting it seems to be one of the hardest things one can do. We are complacently caught in our particular view of the world which compels us to feel and act as if we knew everything about the world. A teacher, from the very first act he performs, aims at stopping that view. Sorcerers call it stopping the internal dialog and they are convinced it is the single-most important technique that an apprentice can learn. Stopping the internal dialog is however the key to the sorcerer's world," said don Juan. "The rest of the activities are only props. All they do is accelerate the effect of stopping the internal dialog. The teacher reorders the view of the world. I have called that view the Island of the Tonal. I have said that everything that we are is on that island. The sorcerer's explanation says the Island of the Tonal is made by our perception which has been trained to focus on certain elements. Each of these elements and all of them together form our view of the world. The job of a teacher, insofar as the apprentice's perception is concerned, consists of reordering all the elements on the island on one half of the bubble. And by now you must have realized that cleaning and reordering the Island of the Tonal means regrouping all its elements on the side of reason. My task has been to disarrange your ordinary view, not to destroy it but to force it to rally on the side of reason."

He drew an imaginary circle and divided it in two along the vertical diameter. He said that the art of the teacher was to force his disciple to group his view of the world on the right half of the bubble.

"Why the right half," I asked?

"That is the side of the tonal," he said. "The teacher always addresses himself to that side and by presenting his apprentice on the one hand with the warrior's way he forces him into reasonableness and sobriety and strength of character and body. And by presenting him, on the other hand, with unthinkable but real situations which the apprentice cannot cope with, he forces him to realize that his reason, although it is a most wonderful affair, can only cover a small area. Walking in a specific manner saturates the tonal," he said, "it floats it. You see, the attention of the tonal has to be placed on its creations. In fact, it is that attention that creates the order of the world in the first place. So the tonal must be attentive to the elements of its world in order to maintain it and above all must uphold the view of the world by internal dialog. He said that the right way of walking was a subterfuge. The warrior, first by curling his fingers drew attention to the arms and then by looking without focusing his eyes at any point directly in front of him on the arc that started at the tip of his feet and ended above the horizon, he literally flooded his tonal with information. The tonal without its one-to-one relationship with the elements of its description becomes incapable of talking to itself and thus one becomes silent. Order in our perception is the exclusive realm of the tonal. Only there can our actions have a sequence. Only there are they like stairways where one can count the steps. There is nothing of that sort in the nagual. Therefore the view of the tonal is a tool and as such it is not only the best tool but the only one we've got. Dreaming is a practical aid devised by sorcerers. They were not fools. They knew what they were doing and sought the usefulness of the nagual. By training their tonal to let go for a moment, so to speak, and then grab again. This statement does not make sense to you. But that's what you've been doing all along, training yourself to let go without loosing your marbles. Dreaming, of course, is the crown of the sorcerer's efforts, the ultimate use of the nagual."Termination of apprenticeship means that a new description has been learned of the world in a convincing and authentic manner and thus is capable of eliciting a new response that matches the new description.[3]

Judy: Response-ability.

John: Samuel Taylor Colderidge was on the edge of the class of discoveries that you're playing with when he wrote the following lines,

What if you slept and what if in your dream you dreamed. And what if in your dream you went to heaven and there picked a strange and beautiful flower. And what if, when you awoke, you had the flower in your hand. Ah, what then?

John: Well, it's time for your tonal to grab again, so come on back. You're probably wondering, "This is obvious," right? (laughter)(drawing on chalkboard) This is obviously second attention. These are obviously the afferent nerve tracks and these are the efferent nerve tracks. You are probably wondering what this is though, right? You know it looks like an amoeba, but this is reality, so in case you've wondered what the hell it looks like . . . (laughter)

Judy: There it is.

THE BIG LOOP

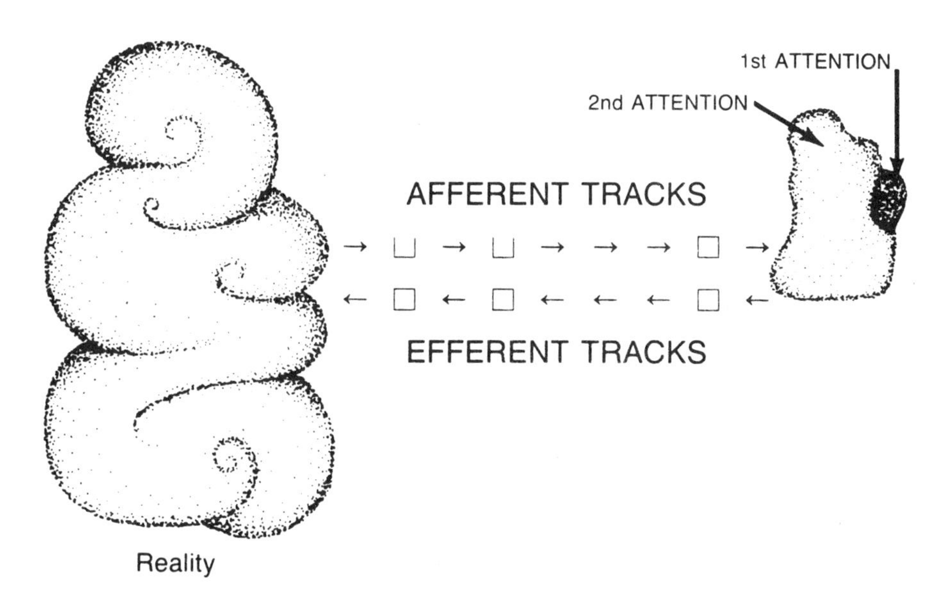

John: It's my best representation, I'll tell you that much. A big amoeba. I did make a factual error as I was talking about 160,000,000 light sensitive receptors in each retina; it's only 130,000,000. So if you feel impoverished by this difference, then elaborate your own retinas. Epistemology is what we're doing. Epistemology applies at the level of personal organization, epistemology applies at the level of social organization within the family group, and higher levels all the way up to and including the spaceship Planet Earth. Using Bateson's description there are profound repercussions of a nontrivial nature when we're talking about lethal values on certain kinds of environmental variables . . .

Judy: . . . which result from epistemological errors in thinking.

John: At the level of physiology there are some astonishing things that can be learned from examination of our nervous systems and it seems to me that one of the cornerstones of epistemology occurs here. We can explore the systematic distortions of our own neurology to come to some wisdom about what corrective actions might be appropriate.

Karen and I had a discussion a moment ago. We were talking about how, in medical school, doctors could be instructed to appreciate the tremendous responsibility of dealing with patients in life and death situations and that it's a responsibility that can not be adequately addressed by first attention alone. Then a great deal of the burden that they carry as part of their professional commitment could be lightened if they understood that in responding to people they have to respond from both first and second attention. The immediate effect of it would be the notion of specialization in medicine would have to be put inside a wiser frame. You could still have specialists but the specialist would always have the wisdom—just as the conscious mind must learn—to refer diagnosis and treatment programs to a larger context, such as the organism or the relationship between the patient and the doctor. In fact, the class of events that many of you have experienced by well-intentioned nurses and doctors in medical treatment is that they are simply responding to arcs of the circuitry which is you, according to their specialty. It would be a fine thing for physicians to have that insight and the behaviors that would congruently accompany such an insight, a fine thing both for the physician and for the patients.

Judy: Epistemology answers the question, "How do we know?" So, here we go. From the world notice that first of all, just as this is "reality" but it's really only a symbolization of it,

this is a symbol of the electromagnetic spectrum. You recognize it?
Can you fill in the gaps?

John: You bet they can. They're in first attention. (laughter) So the eye mediates light waves, that is, it responds to light waves between x and y. Fill in your values. And by the way, remember that the values are not the same for each organism. One of the most astonishing experiences is to couple . . . . . . now there's an interesting ambiguity . . .

Judy: I highly recommend it if you haven't. (Laughter)

John: . . . to form the kind of alliance that Karen was talking about—thinking with another mind. That is, linking up with another thinker so that you set up a circuit. Hooking up so that you're thinking as a team. You're thinking as a single mind even though you start with separate circuitry. You know the concept of mirroring from NLP practitioner certification training. Mirroring is one of the most elementary procedures for linking minds.

Judy: Because two descriptions are better than one.

John & Judy: Herbert, pay attention! (Laughter)

John: In this particular case there are profound differences between what we sense with our visual apparatus and what other species sense with their visual apparatus. So, for example, if you're working with horses it's important to know what class of stimuli the horses are responsive to visually. This may save your ass. If you're out and you see the flutter of a leaf falling, a light color on a dark background, you just identify it as a leaf fluttering. The horse however makes a very powerful response to such things. You may be sitting comfortably on your horse but unless you can recognize what class of signals the horse is sensitive to and what responses a horse is going to hook up to those signals you may suddenly find your horse is four feet to the side and you're sitting in mid-air. And it won't work out real well. Notice how powerfully the horse demonstrates the notion of collateral energy—very little energy in a falling leaf but . . .

Judy: . . . and their maps are very precise. When horses make a visual map they're quite detailed; two days later on the same trail if one branch from a tree is out of place they'll notice and respond.

John: Horses are dumb in the sense that we usually talk about smart and dumb. And I think it's because they do not know how to delete. Like an idiot savant, they cannot not notice certain classes of events in the world.

The analogy between the eye and the camera has helped clarify the process by which the lens of the eye, its aperture regulated by the iris, casts an image on the light sensitive screen of the retina. On this basis the optic nerve connects the retina to the central nervous system in such a way that the map of the retina is formed on the surface of the brain.

John: Remember I said yesterday, "You don't see me, you see an event on your occipital lobe"?

The analogy can be carried too far. Students of the visual system came to assume that the retina was like a photographic film. The individual receptors corresponding to light and its absence like grains of silver salt in a photographic emulsion. That the whole function of the eye and the optic nerve was to form and then transmit a mosaic of the visual world to the brain there to form the basis of visual perception. Anatomical investigations have shown however that there are many more receptor cells in the retina than there are fibers in the optic track. It is thus impossible for every receptor cell to send a separate message to the brain and the concept that the array of receptors is equivalent to the grain of a photographic emulsion must be abandoned. The very intricacy of the retina, the cells of which are variously specialized and richly interconnected, hints at a role more complex than the mere relaying of visual map. The fact is that the retina is more filter than film. It discriminates. It sends on to the brain only the most useful information.[4]

John: You know the visual system we're talking about here? This is in the context of an article called "Vision in Frogs." Take and multiply the difference between the analogy of a camera and what is being proposed here by a scientist who has worked on the visual system of a frog for the more complex organism like yourself—the lack of correspondence between the light waves that are reflected from objects around you and the final transform which exists on the occipital lobe—what we see. We have never seen what's there. We've only seen, one, what the nervous system will allow to pass in terms of transforms that are genetically specified and, two, a contribution of what we have learned to see because it is, as the article says, "useful" information. It's not that we have maps, say, visually, of the world which we can now operate on with first attention in order to come to an understanding. The transform is so distorted by the time it reaches consciousness that we're operating with extremely faulty input into first-attention maps to begin with. By "faulty" I mean that there is no one-to-one correspondence between what's out there and the representation we "see" on our occipital lobe. What's more, we do not know what the rules of transformation are.

Christian: I was at the Network '86 class and I was talking about, even with the machines that we create, they're merely extensions of our senses, hence they're also limited. We only can conceive of what we have some experience of. And so everything that we create in terms of sensing apparatus, even the . . .

John: There are two comments I want to make: First, you say, Christian, " . . . machines are *merely* extensions of our senses, hence they are also limited . . ." Let's consider some machines —say, a vacuum cleaner—here's a labor-saving device which takes a repetitive piece of human behavior—cleaning up some area of human use—and by serving as a mere extension of our body allows the individual using it to accomplish the task more quickly, with less expenditure of personal energy and with more effectiveness than the same job without the device, the machine. Notice, by the way, that the energy savings quality is local—that is, the man or woman working does expend less energy than they might without the machine. If the energy accounting system were more global however, and the amount of energy expended in the mining, transportation, and refining of the raw materials, in the various phases of the manufacturing and distribution of the machine, and the energy costs of the system created to supply the power necessary to run the machine were considered, the term *labor-saving device* might prove to be a misrepresentation. OK, so a vacuum cleaner is " . . . merely an extension . . ." Now what about a radar scanning device? See, . . . to the pilot flying IFR through a storm such devices are not "mere" extensions of his or her senses—they are what allows us to venture into contexts heretofore denied to our species—space, the depths of the ocean, . . . , (pausing) Here's something more interesting —radar is a piece of technology which, indeed, does extend our sensory apparatus but not just " . . . merely . . ." It comes, I hope, as no surprise to you that there are momentous events occurring in our world which have profound repercussions for us individually and as a species at points along the electromagnetic spectrum which are not available to us with our relatively preset sensory channels—these events are simply not detectable. This can occur in a number of ways—the events can occur at a size scale beyond our ability to discriminate—subatomic events on the one hand and the movement of this part of California—the part west of the San Andreas Fault—toward the Arctic Circle on the other—or they can occur in a time scale outside the range of our sensibilities—too fast or too slow for us to notice . . .—it takes a very astute and patient person to watch a tree grow, a rock weather or a stream cut a new bed . . . and an astute and foolish person to detect bullets passing by when fired from a high-velocity silenced weapon . . . and perhaps most exciting, if we examine the relationship between the sections of the electromagnetic spectrum our sensory channels cover and the whole of that spectrum it becomes obvious that our sensors are censors—the preponderance of the spectrum falls into the gaps where we do not sense directly. More of the world in some sense passes by undetected than we can recognize. here is where I challenge your use of the word " . . . merely . . ."—if we are clever we can design technical devices to scan inside the gaps left by our sensors . . . and thereby begin a systematic program of gaining access to portions of the world which are at present shrouded in mystery, veiled from our direct inspection.

I would be remiss as a teacher not to warn you of the possible cost of such a program if it were abused. Technical devices can be used in two ways—as an occasion for learning or as a crutch.

When David Gaster taught me to fly he used to cover the instrument panel and demand that I set up certain configurations of airspeed, engine rpm, attitude, . . . using the out-of-cockpit sources of information and then refer to the instruments for feedback to determine how close to the mark I had come. . . . that is, David insisted that I use the instruments to calibrate my own senses—the net result was that I learned to sense configurations in the air that formerly had been outside my personal range. Take a common thermometer—within the range 98.6° F. to 103° F. the well-trained diagnostician—the old country doctor, for example—could get the information directly, hand on forehead—within this range he or she didn't need to know to the tenth of a degree what the patient's temperature is—the information is more precise than required. Thus the thermometer when used inside this range has two unintended consequences. First, the doctor doesn't touch the patient and gradually if he or she had ever learned to discriminate temperature differences the ability becomes lost—that is, the crutch is being used to stabilize an infirm condition rather than create the context for the body to use its full range of functioning. Secondly, the physical touch—skin on skin—is replaced by as insulator—a mechanical device that offers precision beyond utility and simultaneously robs the physician of other classes of information. Is the patient's skin clammy?, dry? Is the temperature consistent or spotty across the forehead? Information which may be critical in arriving at a differential diagnosis.

I'm proposing that any program which deliberately sets out to create a technology to scan in the gaps left by the limitations of our own senses could usefully have as an ongoing component the deliberate development of human sensing by using the instruments to extend human competencies in these areas. Further, some wisdom is required in considering the long-term effects of using instruments which tends to replace direct human sensing.

When Judith and I built our ranch house, we asked a dowser to help us find water. This man identified with precision the specific place we should drill, the depth to water, and the quantity of the flow we could anticipate. His information was exact. I wonder—if tomorrow an instrument which could duplicate this man's performance were created—how long would it be before the question "Where have all the dowsers gone?" would have to be asked.

Christian—you said, " . . . extensions of our senses, hence they are also limited . . ." and I say, yes and irrelevant. For information to become knowledge it must pass through some human's sensory channels and be coded. It is therefore distorted by the same set of filters information sensed directly is. Yes, however, notice that the argument above goes—the program of using technology to scan in the gaps still has limitations—but importantly, they are different limitations. What we have here is a set of specialized and very limited devices—our sensory channels plus technical devices which in sum give us more access to the world than just our sensory channels. Yes, it's true that any of these technical devices must map from the portion of the world inaccessible to us directly back into representations which are detectable to us—that fall into the portions of the world we can sense—but critically the information being reported is utterly new.

Technology is a multifaceted issue—we will return to it—suffice it to say for the moment from a mistake comes a vision—the new possible world—from the vision, if compelling enough, comes the technology to achieve that new possible world.

Christian—you say . . . "we only can conceive of what we have some experience of." And I say no—the principle that allows us as a species to overcome the limitation you name is called syntax—the boon and the bane of our species.

We need a meta-science whose job is to compute, starting at the level of physiology and neurology, and ending up over here with the influence of language and representational systems, what the contribution we make to the maps that we build is on the basis of the distortions of our own functioning within our neurology. . . . (pausing) . . .

This is supposed to be useful to first-attention organization. It's interesting to explore the notion of transform here. In the frog's visual apparatus (and more so in human visual apparatus) the number of light sensitive receptors and the number of tracks in the optic nerve are not in a one-to-one relationship. Therefore decisions are being made about reality at such a peripheral level in terms of our neurology that if we entertain any hope of mapping "reality," we need now to start to map the transforms. The Parthenon is behavioral evidence that the Greeks had succeeded in partially mapping transforms in the visual system—part of a grammar of vision. At each stage there's a transform. So the optic nerve tracks go to geniculate bodies and the geniculate bodies respond in certain ways to trigger the . . . Notice that even the mood of the organism will have an effect—the mood will determine the chemical composition at the synaptic junction that will raise or lower the threshold so that there are certain things we will not perceive that are in fact there simply because we've raised the threshold by mood changes. Other things—even things that are not there—will be immediately and erroneously recognized because a part of this pattern comes in and if we've dropped the threshold at the synaptic junction somewhere along this class of transforms, we leap to a conclusion in consciousness based on a partial transform.

Let's go back here and look at this more carefully. Well, first of all, notice that the mapping of the electromagnetic spectrum available to our sensory organs is only a small subset of what we know could be mapped and in fact is out there. We can now build instruments which tell us that there are important events going on at other points in the electromagnetic spectrum which we cannot sense directly. That's why getting involved with another species brings home so powerfully the fact that we do not have the same access to the world as other species do. Coupling with another mind, from our own or a different species, so that you can perceive and act together in a loop is an astonishingly educational and humbling experience.

Judy: Gregory talks about it in terms of expanding the boundaries of self so that self really does expand to include other possibilities. One example he used was from a time when he was living in New Guinea and he had a dog and he had a gibbon. And the dog and the gibbon would play games; the gibbon would come and smack the dog and the dog would jump up and they would go through a play ritual where the dog would chase the gibbon around and then he'd finally come back to the porch and lay down. The gibbon and dog would go through the cycle again and again. Bateson says he came to realize that the boundaries of self changed because there became a reality called "gibbon and dog" where behaviors of the dog and the gibbon that had never occurred in their behavioral repertoires were elicited by the coupling of those two organisms.

Don Juan knew that as a young man Carlos had been a hunter —his grandfather had a Leghorn chicken farm and he used to hunt hawks because they'd kill the chickens. So don Juan uses that experience to develop an alternate description of the world. He goes, "You have natural predilections here to be a hunter," and he broadens that description by taking Carlos out and developing a set of experiences that fill out the description. "What does the hunter have to do?" The hunter has to learn about all the habits of the animals, to be able to see better, and to move silently. Then he develops that theme, explaining that when you're entering that reality you can't "squeeze the world." An example of not "squeezing the world" would be when don Juan catches five quail. Don Juan cooks two of them and Carlos says, "Why didn't you cook the other three? We could have had a really good barbecue," and he says, "Because that would be squeezing the world to take more than we need. The hunter goes through the world and he doesn't leave traces around; he touches it lightly and he moves on."

"The art of a hunter is to become inaccessible," he said. "In the case of that blond girl it would've meant that you had to become a hunter and meet her sparingly. Not the way you did. You stayed with her day after day, until the only feeling that remained was boredom. True?"

I did not answer. I felt I did not have to. He was right.

"To be inaccessible means that you touch the world around you sparingly. You don't eat five quail; you eat one. You don't damage the plants just to make a barbecue pit. You don't expose yourself to the power of the wind unless it is mandatory. You don't use and squeeze people until they have shriveled to nothing, especially the people you love."[5]

Judy: Don Juan uses that piece of information about Carlos's hunting experience and develops his second description so Carlos can compare the two. Then he sends him back home to start noticing the difference from the description of his reality in Los Angeles.

John: Now there's a task. The wise negotiator, like the wise hunter, knows better than to squeeze the world. The negotiator whose vision is clear and far-reaching understands that not only must he or she conduct a successful negotiation which both parties can take home successfully but that the negotiation underway constitutes the foundation for a relationship which will promote or destroy further interchange. The hunter who sees with the same clarity and distance will never corner an animal which he or she has not decided to take; furthermore, that live, healthy animal left a way out constitutes a future food source for the hunter. Not leaving a way out constitutes the end of a relationship . . . for at least one of you.

Squeezing the world is only one form of self-indulgence, of course. Not seizing it at all is another. Twenty times a second your eye moves. Can you find that? Can you find that experience? . . . (pausing) . . .

(pointing to drawing on chalkboard) Now, only this segment of the electromagnetic spectrum do we respond to. Instrumentation as we discussed earlier is a way of discovering how limited our access is. I had always shied away from instrumentation because I felt that it was being used as a replacement for sensing directly. It's a form of insulation between you and what you are sensing. And as with any band-pass filter it encourages first-attention consideration of arcs of circuits, that is, parts of people as opposed to the full person. But that's simply a statement that technology can be misused—my mistake. I was operating at the wrong logical level. It can also be used with brilliance and one of the non-trivial applications is mapping from parts of the electromagnetic spectrum that we can't normally get to, back into our filters called sensory channels. The fact that we have an instrumentation only means that we're sensing places or with refinements that we couldn't sense otherwise. Then we subject it to all the distortions that we are heir to by virtue of being a member of the species. As I mentioned, when David was teaching me to fly he made me use instruments to calibrate my own senses. Believe it or not, you cannot tell whether you're climbing or diving—you cannot tell your attitude in the air—by kinesthetics alone, without external visual reference or instrumentation.

Judy: I had a hard time believing this but . . .

John: It turns out it's true.

Woman: I've been in planes. You're talking about up and down, side to side?

John: You cannot tell your orientation with respect to the surface of the Earth unless you have either visual reference external to the plane or instrumentation. Your kinesthetics will mislead you consistently . . .

Judy: . . . they'll trick you . . .

Woman: But not just in the plane—under the hood specifically.

John: Yes, not just in the plane. You must not be able to see outside the plane in order for this effect to occur.

Woman: You're basically saying that if your eyes are closed you can't tell?

John: Correct.

Judy: You think you can tell, but you are tricked very easily.

John: You could be at the top of a loop and you would think you were at the bottom of it.

Woman: That's how pilots sometimes fly into the ground.

John: Exactly. But not for long. (Laughter)

Woman: And not twice.

Judy: Nothing more irrelevant to a pilot than the amount of air above him. (Laughter)

John: Let me give you Gaster's two-dimensional version of the problem I just offered so that you can actually go out and play with it. You won't need an airplane for it. So I'm mapping a three-dimensional phenomena into two dimensions now. Here we are on the river Nile at one of its broadest points. The question is: Is the river moving? The context is the following. We're in a boat by ourselves. There are no other boats available in sight or hearing. The fog has dropped so that we can see roughly ten feet around us. There's no physical reference point available, other than the river. Problem: How do you determine whether the river is moving?

Woman: What about you moving?

John: If the river is moving you're moving with it—there's no doubt about that.

Woman: Give me the information again.

John: No-no, you've got the information.

Alright, when you have an interesting proposal about that solution let us know. Back to what portions of the world we can sense through our sensory channels—not only do we knock out most of the world, in a sense, through the limited receptivity of our peripheral organs, but think about the tempo, something that you're all engaged in as part of this seminar. That is to say if I were a tree what class of patterns would I notice?

Man: Patterns that go very slowly—or quickly, rather.

John: Everything that I presently consider slow would probably be too fast for my perceptual apparatus. Now if I were moving at something approaching the speed of light what classes of events would I be able to sense? Do you remember subliminal conditioning? Somebody was mentioning that yesterday—about the outlawing of subliminal persuasion. Subliminal sensing is relative to the threshold value of the sense organ you're using, consider, for example, juggling 100 years ago.

Judy: One of you said you were walking very slowly on the bridge because the information that was coming in was so different than with normal foveal vision, but also there were runners on the bridge and the runners—it was as if they were not coming towards you, as if they had stopped running but their legs were still moving up and down.

John: Can you use instrumentation as a way of extending the "natural range" of your sensory apparatus? That's one of the nontrivial uses of instrumentation. How else might you learn to extend the range of your sensing ability. If you want a little experiment, go to some public place and stand there and "stop the world." Then sense pressure on your body other than what you can account for in terms of the pressure of the clothing against your body or the way gravity is acting upon you or the movement of the air. And you'll soon discover that you can whirl around and discover someone who's looking at you directly. You can know when somebody is looking at you if you "stop the world" and go internal to sense that class of events. How does a dowser find water? A dowser is doing something which we can't yet recapitulate with technical means. In the bands of perception which each of us inherit as members of the species there are sensations which are below the level of consciousness—they never make it out of second attention for most of us—which would allow us to detect the presence of water. Dowsers have gained or retained access to this portion of the bands of perception—to this particular class of sensations.

Woman: How do they do it long distance using a map?

John: Hell, I don't even know how they do it on the ground. I'm saying the fact that members of our species can do it invites us to recognize that, although these transforms are extremely reductionistic, we're still getting enough into second attention that some of us maintain the ability to sense through all these transforms things that are normally considered outside of the range of human perception. And so it's now an invitation for you to explore that class of events. Go to the Gulf of Bothnia, in Scandinavia for example, and find out whether you sense the movement of the Earth's surface there—a portion of the Earth's crust which was depressed by the weight of glaciers during the last ice age and is still rebounding at the rate of one centimeter (0.39 inches) a year—even the crust of the earth has memory.

Christian: When I hear things like, "extra-sensory," or "supernatural," or whatever, I don't think of them as being outside of what's natural. They are a part of what's natural.

Judy: . . . although outside of what we're typically doing. Notice that this confusion arises when we fail to discriminate between what is possible for us from what is average.

Christian: Right. We just don't have the technology yet or our paradigms aren't large enough or broad enough to be able to encompass these things.

John: Or we're fixated on technology instead of understanding and expanding our senses.

Judy: Right. Just in terms of our physiology, we don't really know what those perceptual ranges, or as don Juan says—the set of human possibilities—what the limiting values are that are placed on us genetically. I'm sure we haven't pushed to the limits of those, especially in this area because we don't even know yet what the possibilities are.

John: Karen?

Karen: I guess another question is: Do we have to know at the level of the occipital lobe or can we know at the periphery?

John: I use the simple example that there are spinal reflex arcs so that heat, in a peripheral sensory organ like a hand, will cause a withdrawal of that organ before the message reaches central nervous system. It goes through the lower spinal chord loops without the cortex being involved until after the response has been initiated So that we can learn and know at the periphery—this is both the brillance and the danger of our species. Because of these possibilities, if we have a deeply held belief . . . that is to say, if we have done some modeling of our experience using this loop between first and second attention, and we start to push that generalization out toward the periphery, when we have pushed it far enough out that we are changing the circuitry, resetting threshold values . . . we can reach the kind of quality of hypnotic deafness that I described yesterday to support your beliefs. Then what have we accomplished when we've done that? We've become supremely efficient—because we've created a situation where we have disconnected ourselves enough from the flux of the world that nothing will pass these bands, these filters, that will upset our homeostasis. Our beliefs, originally derived from our experience of the world, are no longer responsive to experiences in the world. We have just committed suicide.

Judy: At the societal level, as I was saying yesterday about the distinction between somatic storage and extra-somatic storage, you typically have to develop an institution to exercise the filter function that so than no new information is allowed to come in that may potentially upset that homeostasis.

John: How many walking dead have you encountered in your life? I mean that seriously.

Woman: How many walking alive?

John: Yeah, it's probably easier to count the walking alive that the walking dead.

Patricia: I was thinking back to what was said earlier about ESP. Those who have ESP would say that that's exactly what those of us who don't use this much are doing. But in fact those are all sensory inputs that we have but we shut them off from consciousness.

Judy: We've introduced filters somewhere along the line.

John: The only quarrel I have with those people is their epistemology. They are claiming by the "E" in the ESP that it's not in the "SP" And we don't know what the hell's in the "SP" because we haven't done our epistemological homework with respect to known channels yet.

Woman: And I'm using ESP very loosely . . .

John: Loosely, right. And I'm saying there are times to be loose in your thinking and times to be precise. And if you start attributing your experiences exclusively to phenomena that lie "outside" of your normal sensory apparatus you may never discover this part of your heritage. If this looks and sounds like an argument to you let us say that we have coupled at first attention and we are now refining our representations, our models. Words can be dangerous!—because they're one form of filtering. And when first attention indulges itself it's typically with auditory digital symbols. So if I now come to a belief regarding my experiences of remote sensing, if I label it in first attention (the modeler of second-attention experience) as being extra-sensory, I have just indulged myself in the sense that I no longer have to examine my own epistemological foundations. And I will never discover that, if part of the phenomena is in the normal sensory channels, because I won't look there.

Judy: Because you pushed the filter out there. Notice how, at this level of discussion, the terms "filter" and "belief" are interchangeable.

John: Part of the issue for me is that, look, I applaud the alledged ESP competencies—the behaviors are superb when they're actually there. There are a lot of flakes running around the world who claim things for personal benefit and then there are people who can genuinely sense things that I have not learned yet how to sense. Discriminating between those two groups is a nontrivial pursuit in itself. And often it seems to me that they are self-indulgent in just the way I'm talking about. It's important for them because any "psychic" phenomena will have to take a distorted form in a culture that caters to first attention. And that's where we live. So I sympathize with those people because they are proposing something that so much flies in the face of first-attention work that it's typically not valued in our culture. And so it often takes a twisted form. And I'm proposing that they don't have to be outside of first attention in that sense. They can go, "Look what our neurology can do!" I think part of what goes on is that the ones who can authentically do this sort of thing really have to defend themselves against the first-attention onslaught of the culture around them so they define part of their uniqueness in terms of these abilities. Every one of you is in fact unique but if you have to promote your uniqueness as a way of defending yourself against first-attention onslaughts then you can get bent in certain ways.

Marne: When we code experiences in words, and if that can inhibit the experiences by trying to code it in something by putting words to it, then how can one pass on information to somebody else, teach them . . .

John: How did TaTitos teach you how to dance?

Marne: He showed us.

John: Right, so there's an example.

Marne: Right, but, OK, physical . . . If you want somebody to do something mentally and you're trying to get them to get into a certain mental state how would you bring that on? You obviously can't get into them and then drag them in and show them.

John: Ah, not true.

Judy: Language is only a code for experience. The trick that happens, or the problem, the trap, that people fall into is to believe that language is experience. Because we are native speakers of English, we get tricked into believing that we really do understand each other (both horizontally and vertically) when we use language, and we make assumptions based on that. If you go back to the language, when you say something to another native speaker and don't make the assumption that "Oh, she understands me," you will have other alternatives to draw from—language plus whatever. In Kongo they have a proverb, "Every utterance has at least two meanings." And I think that's the trick. Most people act as if they believe that language is experience, when it's only a way of talking about it.

John: And when appropriately balanced, it's a critical, positive function of first attention. The function of consciousness and language is to isolate and delineate, to make precise; and that's one of the functions it has in its interface with second attention. Judith is talking about self-indulgence which results from an unbalanced first attention. If you accept for a moment our contention that one of the proper responsibilities of first attention is to model second attention, and that's exactly what has happened evolutionarily, then of course it's going to use its own code. It's got to. That's the only code it's got. You heard don Juan's comment this morning: "That is a proper and appropriate function of the tonal."

The well-formedness condition that keeps you from pathologically doing that self-indulgently—the difference between a model and a theory—is falsifiability. You seek the counterexample. That will prevent you from making the logical level category error of believing that your words are the reality. They're indicators, they're pointers back to representations at the second attention and back down this tremendous circuit that you engage in with other people and with the environment. There's nothing wrong with transmitting learning and information through words. But remember the rule that I proposed as a well-formedness constraint on verbal communication between organisms: Every verbal communication will be considered utter rumor until it has a physiological basis to it. All I'm saying is that the loop has to go in both directions, and that's what balance between first and second attention is.

Woman: So for everything that is heard, you have the verbal representation and that is the rumor. Then we have our own test of experience and we compare that with the verbal code, adjust, maybe change how we would code it in our own minds so everything that anybody experiences is this continual cycle between rumor and personal experience . . .

John: . . . unless you're talking to the living dead who, making the category error of believing that the words are the experience, will push that generalization out to the periphery so that they don't upset their homeostasis by essentially cutting themselves off from learning anything new.

Judy: Also there are experiences that I don't have words for. There may come a time when I can produce an adequate and useful description of it. But I am still convinced that Marne could pass that information on without words at some point if she chose to and artistically explored the nonverbal codes for teaching and learning.

John: The straight manipulation of physiology will change state, which changes filters, which is a very direct way of changing a person's experience. It's a more profound way than any words. So there are other places to intervene.

Alan: How do you know when you're not self-indulgent?

John: I mean, obviously the question needs more of a context, right?

Alan: Pardon?

John: The question needs more of a context.

Alan: I'm just a little puzzled. I'm sitting here a little concerned about the criteria for self-indulgence.

John: Right. Well, we're developing it. Part of the personal organizational model is for us to discover by experience what the proper balance between those systems are.

Judy: Yeah. You guys *are* the other end of the loop out there.

Woman: I would suggest that perhaps it's having a sense of humor. (Laughter)

Judy: That's certainly a part of it.

Woman: If you lose your sense of humor, you're probably too self-indulgent.

John: Well, let's follow her suggestion. That's really important. What does it mean to have a sense of humor about your own beliefs and understandings, your own experience?

Woman: It means you can switch your perspectives.

Judy: Don Juan talks about self-importance. And he says that, in terms of physical energy, self-importance is the most costly energy using mechanism that a human being has. That's why a warrior practices and takes inventory of his own behavior so that he can let go of self-importance—it uses up too much energy. It's the difference between, as Karen says, coming to the realization that you came to on the bridge where your conscious mind says, "I'm doing it, I'm doing it!"—finding that humorous at the same time, and understanding the paradox—as opposed to going, "I failed." I mean just that difference alone . . .

Woman: Humor is a sense of perspective.

John: Perspective. That means being able to see from multiple positions—even see in different ways. So, for some of you the well-formedness constraint will be: You may never act in the world until you have a minimum of two descriptions. Suppose we define the model (in the sense of model-building) at first attention. The minimum model requires the synthesis of at least two perceptual positions. That keeps you alive. The twenty times a second visual sampling program—the metaphors are profound just in the anatomical structures alone.

Judy: . . . news of difference . . .

John: . . . transform, news of difference, transform, news of difference, transform, all the way back to the central nervous system. So to keep yourself from indulging at first attention, one well-formedness constraint on the proper behavior of first attention will be that you may never generate behavior out of a model, a hypothesis about the world, unless you have built that model on at least a double description. See, it's like choice. If you only have one perceptual position it's like when somebody says, "Oh, in this context I have this choice that I always make." That's not a choice. The only way you have choice is by being able to behave in profoundly different manners. And that's the kind of deliberate exercise of change of homeostatic center that keeps you alive.

Judy: Don Juan talks about that as being a warrior. What does a warrior seek? A warrior seeks power. What is power? Power is knowledge. How does he or she do that? They seek descriptions, multiple descriptions, and while entertaining a new description, they enter it with complete commitment—they have to believe.

Man: Self-indulgence . . . I used to work with the terminally ill. One of the things you learn about working with the terminally ill is you don't put off until tomorrow what you can do today.

Judy: That's exactly right.

Man: Don't put off telling someone you love them because you might not be here to tell them that later.

Judy: Another responsibility in the learning of a warrior is: Don't act as if you're immortal. That's another form of self-indulgence.

John: Death as your advisor!

Woman: It seems important at this stage to chunk up to the societal level and mention that a society that doesn't have two perspectives is committing suicide.

Judy: It's like the cattle-herding African tribe; once the flexibility has been eaten up by the investment, the filter, then you're right.

Woman: I sort of think of putting the government back at the first- and second-attention level and the individuals down at the per . . .

John: . . . at the periphery . . .

Woman: . . . at the periphery. And if we're all being told that we have to believe one thing, the society is gone, dead, done.

John: It's no longer evolving.

Judy: I want to read a passage from Castaneda where don Juan says to Carlos,

> "Warriors fight self-importance as a matter of strategy, not principle." . . . "Your mistake is to understand what I say in terms of mortality."
>
> "I see you as a highly moral man, don Juan," . . . Carlos insisted.

"You've noticed my impeccability, that's all." . . .

"Impeccability, as well as getting rid of self-importance, is too vague a concept to be one of any value to me," I remarked.

Don Juan choked with laughter, and I challenged him to explain impeccability.

"Impeccability is nothing else but the proper use of energy." . . . "My statements have no inkling of morality. I've saved energy and that makes me impeccable. To understand this, you have to save enough energy yourself."

We were quiet for a long time. I wanted to think about what he had said. Suddenly, he started talking again.

"Warriors take strategic inventories," he said. "They list everything they do. Then they decide which of those things can be changed in order to allow themselves a respite, in terms of expending their energy."

I argued that their list would have to include everything under the sun. He patiently answered that the strategic inventory he was talking about covered only behavioral patterns that were not essential to our survival and well-being.

I jumped at the opportunity to point out that survival and well-being were categories that could be interpreted in endless ways, hence, there was no way of agreeing what was or what was not essential to survival and well-being.

As I kept on talking I began to lose momentum. Finally, I stopped because I realized the futility of my arguments.

Don Juan said then that in strategic inventories of warriors, self-importance figures as the activity that consumes the greatest amount of energy, hence, their effort to eradicate it.

"One of the first concerns of warriors is to free that energy in order to face the unknown with it," don Juan went on. "The action of rechanneling that energy is impeccability." [6]

John: "The action of rechanneling that energy is impeccability."

George: I don't understand why Castaneda gave up his argument. I mean, he got discouraged, right?

John: You don't understand it, George, because you were doing the same thing Carlos was doing.

George: . . . (pausing) . . . That's right.

John: The argument between don Juan and Carlos could only proceed from Carlos's presupposition that he and don Juan had to agree about their perceptions of the world. And that's exactly one of the self-indulgent qualities of first attention. Why not embrace the difference?—and from the difference discover new information, a synthesis. Answer: Because of his predilection for self-importance. His perception, his description, has to have priority. Or, alternatively, he has to come to an agreement with don Juan about their perceptions. They have to agree on a single description of reality—a Jackdaw epistemology—which is exactly what Juan is talking about.

George: I find that encouraging. I understand that.

John: It's important to throw a bone to first attention from time to time, George.

Judy: (reading from Gregory Bateson's *Steps to an Ecology of Mind)*

What worries me is the addition of modern technology to the old system. Today the purposes of consciousness are implemented by more and more effective machinery, transportation systems, airplanes, weaponry, medicine, pesticides, and so forth. Conscious purpose is now empowered to upset the balances of the body, of society, and of the biological world around us. A pathology—a loss of balance—is threatened.

I think that much of what brings us here today is basically related to the thoughts that I have been putting before you. On the one hand, we have the systemic nature of the individual human being, with the systemic nature of the culture in which he lives, and the systemic nature of the biological, ecological system around him; and, on the other hand, the curious twist in the systemic nature of the individual man whereby consciousness is, almost of necessity, blinded to the systemic nature of the man himself. Purposive consciousness pulls out, from the total mind, sequences which do not have the loop structure which is characteristic of the whole systemic structure. If you follow the "common-sense" dictates of consciousness you become, effectively, greedy and unwise—again I use "wisdom" as a word for recognition of and guidance by a knowledge of the total systemic creature.

Lack of systemic wisdom is always punished. We may say that

the biological systems—the individual, the culture, and the ecology—are partly living sustainers of their component cells and organisms. But the systems are nevertheless punishing of any species unwise enough to quarrel with its ecology. Call the systemic forces "God" if you will.

Let me offer you a myth.

There was once a Garden. It contained many hundreds of species—probably in the subtropics—living in great fertility and balance, with plenty of humus, and so on. In that Garden, there were two anthropoids who were more intelligent than the other animals.

On one of the trees there was a fruit, very high up, which the two apes were unable to reach. So they began to *think.* That was the mistake. They began to think purposively.

By and by, the he ape, whose name was Adam, went and got an empty box and put it under the tree and stepped on it, but he found he still couldn't reach the fruit. So he got another box and put it on top of the first. Then he climbed up on the two boxes and finally he got that apple.

Adam and Eve then became almost drunk with excitement. *This* was the way to do things. Make a plan. ABC and you get D.

They then began to specialize in doing things the planned way. In effect, they cast out from the Garden the concept of their own total systemic nature and of its total systemic nature.

After they had cast God out of the Garden, they really went to work on this purposive business, and pretty soon the topsoil disappeared. After that, several species of plants became "weeds" and some of the animals became "pests"; and Adam found that Gardening was much harder work. He had to get his bread by the sweat of his brow and he said, "It's a vengeful God. I should never have eaten that apple."

Moreover, there occurred a qualitative change in the relationship between Adam and Eve, after they had discarded God from the Garden. Eve began to resent the business of sex and reproduction. Whenever these rather basic phenomena intruded upon her now purposive way of living, she was reminded of the larger life which had been kicked out of the Garden. So Eve began to resent sex and reproduction, and when it came to parturition she found this process very painful. She said this, too, was due to the vengeful nature of God. She even heard a Voice say "In pain shalt thou bring forth" and "Thy desire shall be unto thy husband, and he shall rule over thee." The biblical version of this story, from which I have borrowed extensively, does not explain the extraordinary perversion of values, whereby woman's capacity for love comes to seem a curse inflicted by the deity.

Be that as it may. Adam went on pursuing his purposes and finally invented the free-enterprise system. Eve was not, for a long time, allowed to participate in this because she was a woman. But she joined a bridge club and there found an outlet for her hate. [7]

TAKING INVENTORY

John: I think it's time to take some inventory. The next step is beginning to take inventory in the sense that we've discussed it this morning. Notice that inventory taking is a proper function of first attention. It has to be a dance between where the information is actually available in its richest form—second attention—and the modeling function which belongs to first attention.

The sorting we're proposing is that you first sort your survival programs out. You don't know with certainty which of the programs buried deeply inside of you are survival programs and which you may safely dispense with—you don't know at first attention. Therefore, the way you approach your task becomes extremely important—the first attention's job is to create a model, in unison with the minds here (Judith, me, and the rest of your colleagues) of how you may respectfully propose to second attention that this sorting be accomplished. It would take a tremendous amount of time and energy, more collateral energy than I think you probably have available, if you were to insist that all of this review occur in first attention. It would be equivalent to specifying to the horse where each foot will be placed in a long journey. I would therefore propose that the proper balance for this task, in first and second-attention circuitry, would be that the first attention propose, just as the rider does to the horse, that a certain destination be the objective; that there are well-formedness conditions on how the horse and the rider may traverse the distance between where they are now and their objective, in terms of insisting that whatever mechanisms you use for this sorting, all survival programs be set aside and protected so that they remain operational during the entire period of the resorting and review.

We're in a part of California which contains a beautiful

species of tree called the redwoods. If you haven't had the wonderful experience of walking through these cathedral-like structures of redwood forests I would urge you to make sure you do. There are two natural methods that I'm familiar with for redwoods to reproduce. One is by sucker plants, and if you've watched trees you may have noticed that coming out of the root ball, just below or just above the surface of the ground, will come new trees. They'll begin to grow out and around. If you walk through a redwood forest you'll notice this recurrent, patterned phenomenon where there's the stump of a giant tree—it's either been cut or has died, been struck by lightning and destroyed—and in a perfect circle around it is a stand of redwoods.

Judy: A whole stand grows around that. That's one way they reproduce themselves.

John: The second way they reproduce themselves is that if the cones produced by the redwoods fall to the ground and are exposed to temperatures in excess of the normal range of temperatures, the daily fluctuations and seasonal fluctuations, in this area, they become fertile and begin to grow. One way to get a huge field of redwoods is to pick an area full of these cones and set it on fire. The Ohlone Indians[8] who occupied this part of the coast of California had a systematic program of burning which they used for purposes of restoring and renewing their environment. They understood the wisdom of context in that sense. Notice that in a forest fire nothing is wasted. The elements are changed in form but not in substance, and the deadfall and the accumulation of material which is a natural part of the reproductive cycle of an ecosystem called a forest are reduced to more elementary elements and made available as a nutrient base for the next season of growth. Notice that once the fire has started, there is no way, except by setting the boundary conditions that it will burn within, that you can really discriminate parts of the field that should not be burned from parts of the field that should be. So the sorting must occur before the fire.

I had a friend who used to have a reoccurring dream—was

it a dream?—somewhere in between the realities, maybe in both—and he used to stand on the edge of a cliff. He would look over the cliff, 80 or 100 feet below, to the roaring surf that would hurl itself against the bottom of the cliff, as the Pacific demonstrated its majestic strength and the wind would begin to blow and it would blow so hard that he could literally lean out over the cliff, supported by the wind, and experience an astonishingly realistic sensation of flying. And at a certain point the wind velocity would become so great that instead of blowing around him, it would blow through him and as it passed through him it would remove all the obsolete structures which had been important in his ability to achieve the stage of evolution he had reached.

John: When Judith and I built our house, the ranch we live on now, the carpenters built a strong, sturdy house. Big timbers. We've had two storms this season where we had one-hundred mile-an-hour winds there. No damage, the house is solid, it's placed well. And strong as the foundation is, if I were to build a windmill structure so that I could have wind power, the foundation that I would have to build for that structure would have to be even more deeply set than the foundation for the house that we live in. Because the house we live in, although it contains dynamisms called Judith and John and Michael and Kathie and Eric, is a stable structure relative to its environment. It doesn't move. There are no moving parts to the house. But a windmill is a dynamic system. The foundation must be set with even more care because with a dynamic system it has to be firmly supported. The stresses and strains on the foundation are extremely amplified relative to a static structure. In both the building of the windmill and the building of the ranch house that we now live in, the carpenters used scaffolding for certain stages of the construction project as any intelligent carpenter would. They did of course remove the scaffolding when that stage of the job was done.

Nearly all of you know how to drive cars. And the way that you learned to drive a car, and the way you drive a car once you've mastered the essential characteristics of operating a car, are a profoundly different strategies.

It's time to take inventory. The well-formedness conditions on the exercise that we've described should include what you learned yesterday about lifelines. Setting context so that the fire burns only in the fields that you choose to burn. The winds blow with the kind of force that you need. And that the balance in the dance between first and second attention be fully respected. It is important that a signal be arranged from second attention to the witness in this exercise, just as in all the exercises, which says, "Pull the lifeline, pull me in, I need to come back." That signal in the participant who is undergoing the transformation has to come from second attention—that's why Larry and I did our dance yesterday. And you, as that witness, respecting the integrity of the circuitry of the person you are witnessing for, should in no way intervene, but should use that as a profound perceptual learning position—one part of a double description—so that later, if it's appropriate, you could offer a second description of the sequence the person went through. But you are not to be active, in the sense of interfering in any way with what has been arranged, except if you receive a second-attention signal, which has been agreed upon previously, to pull the lifeline in. Be back in a half hour. Obviously, you will set in progress certain kinds of functions which we either will complete during this fifteen minutes of clock time (with time distortion) or you will make arrangements so that the process can continue even as you come back to first attention with indicators of the progress of the sorting, the spring cleaning, that's going on. Enjoy your journeys.

John: Second attention in many of you is working very very hard continuing, completing, cleaning up a process which you started during this exercise.

Judy: The strategy of taking inventory . . .

John: . . . occurs on a systematic, periodic basis. Why do you think they call spring cleaning, *spring* cleaning? That's important. Every organizational model, every homeostatic model you achieve, is a trap if it's perpetuated beyond the wisdom of the context in which it was originally generated.

John: I ran across several people who were having a bit of difficulty not in achieving "stopping the world" states but in sustaining the "stopping the world" states. Every aesthetic act requires skill. The development of skill is in a sense a commitment, a personal, disciplined commitment that says I will practice the classes of mechanics until they become so refined and deep in my neurology I need only to think of the practice and the effect occurs. At the risk of the wrath of Judith I will relate that her horse, Shotsey, . . .

Judy: Leave my horse out of it! (Laughter)

John: . . . has a predilection—I call to your mind Erickson's comments about the relationship between rider and horse, and I point out that in the case of Shotsey, Shotsey has a predilection—to eat.

Judy: In fact it's her favorite thing in the whole world. If she could choose to do anything, that would be it.

John: She would eat herself to death—she would founder if we let her go. She is undisciplined in this particular way.

Judy: I asked the vet finally, I said, "This doesn't make any sense to me." I said, "How would this horse survive in the wild? What would happen?" And he said, "She'd eat 'till she got so fat that she'd fall down and the wolves would eat her." In otherwords, she wouldn't survive.

John: And now what is the proper relationship between a rider and this particular horse? We'll be running through one of the fields which is full of lush grass—it's like putting a kid in a candy store as far as Shotsey's perceptual apparatus is concerned . . .

Judy: . . . especially in the spring when the grass is just mouth high. (laughter) It takes every bit of will and discipline that this horse can muster . . . Literally, her body just shakes. (demonstrating) It just vibrates with anticipation of eating that grass. (shuddering and grinning) Huhuhuhnnnnnnn. (Laughter)

John: Now, at a walk, Shotsey could easily and even safely reach over, grab a bite, and keep going. Furthermore, she's gotten very good at disassociating the muscles in her neck and jaw, so that if you were riding with your eyes closed, using tactile feedback only, you couldn't tell at that gait whether she was eating or not because she's disassociated those muscle groups.

Judy: She's so good at taking a bite without ever breaking gait.

John: Now what are the first attention, or rider's, responsibilities toward this horse, because of its predilection?

Woman: Keeping a short rein.

John: Indeed. And for what purpose? At a walk nothing dramatic would occur. However, if the eating programs are allowed to develop at this slower gait, at a run such a program could injure both the rider and the horse. At a run, if a particularly luscious piece of vegetation is within the range of the perceptual program you've allowed her to establish at the walk, she would make that move, thereby throwing the balance point off just enough for both the horse and rider to go down. Therefore in the safe environment it becomes a responsibility of the rider to discipline and to set the boundaries of operation for that horse so that both may move with safety through the world. That's a responsibility of the rider!

While I was circulating around the room during the exercise, I ran across a man who was having difficulty, not in getting the "stopping the world" state, but in sustaining it. Things would happen like: he'd be in for roughly half the amount of time allotted and then suddenly his internal dialog would be retriggered by something in the environment. One of two things is going on here, either the person is practicing stopping the internal dialog to develop the skill further, or maybe it's time to kick a little ass. Or a big one, for that matter. If you forge an agreement at first attention in a respectful, balanced manner with second attention and—that contract is not kept at second attention, you come immediately back to first attention and now you go, "Listen. I've done my part of the dance. If we're going to dance together we're going to dance to the same music. And I've done impeccably at first attention what was necessary to make the arrangements and you did not keep the contract. I call for every unconscious resource to discipline this part of second attention so that the relationship is one of appropriate balance." And it's a perfectly legitimate and in many cases appropriate response if your contracts between first and second attention are not kept when first attention has been impeccable in its part of the operation.

Judy: Do you think it's another form of indulgence?

John: Notice that you can have indulgence at second attention. It's a dance and both bodies are moving in unison.

Alan: Did you say you can have indulgence in second attention?

John: Oh, you bet. (Laughter) Alan, you're thinking in a linear fashion. As soon as you put it in a loop you recognize, "Of course there has to be second-attention self-indulgence because first attention is nothing more than a model of second attention."

Judy: It's a subset, right?

Gloria: My problem was understanding the instructions. First of all, I didn't even understand the idea that we were supposed to come up with a context and sort within the context. I think where I need more help is the first-attention/second-attention balance.

John: Typically. Let me just hit what the high points of what this exercise was. And there no doubt are as many creative misinterpretations of these . . .

Judy: . . . as there are people in the room.

John: The farmer prepares the ground before planting. The caretaker of the forest has a responsibility, both for providing places where the deadfall is left as a habitat for certain kinds of creatures that are part of that ecosystem, and at the same time for cleaning the forest so that it's available for the public to use in an appropriate manner—clearing the deadfall and turning it over in the sense of using it as mulch for the next round of growth.

Without a periodic inventory we become cluttered. We carry obsolete structures, obsolete functions which are no longer of relevance. The context has changed and because of filtering we have not made those adjustments because we are such modeling animals, we cannot not pattern. That is what this is all about. Therefore it becomes necessary for us to build in, as part of our personal ecology, a renovation cycle, a seasonal cycle of change which updates our personal organization with respect to the contexts we're presently operating in. Without such a periodic update we fall prey to the Peter Principle.

Now, more specifically, I propose that there are certain things that are vital to you; the survival programs that you've built up over the years are certainly in this category. They must be protected. They must remain operational and protected during this entire cycle. And now, having made a first-attention request of second attention to remove and safeguard all those vital structures that define the uniqueness of you and guarantee your continued survival and growth, one proposal could be that you spring clean. I offered the metaphor of the fire, the wind—water is a cleansing element as well. You may have preferences as to what class of metaphor you use.

The task was to make the arrangements by sorting and inventorying those things that are essential to your unique definition of self, as well as your survival programs, as well as your learning mechanisms. And then to clean the rest of it in preparation for creating a foundation for your personal organizational model which involves demons at the bottom level who are narrow-band geniuses . . .

Judy: There are spirits out there right now.

John: . . . all the way down to the efferent tracks. I mean we're talking about a deep cleaning.

Judy: Turtles all the way down.

John: Cleansing, a real cleansing, a purification. Now some of you may have completed the entire piece of work under time distortion. You can spend weeks, of course, in fifteen minutes if you've mastered the trick of time distortion. It occurs spontaneously in many of these classes of exercises. Some of you may have set in process the particular arrangements that we've been describing here so that it continues while you return to first attention and enjoy this level of communication as well. In any case, it's important to get a termination signal when the cleansing, purification, whatever metaphor you use, has proceeded to the point where you now have cleared the area for the foundations of constructing a new kind of personal model for yourself. So the maximum length of time I would propose is that this will be complete to the extent it needs to be for the foundation no later than the first waking moment tomorrow morning. That obviously has to include time distortion but you don't have to be responsible for it, I am. I will be happy, along with Judith, to greet you at two o'clock.

Judith: Be there or be square. (Laughter)

LUNCH

John: Whether you know it or not, whether we're just up here talking or you're doing tasks, the rate of change that is occurring in this seminar will far exceed any rate of change that you've experienced in other seminars because we're attacking the circuitry directly. (Laughter) It therefore becomes incumbent on us to offer some guidelines which arise from second attention regarding . . .

Man: How about a dance . . .

John: You can dance. I'm challenging. (Laughter) And it's proper that you dance and it's proper in my function as teacher to challenge in the most direct way I can the homeostatic centers that you've allowed your circuits to become centered on like a thermostat. So it becomes incumbent upon us to offer some guidance as to how to successfully accept what we're doing in our attack on the circuitry—redirecting it as in a martial art so as to use it as the beginning of a dance. There's this lovely and very integrated hybrid form that comes out of Brazil, Capoeira.[9] And Capoeira comes out of Baía, the only place I know of in the New World where the men and women who were torn from their native west African cultures were allowed to keep significant portions of their culture when they were sold into slavery in the New World. In the Baía there were, of course, constraints on how overt they were in the continued development of their own cultures and the Capoeira is one of their responses to those constraints. It is considered, from different perceptual positions, as a dance or as a martial art. And it is a very beautiful form —an integration of those two activities.

Antonio: Yeah, at the beginning it was a kind of a dance and then it became a martial art because they needed to . . .

Judy: . . . keep their bodies trained and strong.

Antonio: Yeah. And they needed to defend themselves from other people, mainly the police.

John: Mainly the police.

Judy: Don't we all.

John: D'accord.

Antonio: And it was prohibited.

John: It was outlawed. That's when it became a dance again, right? (Laughter) So it seems to me that if you watch something like Capoeira you can appreciate how the metaphor that I deliberately chose—an attack on your homeostatic centers—could be elegantly converted by you, with the proper amount of flexibility, into the first step in an interesting dance.

Antonio: I'm surprised you know about Capoeira.

John: I'm surprised you're surprised.

Judy: He knows a lot of things, Antonio.

Antonio: Now I realize that. I'm not surprised.

Judy: Who is that guy?

John: Here, have a silver bullet.

John: George Polya wrote about explicit strategies for thinking —first-attention strategies that I would urge you to examine. Polya is a master in two ways: both as a mathematician who made significant contributions to the development of portions of mathematical theory in this century and perhaps even more especially as a teacher. He noted the profound differences in the mathematical thinking ability of his students and developed explicit strategies which fit beautifully into first-attention logics of the class that we've been considering here.

Judy: Here are the presuppositions that Polya relates of his own thinking about the process of change.

> First, we should be ready to revise any belief, second, we should change a belief where there is a compelling reason to change it, and third, we should not change a belief wantonly without some good reason. The first point needs intellectual courage, the second, intellectual honesty, and the third, wise restraint. Do not believe anything but question only what is worth questioning.[10]

I thought that was very clever for a mathematician.

JUGGLING: THROWING AND CATCHING ONE BALL

John: I want to get you involved in a new activity which is an interesting sample of certain kinds of integration of first and second attention. And what I'd like to do is to use this as an occasion to arrange the balance hemispherically between first and second attention, conscious and unconscious, so as to make each step of your learning process a positive, pleasurable step. (juggling with three balls) How many people here can juggle at least to the extent I can? Alright. So what I'd like you to do is to take them through the very first step in juggling. All you're going to do is practice throwing this thing in an arc that roughly reaches the top of your head like this —back and forth between your two hands. Now that's not a difficult task mechanically. It's the first of two steps—maybe three depending on how you want to count them—that you need to know in order to juggle. Now it's a silly task in itself; however, it's a rewarding task in terms of personal accomplishment. But it's silly, therefore its significance can only be justified in the context of what we're doing here—specifically, you shift attention and disassociate yourself from any previous expectations or personal identity ideas you had about juggling. And it should free you as a child is free to simply play. So what we're doing today is not juggling. We're learning to throw and catch this ball in a certain arc. And so all I want you to do is to have ten minutes of practice in second attention, that is, in a "stop the world" state—centered in second attention with, in particular, no internal dialogue. I'd like you to simply spend ten minutes and the issue of whether or not you actually throw it back and forth between your two hands with a uniformity which will serve later as a basis for juggling is not as important as your ability to sustain, during that ten minute practice period, the altered state of "stopping the world." Would those of you who raised your hand a moment ago, would you stand?—Robert and this group of people, Tom, there we go. Now your job is simply to go around and coach. I would prefer you did it nonverbally. One way to do it nonverbally is to demonstrate. So if I'm doing this, and you want me to do this, you'd walk up, you'd catch my attention and you'd do it; you'd indicate the level at which you want the particular item that you're juggling to go. Another way to do it would be to come around behind me and actually move my body in the form that you're trying for. I don't want you going past this first step. Now you should access your state switching competency so that you can move with some efficiency into your "stopping the world" state. Do you understand your responsibilities? Any questions? Therefore each one of you will only need one of these balls. You had a demonstration of the activity you're after a few moments ago when I was juggling all three but your task for today is to learn the first step, in ten minutes, in a particular state.

Judy: . . . remembering that a hundred years ago juggling was considered magic.

John: So gather around these people who identified themselves, find a place in the room where you can work, shift state, and enjoy your ten minutes.

One of the most important skills that one can have—especially given the differences between a society and a culture, and in particular the added individual responsibilities in a fragmented society—is the ability to develop and sustain certain kinds of representations that inform our behavior which are not necessarily echoed in the outside structure of our everyday life. As we discussed yesterday, in a coherent culture such as the BaMbuti or the Kongolese there is a constant affirmation from the world to the values and representations you create within yourself as a member of the culture. Castaneda would say that the emanations from the outside illuminate the matching bands of perception on the inside which are most closely associated with it. There is a congruity in the experience of an individual in such a culture, one which we may have only experienced for short periods of time, perhaps within our family of origin or within some *hari*-type group (and by *hari* I mean a group of age-mates of the same sex). It's likely that all of you were members of different sorts of gangs at different points in your life, as teenagers, that is, peer reference groups where the bonding was so very tight you might have caught a glimpse and heard an echo of what it would be like to a member of a *hari* in a traditional coherent culture.

John: One of the prerequisites for effective personal organization is an ability to make clean, 100% commitments at each stage of whatever activities you engage in during the day. In Castaneda's metaphor this means being a warrior. If you observe warriors at any moment you will find that they are completely, passionately committed to whatever it is that they're doing at that moment in time. But that as you observe them over time you'll discover that the activities they engage in may not themselves be congruent over time. And yet at each point, although the warrior will do diverse, even unrelated kinds of things, the warrior acts with utter congruency and a passionate commitment . . .

Judy: . . . and a belief . . .

John: . . . a having to believe in whatever they're committed to at that moment. Such is the foundation for what we call demon states.

John: One of the most important functions that we are responsible for as individuals in a fragmented technological society is clean state switching. I work out of my own home. It becomes very very important to impeccably sort business from family. I have two telephones in my residence.

Judy: I can relate to that.

John: If I am working on some business related project and I am called by a family member for some appropriate reason—the horses are loose for example—I have a ritual which has now become automated: I set myself physically, quickly review—I'm talking about split seconds—what I'm doing, where I'm headed, the objective I have, where in the process I have gotten to, and in particular, I may even note what my next step would be if I were to stay and pursue it. So that when I come back I can step back into the same physiology in front of my stand-up desk, in front of that window, look at that note on the paper, and go, "Ah-ha!" and move back into the task with perfect efficiency, the kind of efficiency that I was astonished to witness in Erickson's work when he was out in the second house. He had two houses, one for family, one for consultation, with an intercome connecting the two. A call would come in while he was in the middle of a deep hypnotic session with a patient—this God-awful squawk box would go off in the middle of this deep trance and it would be Betty calling from the other house, "Milton, there's a phone call from Karl in Germany" and Milton (imitating Milton's trance voice) in the middle of this complex syntactic voice song which was designed to entrance the other person would (changing to normal speaking voice) stop and at that moment set his body, turn, change voice, change posture, change direction of voice . . .

Judy: . . . do the telephone call . . .

John: . . . turn back, set, and continue with precisely the same tempo—I used to count it—at exactly the same syllable he stopped at with a precision that was, to me, quite uncanny at the time. Notice the failure to sort and to have rituals that sort these classes of events means that you would do the supreme discourtesy to your family of double tracking.

You have, no doubt, caught yourself many times in important personal relations being partially committed to the moment and partially preoccupied with pieces of business that you might have been doing had you not been where you are. There are occasions where double tracking is powerful and appropriate. There's a whole profession built on double tracking—field intelligence work. However in the set of contexts we're talking about you have to be impeccable in your state shifts. The easiest way I know to accomplish that is to make use of logical levels. The me that jots down that note, and then moves quickly to intercept the horses that are running across the field by this point, is of a higher logical level than the demon who was passionately committed to whatever that first-/second-attention interface task was and profoundly different at the same logical level than the demon who will now pursue the horses and enjoy gathering them up and putting them back in the corral. Notice there is no sense of loss if you make a clean, residue-free shift. The only way you could experience loss or interruption or frustration or boredom or any of these funny words that we use for this phenomenon is by double-tracking . . .

Judy: . . . by not making the shifts cleanly.

John: If you are indeed passionately committed to the moment you do not have the disassociation which is presupposed by things such as boredom and frustration. It therefore becomes an extremely useful tool, a skill which could serve as the basis for any aesthetic act—like daily life. (laughter)

Woman: How do you remember what you were doing before when you get caught up in a new situation?

John: Right. And now I refer to what Judy has written on the board: "controller." Every state has associated with it a class of physiologies and if you have the sensitivity in your own physiology you can use it as a way of very efficiently moving from one state to another and keeping one sorted from the other. The controller at a higher logical level is responsible for clean state switching—another way of describing the well-formedness condition of nonoverlapping demons.

Judy: How did Erickson do it? He'd return to a body position and he would pick up verbally just right where he left off and it was never interruptive to the client in any way . . .

John: . . . because it wasn't interruptive to Milton. Kinesthetic self-anchoring. You understand the mechanics. What you don't have is the structure and that's what we're about to propose we do as part of an exercise. So be reassured that we're moving toward an answer at the experiential level to your question.

Woman: You keep mentioning logical levels.

John: You're about to discover what that means.

Judy: Passion states, demon states, spirit states, I'll let you choose your own word.

DEVELOPMENT OF CONTROLLER-DEMON RELATIONSHIPS

John: You are to find two fully committed states that you already have access to somewhere in your personal history. The constraint is that the two states you choose, each one of which is as close to a full 100% commitment as you can achieve at this point, have to be in an allied area of activity . . .

Judy: . . . in your work, personal life, sports, . . .

John: So you've got a state in which there's a demon who composes written material that, when you get there, hmrmmmmrmm, it happens, you don't do it, it happens. You have another state that's really a demon on the telephone or another state that involves your ability to think in some long-term effective way—planning—or there are two states involved with physical activity, say your ability to dance and your ability to run, or perhaps your ability to swim and your ability to do gymnastics, your ability to ride horses, . . . I don't know. They could be two states that are committed to, say, social relations. How do you handle the class of difficulties that are involved with interpersonal relationships in your family and in your business. One knows how to provoke particularly interesting and new responses and the other demon knows how to mend wounds. They're allied in the sense that the area of behavior which they cover has many common aspects. Now the mechanics are important.

Judy: There's going to be a person, your witness, who's going to calibrate to these states and you do not have to tell them what any of the content nor what that larger framework is.

John: That's personal information. There's no need for them to have that. All they need to know is, you now go into state *A* and snap your fingers when you are in state *A*. And if Judy and I were working together here I'd go into that state, and when I snap my fingers she calibrates to that state. She notices the way I'm moving, eye scanning patterns, physiology, breathing, muscle tonus, all the things that you've learned in practitioner sensory acuity drills.

Judy: Calibrate, calibrate, calibrate. Separator state.

John: As soon as she has that calibration she does what Judy just did. She pulls you out of the state to a separator state, breaks up your physiology, asks you to step into state *B*, the second state.

Judy: Calibrate, calibrate, calibrate.

John: . . . again pulls you out of state *B* to a separator state. So far it's a two-state calibration drill for the witness and a flexibility drill for the person going through the states. It is very important that your witness be insistent that there's minimum overlap between the two states. That is, no residue is carried from one state to the other. That's the point of the separator state. In playing Balinese instruments called gundar, the right hand is the rhythm hand, and the left hand plays the melody. There was a talented pianist who was in the group we went to Bali with some years ago . . .

Judy: . . . who really wanted to learn the gundar.

John: She wanted to so much . . . , she loved the sound. She was a fine learner and she wanted to learn a special form called gundar—a two-handed instrument. She was concerned about the hemispheric confusion that might ensue because she had committed so much passion and discipline . . .

Judy: . . . and time . . .

John: . . . to the piano where the right hand is melodic and the left hand carries tempo.

Judy: Investment, investment.

John: She asked me for assistance. I proposed the following internal organization in a trance state which worked well for her. If you look down at the gundar—it's like a xylophone—there are beautifully cast brass keys. Every one of these brass keys has imperfections, flaws, in them. They are usually a golden brown color, they shine—especially somehow in the tropical light of Bali. There are a lot of stories about why they shine. But however that happens, they do shine. And I invited her, as she sat down to play gundar, to look into the glow that surrounded one of the keys and to discover the most interesting flaw that she could find on that key. If you look at the keys they seem to be warmest and brightest around these imperfections because there's a depth there that isn't there on the rest of the surface. It's an area of difference—of contrast. And I suggested that that warmth could reach out with an invitation to her and she would travel into the light through the flaw in the key and come out in a separate place where all of the learnings and understandings which she achieved in gundar would be stored and she needed only the flaw to enter and she of course would return to the other state when she was finished. In no way could she therefore confuse, either hemispherically or mechanically the requirements of piano and gundar, because they existed in separate realities. This is an example of a metaphoric state-switching exercise. Like, in a submarine, an intermediate double-locking diving chamber, a separator state to make sure that there was no spillage, no overflow from one state to the other because to make a transfer would not be of utility.

Judy: For me it's an issue of efficiency, the time that it would take me to unlearn and relearn, to reorganize my thinking because of the investment.

John: Once you have successfully, by witness calibration, demonstrated you can move in both directions between the two states without residue, you're ready for the second phase. The fact that you were able to choose the two states, that they had some major things in common, that is, they dealt with social relations or they dealt with your profession or they dealt with athletic competency or artistic expression, whatever, means that these two activities—like gundar and piano —will not be operating simultaneously. They will never be running at the same time although they *will* have certain things in common. In the case of aesthetic expression there's a certain artistry to everything you would do in this area of behavior. So now we have a demon state . . .

Judy: . . . and pianos and gundars are at the same logical level even though you would not want to overlap those two states.

John: I want you to either create or discover a controller, because some of you will already have these. A controller, minimally, is the part of you—at the next higher logical level to the piano and the gundar—which determines whether it's appropriate to play gundar or piano. That is, it determines how you switch into those states—in what context is it appropriate for you to enter one or the other of those states. Notice it has to be in some musical environment in order for it to have that choice. It now becomes a question of which activity it will commit to. Notice this prevents you from inadvertently mixing the two. It guarantees there will not be a inappropriate negative transfer of learning.

How many of you are self-interruptive in your activities? Isn't in fact the normal situation one in which you're trying to single track and things have not been carefully sorted, or you do not have controllers to make the choices about their appropriateness and you get intrusions? This is exactly the structural move that will assist you in sorting these. The proposal therefore is that you go internal to second attention, request from first attention that a controller identify him or herself or in fact one be created whose responsibilities are to determine state switching.

May your houses be full of wonderful demons. These demons cannot afford, in doing the kind of powerful, aesthetic job they need to do, to be worried about whether it's time to go to dinner or what "spousie" will think or whatever. The constraints that they live under have to be set and maintained by the controller. It is not the job of a demon to know it's limitations. It is the job of the controller to set and enforce, like the Shotsey and eating example this morning, those particular constraints which define the area of operation for that demon. The controller holds the key and secures agreements from the demons that when released they will operate within their appropriate contexts. The cage for the demon is the context it accepts. And there it can just get in and kick. Notice the tremendous freedom you get through this organizational structure. But there's no self-interruption because the controller handles the switching. The controller can use time driven variables, or completion of tasks, for example, as a way of knowing when to switch out of the state. The controller is responsible for setting the context and enforcing it and determining when to unleash the demon within the context.

John: It would be foolhardy to ask if there were any questions. (laughter) So I won't even mention it. I should think that the arrangements could be made usefully in a half hour, fifteen minutes each, paired with someone you have not yet worked with. There is a funny kind of collusion that occurs when you work too long with the same person. I invite you to seek out someone . . . In fact, best of all, find the person that you know the least in the room. Do that and you will scramble things nicely. I'd like you back in a half hour. Do us a clean job and be back in a half hour.

BREAK

John: Alright. One person noticed in doing this last exercise that they already had a controller who had been doing this "thankless" task for years and had never been recognized.

Judy: Did he say, "Thank you"?

John: You bet he did. (laughter) Another individual who is real demon-like already, discovered that a couple demons overlapped and that the overlap sometimes caused considerable difficulties and wanted to know what to do about that. What's the answer to that?

Man: Separate them.

John: But who separates them?

Group: The controller.

John: It's the controller's job to draw the line. And you go, "You, lovely as you are, you operate on this side," and just kick ass. And on this side, you just get in there and do it aesthetically. So it's real important that there not be overlap because the resultant kinds of confusion states are not to the advantage of either demon. It's a statement that there have been encroachments. If you fail to exercise the full range of your flexibility, whether we're talking about physiology in dance . . .

Judy: . . . or evolution, learning, . . .

John: . . . or perception, then you're going to find that if a variable is not exercised, connected variables will tend to eat up the flexibility that's not used.

Judy: In evolutionary terms that's the idea of the investment. The more the evolutionary investment, the more the previous flexibility is eaten up by encroaching variables. It's just like Pac-Man. (Laughter) There is a range of flexibility which if not used . . .

John: . . . is lost. Use it or loose it . . .

Judy: . . . no pain, no brain. No, that's not it. (Laughter) No pain, no gain, that's it!

John: Moshe Feldenkrais just turned over in his grave. (Laughter)

Judy: You know I just saw a t-shirt the other day that said, "Roses are red, violets are blue, I'm schizophrenic, so am I." (Laughter)

John: Shows a lot of flexibility to me.

Georgine: My controller . . . , I tried to switch controllers, my controller insisted on being able to mix the demons.

John: Yeah, in what form? Wait, that's content. Let's do it this way. Can you create, physically, a context for yourself between now and tomorrow morning where the behaviors of the demons can be displayed for your own satisfaction? Does it require external support, for example, special facilities or anything like that? Can you engage in the demon-like behavior between now and tomorrow morning in some way that's appropriate to context?

Georgine: Which demon? What . . .

John: You have two demons. Their fields of endeavor overlap. The controller claims they should overlap, they should be mixed.

Georgine: No, the controller just wanted the choice. If he ever wants to combine demon states he can.

John: You better talk to that controller's controller.

Georgine: So we just escalate.

John: No, we didn't escalate. Please read Roger Fisher and William Ury's fantastic book *Getting to Yes*[11] for examples—but no, we didn't escalate. We moved up a logical level. Escalation says you stay at the same logical level and one input to you comes back to me in the form of an increased output from you of the same nature. Like the arms race. See, the perception on Russia's part of our military superiority goads them into an increase in military expenditure, which is now viewed by the United States as a threat to, depending on who's talking, national security, the peace of the world, or the armaments people's profitability, I don't know. There's lots of ways of thinking about it. Moves which increase the perception of relative strength on the one side goads the other into symmetrical behavior. That's an escalation. I'm saying something quite different—cleanly move up a logical level and set the conditions at the meta-level to the controller. The controller of controllers says, "Look, if you want that option, you have to demonstrate that it serves some purpose. I will not give you the option unless you present a case for it . . ."

Georgine: ". . . and do it between now and tomorrow morning . . ."

John: Yes. There's an editing function here which will help you accomplish that.

Man: If you have overlap does that presuppose that there's not a controller? Or is it just . . .

John: No. That may be a controller who's not doing his or her job. There may be a controller who has never been instructed in what their actual responsibilities are. In any case, notice that I'm not saying that you can't have overlap. I'm saying in general you won't want to. That's how you get self-interruptive behavior—it's a dead giveaway. And if you are going to entertain the possibility of overlapping demons with their tremendous commitment and passion, you better justify it because in almost every case I've ever run across you get diminution of quality, a reduction in the demon-like qualities of both because they're at cross-purposes. That's the point of sorting out the spheres of influence.

Judy: It's like exciters and inhibiters.

John: That's exciting.

Judy: At the neurological level. That's what gives us edge, right? —in our vision, in our ability to see. If a certain track in the optic nerve is activated there tends to be a lateral inhibition of the adjacent unstimulated tracks. The threshold on adjacent tracks goes up so that it really does take the presence of the edge across those receptors to trigger them. Therefore you get a sharper contrast in the optic track. We've got smart optic tracks. A lot smarter than some of us, I'll tell you. Rosalie. (Laughter)

Rosalie: Backing that up, in terms of this division of tasks, I work with premature infants. One of the things we're finding out is that they don't . . . , it's a question of what do they have developed or not developed when they are born a little bit early. And one thing they don't have developed is the inhibitory parts of their nervous system; they cannot inhibit or delete all the information that comes to them and that gives them a great deal of trouble—they have enormous stress and they can't shut it out. It's almost like, neurologically they needed that extra time in the womb. It's one of the last developing parts of our system.

Judy: Just enough to brown the crust a little. A little more time in the oven. (laughter)

Woman: I discovered something that I even know what happened.

John: I failed again. (Laughter) There isn't adequate confusion here . . .

Woman: I discovered that I had a controller but no cages—no contextual markers. Now what my controller has been attempting to do is when it had determined that one particular demon was appropriate it was running around with its net trying to catch the rest of them. (laughter) And that's easier said than done.

Judy: Then you begin to sort for context, so that the demons are acting in the appropriate context, the "stop the world" state is an excellent place to sort from.

Woman: She has never succeeded because it's not a possible task.

John: A really nice observation. It was reported to me that during an exercise when one of the members of our group achieved "stopping the world"—when there was no internal dialog and foveal vision had been interrupted—they came away from the experience satisfied that they had accomplished the task but a bit disappointed. I think they expected the voice of God or the burning bush or something. I want you to notice that "stopping the world" is only a doorway which begins a class of explorations. You may find the burning bush or God there; I don't know. But I know that simply to open a door and look in for ten minutes and then close the door is not going to give you any indication of the territory to be explored on the other side—although it may be the first step in practicing a skill. A certain amount of personal discipline is required to develop the skills to, at will, cleanly switch states into "stopping the world" so that you can go for extended periods of time with your lifelines in place and explore that territory. May it yield the kind of overwhelming and profound response that this man hoped to have by simply peeking through the door.

Judy: Editing function.

John: Those of you who are familiar with the new behavior generator, this is somewhat similar, yet a bit different. We're going to build a structure with a difference which will make a difference—the structure you've just set.

Judy: Context, context—the controller determines the context for the demon.

John: At the very top there's someone who runs the whole show. Usually this is a part whose sole function is the efficient, elegant, aesthetic coordination of all the rest of the organism. It has no agenda other than that—so it's fully committed to aesthetic coordination. It has technical staff. One of the technical staff is an aesthetically oriented editor. Now I'm proposing as your homework assignment tonight that, with the permission of the controller, you dispatch the editor to this logical level of functioning. The editor would go to the controller in charge of this class of demons here and go, "Controller, how may I be of assistance to you?"

Judy: "I'm from technical staff and I'm available to you."

John: . . . the editor's function now will be to sit down with the controller and let the demon go. . . . you're a spectator in a theatre. You are watching a full Hollywood production of demonology here with your hand on a little button, just like a pause button. And when you see and hear something that the controller indicates to the editor is not as optimal, in terms of quality, efficiency, aesthetics, or whatever, in the demon's performance you freeze frame. At that point the editor and the controller can discuss things and I would say the following questions have to be answered before you edit. One, what's the intent? What's the demon trying to pull off here? Make sure that the controller understands the intent. Two, what aesthetic substitutions for the behavior that was less than full quality and full efficiency would the editor recommend as an aesthetic consultant?

Woman: Say that again.

John: What behaviors could be substituted consistent with the intent you've already discovered in the demon's behavior that would make the demon's performance both efficient and up to quality? That's part of your homework assignment. For the second part of your homework assignment I want you to walk the bridge again. (Laughter)

Judy: Oh, no.

John: (to Judy) They did pretty good. They laughed instead of groaned. (to the group) Therefore you may walk the bridge metaphorically. However, I want you to set your quality requirements, using the appropriate controllers and demons in this internally oriented work, so that this experience has the same reality value that walking the bridge physically had last night. You are striving for the same immediacy in "walking the bridge" while sitting in your hotel room or out in the park or wherever, that you achieved last night in physically walking the bridge. Understand that you have the competency to go to places that you've been as well as places you haven't been and to draw upon those places. Titos was talking about some of the songs we sang yesterday. One of the songs was for people who were far away from home. What's the point of that song? The point of that song is to reach back over time and distance in some very profound way to your special place—your home—and sustain yourself from a distance.

There is a medicine man by the name of Marcellus that we met once in Oklahoma City, a Cree Indian who had the honor of having been accepted as a shaman by the Navaho as well as the Cree nations. He was once called in by the Oklahoma State authorities to a hospital where a Navaho Indian was dying . . .

Judy: . . . and the Navaho was very sad because he was away from the mesas and Navahos believe that their strength and spirit is drawn from these mesas in the Four Corners area where they live. And for him to be away from there meant that he would continue to weaken. The Four Corners area is a sacred area for the Navaho and when they leave it they run the risk of being vulnerable to forces that they are protected from when they're in the Four Corners. So Marcellus took out an eagle-bone whistle and he described to him how sound waves work and that as he blew this whistle it would go all the way around the Earth and pass over the mesas and bring the spirit that the Navajo needed to get well.

John: A short time later the man walked out of the hospital, discharging himself, apparently healed.

Judy: In the model John put up here this morning—where do representational systems fit in? We'll talk tomorrow about this in terms of epistemology. Here's the Polya quote again.

First, we should be ready to revise any belief, second, we should change a belief where there is a compelling reason to change it, and third, we should not change a belief wantonly without some good reason. The first point needs intellectual courage, the second, intellectual honesty, and the third, wise restraint. Do not believe anything but question only what is worth questioning.[12]

John: One closing remark: Those of you who need to change, go change. (Loudly and abruptly) **Except!!** The frog's eye responds only to objects of a certain size. If you move an object of a larger or smaller size than the optimal target object (plus or minus some percentage) through the frog's visual field, the visual receptors are not triggered.

Judy: So if it's too big a moth . . .

John: . . . or too small . . .

Judy: . . . the moth won't trigger the receptors.

John: That is a necessary but not sufficient condition to trigger the visual receptors and the associated capture behavior. A second condition is required and that condition would be that the path followed by the moving object in the visual field, after it has met the size requirement, has to follow a certain pattern that can be specified mathematically. If it doesn't fall within the pattern specified by that mathematical representation the detectors in the retina of the frog's eye do not respond. That's specialization. Do you understand how powerful a perceptual filter that is and how powerful the counterparts might be in the human sensory apparatus? I will point out that every specialization has a cost . . .

Judy: . . . and it is the eating up of flexibility. . . .

John: . . . and in particular, notice the frog will not respond to bugs that fall outside size or flight-pattern requirements and, perhaps most telling of all, they have had cases of frogs starving to death surrounded by dead flies. See you in the morning. (Laughter)

DAY THREE

John: Good morning, good morning. *Erin go braugh,* in case you haven't been properly greeted this morning. There are a number of people who've changed positions in the room. (laughter)

Judy: Isn't that amazing? (pointing to various members of the group who had changed their seating)

John: (to the group) What are you doing?

Woman: Something else.

Judy: Something else.

John: Something else is a good start. Be more precise.

Woman: Perspectives, perspectives.

Alan: Getting another point of view.

John: Double descriptions, right? The minimum well-formedness condition is having double descriptions. You'd be surprised how fixed people get in positions in the room in work like this. Continuously throughout this workshop we have turned to traditional cultures in hopes of finding balance, wisdom, and congruity with respect to the individual, group, and environment. Cultures where we find a first-attention/second-attention balance we can adopt as a model for developing our own internal cultures so as to reflect this wisdom and balance which has been in large part lost in a technically oriented society. So we would like to propose and specify a process—without content or substance—for an optimal personal organizational model. Remember the purpose of such a model is not just promoting excellence but also to promote difference. To specify substance would be to specify the idealized person, one which presumes the development of the individual towards an ideal. Such an endeavor would be incongruent with our purpose to promote excellence and difference—which in Gregory Bateson's words is the basic unit of mind. So it behooves us all to give some deep thought to the metaphor which will serve appropriately as a framework to hang the process of a personal organizational model on.

John: Larry had a proposal . . . (pointing to tetrahedronal figure) You understand this is a two-dimensional representation of a multidimensional creature?

Judy: Bob brought up this same issue. This representation is on a blackboard—it's static—and we're talking about dynamic systems.

Bob: I put the model into three dimensions. I made a basic tetrahedronal unit . . .

Judy: We all know what that is, right?

Georgine: That's some nominalization. (Laughter)

Bob: . . . and put at the four points the first attention, the second attention, the demon states, and the controllers and figured that all the functions can slide around inside. Notice that from any of the four points you can access the other three in one move. . . .

George: I like this one a lot.

Judy: Well, you've got to be flexible, George.

John: Christ, George. Just because you can't fit in two dimensions, you think . . .

Judy: You can't mistake the menu for the dinner.

John: You can . . .

Judy: You can't eat the menu. (Laughter)

John: I can.

John: So let's, as a common beginning point, take a metaphor from geometry: a sphere. The sphere is the most perfect three-dimensional figure according to the Greeks; it has the maximum volume-to-surface ratio.

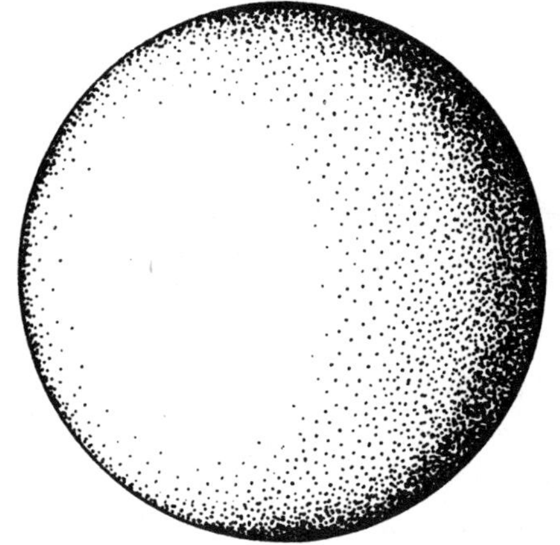

Suppose we use this figure as our basic metaphor. Then, in this figure, the surface corresponds to the interface between each of us and the world. This figure will have to be a special kind of sphere—one with a flexible, dynamic surface. We already know from our discussions of race-car driving, from Bateson's question about the blind man and his cane, and from examples of commitment and passion in our own personal history that this representation of the interface must be dynamic in order to capture the experience of extending ourselves out to the world and incorporating into ourselves parts of the world—including one another by linking minds, as in Judy's example of the horse and rider—achieving that profoundly deep sense of communion with other living systems.

Man: OK, so where is consciousness?

John: Notice that if the surface of the sphere in our metaphor defines the set of contact points with the world and with each other, then reflexive first attention (reflexive self-consciousness) is located at the center of the sphere at the point furthest removed from the real world, as we call it. Moreover, from our own subjective experience we know the sensation of moving around in the circuitry within us—what we used to refer to flatly as parts—thus the sphere will have some internal structure—let's say some latticework which captures or represents those experiences. The actual structure of this lattice will be some interesting result of the genetics of the organism and the class of structures created through experience—the LAD from which Creole springs is a section of the lattice, for example. The main components of this latticework are the crossmodality circuits—the patterns of synesthesia. In this model, committing oneself fully to second-attention circuits will be represented as a conical projection, the apex of which touches the center, which expands, moving toward the surface until it delineates a circular area on the surface.

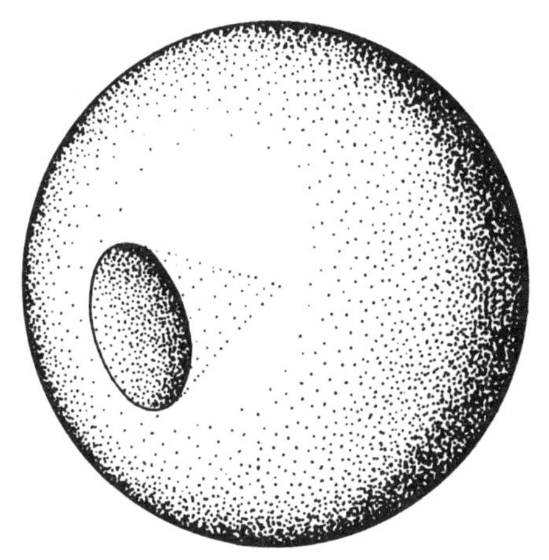

The area on the surface of the sphere defined by the conical projection is the area within which the demon for that function may freely roam—it defines the cage for that particular demon, its context. And anchoring this conical section at the center . . . I don't know what you want to call the center here.

Judy: Mind.

John: The mind.

Judy: Yours . . .

John: . . . and mind. I tend to think of it—because of my present preoccupation with music—as the conductor. Symphony. And these (pointing to the surface of the sphere) are the people who actually run the instruments—right?—they play the instruments. This may be first violinist for example. And this may be first oboist . . . So there's a hierarchical structure within an orchestra as well. Each section has a person who represents that section. Again, there are parts to this analogy that I find really attractive and other parts just seem to miss the mark altogether, right? What does it mean in this case to "hit a discord"? Well, it could be a screwup by a demon.

Judy: Or an oboist trying to play at the same time the . . .

John: (interrupting) Right. Or it could be that it's all . . .—what were you saying yesterday?

Judy: (interrupting) I don't know.

John: (interrupting) It's all timing.

Judy: (interrupting) It's all . . .

John: (interrupting) Timing. Timing. Timing is everything. (laughter) And especially in an orchestra.

OK, so now we have a structure—remember the only justification for any such structure is to arrange ourselves in such a way as to increase choice and lay the foundation for the blossoming of our personal genius—to insure that the base is in place for balanced, aesthetically pleasing experiences to emerge—to make the arrangements which allow us the freedom to live with passion, committing ourselves completely to our pursuits. This is in part the justification for our examining traditional cultures—to appreciate what arrangements we might make to provide the key to excellence. Now what processes, what characteristics, will this model have? . . . First of all, awareness we attribute awareness—raw animal awareness—the ability to sense and respond to the world and to sense and respond to signals arising within the organism itself. Biologists sometimes refer to this characteristic as irritability, philosophers as sentience. Note that these terms are subject to all the usual transforms or distortions of our species. For us to consider an organism sentient, it must react to some stimulus we can identify within the range of our sensing apparatus and within a time frame in which we can maintain attention. So we have the sentient sphere—the child before the acquisition of language, our proto-ancestor before the dawn of consciousness, each of you when fully committed to Kongolese dance—a model of a being alive and in full contact within itself, i.e., with no internal divisions, and with its environment. We say that this organism is associated within itself and with its environment, that is, this creature is living in complete circuits, not arcs. Some of these circuits are complete within the organism itself, some involve arcs of context as essential portions of larger circuits that the organism participates in—the food and water cycle between environment and organisms, for example.

> We sense, from the moment we are born, that there are two parts to us. At the time of birth, and for a while after, we are all *nagual.* We sense, then, that in order to function we need a counterpart to what we have. The *tonal* is missing and that gives us, from the very beginning, a feeling of incompleteness. Then the *tonal* starts to develop and it becomes utterly important to our functioning, so important that it opaques the shine of the *nagual,* it overwhelms it. From the moment we become all *tonal* we do nothing else but to increment that old feeling of incompleteness which accompanies us from the moment of our birth, and which tells us constantly that there is another part to give us completeness.[1]

Summon up the image of a young deer grazing happily in a meadow next to a stream. How the hell did we get from there to McDonald's? Ever since the industrial revolution, social philosophers have been making the complaint that our technological competencies are running well in advance of our social competencies—we are unbalanced in that technology is developing much more rapidly than our ability to take effective action socially, for example, questions such as what technical paths to explore, which are to have priority, and how to apply the tremendous technological advantages we have achieved with enough wisdom to enhance the human values we deem appropriate to promote. And I say that such comments reveal a lack of understanding on the part of such social critics—they are complaining about the deep cybernetic nature of our species and fail to recognize the nature of the relationship between technical advance and loss of wisdom, or, as we have been suggesting, loss of contact with context.

> . . . man's habit of changing his environment rather than changing himself. Faced with a changing variable (*e.g.,* temperature) within itself which it should control, the organism may make changes *either* within itself *or* in the external environment. It may adapt to the environment or adapt the environment to itself. In evolutionary history, the great majority of steps have been changes within the organism itself; some steps have been of an intermediate kind in which the organisms achieved change of environment by change of locale. . . .
>
> Man, the outstanding modifier of environment, similarly achieves single-species ecosystems in his cities, but he goes one step further, establishing special environments for his symbionts. These, likewise, become single-species ecosystems: fields of corn, cultures of bacteria, batteries of fowls, colonies of laboratory rats, and the like.
>
> . . . the power ratio between purposive consciousness and the environment has changed rapidly in the last one hundred years, and the *rate* of change in this ratio is certainly rapidly increasing with technological advance. Conscious man, as a changer of his environment, is now fully able to wreck himself and that environment—with the very best of conscious intentions.[2]

When we propose looking to intact traditional cultures for the kind of balance and aesthetics which will guide us in creating personal culture, we are implicitly making a claim, namely, that there is a wisdom to the organization of traditional cultures which does not exist in our society. And the wisdom we refer to is the long-term success of such cultures in staying in a balanced circuit with their context. Such cultures have proven to be successful by their ability to dynamically balance themselves in these contextual circuits over centuries. Back now to that idyllic setting with our complex and congruent deer beautifully balanced with its environment and to the question of McDonald's. There is a magic moment here, astonishingly important for the development of our species and the history of our planet and we name it syntax. We must beg your indulgence here, or as Indiana Jones says, "Trust me!" Specifically, accept for the moment that there is a process which severs the bonds which tie us to the sensory world and allows us to dream, allows us to generate possible worlds —representations which have never been experienced in the world by the representing organism. Tie a knot in your handkerchief for a moment; I owe you an explication of this process which is based on our syntactic ability, and you will have it—but not yet. Grant me those representations of a possible world in the representer which did not arise from sensory experience and the trade-off between technology and wisdom becomes understandable. You see, as soon as you give me that class of representations (the possible but never experienced worlds) I have, one, technology as our response to the difference between actual worlds and possible—technology is the bridge between our dreams and our waking experience and, two, loss of wisdom—as we initially entertain representations of possible worlds—at that point we have stopped referring ourselves to the wisdom of context. We have severed the tight bonding between us and context—we are now creating new contexts—possible worlds. When we make the technical step of constructing the possible world—we are simply making a concrete substitution of context—i.e., placing the actual with the formerly possible—we are simply ratifying a new relationship—one we achieved first internally. We cannot create what we cannot dream. This is the sense in which the social critics have missed the boat. Technology is the external result of what first occurred as an act of mind.

Women: So this is the beginning of disassociation?

John: The notion of disassociation is a critical one and deserves some careful consideration. Note, first of all, the predicate *disassociate* is a threeplace predicate or relationship—*X* disassociates *Y* from *Z*— take a couple of examples—NLP is well known for its startlingly rapid success with people who are phobic, and as you know, the key here is disassociation —so-called V-K (visual-kinesthetic) disassociation. More specifically, the person wishing to change their response from one of terror to one of resourcefulness is guided by the practitioner to commit to a state of resourcefulness—a fully physiologically defined resource state. When the practitioner verifies the client has entered such a resource state, the state is stabilized through the mechanism of an anchor. The client is invited to maintain the feelings (the kinesthetics) of the resource state while seeing and hearing the full visual and auditory representation of the phobic context. The person previously phobic of snakes sees and hears representations of snakes in appropriate contexts while maintaining the feelings of utter resourcefulness. (The anchor, used judiciously by the practitioner, ensures the feelings of the resource state are stabilized.) Visually, we can represent the pattern as follows:

The Phobic Client

$$A \langle\langle A, O, U, K^1 \rangle\rangle$$

A	A	O	U	K
the word "snake"	the sounds of snakes,	the odors of snakes,	the sight of snakes,	K^1

where K^1 represents the set of feelings associated with the learned phobic response to snakes

The Resourceful Client

$$A \langle\langle A, O, U, K^2 \rangle\rangle$$

A	A	O	U	K
the word "resourceful"	the sounds of resourcefulness,	the odors of resourcefulness,	the sights of resourcefulness,	K^2

where K^2 represents the learned feelings of resourcefulness.

Now, by the precise use of an anchor the practitioner can decompose or break up the 4-tuple, or rather, the experience represented by the 4-tuple, and make a substitution, in this case substituting K^2 for K^1, the feelings of resourcefulness for the feelings of overwhelming fear. Thus at the conclusion of the V-K disassociation procedure the client's state, his or her response to snakes, is represented as:

$$\mathbf{A \ll A, O, U, K^2 \gg}$$

the word "snake"	the sounds of snakes,	the odors of snakes,	the sight of snakes,	the feelings of resourcefulness

The client, has disassociated his or her originally learned feelings of terror (K^1) of snakes, from the odors, sounds, and sights of snakes,—the single bundle of experience has been broken up and the visual/auditory/olfactory experience of a snake simply produces feelings of resourcefulness. Obviously the client still has a learning task—that of using the feelings of resourcefulness, (K^2) now associated with snakes as a base from which to learn appropriate, respectful, and safe procedures for dealing with snakes. Such a therapeutic example demonstrates the tremendous personal evolutionary advantage of having the choice of disassociation. Coupled with the skill base associated with anchoring, disassociation gives an individual the capability of transforming personal history from a set of limitations to a veritable treasure house of experiences, portions of which can be disassociated and recombined with portions of other experiences both to escape the accidents of personal history and to create entirely novel experiences. So the breaking up of a bundle of experience by using anchoring as the decomposition tool is a familiar example of disassociation. But within this example are other forms of disassociation as well. For example, when the client is watching and listening to the previous experiences of snakes they are disassociated from the present world timeline; they are reliving an experience, one from a different time and space. Typically, a client is so involved with these historical representations that they are oblivious to (disassociated) from the sights, sounds, odors, and feelings of the actual physical environment they are located in. They report later having contact with only the practitioner's voice and touch (the anchor). Perhaps most important for our discussion here is a technique which is often employed in this type of phobia work, namely, after the feelings of resourcefulness have been accessed and anchored, the client is sometimes invited to entertain a representation of themselves going through the reference experience—that is, to see and hear a representation of the original experience—from a perceptual position other than the one which they originally occupied in the experience. In other words, the client is asked to create and focus on representations which include a representation of the representer. This special state we call reflexive first attention. Consider the consequences of such a move—suddenly the client is freed of the overwhelming feelings of having to cope directly with the sights and sounds of snakes and instead, can, like a director in the theater of the mind (supported by the anchored state of resourcefulness), propose a new class of responses, watch and listen to them, make an evaluation of their effectiveness and aesthetics and (with the proper NLP skill base) select and integrate new behavior. Life with such a state of reflexive first attention available becomes a chess game. As long as the human involved has the requisite skill base, he or she becomes literally self-programming—an organism who has achieved some choice with respect to their own personal evolution. With this move trial and error are superseded by questions of aesthetics and balance. This personal bootstrap program is at the individual level. What possible worlds are socially . . . and like the social issues, simply to have created a representation of an important difference—whether going to the stars or how to handle in a balanced way the anger of a close friend—is no guarantee that the world will be different—both socially and individually the representation will remain sterile unless there is a supporting skill base or technology—one which we can use to create the bridge to achieve these dreams in the waking world. Once again, a warning is appropriate—to disassociate from the larger circuit of our connections with one another and the environment has a cost—the suspension of feedback from the world which contains the wisdom of context—wisdom is in the full circuit—thus we incur the debt of referring whatever choices regarding new behavior (at the individual level) and new social programs to the larger circuit for ratification. We are saying that initially the ability to disassociate both frees us of the constraints of our personal history (individually and socially) and robs us of the wisdom of the whole circuit. Thus the new behaviors, the new programs we can design and implement must be referred back to context at a higher logical level before implementation if we are to act responsibly with respect to one another and our physical context. The trade-off, then, between disassociation and wisdom is necessary only if the two remain at the same logical level. Access to the next higher logical level offers the possibility of a return to the wisdom of a referral to context. To talk usefully about logical-level shifts and how to accomplish such shifts requires a more precise representation of the phenomenon of attention. Ah, attention—here we arrive at what is considered by some to be the supreme accomplishment of our species.

Judy: (reading from Castaneda)

Don Juan reminded me that my argument had no basis for him, and that, long before, he had already made the point that there was no world at large but only a description of the world which we had learned to visualize and take for granted.

"The *tonal* is everything we know," he said. "I think this in itself is enough reason for the *tonal* to be such an overpowering affair." . . .

"The *tonal* makes the world only in a manner of speaking. It cannot create or change anything, and yet it makes the world because its function is to judge, and assess, and witness. I say that the *tonal* makes the world because it witnesses and assesses it according to *tonal* rules. In a very strange manner the *tonal* is a creator that doesn't create a thing. In other words, the *tonal* makes up the rules by which it apprehends the world. So, in a manner of speaking, it creates the world." [3]

John: The ability to focus ourselves, to attend to parts of the world—internal and/or external—is simultaneously the ability to delete, to ignore other parts of the world. It is the process referred to as figure and ground—this focusing with

its simultaneous wholesale deletion is our escape route from the limitations of animal awareness—a type of consciousness, too tightly tied to the sensory world—it's what distinguishes us from an idiot savant. *Concurrently* this achievement is our curse—by focusing ourselves, we escape from the demands for attention arriving through the senses and by the same move we lose our connection with the wisdom implicit in context. So this attention is what we have been referring to as first attention or what most people call consciousness. See there's this funny thing. If you have a flashlight in a dark room, whatever the light illuminates is illuminated and whatever it doesn't illuminate isn"t illuminated even though the light may change direction. The area it illuminates is sharply defined. Now if we attribute consciousness to the flashlight the flashlight will immediately arrive at the generalization that the world is always illuminated. (laughter)
We do know some things about this process called attention. We know, for example, that the illuminated circle—the portion of the lattice illuminated by the flashlight is precisely seven plus or minus two chunks of information in area.[4]

Notice as soon as we start talking about the flashlight illuminating the latticework we are proposing an important difference between attention and the internal structure of the sphere—namely, that attention is an operation defined on the lattice and is therefore at a higher logical level than the structure it illuminates. So the question of interest to me is what are the consequences of applying this operation attention to the internal structure of the sphere—What can attention do?

Suppose you're in an unfamiliar environment—a forest, say, —and you hear a sound the source of which you cannot identify—what happens? You attend—you simultaneously drop the threshold on all filters which could pass information on the location and identity of source—the sudden raucous cry of the steller's jay, the sway of pampas grass, a whiff of wild azalea on the breeze, the cessation of the cicada's song —your senses reach our for news, for difference—you are committed. . . . and you raise the thresholds on all filters not relevant to locating and identifying the source of that sound —you don't know at that point whether you're hungry or thirsty; lost or perfectly oriented; tired or refreshed. You are living in all and only those circuits which connect with sources of news from the environment.

You are driving to an important meeting—one of consequence to your future plans. You stop at a traffic signal—while you wait for the light to change, you commit minimum attention to the color of the light, the feel of your car vibrating, perhaps the sound of the engine and you attend instead to representations of the upcoming meeting—what your objectives are, the responses likely to occur to those objectives, the goals of other members of the meeting group . . . you literally see and hear possible futures and your feelings are responses to the hallucinated environment—the internal context. Suppose in your preview of the meeting you see and hear someone make a response which stops you—you suddenly feel stuck—so now you make the meta-move—you rerepresent the meeting so that you are a director/author of a stage play, the subject of which is the meeting. Your perceptual position is outside the direct influence of the actors in the play, however, as director/author you may change the behavior of the actors until you are satisfied. The fact that one of the actors looks and sounds exactly like you makes no difference. You have achieved meta-position—by moving up a logical level of representations you make the previous context you were responding to—the meeting—one of a subset of a larger frame—the theater. This larger frame defines a context in which you have the freedom to vary the behaviors of the actors until you achieve what you want. With such representational maneuvers you are patterning, you are constructing models which will guide your future behavior. Notice how far from the larger circuit of the actual world we come—not only are we representing something which hasn't occurred yet but we are operating as if life were but a play—this freedom has its cost—we are responding to representations which themselves have no direct connections to the world—we are divorced from the wisdom inherent in the larger circuit. Modern man, changer of his environment—to quote Bateson—creator of his or her own context insofar as he or she responds to these self-generated representations of context solely is devoid of wisdom—a blind pilot with no instrumentation—we have climbed the tree of knowledge and eaten of the apple of disassociation and we have lost the garden—but surely this is not news in a world where people insist on allegiance to symbols such as words, flags, . . . to the point of destroying those who refuse to accept those symbols. Wisdom is however available just in case we can maintain a dynamic Learning III position—one where we go back to the world without hallucinated and overly simplified models, suppress the evaluative function and note the differences between our model and our experience . . . and subsequently change the model. To filter out the world because it fails to agree with our model, our expectations, is to eat the menu—you can say you had scampi for dinner but both the shrimp and your stomach know the difference. . . .

But this discussion is unbalanced. Back to the forest. The first time you found yourself in the forest and the last time you found yourself there you behaved in profoundly different ways—some of the things you watched and listened and smelled for initially offered no useful news of difference and you suppressed them—you no longer attend to them. Other portions of your sensing circuitry yield high-grade information so you have lowered the threshold even more. Perhaps in that interim period you went into a forest with an individual highly skilled in woodcraft and through careful observation you noted and successfully used these sensing procedures—ones entirely novel to you. You learned—you created a model of forest sensing. If you understand that attention is the systematic variation in the threshold values of filters on channels of information potentially available to you, then it follows that you create models through this process of attention for each and every state of consciousness you achieve. These models are partially determined by the world and therefore responsive to the wisdom of the larger circuit (where connected appropriately) and partially the unique contribution by you. Learning III occurs when the organism recognizes the wisdom in subordinating all models to experience not because Karl Popper says so but because experience is the source of certain kinds of corrective wisdom. Thus epistemology is no longer an endeavor to arrive at a proper, true, or even useful representation of the world but a dynamic endeavor where we engage the world from multiple positions —it begins with the recognition that multiple descriptions of the world, even those inconsistent one with the other, are the foundation of wisdom—that we may achieve some balance not by obliterating difference through statistical averaging but by promoting and experiencing difference—this is the dance of life. . . .

Attention, as you have no doubt guessed, is another name for "I" and the states which can be differentially achieved through the disciplined and skillful employment of attention are the range of human possibility. "I," or attention, is a function which is defined on the lattice and can operate to produce states ranging from the demon-like narrow-focused, sensory-based states of the race car driver to the sensory independent, future-oriented states of the corporate planner. Each of these states has its model of the world—all of them subject to the epistemological considerations we're developing here. Now what is the relationship between attention and disassociation? That's right—they're inverses—one is the flip side of the other.

Judy: Many years ago Gregory Bateson upon the occasion of reading *Structure of Magic* asked the following question, "Is 'I' a nominalization?" At the time we responded with a resounding "No! 'I' is not a nominalization, 'I' is a pronoun." Perhaps we owe Gregory an apology and certainly we'd like to make some corrections and comments about this question of nominalization and "I." Gregory Bateson himself had stated that the discovery of representational system coding in our neurology seems obvious when the argument starts from linguistics instead of starting from cultural contrast and psychosis. Nominalization as a linguistic process is a complex transformational process where by a process word or verb in deep structure appears as an event word, or noun, in the surface structure. However, every model has its limitations, and the linguistic model did not facilitate our thinking of "I" as a nominalization. No doubt we missed the spirit of Gregory's question—it was not designed to be a technical linguistic issue at all—but a question about "I" as a process function which sustains a mobility internal to an individual or culture for health, learning, growth, and balance. If this be the case then we were accurate in our assumption of "I" as a pronoun, but irrelevant to the spirit in which the question was posed. "I" began to take on a new meaning so to speak, "I" had begun to develop as a function. Another important point is how this function of "self" of "I" relates back to the old notion of parts. The idea of parts is essentially a static notion —in the individual it becomes an impoverished metaphor when compared with the notion of "I" as a function. The only echo of parts in this new model is that we all have homeostatic centers which need to be rebalanced to facilitate a sense of wisdom by developing a fuller and more dynamic understanding. Just as the concept of nominalization suggested a possible filling out, a search for congruity between language and more primary representation within the individual—the function "I" suggests a rebalancing both within and without the individual with respect to group and environment. In other words achieving congruity and balance with respect to context. R.D. Laing is well known for remarking that schizophrenia is a congruent response to a highly fragmented technical society—we have criticized Laing with tongue in cheek for being so conservative—schizophrenia gives a person only two models—we've insisted in the past on multiple personality or parts as a minimum requirement for dealing with a fragmented technical society. This new proposal is a more radical critique—it proposes not fragmented parts—but a balanced personal organization in which the individual can occupy any set of circuits within the lattice of human possibility—in fact, the only reflection of parts in the new model are circuits which have been occupied frequently enough by the individual that physiological investment has occurred. Unless the individual deliberately stretches the range of their circuitry, their flexibility will be eaten up by encroaching variables, they'll get comfortable and they will slip altogether too easily into the same circuits—the ones which constitute their homeostatic centers—their parts. And then the coroner's report comes in—yeah, that's right—the individual comes to first act as if the information reaching them through the perceptual filters is the world and terminally they believe it —and so must defend these homeostatic centers against news of difference by raising thresholds—yep, the living dead have arisen.

John: Thus far we have developed one possible structure for the personal organizational model, defined the functions of "I" within the latticework of the model, and suggested that each person give some consideration to an appropriate metaphor for themselves to serve as the initial structure.

Woman: So how do we know if the metaphor we choose is appropriate?

John: As with any structure certain design principles must be developed as the structure is built, or after the structure is fabricated it must be subjected to a set of conditions to determine whether it is well-formed. The following are design principles and well-formedness conditions that have occurred again and again in both working with people considered genius by our society and in the development of the personal organizational model.

The first condition to consider is where we get our news. News comes from difference and difference comes from multiple (at minimum double) descriptions of the world. So now before acting in the world we propose upgrading the well-formedness condition from double description to triple description. You may not make a change unless you appreciate enough context to occupy three positions: where you yourself stand—the position of your own referential index in the experience (or the experience you are planning); the position of some or all significant others who are part of the relationship at the same logical level, namely, other human beings, or if it involves other species for example, an animal trainer with a horse, or any living system. Last but certainly not least, meta-position, as that higher logical level gives you the kinesthetic dissociation so you can escape the tyranny of the physiology you originally occupied. In other words the wisdom exists in the whole circuit, so it is the whole circuit we must consider in gaining our news of difference, the basis for acting with some wisdom in the world—we must consider the "contextual side" of the loop.

This concept of multiple description allows us to cyberneticize any format. Let me tell you a story that Bob Dilts told us the other night. He was over and we were running this material by him and having a wonderful time. We were talking about changing personal history.

You all know the change personal history format, right? It goes, "What do you want to change?" "I want to change X" Anchor that kinesthetic sensation. "When was the last time you had this experience?"—you see the physiological shift and you anchor it. You hold the kinesthetics constant, which takes the person back down through personal history to the "conditioning situation of origin." It's always mythological but it's exactly the mythology that they need because it's the one they live by. Then you add resources to it until you see the physiology shift. You know you've all done that. You bring them back up through personal history, have them change their personal history on the way back up, and here they are, right? (laughter) And now you can test. That's pretty much the way I do it. And watching and listening to Judy, that's pretty much the way she does it. What Bob has done is he's cyberneticized that format. And here's a challenge for all of you who have some mastery of the technology. Certainly in my work, in doing change personal history in the format I just loosely described, I'm very pleased with what I get done. But notice that as a first-attention requirement, the modeler requirement, we have not done an adequate job. What's the difference? Now let me tell you how Bob does it, You ask. "What do you want to change?" and anchor that. So far it's the same thing. Have them go back to the point of origin of the behavior they want to change. Now Bob has them reexperience it, stops them . . .

Now, there's a presupposition here—right?—that that behavior was looped in with some other aspect of the environment. A person, an object, something. If it's a phobia, the phobic stimulus.

So, the first move is reexperiencing it from the position that the person occupied, their own personal referential index, their own perceptual position. He pointed out to us that if you take the person back to a time when, say as a child, an adult was shaking *them*—and this was a traumatic experience, so the person never objects to things in public because of this almost phobic conditioning experience—when the person goes back to that situation Bob goes, "Are you back there?" and they go, "Oh, yeah!"

Now the piece of the behavior that they'll exhibit is other person's referential index—the other perceptual position.

Woman: Which perceptual position?

John: The one of the adult shaking the child. The adult shaking them as opposed to the child being shaken. They're taking the "contextual side" in this situation. I see and can physiologically identify when they've done that. I don't comment on it. That is, this is an essential part of the loop —an arc in a ecological piece of work of changed personal history. It has to be part of a circuit. I identify it physiologically. I sit there and watch this thing happen and am amazed once again by the elegance of nonverbal communication and I don't name it. Bob now insists that the person overtly occupy both positions. First, they get the position they naturally choose—they come to an appreciation from that perceptual position of this situation, say, from the perspective of the adult involved in the original situation. And then he has them switch into the child position and notice what that was like. They already know that all too well, that's the phobia. If there are significant others . . . do those too. If there are none, then they move to meta-position, standing to the side with Bob and watching the dance.

Judy: Bob Dilts has come closer to achieving an adequate first-attention description in that he has included the context, considered the whole circuit in the format called change personal history.

So descriptions produce news, but only if we suppress our evaluative functions long enough to receive the news. The

American Indian had a saying that nicely illustrates this point: Do not judge your neighbor until you have walked a mile in his moccasins; do not evaluate until you have, through multiple descriptions, gained news of difference. Many times we take on a new or different perspective—as the medicine wheel suggests—but a new description presupposes more than a new perspective. A new perspective is static where we are insisting upon dynamic representations. It is not enough just to occupy the posture of the other individual or living system, but you must introduce typical movement. Through movement we evolve the dance, the dynamics, and develop a double description—so walk some in the other's moccasins before evaluation.

Often John and I have talked about states from which news of difference can be obtained and from which a new description of the world can be developed. Like learning a new language (a new description) a clean state which both protects and supports the new description is useful. For the purposes of this workshop we have developed the "stop the world" state, where language and foveal vision (two important filters for stabilizing our present descriptions of the world) are suspended to gain news of difference. It is a special state for collapsing the world of stability. Contextual markers, those external and internal signals which allow us to know that the state is appropriate and in the right context, as well as the concept of lifelines as a way of knowing that if the world demands our immediate attention while we are occupying new circuitry in the latticework of ourselves we can meet those demands with competence. It allows us the freedom to change the state if necessary. Scanning for difference also involves waiting to evaluate or judge the news until it has become a dynamic and robust enough description to offer us significant news of difference. This brings us to the question of assigning stability and entropy in the model. Where do we want stability and where do we want surprise and news of difference? When we scan for difference we do not want to evaluate news at the periphery where we interface with the world. If we place our filters at the interface we are unlikely to get any information that would lead to a new description.

This is not a question of not having filters; our neurology alone insures that filtering will occur. The question is: Can we suspend some and maintain different ones and get news of difference. So while scanning for difference, stability at the interface would not be useful, here we want surprise, flexibility, and news. Placing filters at other positions along the continuum moving towards first attention may also be costly —in as much as we may be evaluating news of difference and shunting it off before it reaches our attention. On the other hand we don't want news all the time. So we propose with this model placing stability in the structure of the model itself and entropy in the substance—in particular, news of difference.

It is important to again mention that these models or representations are limited, are arcs of a more complete circuit. So how can we further assure that our representations are carried back to the world of experience and examined for difference that may make a difference. Understanding that if we do not have a periodic review or a periodic suppression of our filters we fall prey to believing our representations or models are the world. It is only by carrying these representations back to the world that we come close to achieving some wisdom in as much as we have reassociated them to context.

Two other possibilities we may suggest are, (1) playing to your weakness and, (2) seeking counterexamples. If I can already do something successfully, whatever that may be, then I want to develop those places where I am weak, and in those places where I am successful I want to be alert to those times where behaviorally, although I responded the same as before when I was successful, the outcome was counter to my past experience of the matter. These will be places where news is just waiting to be discovered.

Every aesthetic act proceeds from a foundation of skill. To implement this model requires a well-developed skill base—one such base is the NLP technology. It can serve as a bridge from your present personal organization to a balanced, aesthetically pleasing structure in which you can live with passion and balance. In this sense it is the counterpart of the industrial technology which formed the bridge from our dreams of flight as we walked the Earth to the actual flight to the stars. If the geometric metaphor we've developed here has isolated the issues to be addressed and the variables necessary to effect such changes then it has served its purpose and we recommend you use an interim aid in the process of developing your own personalized metaphor.

Rosalie: Can we go back to a question about meta-position?

John: You understand that for any editing change or any organizational change, now the well-formedness condition is that you occupy, minimally, the perceptual position of at least three positions; your own referential index, the most significant other in context, and meta-position. You might want to cover all living systems. You might want to have second attention pick some subset. You might deliberately ask for the most important nonliving system's perceptual position. Lots of possibilities. That's your personal aesthetic. By mentioning and isolating the variable I place the decisions in your hands. And I'd like you to try different variations on the theme. That's essentially the editor position.

Rosalie: Why do you limit it to every living organism?

John: Because I make a profound distinction between living and nonliving systems.

Rosalie: Can I tell you a story?

John: Do I have a choice? (Laughter)

Rosalie: On one of my fantasy trips a while back I was playing the gestalt number, in essence.

John: Dreamwork, dreamwork formats.

Rosalie: Yeah, dreamwork formats. So my problem was that I was being left. And I felt like I was being deserted across the board. So I played myself and that wasn't too comfortable. Then I played the deserters and that wasn't too comfortable.

Nothing seemed to help, you know? Everything was lousy, the house was lousy, there were newspapers, it was dirty, you know, everything I didn't like. So you know I played every living thing there and I hadn't gotten me anywhere. So I said, "Well, what else is there left to play, you know? I can play the toilet, I can try that one." Didn't get me anywhere. I tried the house. When I tried the house, it was a dirty, disgusting house but it had this dirty window and all of a sudden when I was the house I was aware that there was sunlight coming through this window. And that, you know, I could bask, as the house, in the sunlight coming through the window. And I went through the window (it was night) as a bird. And it was like it was night and it was black but it was like going into the light. So it was through being the house, the inanimate system—because I tried all the others—that I went through this totally transforming experience and I just didn't look at it the same way, you know, it was just too little.

John: The minimum requirement is that you identify with every living system and then go to meta-position. I didn't hear you go to meta-position, number one. Secondly, I certainly would have a bunch of fallbacks so that if I went through every living system in the context and it didn't do me any good I'd sure have something to try—anything else in the area. I'm just exploring what the minimums are. There's a certain aesthetic to what you did. One other thing I want to comment on. How did you know when you got what you needed? You understand that's an epistemological question?

Rosalie: Because of how I . . .

John: . . . felt.

Rosalie: . . . felt.

John: Right. Now, a caution to the organism undergoing change. Your feelings are an important part of everything you do and not to notice them and not to use them as an integrated part of your experience is wasting a tremendous resource within you. You would end up with the kind of disassociations which are all together too common in the technical culture where a person goes hollow, they lose their soul. However, kinesthetics is not the only representational system. It may be your preferred one, or it may be your preferred one in context, but it seems to me just as the well-formedness conditions are at least three descriptions and, minimally, identification with living systems, that the classes of understandings which we talked about on morning one, horizontal understandings (representations in all representational systems) and vertical understandings (connections to context), are also well-formedness conditions on what you do.

Judy: It is only in a society where feelings are considered to be the involuntary representational system, that so much attention is paid to the kinesthetics. If we go to another culture where kinesthetics are voluntary they would be amused at this representation. They would be fascinated by the visual images as we are on feelings because in those cultures that's the system that's involuntary. So I'm proposing that there are biases . . . Remember what we said on day one: The genetics sets the range within which the organism can develop. We're accepting that as a given for the moment. What actual phenotype—that is, what personal organization—occurs is some skewing within the range that was set by the genetics. And one of the most powerful skewing influences is the society. Here is a powerful example of the skewing in our social system culture; the kinesthetic representation—feelings—are considered to be involuntary. It seems to me that if you want to operate in the range of human possibility as opposed to "personal alternatives" or even cultural alternatives you want to rebalance in just the ways that we're proposing here.

Woman: Visually, auditorially . . .

John: Absolutely, all of them. They're all your allies, they're all your assets.

Woman: I work in a developmental preschool with children who are making what I used to refer to as "ego shifts" and changes. The part of our work that we're really getting interested in now is how we, as a society, are influencing children's need to play out these roles. We find in children's play that they do experience things with the kind of projection you're talking about and in order to integrate those experiences they have to act out in some way or act on their environment and some have a greater preference to get into their feelings. Others really seem to need the verbal interpretation of what they're experiencing. And it's a real critical issue if we're going to begin educating children at younger and younger ages to take responsibility for what sort of biases we're offering them as to how they interpret their feelings and organize their internal states.

Judy: Yeah. It's certainly an evolution. That's what you and I were talking about yesterday, how you have the technology and then you have to wait for wisdom to catch up to it. And then you have wisdom which allows you some space to create some more technology and then you have to wait for the . . . It's just a constant evolution and you don't know what you don't know.

John: I had a close friend come to me . . . , had a daughter. She was about four at the time. He was being persecuted by my need to play music all the time, even when we were sitting there talking . . . And he said, "This thing you're doing, this new demon of yours for music, for percussion, for rhythm . . . , I like it. It seems to add a dimension to you. I'm struck with the responsibility I bear toward my child. This is the first time you've played music. And I assume that you in some sense wish you could have started earlier." So my friend says, "I'd like to expose my child to music now, seems to me to be appropriate. My problem is, one, the educational system. If I turn my child over to a standard music teacher God knows what's going to happen. And further, should I choose a drum? Should I choose a kalimba (African thumb piano), should I choose a horn of some sort, should I choose a stringed instrument? My problem is that if I choose one, it excludes the others."

You're faced with a wide range of alternatives. And this is particularly true in a technological society whose members do not have a shared culture. In a traditional culture, the paths are already made manifest and the children are already encouraged to move through these different and relatively well-defined paths by the whole tribe. But here we're overwhelmed with choices in some sense. You remember Fromm's book *Escape from Freedom.* So the issue for my friend now becomes how can he execute his responsibility as the parent —both to protect the spirit of this child and to expose it to certain classes of learning experience. Now everybody has their own solution . . . seems to me that the worst solution is to do nothing. That way the child gets no experience. You rob the organism of a profound learning experience. There are better things to do than just flipping a coin though. You could, for example, expose the child—accidentally from the child's perceptual position—to a number of events. Say you have Uncle John come over and sit around and play kalimba. You have Aunt Judy come over and dance. You have Uncle Titos come over and play drum or Sonny could play horn.

Judy: And she'll choose.

John: . . . and all you're doing is reading the second-attention unconscious responses to discover what the natural predilections of that child are. There will be preferences that organism will express. So you do not confront the child with any conscious decisions. The child is not competent to make that class of decisions. But what you do is you expose the child to a wide range of experiences in this area and read the unconscious physiological responses the child makes. So now your responsibility really begins. Because you've got to find someone who can teach the child without damaging that child's spirit. Maybe it's you. Maybe it's the child him or herself.

And the real responsibility comes in the next step and that's balance. If that child developed a demon for kalimba at some point up the line . . . First of all you make it an honest endeavor. If the child chooses to do this, once they're engaged in it, I myself would set certain quality standards. They may not leave that until they've reached a certain minimal competency. Now, I'm not going to say that to a child because that is to invite rebellion but I will certainly manipulate the context appropriately so that there are contingencies based on their continuing play up to a certain minimum quality. I now have to go, "They are overdeveloped in ballet" or "They are overdeveloped in kalimba" or at a higher logical level "They are overdeveloped cognitively—they're wordsmiths." "What do I need to balance?" And now, I again manipulate the context so as to create access to a new order of events which are biased by me, deliberately, without conscious perception on the child's part, to offer them choices within a class of experience which will rebalance them.

Woman: That's where the integrity comes in.

John: Yes, and one aspect of integrity is an appreciation that you're in that loop. You're not outside that loop. You may be covertly manipulating the context but at some level of representation that child knows exactly what you're doing. And the fact that they can't verbalize it has nothing to do with their appreciation of the situation. Ultimately at some point—just as yesterday your baby sitter played your controller in the first phase of the exercise and then you took over that function and they moved up a logical level in relationship to you—you as a parent, as an adult in bringing along these amazing little organisms and learning from them at the same time, need to occupy certain positions in the personal organization as part of the child's ability to have experiences that are coherent. As soon as they can handle that function you move up.

The final one, and a very hard one for many people, particularly since teenagers are very very good at finding exactly the buttons that they need to push . . . , the last generation's buttons. I think that some of at least the visual part of punk, I like think that's wonderful. But mostly I love to watch the relationships they declare with people walking by—the response the punkers get from other people. Every generation goes, "Oh, we weren't that way when we were kids." Nonsense! Remember "Elvis the Pelvis?" My parents' generation, they were real worried about that one, right? The substance of each generation's declaration of independence may differ but the pattern certainly is predictable.

The final one—the move that signals symmetry. You turn over to the maturing child the decision-making in terms of the balance between purposive first attention—which is often the last place you're probably going to occupy in their hierarchy —and second attention. The young adult decides even the context. Castaneda proposes the worthy opponent—a person or a context which serves as a stimulus for the child to make a full mobilization of resources. Doesn't seem to me to be appropriate very often to be your own children's worthy opponent. That's one of the things I like about the west African model. The uncles of the male child are his worthy opponents in the areas of discipline and performance.

Judy: The idea of the worthy opponent is essentially that if you're never tricked you'll never learn.

John: And if you're never pushed, never stressed by your environment you're not going to develop certain classes of resources. There's an old rat experiment[5]—I think Rosalie has lots of information about this—where they took baby rats and they handled . . . , one group they just handled a certain number of minutes a day and messed around with them. Another group they handled and shocked and beat on. Where do they come up with these ideas anyway? I guess they're working something out. (laughter) I don't know what it is. I'm glad it's with rats, that's all I can say.

Rosalie: Not always.

John: And another group they left in the cage, alone, with adequate food, shelter, all the wonderful things that parents tend to believe, parent rats I assume (laughter), are appropriate for baby rats. Now, this is during some critical period, 21 to 40 days after birth, blah, blah, some specified period . . . , and then they let them be and then when they became adults they tested them for things like how well they responded to new environments and so forth. Do you want to guess?

Man: The shocked rats.

John: The shocked rats what? They did well. The shocked rats were absolutely impeccable in their insistence on exploring an unfamiliar environment. The handled ones did as well. The ones that had been left alone cowered in the corner, defecating, urinating all over themselves. (Laughter) In a sense, inappropriate stress is better than no contact at all. I can also think of certain incidents that I went through as a teenager which are part of the foundation of my resourcefulness. And I know adults who are still whimpering and whining that these experiences are the thing that crippled them, that defeated their ability to become the personal genius they could have been. Perception and meaning are contributions from the organism not from the environment. The experience, the raw experience itself, the environment has a great deal to do with. But what it means to the organism is within your control to an extent which would surprise and delight you.

There's another thing that I know you know a lot about. You all have old demons.

Group: What?

Judy: Old demons.

John: Old demons. Demons you've had for so very long . . .

Judy: . . . but are not necessarily . . .

John: . . . relevant . . .

Judy: . . . to who you are or what you do now. But nonetheless they're there.

John: The demon who could climb trees when you were a young girl or a young boy. I mean the demon who knew how to go out and dig for frogs. I don't know. Notice that you don't spend a lot of time climbing trees or hunting frogs, which may be an invitation from the world—a statement about your getting a little too solid for your own good, a little too adult. However you think about that, there will be, because of the evolution of both internal context and of external context, demons who no longer have a relevant function.

Judy: What are you going to do with them?

Man: Promote them.

John: Promote 'em to what?

Robert: To a level of incompetence. (Laughter)

John: And that's exactly what old demons end up doing if you don't put 'em where they can be useful. It's the Peter Principle in internal organization.

Judy: In some African tribes they have a concept of the *Wazee* which are the old wise ones. They're available—waiting for somebody to indicate that they need some information about something that they know about because they're old and wise; they've seen and heard a lot of difference.

John: If the *Wazee's* counsel is not sought, they'll come around and get involved anyway—whether you want them there or not.

Their very presence can be a stabilizer. They act with a wisdom which is the result of having been a demon, of having executed their field of activity brilliantly, and of understanding that the context has shifted so that they moved to not only a different logical level, they moved lateral to the rest of the personal structure. You can't waste something as powerful as an old demon. It's just foolhardy.

Judy: You might need it anyway. You never know.

John: Now there's a second way to use old demons—use them as trainers.

Judy: Say what?

John: They train new demons. They're like a prototype demon, right? So I have trainers in my technical staff—the difference between the learning curve and the learning circle. I notice in learning drumming and percussion that there are things that strongly remind me of certain other experiences. I'm going through the same kinds of things I went through in athletics, interpersonal relationships, . . . There are things in common about that. Therefore there are really powerful generalizations that come out of old demons that could be applied to accelerate the learning cycle of the new demons as I develop them. Antonio.

Antonio: I was thinking about that. You know, I have a soccer-playing demon.

Judy: I bet you do.

Antonio: I have another one to do psychotherapy. And when I am doing psychotherapy like I am playing soccer—I am really good, you know, and the things go so easy.

John: Yeah, you get a kick out of it, right? (groans from group) Just relax. Everybody has their own brand of humor. I was trained by Erickson.

Antonio: What I've been thinking about is: Is one demon training the other one?

John: Or even temporary alliances. Have you also noticed that in doing psychotherapy there are sometimes when using the soccer metaphor or the soccer demon is inappropriate?

Antonio: Yeah.

John: The soccer demon—a beautiful demon in you; I've seen that sucker smiling out from behind your eyes—comes up when you dance as well. It would be a tragedy to collapse the psychotherapy demon with the soccer demon. There are areas of application that are inappropriate. How many men or women are there on a soccer team? And isn't the class of relationships on a soccer team a mirror image of some of the most powerful organizations in terms of group work? Notice that the thing that's lovely about soccer is that you never stop moving—one of the most demanding sports, in terms of just straight physical energy. And the fluidity with which a soccer team that really knows how to play as a team can play is phenomenal. You can take the best soccer players in the world and put them on a team and I would rather watch a practiced high school team play because of the tremendous coordination and interconnectedness that people who have played together have. You know, when you're playing your peripheral vision is superb, in fact, it gets uncanny at points. You even know where people are behind you because you can count on certain predictable patterns that you've used in practicing together.

Judy: You have eyes in the back of your head like the nuns did when I was in Catholic school. (laughter)

Antonio: I had many experiences of kicking the ball and knowing where the ball was going to be before it got there.

John: Yeah. You appreciate the metaphor. You do want that demon on call so that if the psychotherapy controller determines that this is case which could be appropriately handled by a soccer metaphor they go, "Whhsssssstt! Here comes Pele. Here comes one of the *Wazee* to sit next to the psychotherapy demon." "Do this, do that, act now." Let me ask the question for the morning: How many people set up dreaming last night?

Man: Set up dreaming?

John: OK, let me ask the question the other way: How many people did not set up dreaming in the way we proposed the night before? As I said, maybe this got done during dreaming. You could even do a check. Let me add, if you find that in fact this organizational structure has already generalized itself, or as Carol said, a couple tweaks here, a little discrimination and refinement there, and you're home free because you've had most of it when we started, then now it becomes time to recognize this is a bare-bones, skeletal structure. It will provide the balance for the foundation for some personal genius which is what we're doing here but it's not yet aesthetic. Does your aesthetics consider that you could take this underlying structure now and notice it could be tribal? I mean what metaphor do you like? Have you ever been on the ocean and watched schools of dolphin playing from horizon to horizon? Is that a metaphor that appeals to you? Have you ever seen a soccer team that was really well coordinated operate? Have you ever watched Baryshnikov dance with Elaine Kudo creating a magic which was difficult to believe? The aesthetics, aesthetics.

Susan: Also, what you're talking about in each of those examples is the interaction between systems.

Judy: That's right.

Susan: So, I don't know if I can verbalize my question, but where does the dimensionality come in if there's one individual . . . ? The sense that I got a little while ago—and now my first attention has had too long to chew on it but if I go back to what I got then—it was like the demon states . . . Like if I'm in my demon state and you're in your demon state and we're drumming in the drumming circle, it's as if we become one mind . . .

John: . . . one mind, absolutely.

Judy: . . . at another logical level, and you've extended the boundaries of self to include other selves. Also, each drummer has played a part which when put together creates a new song; from two descriptions comes news in the form of a song not manifest in either part singly.

Susan: . . . at another logical level.

Judy: In playing drums, notice that it's cooperative behavior at that next logical level.

John: When you're drumming that as you're playing one part. This part has no meaning except in relationship to other parts.

Judy: . . . which is a special kind of double description and from it you get a song.

John: And the underlying skill level must be developed enough that I can hear and feel what Susan over there is doing as I'm deliberately playing something that pulls on her. The tension in the drumming and the percussion is where the song comes from. So that you've got to be able to hold your position in this relationship with a stability, an integrity, otherwise no song comes.

Susan: So the song is a function of the tension. Is that what I just heard?

John: Yes, that's what you just heard. If they were the same parts there wouldn't be anything there. The fact that we're playing different spots in the rhythm and pulling and pushing on each other, that tension gives rise to the song, and where in the spots we're playing gives variation to the song.

Woman: Once this structure is in place in the individual it also then gives a reference to deal with the outside world because as you have to interact at different levels inside you then you recognize where the outside person is.

Georgine: To me, it allows total freedom. Because now I can mix and match whatever I want to in my own personality and I can play with something and bring it up or increase it or diminish this one and bring up something else and I have a home base to go back to.

John: Yeah, it's home base.

Larry: Is it possible that you could get just as stuck in the meta-position as in the demon state or the . . .

John: OK. So let's talk about "personality types" with the understanding that "personality" is a pseudo-phenomenon—a secondary consequence of personal organization like the human chin as a unit of evolutionary study—a nominalization which has only linguistic validity. There are people who indulge themselves by living here—so completely committed to responding to the stimuli from outside of themselves that they have no direction to their life. The first class of people who live here, they're spontaneous, they're warm and wild. I mean they're people who, they're fun to be around, they'll make you crazy after a while, but they're a lot of fun to be around, right? You never know what's going to happen next with somebody like that. But whatever happens is going to pretty amazing. And if you can apprehend difference without evaluation it's an astonishing state of affairs. We're setting up personal structure. Do you understand in coupling, in the sense of relationships with other people, that unless you have an integrity to your own circuitry you can only fall into the holes in their circuitry.

Judy: Fill in the gaps.

John: A generative relationship of challenge and excellence with you and another person is possible only if you have integrity to your circuitry.

Judy: Don Juan says, "People get obsessed." A warrior will go through apprenticeship. Maybe there will be some point in the apprenticeship that will be so overwhelming that he'll never move past that because he's obsessed by it. Or maybe he'll make it to warriorship and going through his descriptions will fall into some description that he gets obsessed about and not move past that. Don Juan would say it's another form of indulgence.

John: There are people all over this country, Canada, and Europe who are stuck at stages in my personal evolution.

They are doing the same damn things that I happened to be doing when I had contact with them. And they're having a good time there and they're not going anywhere.

The opposite end of this continuum is the person who can't get out of first attention. What "personality" characteristics does this person have? They're cold, aloof, rigid . . .

Judy: Very objective, though.

John: Very objective.

Judy: Probably science or something.

John: Plausibly business. At any rate being unable to escape from first attention means that you're not going to have anything spontaneous in your life. If you get surprised by something it will upset you as opposed to delight you. Then there are people who are so good at moving the function of self around that they're constantly confluent. By confluent I mean they have the same emotional state as whoever they happen to be around. Traditionally in this culture women are suppose to have this position with respect to their husbands, right?

Judy: No. (laughter)

John: On the other hand there are people who never can identify with another living thing and they live an incredibly impovershed life. I'm not sure which is worse, constantly being at the mercy of the winds of whatever emotional storms are in the local area or never participating in the world. Notice that every one of the functions that we could talk about, if it's extended outside a healthy range, has "personality" characteristics you could easily identify.

Georgine: The other possibility I see is that the person who has those two poles as their options so they go one way for a while and then they recognize that there are problems with that way so then they go completely the other way and go that way for a while.

John: Flip-flops—that's a threshold phenomenon. You're getting close to multiple personality. See, if you draw a line through your circuits so that they are disconnected into two or more distinct sets of circuitry—relatively complete within themselves but unconnected with one another, you've got a schizophrenic. That's the alcoholic. Now you've got people who are often amnesiac for their experiences on both sides of this. And the problem is thresholding. That is, they do not know they're doing one when they're living in the other. Remember I mentioned the woman who wanted the situation where she was married to this man who had certain irritating characteristics. She didn't want to know about them until they reached a certain threshold value. And of course what happens is her whole life is like this, right? Six months of idyllic relationships. (indignantly) "That was all deceit!" Then. (affectionately) "Here he is! It's Prince Charming again," you know, for six months.

Judy: . . . threshold . . .

John: . . . a really powerful threshold phenomenon. And notice the violation can only occur if you draw a line through circuits so that you're left with arcs. Remember what I read from Bateson. The conscious mind, because of its seven plus or minus two constraint, can only consider arcs of circuits and if we reify the arcs we've just created personality types. We've drawn lines though circuits which are essential for our further development.

Man: Does that apply to diet as well?—to people that are gaining and losing weight?

John: They go up for a while and then they go down for a while?

Judy: It's in a different system . . .

John: . . . meaning, "What code did they put each threshold in?" Disease . . . Anybody who went through medical school knows you had better pick your strategies for learning and understanding in medical school and make them anything other than kinesthetic.

Judy: If you use a kinesthetic strategy for understanding disease —you have medical school students who manifest symptoms of every disease that they study.

Woman: What's even worse, they give it to their kids.

Woman: It seems to me that what you've been describing is a way of putting our demons in the proper context so that we function ecologically within us which we then take to the outside world, function ecologically in the outside world . . .

John: So we have the balance.

Woman: . . . so you no longer need the culture because you've internalized it.

Judy: Yes, in a traditional, coherent culture, the culture would maintain that congruity between inside and outside. In a society you don't have the maintenance of that congruity outside so we are proposing that that becomes your personal responsibility.

Woman: So you're creating your own culture.

Judy: Yeah, you're creating your own internal culture. This is where your NLP comes in—the skill base.

John: Seems to me first attention is responsible for formatting. And that's why I absolutely defer to Francis's request because his first attention has to make the arrangements. There is a richness to second attention but it's typically an unorganized richness. The function of first attention . . .

Judy: . . . is modeling. . . . with language and with consciousness you get a precision and a delineation which is purposive and therefore not particularly wise but very powerful. This chair here doesn't weigh very much. But if I took this chair and took one of the legs and shaped it to a very thin point and balanced the chair on that point you could bring tremendous pressures to bear on that single point. That's what demons are. They're so narrow-band focused that the whole resourcefulness of the organism is expressed at that single point. That's why you can just ease your way through otherwise very difficult situations.

That makes a lot of sense to me. And that's another place where old demons go. Where do old demons go?

John: On the other hand you notice there are important cases in your work with the technology of Neuro-Linguistic Programming where you want to keep parts separate. You don't integrate them because they have nonoverlapping domains of application. So this is a really important well-formedness condition. And notice, NLP alone is nothing more than a technology. It can be abused or it can be used for superb pieces of work in terms of human excellence. The point is it's a technology and until there is a context which has both some wisdom and some aesthetics to it, you're a damned "plugger." You're just plugging along without any vertical, contextual understanding. It's as if you have this wonderful, wonderful box of tools back in King Arthur's court but you have nothing of value to do with it. And part of what we're about here is putting that aesthetic frame around it.

Rosalie: This is the question that I had when I woke up this morning, exactly what you're talking about. In terms of, Kierkegaard talked about how you moved from the aesthetic to the ethical terms. And always a question for me is: What happens if you don't? In his view you became "demonic" if you didn't. I was never quite sure what he meant by demonic, however . . .

John: I always used to get so depressed when I read him. I could only read him for short periods of time.

Judy: Kafka didn't have any fun either.

Rosalie: It seems to me in the development of NLP you have been meticulous in formulating it as a technology without having a content.

John: Right, absolutely. Substance is the individual's concern. Our job is patterning.

Rosalie: Now, as you start this workshop, people come from whatever framework they have . . .

John: . . . if any . . .

Rosalie: . . . if any. Now as you start up this particular workshop, what particularly interests me is that you're using your technology, it appears to me, like a technology that's been developed in many religions. It's usually been within a cultural context that this technology has been developed (at least aspects of it). It has not been within the context of a society that this technology has been let loose. So even if so-called meditation is a technology for getting to achieve certain states, it's given to you within a context that's extremely cultural, one or the other.

John: . . . which has aesthetic and balance and . . .

Rosalie: . . . which has an overall framework within which one shapes the use of the technology. So you come here and you have a society as opposed to a culture. You present a technology, you know, that is not put within the ethical framework of a culture, and you have an H-bomb. And my question is, "What are you doing?" (laughter)

John: No, you have the tools to build an H-bomb or the finest agricultural support system which is relevant to balancing the population-food cycle problem. The critical difference here is one of logical level. There is an important difference between religion and NLP when appropriately mastered, integrated, and applied. Every religion I know of offers two things: first a set of practices, disciplines, and behaviors which identify the members of that religion and shape, when successful, their perceptions and consciousness. Secondly, a religion offers security; it says that out of the many paths we as humans could tread this specific path defined by the practices, disciplines, and behaviors is the correct one, that if you follow these directions you will be rewarded. Neuro-Linguistic Programming is an epistemology; it is not allowed to make substantive decisions, to offer the comfort of "the correct path." It offers the opportunity to explore, it offers a set of pathfinding tools. It is for you to select and explore these paths, whether you find comfort or challenge or hopefully, I would say, the comfort of challenge. . . . (pausing) . . .

And as you are correctly pointing out, the concentration of power that the technical competencies of NLP bring to the field of communication are strongly reminiscent of the technical concentration of power achieved through industrialization. That constitutes both an opportunity and a danger. The finest compliment that I ever got from Bateson, was the statement to me that NLP was a set of Learning III tools. Now, if that's true then it becomes incumbent upon me, Judith Ann, Richard, Robert . . . , the co-creators of this technology, to make some statement about context. As you say without that movement to some ethical considerations, we have not done what is considered a socially responsible job. Remember our opening statement. Examine a homogeneous, coherent culture. You'll notice that the representations externally and the representations internally match. There's a congruency which allows a set of wisdoms and balances both within the tribe and between the tribe and its environment that has a kind of ethical, moral characteristic. The result of that discussion, I remind you, was our proposal that in a fragmented, technical society which doesn't have that kind of matching between the "emanations from the outside and the emanations from the inside," it becomes incumbent on the individual to develop their own personal culture in the sense of the ethical frame within which they employ the tools. It has to have a wisdom to it which, we're proposing, would be referenced to context and would have an aesthetics to it. Now there's no way in hell that I'm willing to be substantive about what you "should" or "shouldn't" do. I'm proposing a class of well-formedness conditions which addresses a issue vital to each of us. Since there is no shared culture, how do we behave with this tremendously powerful technology in a responsible way?

Rosalie: Does the use of these tools themselves . . . ? Obviously, as you use these tools themselves, you are transformed.

John: Yes.

Rosalie: But the direction within which you are transformed . . .

John: That's what we're talking about, Rosalie. Now the delicate balance is that we're not interested in proposing what the "actualized human being" should be, or what the actualized society might be. We're saying we can learn from coherent traditional cultures. What kind of balances and checks are built into that system? So, it now becomes incumbent upon us—and I'm talking about the big loop here—to build a class of well-formedness conditions that addresses precisely the issue you voiced.

Rosalie: Thank you.

John: Do the second-attention check. I want to release you for a full hour in the world. Not in this place. I want you to go out in the world. I want you to spend the first twenty minutes doing a check. Is this program in place? What portions of it require further structure? Is it in progress? When can I expect a completion on this portion of the structure? Whatever you need to do to reassure yourself. The question becomes epistemological: How do you know you've made the arrangements? If my dad and I are going to work on a car, I know he knows a lot more about it; he has a lot more experience. Suppose he tells me to change the shocks in the front end. I'm not going to bother to ask him, when he walks around from the back and says, "OK, let's go," whether he's done the shocks on the rear end. He knows how to do that. He knows it better than I do. He's going to get it done faster and more efficiently than I do because he's more skilled at that. The fact that he says, "Let's go" tells me all I need to know. To belabor the point by going, "Well, did you make sure you tightened the bolts, Dad?" . . . You know, he's going to go, "Sshhheeeee!" and walk away.

What I'd like you to do, after you've played with your regular strategies, is switch strategies.

Peggy: I found when I first started to do the strategy that my partner did which was, "Hey, guys, are you all ready to go?" there was a kind of overwhelming thing like, "Well, we're not sure." So it was like, "Give me an analogy." And I went through with just one situation with one demon . . .

John: . . . and then generalized.

Peggy: . . . but then after that I could go to that strategy. It streamlined.

Judy: So it was like the second attention requesting, "First attention, give me some more specific information." That's good balance.

John: When I used to do therapeutic work, if I had a person with multiple phobias, I would say, "Give me the one that you think is least likely to change." I would do that one really slowly and carefully, warning second attention to pay attention because I had a job for it when we were done. Since that was the hardest one, when we'd get it done and they could test it, they'd go, "It really works!" And I'd go, "Now, second attention, did you understand the steps? They are . . . ," I'd backtrack, and then I'd say, "Do the rest of them tonight in a dream."

Judy: Learning to learn to learn. Gregory said that's what NLP tools are about—that really places them in terms of epistemology, as quite an evolutionary tool.

Marshall: Often we use our kinesthetic system as a check to see what's right and what's wrong. The speller makes a visual and then checks it out kinesthetically. Sometimes when we do behaviors or we get new ideas, especially new ideas that come in, our kinesthetic sense—our homeostatic sense, if we're a very structured person, comes in there and says, "Hey, that's wrong," not different but wrong, and we rob ourselves . . . So you might want to . . .

John: . . . develop the ability to find difference without evaluation. So the kinesthetics is not telling you that your new idea is wrong. It's telling you that it's different than the homeostatic level you've already achieved.

Judy: Ultimately it may be a question of right or wrong, but the issue of where along the continuum you make that evaluation is important . . .

John: . . . and the signal which you labeled as wrong, I'm saying is simply difference. And there is a next step which says: Difference, if acted upon, will require effort. We're going to have to shift our homeostatic level. Now there's two attitudes about that. One, if you're a creature of comfort, you are going to go, "Awww, I don't want to move," unless there's some higher level principle which says, "I've got to move. I'll rust if I don't." The principle of pushing your homeostatic center back and forth syntactically has tremendous support biologically. How do you loose flexibility somatically?

Man: You contract by not using . . .

John: You contract, that is, you pick the perfect value for your state, your class of states and you go, "Oh, man, this is the most balanced thing . . ." and at the moment you make the choice it probably is.

Judy: You've made an investment . . .

John: . . . in maintaining it.

Judy: And those little guys I was talking about yesterday come and gobble up flexibility, right?

John: The Pac-Man?

Judy: It's used up in some other part of the system.

John: So that you use it or you loose it. So there's a meta-rule . . . You've heard some of my meta-rules: Never do the same thing twice. Let me repeat that. (laughter) There's another meta-rule that says there is an inherent satisfaction—not only at the level of direct kinesthetics, because if you use comfort exclusively at that level as the indicator you may never move —there's a meta-level satisfaction kinesthetically to moving. Notice exercise is a twentieth-century concept. A hundred years ago it was an integrated part of our life. That is, we had to work—to do physical labor. Now we have labor-saving devices to reduce our physical effort so that . . .

Judy: . . . people have to exercise. When they get done working.

John: If we get locked in there's no easy way out. That's why there is, at the higher logical level, a rule that says: Exercise the variables that you have decided are critical for your ongoing flexibility and balance. Even if there's no "justification" from the environment for it. I mean, why do people run? Why do people do exercises? It's because there's a recognition at a higher logical level that doing that class of events maintains a flexibility which leads to choices which will pay off, not only in the survival of the organism, but in the enjoyment of the world that we live in. I would even maintain, for example, in dancing or percussion or singing, there is an inherent satisfaction at a higher logical level than the issue of effort expended and comfort achieved. There's something deeply satisfying about moving rhythmically using voice and body which extends into the world outside of the dance studio in obvious ways. And the important thing is the notion of detecting difference without automatically evaluating. Evaluation has to take place at a different logical level than the detection of difference. That is, at the level of comfort, you know, you're never going to do anything. But at the level of the demon that says, "Keep those options open," . . .

I want to meet back here at quarter-to-two since we've run

in a bit—we'll start the afternoon session. I would urge you to find yourself a witness who you can work nicely with. I would even recommend that you shift witnesses—part of what's going on now is I want you to bump into each other a little bit, just as Rosalie and I bumped into each other this morning. We're very different. The difference can lead to tremendous advantages for both of us if we are respectful in our exchange. Because she offered, just as Francis and Curt here offer, profoundly different approaches to the same class of events and . . .

Judy: . . . because the new information is in the difference, right? That's the basic unit of mind. News. News of difference. That's where new information comes from. Remember the well-formedness conditions on acting in the world? You need at least three descriptive positions, that is, three descriptions for synthesis, if you're editing, changing behaviors, or any of that material. And this really fits in with Polya's notions that I read yesterday. It's not even obvious to me that you have to make a discrimination between when lunch begins and when you're doing what you're doing.

I urge you now to engage in an epistemological exercise. The exercise says: Check on the status of your personal reorganization. Have you got this arranged? Are the arrangements done? Are they done for some subset of circuits that you could now exercise? Find some place where you've made the arrangements, or in the case of George: What would be nice and appropriate, George, is to pick an area of your behavior where you're not satisfied with the quality. Get your demons lined up, get your controller in position, use spatial sorting . . . If you watch TaTitos make a move, and then watch almost anybody else in the room make a move, there's an effortlessness to what he does. That came from doing a lot of dancing. So that pretty soon just the thought of making the shift triggers the physiological shift and it's not an overmuscled move; there's an elegance to it. And check your description. Make sure you have all your description . . .

John: . . . especially when you are setting up this level of structure make sure you get descriptions from the demons. Make your arrangements and then answer the question by some dance between first and second attention. In other words, you're testing. One answer to the epistemological question, "How do you know you've got the arrangements made?" is to go out and exercise the functions. So I should be happy to see you all at a quarter of two this afternoon.

LUNCH

John: I nearly had kittens at lunch when Judith Ann and I started discussing all the other things that we need to do so I'm going to step up the pace a little bit. I'll need your cooperation in doing this. There's about a million things we want to do here before we're going to be satisfied, and we've got to do 'em in a loop with you, so . . .

John: . . . feedback time from the exercise:

Woman: I had a wonderful time. Discovered that the places in one demon state that were giving me difficulty were because first attention was trying to do what demon and controller were responsible for . . .

John: Balance.

Judy: That's very nice.

John: There's a balance here which is really an assignment of function.

Woman: The strategy that worked for me in that exercise was the "stopping the world" state where my vision went way out to here and it was all there for me.

John: Bravo. Nice collapse of a couple of techniques.

Judy: We all have those times in our life where we know that we're competent, confident, functioning human beings and low and behold, "I can't get anything done. Why can't I get anything done?" Any time that it gets "too complicated" or "too complex" you're using too much consciousness, first attention—a good indicator that some re-balancing would be useful. What's going on here? Components are not getting sorted out, neither by function nor by logical level.

Robert: You were saying, about nonoverlapping demon states, that there needs to be a controller that's involved with making sure that they don't overlap.

Judy: Yes, that they respect context.

Robert: Now, when I was thinking about it, I was thinking about it in terms of music: singing. I was thinking about one demon state being like rhythm and another demon state being like melody, another one like lyrics, and so on.

Judy: Chunking down.

Robert: Chunking down into that. And then it seemed to me that there was a controller that would make sure they didn't merge and then there seemed to be a need for a synthesizer above that to make into singing.

Judy: . . . where they all merge, as the drum parts make a song.

Robert: . . . where they in fact all do weave their separate threads. I mean I can just do rhythm but I wanted to install some synthesizing part. That really made a great deal of difference to me because I never had thought of it before because I needed a lot of work on this one, I'd clean this one, I'd clean that one up and then put them all together. So I had a controller and above the controller a synthesizer.

Judy: And it's in that sense too that, as I said earlier, it becomes less complex at that point.

Robert: . . . less complex as a result of . . .

John: Well, for singing you only have to go to that logical level. If you want to now exercise one of the subvariables, you'll have to go deeper. But you don't have to handle the multivariables because . . .

Judy: All as distinct units, right?

Robert: The synthesizer I put above the controller.

John: So if we put a synthesizer here, let's say, that covered this much then your first attention . . . We're using the metaphor that identity of self is a function that goes down into subcircuits. You never go past here for singing. Now the notion of nonoverlapping demons is still respected. None of the demons inside of this area of operation overlap. They're used simultaneously, concurrently, parallelly. And also you're respecting nonovelapping in the sense that while you're singing you're not eating. Antonio's example is really parallel to what Robert is talking about. We were talking earlier, he had a similar question about this and I said, "Look, think about it this way. When you first start playing soccer you practice passing, you practice shooting at the goal, you practice team plays, you practice sprints, you practice running." There are subcomponents. Maybe Antonio was always a sprinter. Maybe he always had good peripheral vision, this was something he learned as a kid. But he had to work harder at some other aspects of it. When he plays soccer as when you sing he never goes down to those variables. In a sense, this is an indication that you could use the NLP technology: anchor state *A, B, C, D* then squash them together. But on the other hand you wouldn't want to squash singing and eating.

Judy: Yuck. (Laughter)

John: That really is disgusting.

Judy: Really! That really chokes me up. (Groans)

John: Hey, Thomas, is there any truth to that rumor you were telling me about last night?

Thomas: I think there is. The one about . . .

John: . . . the airplane, yeah . . .

Thomas: . . . Gorbachev and Reagan and Marcos all on the same airplane? No, there is no truth to the following rumor that Gorbachev, Reagan, and Marcos were all on the same airplane and it developed engine troubles. They searched the airplane and found one parachute. They decided to take a vote on who would get to use the parachute. All three of them cast a vote and when they counted them it was fifteen to nothing in Marcos' favor. (Laughter)

Judy: Nope, just a rumor.

John: No truth to that rumor. So, there's an important issue—when do you collapse what we used to call parts or demons and when you keep them sorted. And it seems to me that those decisions are not hard to make when they are mapped onto this structure. I want to go back to George's thing and sort this. As Judy said, it sounds like logical levels. This is similar to what I was proposing when I said I may waver on the edge of which demon I'll commit to, or even which controller should operate in this context, but once, by an act of the will, I move . . . Will is overcoming inertia—when I overcome inertia and I am completely committed. . . .

Judy: . . . considering the consequences—arranging the lifelines.

John: Georgine was talking this morning. She has had good success in working with athletes. She has been invited to address a majority of the European and United States figure skating coaches about her technology. She said to me, "There are times when I don't want to respect context. And there are times when I get so excited about what I am able to do that I just blow people away." I said, "Now, understand, your enthusiasm is a strength. It's a demon that has to be tempered. It doesn't mean that you shouldn't blow people away with your enthusiasm and your fervor and your commitment and your ardent ability to demonstrate by your own behavior what a demonic thing this is that you're capable of doing with people. But you either have to make a decision to respect the context or be prepared to deal with the consequences of not respecting the context. And for me to say that you should do one or the other is to play God." That's substance. That's the so called meta-programs that people have been playing with. Those are content areas. And in so far as you engage in those you're engaging in substance. That's religion. What we are doing here is not religion, it's patterning. It's important to understand you may make any class of decisions you want but as a responsible individual in a culture-free society—funny way to say it—we have certain responsibilities and the responsibility it seems to me that we all have is either make decisions that respect context or be prepared to deal with the consequences.

George: If the issue of will is going to be outside the system then whenever you are going to have overlapping demons it's going to turn out, to some extent I think, to be an issue of will in terms of what you're really committed to. I'm thinking of yesterday. The person I was working with had, when he was with patients in the consulting room he was thinking about his writing and when he was writing he was thinking about the patients in his consulting room. Clearly . . .

John: Standard technical organization, right?

George: Same problem applies, though—which activity is he really committed to?

John: Neither. That's exactly the problem.

Judy: That's exactly the problem and of course the quality of both is diminished by the mix. You're not committed to either state. It's the context, right? If he's with a patient, should he be writing then? Is that the appropriate context to write? How much information from the world of this patient is he losing in that context?

George: So organizing a pure demon isn't where it's going to work. Somehow something else has to happen. I'm trying to figure out how to organize the demons . . .

John: One point of organizing demons with this strategy is that you never have to run across the double tracking situation that you just described. You're describing double tracking. You've heard me give the standard example which gets everybody's experience. So here it is, it's a lovely Saturday afternoon, right? And you want to read this technical report and as you sit there you read the same paragraph a dozen times. Unfortunately, you would even fail a recognition test on what the subject matter is about. Your body is restless. You've been making images of what you could be doing if you weren't reading, . . .

Judy: . . . "go play a little tennis," the little voice says . . .

John: . . . and the result is a reduction of quality in all respects. You're not playing tennis even though you're thinking about it. Your body is restless, it's not getting its exercise. You've just wasted an hour and you've gained absolutely no news because of the noise in the system. That's because you have competing demons. And now you go to the tennis court of course and just as you throw that ball up and you're coming around with this beautiful overhand serve a little voice goes off and says . . .

Judy: . . . "Oh, shit! I have a test tomorrow."

John: . . . "You never finish anything."

That's double-tracking. Now there are occasions where double-tracking is a useful skill. So I'm not saying that you should or shouldn't double track. I'm saying understand the . . .

Judy: . . . contexts and the consequences—the circuits internal to yourself and how they extend to the outside in your lives, in family, business, et cetera.

John: Every human being I've ever met evaluates their experience. Some human beings evaluate their experience at the periphery. They are called "the living dead."

Judy: That insures that no new information gets in. You're never going to know if there was a difference to begin with.

John: Other people wait until they get at least three descriptions before they now make a synthesis and a resultant evaluation. Those people learn—even if they make the choice to persist in the behavior that was present before the three descriptions were synthesized—they learn something about the world. They have not filtered at the periphery. They have filtered at a point where they can make use of the representations. Those people stay alive. Where you filter is important information for you, if you're going to move in a coordinated fashion through the world—for example, how you hook up . . .

Judy: . . . with another unit of mind . . .

John: . . . or with a lot of other units of mind, . . .

Judy: . . . aggregates of mind.

John: The long term effects of overspecialization: I have listened to five cases from you all, since we broke for this morning's exercise, which are examples of people playing arcs in other people's circuits in relationships.

Judy: Filling in the gaps.

John: Again, I don't say that's good. And I don't say that's bad. I say there are consequences of having your own integrity as a unit of mind, that is, when your circuits are complete within themselves. There are activities that require more than one unit of mind to accomplish . . .

Judy: . . . and two descriptions are better than one.

John: . . . and if you have integrity to your own system you will never get caught in the situation of playing an arc in somebody else's circuit. My maternal grandmother, Anna McCleavey, married Philip O'Mara. Philip was the perfect grandfather for me: wooden leg, a factory worker at Ford's plant in Detroit, liked the bottle. This is St. Patrick's day so we can talk about Philip. He liked to drink, he loved to play cards, smoke cigars, and curse. He was soft at heart—all the grandchildren knew that underneath that exterior they could get to him really easily—but boy, what a gruff and amazing man he was to a child.

Judy: He liked to put the dollar bills in his wooden leg, you know, so they had to . . . (Laughter)

John: . . . come and take them—the perfect capitalist move, right? Deconditioning our response to amputation by feeding us money out of his wooden leg. (Laughter) They had a happy marriage for forty, fifty some years. Now can you predict the personality characteristics of Anna?

Woman: Yeah. Of course, just the opposite.

John: Sure. So she was perfectly groomed, courteous, cultivated voice, Mass every morning, the whole nine yards.

There is a phenomenon that I think all of you can find easily in your own experience of the world. If two people, whether it's business or marriage or brothers and sisters, have a close, continuous relationship over a long period of time there is an overspecialization that occurs—unless they are extraordinarily conscious and have a balance system much like the one we're designing. They begin to play arcs in each other's circuits. They represent circuits in one another. Circuits that are in each of them but may atrophy over the years to the point of becoming nonfunctional, just as muscle disuse will cause atrophication. That's different than eutrophication, right?

Judy: Dry up. (Laughter)

John: That's very very good.

Judy: That's eutrophication.

John: So, I have found in working with people who suffer grief and loss, that the finest prognosis, the finest indicator behaviorally . . . You notice that often, when one half of a couple is gone, the other member dies within a short period of time. Others seem to recover fully and live a satisfying life. And this is the difference: Within a week after Philip was dead I heard my grandma . . .

Judy: . . . curse . . .

John: . . . and throw one of the grandchildren out of the house. And she missed morning Mass three days in one week. I cheered in my heart because I knew she would (and indeed she did) live a long and happy life after her husband died. Because she was able to restore her integrity precisely the metaphor we're using by reactivating arcs of her own circuitry which had been played by Philip for years. She recovered her integrity and had a lovely and full life subsequent to her husband's death.

Man: You know what they say.

Judy: Parts is parts. (Laughter)

David: She developed a wooden leg.

Judy: No she didn't . . .

John: . . . but she walked funny sometimes.

Woman: One of the things that I found as I was doing the exercise is that I tend to get confused about how I'm evaluating things. And that's when I get . . . It's double-tracking because I start to evaluate being in one demon's state as inadequate because it's not doing a bigger function which is higher up.

Judy: Next logical level.

Woman: But what was important for me is that I discovered that the controller can help me sort. To say you don't have to worry about accomplishing that piece of the bigger picture right now because you're just doing this one little thing.

It's a kind of permission for me. It's like giving myself permission not to worry about the whole thing at once.

Woman: You keep speaking about logical levels. It reminds me very much of chunking. What specific logical levels are you talking about?

John: The question is, "How do you identify logical levels? How do you move around in logical levels? You know the linguistic rule of chunking up and chunking down.

Woman: I wouldn't mind hearing it again.

John: OK, so I say to José, "Boat. Chunk down, please." Now he has to go internal, which is what he just started to do, and say, OK, there's a set, a category of items in the world called boats.

José: Canoe.

John: And he picks a member of the set, canoe. If I said, "Boat . . ."

Judy: ". . . Chunk up . . ."

John: . . . he goes, "Hm, what is the set of boats a member of? What set is the set of boats a member of?"

José: Things that float . . .

John: . . . or means of transportation over water. Stuff that will save your ass if you are at sea. There are lots of ways to define it. And so it has that flexibility. But nevertheless it's the inclusion relationship. In the organizational structure we're proposing here each demon has an area of behavior in the world that it's responsible for . . .

John: Now, they are all controlled by a controller here who's in charge of this whole area of the world. So the domain of the controller is this whole class of behaviors which is the sum of the behaviors of its constituent demons. Just as the category "boat" covers canoes and rowboats and dories and skiffs and sailboats and steamships and . . .

Judy: A steamship is not a boat.

John: Not to the nautically inclined.

Woman: How is it that you defined . . . ? I think that part of the homework assignment was to find what category fit in what. It's like in color charts . . .

Judy: That's sorting.

Woman: . . . you have different color blues.

John: So the question is . . .

Woman: So the question is how do I . . .

John: . . . you take what's common. This controller is defined by what is common to all the demons that it controls. One category could be social relations. So you want all the demons the demon that connects you to your very significant others, the demon that connects you to your business associates that are significant others in that context, the demon that can make a connection of really powerful identification, on the spot if you need to, with a patient, for example. They all deal with social relations, your relations with other people. I would have a controller who decided which one was appropriate in context. Notice that there are already definitions of difference in context. The demon that runs the relationships with patients is already defined by working in your office or in some substitute for your office. So that's easy. Now you've got to define the context for the other ones to make sure they're nonoverlapping. That's the sense in which you've got to do sorting. And that's a first-attention/second-attention dance. By the way, I keep saying that the formats and proposals come from first attention. That's strictly speaking not true.

Curt was proposing that the first attention goes, "Second attention, give me an indicator of where we ought to go next."

George: Well, let's go back to this issue on social relations, the way you sorted it is by type of social relation, rather than by the sequence of what goes on.

John: That's arbitrary.

George: But that makes quite a difference in how you wind up.

John: That's why I'm insisting that that's a substantive sorting issue. And each of you must find your own categories. I'm calling your attention to a task and offering you an example. I do not intend the example as a format.

It's not my intention to tell you exactly where to turn right and left, where to eat lunch, and when to use the park facilities. There's no adventure in hiking when you know exactly where you're going and what you're going to see when you get there.[6] Honest, folks, the best hiking guides are your feet and your eyes.

I intend it as an invitation for you to use the first-/second-attention dance to discover what the relevant sorting principles for you are. Meta-programs are content categories. You're asking me to indulge in those and I'm going, "No, I won't." I will give you examples to get you started. I will propose strategies to dance between first and second attention. But I consider it to be less than professional to engage in these so-called meta-programs. They're substantive. They are impositions of other people's belief systems on yours. And I will not engage in that.

Carol: It seems to me that whenever I'm interacting with other people in various contexts I would want to be in a passionate state. Because that's the optimal level of functioning. Yet I wouldn't want, necessarily, to be in a passionate state when I rest or when I evaluate. But we always want our demon there so we can be in the present.

Judy: Well, I was talking earlier about comfort. I can get real uncomfortable being comfortable all the time—I really would—and those feelings are not on the same logical level.

Carol: They're not?

Judy: I would be uncomfortable about being comfortable all the time.

John: . . . turning into a slug.

Judy: I mean Milton used to say, "It's too damn comfortable in here." And I'm talking physiology. I'm not talking about evaluation on top of that.

John: You're talking about straight effort, that is, a minimum expenditure of effort, right? If we call that "comfort," just for this discussion, then I am absolutely discomforted by extended comfort in that sense.

Carol: OK.

John: Notice that these have to be different logical levels. I'm applying the evaluation of this demon of keeping me absolutely comfortable. I'm saying, "Ah-ha! No balance here."

Man: No boundary.

John: No boundary. Another nice way of saying it.

Carol: But if the demon is contextualized it won't go into the wrong . . .

Judy: Right.

John: Exactly.

Carol: Then it's just living with passion in every moment, right? (applause)

John: Do you understand how you can be passionate about resting?

Carol: Yeah, boundaries.

John: Remember, when it comes to survival programs, however, there are no contexts which such programs will not interrupt to *ensure your continued safety.* So, that is now a function called self which I can apply to any context.

Some years ago Arch McGill was brought in as the number three man at AT&T before the split up of . . .

Judy: . . . the monolith.

John: When McGill came in he spent some time just wandering around to find out what this thing—this sprawling monster bigger than all but three nation states—was. McGill then went out and did something which I really respect. He went out and hired a couple of dozen people who came to be known as McGill's Raiders. McGill's Raiders had one function and one function only.

Judy: Can anybody guess what it was?

John: "Shit disturbers" was the way they referred to them irreverently.

Judy: Get in there and mess things up. Their job was to throw monkey wrenches into the machinery. To rattle the cages. To dig people out of the various offices they had ensconced themselves in.

John: Now the proposal here is that you would have another sliding function, like self, like survival programs, which would be dispatched from technical staff any time you got reports or indications (and these can be kinesthetic, they can be visual, they can be auditory, they can be solicited, they can arise spontaneously if you set up the system of reporting properly) that there has been no variation in your behavior in a particular context. You immediately dispatch one of your agents of entropy and their job is to go down and just stir things up. Do you understand the importance of that? What is the consequence of *not* doing that?

Man: No surprises.

Judy: No surprises, specifically in the most insidious form possible. If you make evaluations and you push them out to the periphery, soon you have no news of difference upon which you could base any change. And the world seems to be the most perfect of all places. And you begin now to commit the major sin that we commit against each other. Taking each other for granted. And getting bored.

John: And you're dead. They just haven't buried you yet.

Judy: One of the things that I think makes John so different is he doesn't play to his strengths. He plays to his weaknesses.

John: It took me about forty years to figure this out. So if there's any wisdom to it I'd be happy to offer it to you. I'm up here drumming and I hope to get to dance today. I have absolutely no natural talent for rhythm, dance, any of these things. And that's why I chose them.

Woman: It's not taking each other for granted. It's taking ourselves . . .

Judy: . . . for granted, right.

Sharon: It seems like there's a piece in there that would be useful for me to have you make a little more explicit: How do you notice when you're taking yourself for granted? Or how do you know that you need a difference? It seems to me that there are times when I've gone, like you said, "It took me forty years." How do you know at twenty years instead of forty that you need to look at it differently and how do you sort of jar yourself out?

John: Here's an assignment for anybody who thinks that this is important. We're not going to have time to do it within the frame of the workshop so let me give you the sequence of experiences that will be one of two ways of answering that question. What you do is, first of all, you get into the context with someone who you don't know or don't have to ever see or hear again, or with whom you have a solid enough relationship that you have the ability to vary your behavior without them taking it as a comment on the relationship—a feat which is almost impossible in all mammals.

Judy: But it can be done.

Woman: Find some frogs.

John: There you go. Now, pattern interruption—as soon as you detect a pattern or a redundancy in the behavior of another person then you have the ability to interrupt that behavior. By the way, in terms of rebalancing in couples this is an important move. As soon as you notice that repetitious behavior then you can do whatever is not expected in the sequence and you get that pattern interruption. So you have succeeded in surprising someone. Do that a number of times until you really have a sense of how you went from observation to pattern interruption. Then you make a first-attention request of second attention . . . and there's two pieces to it. One is that sometime between the hours of such and such in a non critical situation—not if you're doing heart surgery or something—you would surprise yourself. The second part of the arrangement is that when that experience of surprising yourself occurs, your second attention will automatically mark for you, kinesthetically, the state that you entered from which the behavior of surprising yourself flowed.

Woman: Say that last part again.

John: That you would automatically anchor the state that you went into from which the behavior of surprising yourself naturally flowed.

Sharon: Uh-huh. Thanks. That's the piece I needed.

John: It's a really interesting paradox that you can use first attention to arrange to interrupt first-attention pattern.

Woman: That's where it seemed impossible.

Judy: In the paradox.

John: The other way is triple description. Suppose you did an inventory at the end of a day, or a week, or a month, whatever period you think is appropriate for review. One thing you could do is notice that there has been no variation in your behavior in context *A* for this period of time. So then you call in the editors. By the way, do you notice there's an awful lot of tedious work involved, I mean there's a lot of effort involved in this. Be heartened folks. Practice makes it streamline; you will be able to arrange these circuits to be triggered by the passage of time.

Judy: The same thing that's going on now.

John: The point is to get it sorted out. And then use that state appropriately. So you might even turn it over to second attention and have it determine which demons have not made much variation or which controllers are constantly calling on the same demon and assigning the task to the same controller, etc, etc, etc. Also, an inventory of where your weakness is will tell you what kinds of projects to select.

Alan: So a feeling of weakness immediately puts up a signal, "I need to do this."

John: Not a feeling of weakness—that's a kinesthetic sensation and you're playing to your strength. It's like perceptual filters. How would you know if the difference is not getting in? That is, if you constantly unconsciously choose things you're strong in then you'll never have the sensation of weakness that you were talking about. In addition it's not an adequate signal system—the design principle it violates is the one which governs your oxygen exchange; an excess of CO_2 . . .

Judy: . . . not the lack of oxygen . . .

John: . . . in the lungs triggers the intake of O_2. So you don't use signals of weakness to know where your weaknesses are.

That'll kill you as surely as if you were organized so that a deficit of oxygen in the lungs triggered the intake of oxygen. You could easily get past the lethal threshold and die. Consistent with double description, you use a second variable to evaluate the first one. You never have the police investigating themselves. That's a really important design characteristic. Do you understand how you would never know that you didn't know? As Judy read this morning, the first attention does not know the unknown. In fact, it so little understands the unknown that for it the unknown doesn't exist. The perceptual filter that says, "I'll let no information in in this category," when pushed out to the periphery allows the consciousness to go, "God, things have been wonderful in this area for years now." How many times have you watched and listened to a couple or a friend behave and they are oblivious to things that are painfully obvious to you? But they don't know that they don't know because they don't know. (laughter) And that's the point of double and triple description. It insists that you perceive it from multiple positions.

Woman: There's a second-attention self that you have to use to change the first-attention self. When I start wondering how I should carry out this personal reorganization at first attention, I can't figure out how to do it because it's such a collosal task if approached through the first attention. You've got to rely on second attention.

John: That's how you resolve most of the paradoxes you'll run into in first attention; you go to second attention. Because that gives you a second position.

Judy: Because first attention is so limited. It's just the trickle of all possibilities that ends up there. After all the transforms have occured . . .

John: Closely allied with the notion of agents of entropy is the notion of news. Where do you get your news? In fact, the principle of playing to your weakness, that is, choosing tasks and projects which address your weakness is an example, a meta-example of how you sort for news. Every organism, every culture, that's well organized has a surplus. The surplus is sometimes used to support a priviledged class like a priesthood or something. But somewhere in the system, there's enough surplus that you can now extend the boundaries of self by exploring new areas of the world. And the interesting thing is, you better build a function in that makes sure that you're getting news. A meta-principle on how you choose the news is: Choose the news that's most different from the present state. That is, play to your weakness; play to your undeveloped parts.

I have a puzzle for you. And I'll proceed by way of metaphor. I am fortunate to live in one of the most beautiful parts of the world, the Santa Cruz mountains. Judith and I have a ranch there. We each have our own horse that we've trained ourselves and there are hundreds of miles of trails that we can ride. The ranch borders on a *Refugio,* a timber and animal preserve, so we can ride all over those trails. Lovely. Overlooks the ocean, redwood trees, the whole thing. It's a magic place to live with a magic woman. I'm out riding with a friend who's come for a visit, who borrows Shotsey. You all know about Shotsey. "Needs a lot of discipline, that horse." (Laughter) So my friend and I are out riding through these idyllic settings and we ride up straight up to a fence and we're both sitting on our horses and here's the fence. Overlooking the fence we look beyond and we see the beautiful ocean. And I look at the fence and I look at my friend and I go, "You know, six years I've been riding out here now and when I first started riding out here one of the very first things I ran into was this fence. When I ran into this fence . . ."

Judy: . . . it really made him mad.

John: You bet. And I went, "What the hell is this thing doing in my way?"

Judy: I said, "You can't cut this fence, John. It's not your boundary."

John: And when I ran into the fence I really was outraged that somebody would put up this barrier to my exploration of the world. So when I ran up against the fence, my first response was traditional. "Ehh, cut it!—grumble, grumble."

Wiser voices occurred to me at that point and said, "Well, wait a minute. Consider context. You yourself are a property holder. And if somebody who was not respectful of your property came up to your ranch and started doing things . . ."

Judy: ". . . like cutting your fences . . ."

John: ". . . it would justifiably anger you. So it seems to me that a second description, a referential-index shift, is required." Well, it would have been really discourteous for me to simply cut the fence and go on. And I said to myself, "Well, you know there are hundreds and hundreds of possibilities I have not yet explored on this side of the fence. Seems to me that while I'm solving this problem of being both respectful to context and true to my own exploration needs that I've got wonderful things to do." And so for six years I rode this side of the fence.

One interesting thing about horses is that they are too smart by half, in the sense of representational fidelity—if you ride a horse down a trail and go back a year later and a branch has fallen from a tree and is lying on the side of the path and you're cantering along, you better know how to sort for difference the way horses do because your horse will shy at that thing. Horses are very very good at this sort of thing—keeps them from becoming very clever. I mean they hold eidetic visual representations for a long time—idiot savant kinds of behavior. There's a sense in which a horse never goes down the same trail twice. And in a way that we'll operationalize tomorrow and the next day, I have now learned to reach out and change my sensory filters at the periphery in such a way that I also have the choice of never going down the same trail twice—although for profoundly different reasons than my horse. In fact, we can, together, not go down the same trail twice in different ways at the same time. . . . (pause) . . . It's very confusing.

And now as I sat looking at this fence with my friend, I pointed out to him that this is the balance question—the aesthetic question in my life at this point.

In the aesthetics of your life, how much do you change your perceptual filters so as to stay engaged in getting news, and how much do you confront, challenge, and change the obstacles that the world seems to place in your way? And it seems to me, posing the question seriously might be the beginning of this funny thing we're talking about called wisdom. I happen by predilection to be an explorer so I know I'm going to cross that fence. The only issue is how I'm going to do it, and when, and under what circumstances. But the issue about varying your contribution to new experience, versus directly challenging the world is an outstanding aesthetic question. It addresses the issue of where you get your news.

Judy: Is that how no news is good news?

Antonio: Well, I guess my problem is that I always have a good reason not to cross the fence.

John: I propose that some of the reasons are reasons of wisdom in context and some of the reasons that you don't cross the fence are very much like how some people prevent themselves from expressing their personal genius—by not making the appropriate arrangements or by not being willing to accept the consequences of crossing the fence. And I don't know the answer to that. I'm convinced from the little you gave me that there is some sorting that you could do to clarify your position with respect to some of those fences, some of those obstacles. And I think you would end up deciding not to cross some. But others you could be willing to cross if you did the sorting and made the appropriate lifeline contextual marker arrangements to give you the freedom so that when you cross, you cross with passion . . . and—you know lots about passion.

JUGGLING

OK. We got to do our ten minutes of juggling. Yesterday we did this: We went from here to here and then we went back, right? And then we were trying for an arc that roughly goes right over the top of the head and has a lot more uniformity than I'm demonstrating at the moment in both directions. So remember the state we're after is this one where you're using peripheral vision and there's uniformity to your throwing. You already know the first step which I demonstrated. Today's step is actually the only other thing you need to juggle.

Judy: All you need. It's really true.

John: Because you're never holding more than two balls . . .

Judy: . . . at the same time.

John: Watch. (juggling three balls) Notice where the third ball is all the time. The only time you hold three balls is when you're starting or stopping. So all you really have to do is manage the two-ball problem and then you leave the other one in the air all the time. I'm sure this is utterly convincing to you. (to Judy) They looked really overwhelmed by that explanation. (laughter) Remember the important task is not the physical one; it's sustaining the "stop the world" state while you're practicing. And with their permission I'd like Poppy and Robert and the same crew to do nonverbal coaching again today. So what you're doing today is you're going to throw one and you're going to wait until the last possible moment and throw the other one past it. I demonstrate. Now. So I wait until it's almost there and I throw the other one. And then, of course, reverse the direction. The longer you can wait to throw the one from the hand that's going to catch it the easier it's going to be for you to juggle. You can see this little chunk here because I'm doing it nice and slow. Now see if you can find that chunk inside of the three-ball problem. You see how the two-ball problem really solves the three-ball problem? But today's limit on your training is going to be simple; it's going to be the two-ball problem. Yeah, I want you hungry, that's right. (laughter) Are there any questions about what today's task is? Remember the most important aspect of this is controlling your state. Enjoy your juggling for the day.

Judy: (pointing) Yes, did you have a question?

Man: The nominalization "balance" is . . . I need some help with . . .

John: . . . well, let's do it this way. You want some stability in your system. And you want comfort. Those are a couple of things we talked about. But where do you want the comfort? At what logical level? I can be comforted in knowing that I am physically fit. I mean there's a comfort, not in the direct experience of laying around, but comfort in the sense that I have learned to use my body with skill for certain kinds of physical activities. So comfort can apply at lots of different logical levels. Well, so can balance and stability. So the issue here is where you assign stability. For example, when I move across languages and cultures there's some core me that's the same. But it's not in the circuitry linguistically or behaviorally. The demon states are profoundly different in Italian, German, KiSwahili, et cetera. So there's the sense of stability you want, right? On the other hand, the point of agents of entropy and the point of news is to keep flexibility in the system. The point of the agent of entropy is to come along and push on the structure so it demonstrates a resiliency and flexibility and maintains that flexibility.

Judy: So you keep extending the range of your variables so that you don't stay at one value so that your flexibility gets eaten up.

John: I would say that one of the most important differences between us or between any two people, is just the question that you've asked: "Where do you assign stability?" And: "Where does flexibility occur?" And that is a question of balance. See, you don't want all new news all the time. I go into states where the world is entirely new and I don't know anything. In fact, that is one of your assignments for tonight. I want you to have an experience without meaning.

Man: Is that the same as a meaningless experience? (Laughter)

John: It's not the same as a meaningless experience, no . . .

Judy: . . . they are really profoundly different animals.

John: Let me give you an example. I'm at the IBM data processing building in Fort Worth and I'm negotiating a contract, believe it or not, with a guy named J.R. He's going to execute the training. I'm doing the set up and the contract so that he can go in and execute the training. One of the best team of negotiators I've ever worked with. This team was actually sorted by representational system. There was a guy who sat there listening all the time, the same one who asked all the questions. Another guy sat there in the land of images and whispered things to him. Click, click, click. They were perfectly coordinated that way. The visual guy would listen to the auditory guy ask the questions and he'd say, "Ask about the . . ." And finally the auditory guy turned to the visual guy and he went, "OK." And the auditory guy turned to the team leader and he went, "Alright." And the team leader at this point (this was about three hours into the negotiation) literally shifted his body orientation to face the kinesthetic guy who's sitting there at the end of the table, waited, and the guy said, "I think we should move on it. Feels alright to me." Team leader says, "OK, let's do it." These guys were good. And they didn't know, at the meta-level, how well they were doing. But they knew at the level that counted, namely behavior.

After three or so hours of negotiation we agreed to specifics and then I went down . . . The DP building is one of these interesting perimeter buildings—a shell of a building with a garden in the center. It's all glass on the inside and there's the garden. It's about 12 or 15 stories or something like that. I went into the interior and there was the garden, a pretty garden with waterfalls and I was just saturated with businessese and English and wearing ties and being civilized and all the rest of this stuff. And so, what I did at that point was shift consciousness and became a WaDogo (a tribe of East Africa that I lived with). I was standing there feeling very strange. And before I shifted I had asked my friend, "Look, there was a paper they were supposed to give us. Would you go back and pick up a copy? I want to take a copy home." And he said, "Sure, no problem. I'll be right back."

John: As soon as he left I shifted consciousness. So there I was, a WaDogo warrior in this garden, water . . . , it all seemed pretty nice. Until I noticed this guy who I somehow knew I was connected with, as he moved away from me and walked up to the wall. There was this spot on the wall. And he pressed the spot on the wall and the wall opened. And he walked into the wall and then it closed and crushed him. It closed and went, "ccrrrrrrssssssshhht!" I was horrified. I started looking around to make sure there weren't any of those things near me. A few minutes later, I watched in amazement as the same part of the wall opened and two women walked out. (laughter) Now, that's not a comment about equality or lack thereof. It's just a statement of my perceptions.

Man: Double description.

John: Double description.

Judy: So they're really different. Having an experience without meaning and having a meaningless experience. They're not the same.

John: Do you understand the way that that perception happened? In my world, the one I had committed myself to by going down into my circuitry, I didn't know anything about elevators. That didn't exist along the coast of southern Kenya and northern Tanzania. I witnessed events at the sensory level which had no meaning. That is, they were not associated with any previous experiences and maintained value only at the level of sensory description without any evaluation and any meaning. And, by meaning, I mean the automatic movement in each and every one of us as humans to associate our present ongoing sensory experience with representations of some class of similar experiences internally.

Judy: Your homework assignment tonight is to have an experience without meaning.

John: OK, now Consuella is puzzled by this so I better talk further. Now, if you happen to be so fortunate as to be a polyglot, polycultural, and you can find things that don't exist in your other world here in this setting, then all you need do is make a complete shift—you can actually use the paradigm that I offered you that occurred to me by accident. So some of you are fortunate in that sense. If you don't happen to be a fully fluent in another culture and language or if you can't find enough difference between this culture, this urban setting, and other places . . . For example, Consuella comes from Milano. There are lots of things that are common between San Francisco and Milano. So it may be difficult to find a class of differences there.

John: Jessica, is another approach. (to Carol) Isn't that your daughter's name? Carol has a two year old daughter, Jessica. Have you done the exercise with her?

Carol: I haven't. I will tonight.

John: If you have access to preverbal children it's quite easy. You extend self to identify with the child. Make the first-/second-attention dance arrangement and make sure that the contextual markers, safety lines, all the rest, are set up just like you've been setting up here. And then spend fifteen minutes identifying with that child. The movements, the breathing, the scanning patterns, the orienting responses. You'll have lots of wonderful experiences without meaning. Set up your lifelines, set up your contextual markers—commit to the state.

Susan: Over in Chinatown there's a Korean restaurant where the menu is in Korean and the foods are different.

Judy: It certainly holds lots of possibilities because there are differences there that are different than any differences you've ever encountered before. And that's what you're searching for.

John: The dreaming I propose, is to take one of these first attention representations (pointing to sphere on the board) and go, "OK. What is second attention's representation of a more dynamic, multidimensional nature than this? What could we possibly use as a visual symbol for the kind of organization we're after?"

Judy: This is your own metaphor that we were talking about earlier. This is a sort of skeleton of the thought. And then your task is how to develop your own metaphor around that, how to flesh it out.

John: How do you get your aesthetics into it? So, one alternative to the sphere would be Larry's proposal or one of Bob's figures. Whatever you do, make sure you validate the representation with both first and second attention. There's one other thing that I want to mention in closing. Phil pointed out something really interesting. This morning he was doing this exercise of going to the bridge. When he got done he was talking and he went, "Wait a second." And he said to his first attention, "First attention, what criteria are you using for constructing the various clusters and what criteria are you using for driving the system? What are the major criteria, the well-formedness conditions?" And the first attention said, "Well, security and success." And he was horrified. And he went, "Whoa, wait a second! There's a whole lot of other things I want. I want joy . . ." He had this conversation and got a nice validation from first attention. His question, which was really interesting, was this: who was he when he was talking to first attention?

Group: Uh-huh.

Judy: Ah-ha.

John: And now maybe some of you understand the notion of a meta-model. See, a meta-model simply says go up a logical level. That is, what category could include the last level that we were operating at? He went one level up from first attention. That is, he split first attention.

Judy: Another logical level.

John: He was modeling the modeler and discovering what criteria the modeler was using for running the model.

Judy: Good idea. (Laughter) It is turtles all the way up and down.

John: I'll see you all in ten minutes.

DAY FOUR

Judy: Good morning.

Group: Good morning.

Judy: Did everybody have a good rest last night? Not even close, eh?

John: Have your sleep patterns been changed? (laughter and groans)

Judy: By the way, so have mine.

John: Not mine.

Judy: Not John's, though.

John: I don't sleep.

John: There's a famous Balinese painting that was analysed by Margaret Mead and Gregory Bateson. It's discussed in an article titled, "Art, Grace and Style in Primitive Art in Bali."[1] Gregory points out that one of the characteristics of an aesthetic aesthetic act, whether the result is static—a painting or a sculpture—or dynamic—dance and music—is that the result is static a visual is that it is multidimensional, multifaceted. Notice some of the differences in terms of coding systems. You cannot have an auditory experience that doesn't have some dynamics to it—because difference can only arrive in sequence. But it is possible in a visual art to have static representations.

John: In this particular painting the overt subject matter is a cremation—a very important social, political, and economic event in Bali. Bali is the only traditional culture I've ever visited which has been impacted by the internal combustion engine . . .

Judy: . . . which is no light impact, by the way . . .

John: . . . where they had succeeded in using that impact to reinforce traditional values. You will find these vehicles called *Beemos,* . . .

Judy: . . . little open-air buses that drive around . . .

John: . . . and you sit in the back and go along the highway. Unless you make an express run from somewhere on the island straight down to Dimpansar, to the airport, or the government buildings, you'll find that if you wish to make a trip, say from point A to point B you are obliged to take a *Beemo* from point *A*, you get to point *A*, and the *Beemo* stops and you get off . . .

Judy: . . . get another *Beemo,* go to A_2, get off, catch another one to A_3 . . . , A_4 . . .

John: . . . dot, dot, dot, *Añ,* and finally, *B.* And now if you look at the old tribal/family/political boundaries of the area you've traveled through, you will find that those switch-over points coincide precisely with the traditional division of the landmass in Bali.

Judy: Everyone we met in Ubud—the part of Bali we stayed in—is an artist.

John: The normal socialization process in the part of Bali leads to a competency in dance, in making music . . . . . woodcarvings . . .

John: . . . masks, paintings, or shadow puppets. They distinguish different kinds of paintings by the state the artist is in when the artist does the painting. It's a rich, rich artistic culture. The people we met in Ubud in the normal socialization process have achieved a level of competency in artistry which we would consider professional in our culture.

Judy: Of course the real pros in their culture are different; they are the ones, of course, that excel and go on to specialize in those forms of art.

Judy: I don't know if you've ever seen Balinese paintings; they are incredibly busy. And if it's a *satori* painting—which is a painting that comes already done into the mind of the artist through a special state.

John: In this particular painting—the one Gregory discusses—there is a background which is a pattern of a leaf of a plant which is ubiquitous on the island. And the interesting thing—again, like the claws of the crab—is the proposal of uniformity which comes from the edges of the painting using the leaf patterns *and* which is defeated perceptually as the artist subtly introduces variations toward the center of the picture. There is a subtle proposal about the absolute symmetry and uniformity in the claws of the crab which is defeated by the difference in scale between the two claws. This defeating of the proposed symmetry leads to a certain tension within the perceiver which is in part the artistic value of the painting.

We happened to be present when one of the princes of one of the old families of the island died.

Judy: Big party.

John: Cremation is a joyous occasion. Cremation is the only way in which the soul of the dead person can be liberated so as to continue on the cycle of reincarnation. You will find situations where families—because of the expense of the cremations (the outlay of money is tremendous relative to their incomes)—will actually bury people in the earth for a period of time until they can put together adequate money for the cremation. They will disinter the body at that point and cremate it.

Judy: Now this ceremony was for one of the old princes. Think of a tropical setting . . .

Judy: . . . not a very big island.

John: . . . but lush, green. Temperatures running in the eighties, nineties. Humidity is up in the eighties. And a gathering of two or three thousand people—right outside the temple where the bodies were in residence before the cremation started. They built a tower for the cremation which was forty feet high and the base was forty feet on a side, a square. And this was carried by eighty men. It was made out of bamboo —a very light material. However it was strong enough to carry an . . .

Judy: . . . an entire gamelan . . . or Balinese orchestra.

John: . . . on the cremation tower, on the bottom section. The tower of course was quite high. Now you have to be careful about demons in Bali. They have a different kind of demons than the ones we've been training here.

Judy: They have to make a run to where the cremation will take place, actually running while carrying this structure.

John: They had men with axes in front . . .

Judy: . . . cutting trees down . . .

John: . . . all along the boulevard because this was such a large tower. That's the only way they could get it out to the cremation site . . .

Judy: . . . it was so wide.

John: Imagine the gamelan sitting on this thing, eighty men carrying this tower on bamboo poles, and a crowd of two or three thousand people jammed into the streets. They pick it up and they tilt it and they whirl it around and start to run down the boulevard.

Judy: And every time they come to a crossroads they have to tilt it and whirl it around, just to throw the demons off the track.

John: Why? Because demons can only travel in straight lines. (laughter) Hey, you laugh. A good friend who is a fine gamelan player . . .

Judy: . . . who lived in Bali studying with the master musicians had gone in front of us as an advance party to make arrangements for our group and had constructed an outdoor pavilion, a thatched roof area with earthen floor and open sides, where all the gamelan instruments could be kept.

Judy: Now this had not been blessed yet in the official Balinese way so our host Ketut Madra made a request that no one play the instruments until the following morning when we, and the instruments, and our whole program, and what we were going to do had been blessed . . .

John: . . . by the local priest . . .

Judy: . . . in the Balinese way.

John: And our friend went into the pavilion the evening before, just to tune up a little on gamelan. Within a few moments the instrument he was playing broke and he so severely cut his hand he was unable to play gamelan for some days afterwards. So God, like nature, is not mocked in such situations. And deviations from certain classes of behaviors are always compensated for in some way or another.

Judy: Trance is very highly valued there in Bali. One of my friends who was there wanted to make a complete entry into the culture and wasn't exactly sure how, specifically, to do that. She was playing around a little with the language, she had made some Balinese friends, but she hadn't yet met her needs for entering the culture. We were getting ready to go to the funeral and I had mentioned to her—because we were all dancing as well as playing music every day—that little girls are taught to do the dances from the time they are very small; their parents start to mold their bodies in those positions that will later be the dance. I told her that I had read in Bateson about how very often at some point in their training the little girls would start to dance and they would go into a trance and fall down. And their mother or some older woman would pick them up and put them back in the body position that they had just been in. Then they would remember and continue to dance on through the dance.

John: From that position.

Judy: From that position.

John: Direct kinesthetic programming. Those of you who've been trained in our certification programs in hypnosis know that this kind of a movement (demonstrating) is typical only of unconscious kinds of states.

John: The movement of the hand and arm to the face under normal states of consciousness and the movement in the altered state—which is a good indicator of the depth of the altered state—are profoundly different kinds of movement. Clonus (the small, rather jerky, uneven movements) is built into many parts of the dance—every dance that I witnessed in Bali. Thus the dance itself contains physiological requirements to alter state.

Judy: So I told my friend to consider trance itself as a way, . . .

John: . . . an entry point, . . .

Judy: . . . into the culture. So we went to the funeral; it goes on all day long and it's a very happy affair. I'm sitting on one side of the road and I look across to the other side of the road and there's a pavilion bigger than a bus stop. And there are probably a hundred women in there. The gamelan is playing and there's a lot of chanting going on. And I look over and see my friend; she's dropped into a trance and fallen over . . .

John: . . . committing so completely that she temporarily lost her balance . . .

Judy: . . . and when she came out of this trance she found herself sitting between the legs of an old woman who was holding her up and my friend had a baby sitting in her lap. No verbal communication at all. When everybody got up to run down the street with the funeral party, they just grabbed her and took her with them. She ended up at somebody's house that night having a feast, and never uttering a word . . .

John: . . . but communicating quite well.

Judy: . . . and making friends that she enjoyed for the rest of her stay there.

John: This particular painting that's analysed in *Steps to an Ecology of Mind* by Bateson has a number of interesting features to it. It makes the point that any aesthetic act is a multidimensional affair. Artists resist anyone assigning meaning to their production. Although it may indeed have meaning in the sense that the critic or the commentator propose it doesn't have *only* that meaning. That is only one of a number of meanings that the piece of art has. This painting is particularly amusing in this regard. It shows a tall funeral tower and the leaves and the trees and so forth behind it at the top of the painting. In this particular school of painting in Bali it takes six applications of paints—which they prepare themselves—in order to get the kind of translucence that these leaves have. And as the leaf pattern comes closer to the center suddenly the symmetry, which has been uniformly distributed at the edges, begins not to be quite as symmetrical. As in the case of the claws of the crab, a symmetry, a uniformity is proposed and then pushed slightly off balance as a way of capturing attention . . .

Judy: . . . knowing the rules and bending them.

John: Now, as Bateson says, there are several interpretations to the painting. First of all, we could consider it a painting of a cremation because that's what the overt, manifest content is.

Judy: Or a statement about the social life in Bali. In Balinese culture, stability is not achieved by a solid foundation; it's achieved by mobility at the bottom. In one of the dances a small, prepuberty girl will stand on the shoulders of a man and balance there, holding on to the man's hands. The girl is typically in a deep trance and, in fact, directs the man by leaning. As her weight goes forward, in order to maintain the stability of the entire system, the man has to move under the weight—like a good cutting horse moves under a rider. So that at all points the stability of the system is based on mobility.

John: The reflection of that in the painting is that the lines in the painting are sharply defined at the top of the painting but there is a fuzziness, a lack of resolution, a lack of division, at the bottom of the painting which could, as Gregory pointed out, be interpreted as a commentary of the social structure of Bali. This in fact is perfectly parallelled in Balanese culture in that the lower castes shift, balancing for the upper castes as they lean in one direction or the other. There is yet a third description of this painting. If you step back and forget you're looking at a Balinese painting the cremation tower looks like a huge phallic symbol. And the foliage and the trees at the upper part could easily be seen as female genitalia. So this work could be interpreted as being a sexual commentary as well. However, the thing that makes it a piece of art, according to Gregory, is the fact that all three of those interpretations, and perhaps more that he didn't comment on and I couldn't consciously find in first attention, are available to the perceiver whether or not they ever enter consciousness. Every aesthetic act is a multidimensional affair.

The Balinese know how to do something which makes them unique in my experience; they know how to finish things. They are the only people I've ever met who know how to finish something as well as they know how to start it. This is true in their social relations; it's true in their art. For example, in playing the gamelan you strike with one hand, dampen with the other and how cleanly the sound is dampened is as important as how cleanly the sound is initiated. Typically, in music in our culture, the attack is the focal point; a certain consideration is also given to duration. In Balinese music the cleanness of the damping is as important and is what often distinguishes more accomplished players from someone who plays more casually.

Judy: And the gamelan has an interesting organization; the person least trained at music and most self-conscious about what they could do . . .

John: . . . initially at any rate . . .

Judy: . . . was the person who was given the critical part.

John: There is what is called a "God gong." If you complete the arc that I'm making with my arms, a very large gong this size (gesturing to indicate a gong about three feet in diameter) that hangs from an ornate structure.

Judy: . . . and it never touches the ground . . .

John: . . . and it is struck with a large mallet . . .

John: . . . and sets the time signature for every other instrument in the gamelan. It was immediately assigned to the least musically sophisticated member in our group as a natural part of the affair of putting together a community of gamelan. Not only that, our fine teacher, Suecha, taught to the fastest learners in the group . . . There was a group of three or four of us that had, either because of committtment, or the ability to control our trance states, or because of background, quickly developed a fine learning strategy for this class of instruments and could move relatively fast. He taught to that subset of our group. And when members of the group who were experiencing the traditional Western frustrations about not being able to keep up with what he was teaching approached him requesting a separate session where they could catch up, he turned to the whole gamelan, the whole group of us, and said, "No, that's the responsibility of the other members of the gamelan." So, by deliberately teaching to the strength in this case, he forced a coming together of the group so that we ended up playing twice as much gamelan each day; we would spend an equal amount of time before he arrived teaching the members who hadn't been able to master what he had taught the day before, exactly those melodies and sequences.

Judy: Another beautiful thing about the gamelan is that there is a part for everyone. Everyone has a part.

John: And each of those parts are equally essential to the overall production of sound which is the sought-after experience for gamelan.

Judy: I had a teacher at U.C.S.C. once. I was very lucky to have this man as a teacher. It turns out that this is the biologist who was running the Oceanic Institute in Hawaii when Gregory Bateson was doing his dolphin research there. I just took bonehead vertebrate biology which I assumed was going in and learning ten weeks of Latin-based taxonomy and much to my surprise it turned out that while we did have to spend some time learning the Latin terms of classification, classification was not what this teacher did. He started out as a desert biologist. I think he came from Arizona or New Mexico somewhere. He said that he used to take graduate students out and sit on a fence to watch lizards. And he would say, "All I want you to do is watch what these lizards do and write it down in a notebook."

John: Inventory, first-attention inventory.

Judy: Pretty simple. And he said he would sit on the fence with the graduate students. Plenty of lizards to look at, no problem there, and they would begin to write. And after two hours the graduate students would get done. They would have about two pages of notes. When he'd get done, he'd have twenty pages of notes. Now what do you think the difference was?

Woman: He saw with new eyes.

2nd Woman: Chunking well.

3rd Woman: Precision.

Judy: Yes, all those things, and in his words, "Those graduate students were thinking in their minds about what the lizard was supposed to do."

John: Descriptions they had arrived at by reading other people's reports prior to the experience.

Judy: Thereby missing what the lizard was actually doing. It turns out that this same man becomes the number one marine biologist in the country after being a desert biologist. There had been a lot of theories for a long time about the sperm whale, you know the giant organ, the spermaceti organ in the sperm whale, what that was for. There were several theories to account for its function. I don't remember what all the theories were—one of them which was ballast; they thought it had something to do with ballast for deep diving. They don't have very many sperm whales that sort of wash up on the beach so they could check it out. But one day one did wash up and they called this man immediately and said, "We've got to figure this out, we've got to come up with some decision about which of these possible theories is accurate."

Judy: So he shows up. What does he know? He knows the context in which the whale lives. And he knows—he's looking at the anatomical structure right in front of him as he opens up this dead whale's body—to look at the structure of this organ and try to make a decision about what its function is. And he begins to put clues together. He goes, "Hmm, at one end of this structure . . ." He called them monkey lips because it they look like a circle with lips. It could make noise there. And at the other end of this giant organ there was a membrane that sound could bounce off of in this huge thing of liquid inside this giant organ which fills thirty-five percent of the whale's body. It's enormous. So he says to himself,

"That's a perfectly good noise maker." So he maps, literally, from the environment, the context, to the structure of what's there and develops a theory of function which turns out to be correct. It's a sounding mechanism. Now one of the things that made him such a good biologist was that if you gave him a context and you gave him a function, he could probably make a real good guess about what the structure was like. If you gave him a structure and you gave him a function he could tell you what the context was—by being able to map across.

John: Notice that with practice, a double description, if the perceptual points are chosen properly, allows you to make really intelligent guesses about a third perceptual position which you could then seek in the world. Perhaps the best antidote to hard-wired beliefs in the perceptual filters is the ability, not only to make interesting guesses, but to take the guesses seriously enough to go back to the world and seek evidence for or against the hypothesis which you formulated, iteratively, recursively, again and again and again. But those two things are not in and of themselves adequate to protect yourself from becoming part of the living dead. There's a third principle involved here. The third principle is that you seek a counterexample. That is, if you understand the notion of perceptual filters, whether we're talking at the level of the distortions of consciousness as second attention is mapped into first attention, or you're thinking all the way out to the periphery of the class of summations that occur in the optic nerve as you move back from the retina toward the central nervous system. Recognize that over time that your beliefs, the hypotheses you formulate, if you go seeking confirming information, will structure the input by perceptual filters in such a way that they are band-pass filters that will not allow information of difference to pass.

Judy: Difference is what makes a difference.

John: You could die with dead flies all around you. (Laughter) The first time I ever ran across the counterpart of the receptors for bugs in the frog's eye was a really brilliant example.

I met a woman in a workshop who could walk into a field of clover and return within sixty seconds with a four-leaf clover. And it was quite obvious how she did it. Even she was explicit. She formulated in her internal visual system a template, a silhouette of what a four-leaf clover looked like, emphasizing those features which make a four-leaf clover distinct from a three-leaf clover. And she would simply go into a mixed state where the template, as it were, was pushed out to the periphery, so no reflexive consciousness was required (far too complex for first attention to be involved) until there was a match of the template she had deliberately set up (notice, using first attention to make the arrangements) at the periphery with the coincidence of the same form from the environment. Her ability to do this with refinement led to this rather extraordinary and amusing talent she had of being able to find four-leaf clovers.

Judy: Now I have an older brother who is a real naturalist—one of these guys that can go out and look around and say, "Yep, right about over there." Then he'll walk over and start kicking the dirt around and find arrow heads. And I asked him one day, "How do you do that?" And he says, "All I'm looking for is anything different because my eyes are so thoroughly trained to see what is normal in this environment," where he lives, in Missouri, the areas that he goes to, that he just looks for difference. Actually he says, "I make a rapid scan of the area to see what is out of place or does not fit with what I know. When I detect a difference, I examine it more closely."

John: Notice he moves around as he looks for difference. That is, he adopts different perceptual positions. If you can do double description, your epistemology is at least superior to that of a jackdaw. (laughter)

Judy: Konrad Lorenz is a famous animal ethnologist, behaviorist.[2] There is some beautiful research he's done; he sounds like a real amazing person in a lot of ways. One quality that really intrigued me was his apparent ability to communicate with animals. He is able to extend the boundaries of self with animals in a really phenomenal way in that he comes up with amazing information about the possibilities in those worlds. And that when teaching, he can draw an animal on the board with great precision and by changing some little aspect of that drawing . . .

John: . . . a small arc of what he's drawing . . .

Judy: . . . a picture of a dog being in a submissive posture, just some very small change will change this dog into an attack posture. What's interesting is that he cannot draw a human figure. He can only draw stick figures for humans. I think that's a interesting puzzle. Consider the primitive cave drawings. Primitive man could draw pictures of antelopes and other animals but only stick figures for people.

John: So, I'm sure you're delighted that you have reached an epistemological status superior to that of a jackdaw.

Woman: What's a jackdaw?

John: A jackdaw is like a crow. A large raven-like bird that Lorenz did lots of research with. There were a couple of interesting things he found. And by jackdaw epistemology I mean the following: when jackdaw A wished to signal to jackdaw B (when Lorenz was approaching the area that they were in) that Lorenz was not to be trusted . . .

Judy: Jackdaws disappeared, somehow, when Lorenz was about. (Laughter)

John: So given a jackdaw epistemology, it became obvious to the jackdaws that . . .

Judy: . . . this guy eats jackdaws.

John: Now, here's the problem: If you were a jackdaw and I were a jackdaw and Judy had the reputation of being a jackdaw eater, how would you signal me if I were naïve, that she was a jackdaw eater?

George: I'd try to eat you.

John: So you, as a jackdaw, would make movements and gestures and communication analogically toward me as if you were trying to eat me in the presence of Lorenz. There's no doubt that you've achieved an epistemological position superior to that of a jackdaw because what jackdaws uniformly do is they attack Lorenz. They demonstrate their own perceptual position in the relationship and there is no indication in their behavior that they can switch referential index—the underlying move that you made in order to offer me the signal that he proposed. They can only occupy one side of the loop, the side that nature has placed them in in this niche, in this relationship to other parts of the environment. As Gregory says when your cat brushes up against you . . .

Judy: . . . it signals, "Dependency, dependency." (Laughter)

John: Would you like to elaborate on that? (Laughter)

Judy: Not me, that makes me crazy.

John: How many here who have had pets—say, dogs and cats—have ever had a dog or a cat come up to you and take its paw and stroke you? Really! Then you certainly have epistemologically sophisticated animals in your homes. The cats that I've watched come up and will push their body against yours in precisely the way that they want you to touch them. Not from your perceptual position of stroking, which would mean they would bring their paws up and stroke your body as they wish you to stroke them, but they move their body against yours as if you were stroking them so as to call for the complimentary response, namely that you would reach down and stroke them. "Dependency, dependency."

Judy: We have a little cat called Echo. And for a long time I tried to get Echo to go down to the corral with me. It's not very far but some cats don't like to get too far away from the house or other protective cover. They're outdoor cats but still they don't like to get too far away.

John: This, by the way, is one of the pitfalls of having a single reference point, single-description epistemology.

Judy: So over time, the cat learned to follow me down because the sequence was I'd feed the horses, and then the dogs and cats are fed, so they all would get excited as soon as I'd start to go feed the horses. So this cat would always go, oh, about halfway down and then she would run back. She wouldn't go all the way down but each day a little bit further, a little bit further. This took a long time; we're talking—about a year. Finally she got all the way down and immediately walked up to the horse and started to rub up against the hind legs of the horse which scared the horse who then punted her about sixty feet. She'll never go back down there. (Laughter)

John: Because, like Kenge coming out of the rain forest, "The air is bad, the earth is bad and I'm not getting out of the car until we leave this place." (Laughter) Single-perceptual positions lead to really hellacious and restrictive kinds of epistemologies. There's a Swiss psychologist by the name of Jean Piaget who has done some quality work with children, especially on the development of epistemological structures. His claim is that there are interesting developmental sequences where there is a correlation between language development and certain other kinds of symbolic representations, such as patterns which occur in arithmetic or physics, where children learn conservation of mass, conservation of energy. According to him, the signal that a child has achieved adult maturity in terms of its cognitive development is that you can hold up an object like this, show the child both sides of the object which are different colors and then after the child has examined the book adequately you can go, "What color do I see?" Now what this requires is two things: Memory, both storage and retrieval, and more importantly . . .

Judy: . . . referential-index . . .

John: . . . shift. What is presupposed by this, in terms of the NLP technology you are familiar with? It requires double description and the ability to understand, from what is available, what my perceptual position must be. It's the medicine wheel again.

Judy: Or having the structure and the function and figuring out what the context is. Or having the context and the structure and figuring out what the function is.

John: Is there any evidence, anywhere in the animal world, for referential-index shift, for achieving second position?

Karen: I have a story that fits so beautifully into what you're saying that I'd like to share it. I have a friend who's a biologist at Brown University who has gotten quite a bit of attention recently for his description of the evolution of wings. He used to work at Berkeley and began by looking at the paleontological imprints of insects with "vestigial" wings—ones which did not work for flight. Maybe some of you have seen the research. It's been in *Scientific American.* His question was, "How did the insects go from having these little buds to having something that allowed them to fly?" People have been studying this and wondering why did insects begin to fly. His genius came in broadening out the frame of his question with respect to function—what could be the use of those appendages? And what he finally discovered was that it was not in order to fly that the wings were developed but rather in order to absorb more heat which gave the insects an evolutionary advantage. It could reproduce better and it could survive in an environment which was cooler and it was only a secondary consequence that the insect indeed began to fly.

Judy: When the wing surface got big enough it got lift. That's great.

Karen: So what he had to do is think outside of the function of the wing in order to discover how it got there. Which I think, again, is taking another perceptual position.

John: Double description. "What other possible function can this thing have?"

Judy: So if you take a sea urchin cell, just fertilized . . .

John: . . . first division, . . .

Judy: . . . two cells, . . .

John: . . . what could be more fragile?

Judy: You poke one cell. Do it in . . .

John: . . . destroy it.

J & J: What do you get?

Judy: Half a sea urchin?

John: What the hell good would half a sea urchin be, George? —you couldn't even put it on sushi. No, You get a complete form.

Judy: You get a whole sea urchin but it's one-half the size of a regular sea urchin.

John: If you wait until the four-cell stage—two divisions—and you destroy one, two, or three of those cells you get a correspondingly reduced but perfectly formed sea urchin.

Judy: This is from *Biology: The New Science of Life,* by Rupert Sheldrake[3]—my candidate for agent of entropy in biology. He goes, "Hey, let's mix it up a little bit." "How about all these things? Nobody knows about this. Nobody mentions these things." How do you get a giant one then, John? (Laughter)

John: You take two sea urchins—that's right—and do a visual squash; integrate them. (laughter) It'll be twice as big.

Woman: That sucker's going to have you for sushi. (Laughter)

Judy: . . . and it works. You get one twice the size.

John: Perfectly formed. Laws of form, laws of form. Regeneration phenomena: You take a newt and you pick some trauma that would be unlikely to occur in a natural setting except by the most unlikely and fortuitous possible circumstances—for example, you excise the lens of the eye from the newt.

Judy: Within a month . . .

John: . . . a portion of the cornea has extended itself and a new lens is produced. There's no apparent diminution of quality of vision in the newt.

Man: Doesn't the bee have a referential-index change when it comes in and communicates to the other bees where the flowers are?

Judy: . . . when it does the wiggle dance?

John: I think that it's always oriented, not to the spectators, but relative to compass direction. So I think not. I will tell you the only one I've found that comes close and it's really interesting. There was a man named Köhler[4], a German researcher who got stranded on the Canary Islands during the First World War—stranded in the sense that the islands were cut off by marine embargo from Germany, his native land—and . . .

Judy: . . . there were chimpanzees there at the Primate Study Station . . .

John: . . . so he took the opportunity to do primate research and found some fascinating things.

John: Now there can be no doubt about the existence of internal representational maps of the quality and type that we have in our representational systems in other species—the Umweg problem for dogs, for example, where you have a very hungry dog and you show that hungry dog food on the other side of a barrier which he can't directly cross. The dog will have absolutely no problem finding a way around the obstruction.

Think of the presuppositions that are involved in finding the way around the obstacle—a detour whereby the organism has to move away from its goal in order to reach it.

John: There's a discontinuity in cognitive sophistication in the bird hierarchy as indicated by their behavior.[5] Take a situation like this, where you have a room where there's an escape hole in the roof so that birds can fly to the outside. You take a transparent screen—say, chickenwire—and you line it from ceiling to floor along the long axis leaving an opening at the far end. Then put the nests of the birds that you wish to study here immediately next to the escape hole but separated from it by the chicken wire. You've created a situation similar to the Umweg problem in that the most direct route has been blocked. . . .

Both species used the same initial search pattern. They would fly directly into the wire and discover that barrier . . .

Judy: . . . and then start to circle . . .

John: . . . flying in an expanding spiral in a systematic exploration of the environment . . .

Judy: . . . until they would find . . .

John: . . . the way out. Now the interesting difference between these species emerged on the second day. One species, the starling, I believe, flew directly out and around the barrier the second day.

Judy: Yes. The other species had to go through the same sequence that it went through before every day.

John: Back to the Canary Islands. In the Canary Islands research Köhler[6] constructed a situation where along two sides of an open quadrangle were cages for the chimpanzees, and one day Köhler and a couple of his coworkers, in full sight of all the chimpanzees, at noon on day one, marched out to a randomly chosen spot in the quadrangle, in full view of all the primates, dug a hole, took this beautiful stalk of bananas, put it in the hole, and filled the hole with earth leaving a little mound of dirt marking the place where they had buried the bananas. The chimpanzees were engaged. (laughter) The researchers waited until late that night and verified that all of the animals were asleep. Then they went out and carefully moved the mound of dirt to a second randomly chosen spot in the area making sure that none of the animals had witnessed this act of deceit. Then the next day at noon, twenty-four hours after the initial information had been offered, they took the chimpanzees one by one out of the cages, denying the other ones visual access by shielding the cages so they couldn't see the activity of the chimpanzee undergoing the test, and released them one by one into the quadrangle. In every case the obvious occurred—what you would predict. Seeing the mound of dirt the chimpanzee would run to that position in the yard, frantically dig a certain depth . . .

Judy: . . . no bananas. What a drag . . .

John: . . . and would sit there (laughter) and finally after a period of time would be removed from the area and a new chimpanzee would be brought in. But one of the chimpanzees did a really astonishing thing. It went through the first part of the trial, ran pell-mell to the little mound of dirt, dug futilely for the bananas that weren't there. No bananas. Sat there like the other chimpanzees looking around and thinking about it. (laughter) Did all the appropriate chimpanzee things . . .

Judy: . . . and then what do you think he did?

John: Anybody got a guess as to how this one solved the problem?

Woman: Did he go back to his cage and . . .

John: Yes, he plastered himself against the cage, assuming a perceptual position quite close to the one he had occupied the day before—I'm sure if an NLP-trained person had been there he or she would have seen pupil dilation (laughter) or a movement of the eyes up and to the left—ran along a direct line from that position to the unmarked position in the yard where the bananas were buried . . .

Judy: . . . found those bananas . . .

John: . . . and pulled them right out. (applause) I'm not sure how to interpret that. (referring to the applause)

Judy: The things that you can do on an island during a war!

Marshall: Did he really run for governor of the island?

Judy: No, the monkey did.

John: So this report supports in a rather dramatic way the contention that other species do use internal representations. Now the one possible counter example I know of to the claim that there is no referential index shift in animals occurred during this same period of experimentation. They created a situation like this. (drawing on chalkboard)
There was a simple enclosure and on one side of the enclosure were bars that ran halfway down the wall and then there were solid walls on each end. On the other side, over here, the facing side of the box, were bars that ran all the way to the ground. They fastened a stick on a chain here to the half wall side of the box. They took the juiciest bananas they could find and they put them down inside the box close to the half wall side so that the animal could not reach the bananas by extending its arm from this side. Since the bars went to the ground on this side had they been able to seize the bananas from this side they could have dragged them over and easily eaten them. And they watched what happened. And of course there was the usual reaching futilely from both the open side, that is, the side where the bars ran to the ground and from this side as well; in both cases all such attempts were unsuccessful. Then the chimpanzees began to play with the stick trying to use the stick to bring the bananas up from this half wall side,

also futile. There was a solution and one of the chimpanzees found it. The report goes something like this: "Chimpanzee holding stick, was looking at bananas, had stopped prodding them, was holding the stick and looking at the bananas, looked up over the bananas to another chimpanzee who was on the far side, took the stick and pushed the bananas away from him to the chimpanzee on the other side—who was then able to seize the bananas, ran right around and the two of them ate the bananas." Now that's as close as I can find to an example of referential-index shift reported in experimentation in other species.

I'm claiming that one of the three characteristics that distinguishes us from other species, and, for better or for worse, makes us dominant on the planet at the moment, is reflexive first attention. Or more specifically, first attention can model not only second attention, it can also model itself. This is called reflexive consciousness. And in particular, I know of no evidence anywhere in the literature on animal work, that indicates that they, like us, can not only build models, but can build models that include a representation of the modeler, that is, themselves in the model. That's the distinction which defines reflexive consciousness.

Now notice what occurs when you are able to do that. If you seize that opportunity, one, you never have to do anything for the first time in the real world. You can rehearse it, prepare it, work out the kinks internally. You yourself, through disassociation of this nature, can become your own planner and coach. That is, you can mentally rehearse before entering the context in question; you can try different patterns of behavior in the hallucinated internal context: you can select the classes of events that you actually wish to participate in in the world We've already talked a lot about the costs of reflexive first attention. It becomes so fixated on itself it dismisses the unknown because it can't know it. And so it becomes important in our work here to distinguish three kinds of attention now: Second attention as we've always talked about it, and then two kinds of first attention—reflexive first attention where you are disassociated and generate representations which include representations of yourself, the representer in the representations, and first attention proper, which is that sliding definition of self that you can use to extend or shrink self in different portions of second attention so as to achieve 100% passionate commitment—when it's appropriate and you judge it to be so in the context you're operating in.

John: Here's a puzzle for you. How long do you think any mammal—pick your mammal—can survive without drinking water.[7]

Tom: Kangaroo, kangaroo rats don't need water.

John: Kangaroo rats don't need water? Are you crazy? Ever?

Jack: Ever.

Judy: Even if you give them watermelon seeds?

John: In fact, not far away from here at Stanford University they proved exactly what Tom and Jack are telling us. Desert kangaroo rats do not need to drink water. Not only do they not need to drink water . . .

Judy: . . . they won't bother.

John: If you put nothing but dry barley seed in their cage—no water—they can live an indefinite amount of time, a full lifetime, on just dry barley seeds and no water. And 65% of their bodyweight will always be water.

Judy: If you take them, put them in another cage and give them nothing but watermelon and watermelon seeds, they'll still be 65% water.

John: Now there are a couple of really fascinating adaptations they have made. One is the fact that in their natural environment they are entirely nocturnal so that they never expose themselves to the high grade evaporation environment of the daytime desert.

Judy: They stick pretty close to home. They don't travel too far either . . .

John: . . . never more than a couple of hundred yards even at night. The humidity in their dens runs roughly around 60% with a mean temperature of around 75° Fahrenheit. They have an advanced kidney system. The maximum nontoxic level in humans for urea in urine is approximately 6%. And in the desert kangaroo rat it's 24%—400% of what we can achieve without toxicity. They do this by means of an organ that's sort of a satellite on top of the kidney called the Organ of Hinley?

Judy: Loop of Hinley, I think. Is that right, Jack? Does that sound right?

Jack: We have those too.

John: We have part of them? The efficiency of the system is obviously different. But how the hell do you think they maintain 65% body weight water with absolutely no water intake?

Judy: This is a wonderful question.

Woman: Do they recycle it?

John: Yeah, absolutely. However they can't recycle any more than they get and they're getting none.

George: Oh, there's water in the barley seeds.

John: 13 parts per million or something.

Woman: What about light?

Judy: Well, they're nocturnal. Is that what you mean?

Woman: Alright so they're nocturnal but if their cages were lighted and they did not have the opportunity to be nocturnal could they maintain 65% . . . ?

John & Judy: They do.

John: They do. At 75° Fahrenheit, 60% humidity.

Woman: What do they eat?

John: Dry barley seeds.

2nd Woman: They'd have to synthesize it—hydrogen and oxygen!

Judy: Hydrogen and oxygen.

John: There you go.

Judy: They oxidize; they make their own water.

John: They oxidize their food and when they oxidize their food the natural by-product of oxidation is H_2O. Adaptations. Flexibility.

Judy: My favorite one is the cheetah[8], you know, and all the adaptations of muscles and bone that allow it to run so fast? There's also the adaptation in the spine. The flexibility in the spine is so great that without legs the backbone could move at six miles an hour; it's got that much flexibility.

Woman: How did they test this?

Judy: They had an old cheetah named Slinky . . . You go like this and let it go. (Laughter)

Philip: What are the other two things that make us unique as humans?

John: I like somebody who keeps track of numbers like that. I'm claiming one is the ability to model ourselves, to create a very special class of representations: representations which include a representation of the representer—what in NLP we normally call disassociation—where first attention is modeling itself.

John: I have an obligation as the teacher in this context to remind you that disassociation has a price. It can be cost effective and it is, if you remember to tie a knot in your handkerchief.

When you disassociate, it should be an act which is validated by an automatic program you've set up with first-to-second -attention cycles. You've essentially made an arrangement from first attention that second attention will automatically kick you out of a situation where you need to be in a disassociated position in order to cope effectively.

Judy: And it's also another perceptual position that you can learn a lot from.

John: And I'm thinking even in terms of professions such as the medical profession. If you're going to assist at the scene of a tragedy where there are other people injured. Your ability to identify with and extend self to include them at that point is not only useless, it could actually impair your competency in dealing with the situation. To feel what somebody who is injured is feeling as a way of helping them is not very helpful. To be able to automatically disassociate and take the class of actions you've learned are appropriate for saving that individual's life is.

Alan: Is that dissociation or just a limiting of the self?

John: Disassociation is a function. When we're sitting at dinner having an intimate conversation we're very much sharing circuits, in the sense of working together. I can disassociate from the other person and withdraw the definition of self to include only the circuits which are minimally required for my integrity, or I can extend it. There's a second sense of disassociation which is a disassociation from the normal circuitry but at a meta-level. We've talked about going down inside the circuits to become demons. The other end of the continuum is to disassociate from the circuitry that supports us. That is, limit self temporarily to be an observer in an outside position. Your editors, for example, have this quality.

Judy: Right. That's when you model, when consciousness can model itself . . .

John: . . . reflexively. So they are both classes of disassociation. So disassociation can also be usefully thought as either extending or shrinking self, that dynamic function we've been playing with.

It reminds me of R.D. Laing. He once gave a definition of repression as forgetting something and then forgetting that you forgot it. And when you do that it's very much like a perceptual filter that you've pushed out to the periphery. You don't know the difference because the difference is blocked so far in advance of second attention or first attention. How could the world be any different? It's the problem of not knowing what you don't know. If I were to propose fostering a quality in your work I would say that not only to know what you know but more importantly to know what you don't know. That's how you essentially move throughout the world rebalancing yourself by playing to your weakness.

Judy: It's where you find the edges too.

John: So the cost of disassociation is in some way to become less human, I think most humanists would say. If it's done with the proper knot in your handkerchief, so that you don't forget what you've done, you can step back into a fully associated, participatory, spontaneous, warm state and participate fully as another member of your community in a fine and deeply satisfying manner. How often, in your work in business, Phil, do you run into men and women who by the pressures of business have learned to disassociate their kinesthetic system and have forgotten how to get back? They're trapped. They're trapped at the top end. They can't get back. They certainly could but they don't know how.
So that's one, the one I already talked about. The second one is humor—and I say that laughingly. (groans) The third one is almost as amusing it's syntax. It's one of the first distinctions we drew in this seminar. I know of no examples of communication systems in species other than ours which are syntactic. Now there's a huge caveat that goes around this discussion that says, "How the hell would we know . . . ?"

The lack of overlap in the range of our sensory receptors . . . —when was the last time you had a meaningful exchange with a termite?

Right, an epistemological caveat. It's through our neurology anyway that such information would have to pass . . . I know of no evidence for any communication system in other species where the sequence of the signals makes a difference in the meaning of the message. On day 1 we talked about the pair of sentences:

The cat chased the rat.

The rat chased the cat.

There is no specific place to point to the difference between them. As a matter of fact I gave a misleading representation there. He said the difference in meaning was a result of a difference in the sequence of words. That's only part of it. Notice, that's linear thinking. That's a first-attention statement. What is the context that this has to be referred to? And the context, as de Saussure,[9] a Frenchman from a hundred years ago, pointed out that words only have meaning in the context of other words, that is, by contrast. So "The cat chased the rat" and "The rat chased the cat" are profoundly different in the sense that their sequences are different, their meaning is different. There is a tendency to attribute the difference in the meaning to the difference in the sequence only (as I did the other day); but that has to be put in the context of what other sequences are well-formed in the language. So notice I can say, "John took his hat off," and I can say, "John took off his hat." They mean the same thing. They have a different sequence. So not all sequence differences lead to meaning differences and the study of what sequence differences lead to equivalent meanings and what sequence differences actually make a difference at the level of meaning is one of the things a syntactician does in the analysis of a language.

Judy: What about negation?

John: I *don't* want to talk about it. (Laughter)

Judy: That may be a difference too.

John: How does any other species signal negation? How does a dog say, "Let's not fight." No, see if a dog goes into submission posture it is making a positive statement. It's saying, "I defer to the dominant animal."

Man: So they will do anything else.

Woman: But it's a positive statement.

John: OK, but when you do anything else you have not mentioned the thing that you wish to communicate that you are not going to do.

Man: So if the other dog says, "Come on, let's do this," in a sense, by its behavior, and the other dog chooses to do something else, is the negation.

John: I accept that. But the point is that neither dog has said, "Let's not fight." A dog has said, "Let's fight," and another dog has walked away to do anything else. I can say, "Let's not talk about this any more." Now we may talk about it or not talk about it but I've communicated effectively what I set out to do.

Judy: We can negate our representations. That's the issue.

Marshall: The dog would bare its teeth and then it would move back. It would start in attack position and then it would counter it with a nonattack position.

John: That's the classic analysis. That is, a part of the whole attack sequence is offered but there's something not quite right about it; it is either reduced in intensity and/or other parts of the attack sequence are not presented.

John: It draws a line, in Bateson's sense, through a piece of instinctual behavior. What a remarkable accomplishment! It has digitalized or chunked-down internal to a single line of behavior. Notice the entire sequence is iconic; it demonstrates the part-for-whole relationship.

Man: So the dog doesn't negate the message. The dog acknowledges the message.

John: The dog that offers the bared teeth . . . It mentions the possibility of attack and then does not carry through on it.

Judy: If you think about the whole escalation, the whole behavioral loop would be the fight. He mentions it and stops it.

John: The Nobel Prize goes to whoever of you can figure out how you get from that to negation—digital negation in language.

Alan: That pattern is often used as a warning though, by animals.

John: So there's an ambiguity in the message even. Not only that, notice that animals could make a horrible mistake. If you happen to pick the first signal in the instinctual sequence there is no reason for the other dog to withhold its response; it's part of the loop. So part of the condition for the dog effectively choosing what part of the sequence to use as the signal is to use anything but the first or the last part of the sequence. So, being out of sequence is another way that is typical for passing this class of messages in other species. Now if I say to you:

The cat chased the rat.

how do you know what that means? I've used an auditory-digital representation and everybody here who is fluent (native speaker and non-native speaker alike) understands what that means. How do you know what that means? What event occurs internally that allows you to seize the meaning? What is meaning in this context?

Man: Internal representation.

John: So you access some class of internal representations. How many did it visually? Hold that picture for a moment. Put it someplace so you can bring it back in a moment because I want you to tell me how you know the meaning of this representation:

The cat didn't chase the rat.

What in particular is the relationship between the first picture and the second picture?

Woman: Movement. This was . . .

Man: . . . static, yeah.

John: OK, so in one case you have one that shows the movement —the cat is chasing the rat—and the other one in which they are in the same position but stopped.

Group: No.

John: Or are they sitting side by side?

Man: I have them going in opposite directions.

Judy: Wrong turn.

John: Do you have them going in opposite directions?

Consuella: I have a slash mark across them.

John: A Batesonian! (applause) How many people got a big X across it? How may people stamped some other symbol over the top of it? Now, do you understand the difference between the cat sitting down or running in different directions as opposed to the overlay, the slash mark? . . . pause . . . Logical level difference.

Judy: International traffic symbols.

Alan: Could you develop that? I didn't quite get that.

John: So notice that if I offer sentences with negations to George as opposed to Robert as opposed to any of the rest of you, my intended meaning, that is, the class of representations in me from which I generate the auditory message, the digital message, is not the one you receive at all.

Woman: Say that again, please.

John: The implications of the representational difference between the visual images of animals running in opposite directions versus the cat sitting and watching the rat go by (or whatever other variations on the theme fall within that class of pictures at the same logical level) mean that the meaning that each of you create is in a deep sense profoundly different both from what I intended and from each other. If you are looking for a place where there is tremendous slippage in communication, here it is. The point I'm after, however, is that those differences in the picture are differences at the same logical level. That is, George saw the cat chasing the rat, movement, and then he saw the two animals with movement running away from one another. You (Robert) took the movement out. You (referring to another group member) took the movement out of half of it, the relationship. Those are profoundly different representational maneuvers although they're all at the same logical level. Now Consuella is going "slash" across the original picture. The previous representation is held constant and the entire proposition is negated by a logical level move one logical level higher than the actual picture—the original representation.

Alan: So it's worth getting explicit about, is that what you're suggesting?

John: I'm not saying it's worth anything at the moment except noticing that it defines a well-structured piece of research which will ultimately be a critical part of the study of the distortions induced by the interface between language and the primary representational systems—in this case, we've focused on the loop:

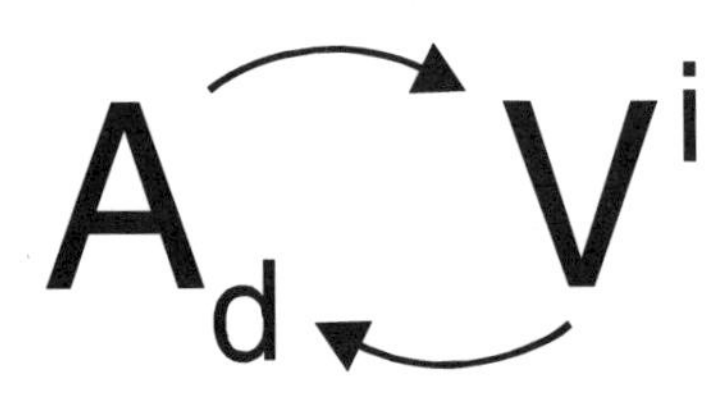

Epistemology is the study of the sequence of dynamic transforms connecting the world with our models of the world and the language/representational system interface—surely one of the most accessible and least appreciated in the sequence of transforms. An explicit model of the distortions, the transforms induced by this set of mappings, language and consciousness is badly needed—consider, for example, the consequences of what we have just discovered relative to negotiations at the international level. Who knows what representations Reagan or Gorgachev has when the other says, "We will not attack you with nuclear devices!" Does the other access, consciously or unconsciously, images of the other one attacking with biological agents, or conducting an economic attack, or representations where the USSR is not attacking but China is—or what. Without some epistemological work, we are on totally shaky ground—and the consequences are unacceptable.

Consciousness and language are going to continue to be used to interface between me and you in a community, and in the world, for making making decisions. If there is to be any wisdom, some respect for context, then it is incumbent upon us to elucidate the specific distortions induced by these classes of transforms. As far as I know, we are better qualified than anybody in the world at this moment to accomplish this task. And here is a difference which is profound.

Judy: Just one. There's a lot of them.

John: We're operating in the same language. What happens if we move across languages.

Judy: Yipes!

Woman: How does putting a slash across the picture make it a different logical level?

John: How? Yes, how. That's what I'm asking you. What is the difference between removing movement from the image and putting this slash over the top . . . ?

Rosalie: Difference in perspective.

Woman: One is from outside the position.

John: One is a manipulation of the representation so as to change it within the representation, to remove movement—a manipulation at the same logical level. In the other one you hold the representation constant and put a marker over the top of it that says, "Not this." It's a digital move. It's a shift in logical levels.

Judy: Isn't epistemology fun?

John: Trisha.

Trisha: John, isn't that really more pure because . . . ?

John: I don't know what "pure" means in your sentence.

Trisha: So Consuella came up with a picture; she slashed it, negating the picture. Several others of us didn't achieve the cat not chasing the rat without the cat and rat in another relationship . . .

John: . . . doing something else. Exactly. Thank you. That's well said. The relationship that George got and the relationship

Robert and Marne got were profoundly different and that's the sense in which we never understand—we don't access the same class of representations—in responding to verbal messages. And negation is a very powerful demonstration point in this area.

Woman: The part that I have the question about is how did that, when you said, "The cat chased the rat," and, "The rat chased the cat," how did that line negate that because that picture was still going on even though it had a red line through it?

John: Because you put a marker over it from a different logical level—like the knot in the handkerchief—that said, "Not this."

Judy: Or the way I think about it it says that this is the loop: The cat is chasing the rat. She goes to the next logical level.

John: This loop, this relationship, does not exist—slash!

John: There may be other loops and that's what George and you, Marne, and Robert and the rest of you who had different kinds of pictures at the same logical level, chose to use as the way of representing negation. That is, you are saying, "Some other relationship." It's very close to the baring of the teeth.

Woman: I don't understand how that negates the picture.

John: I believe you don't understand that.

Judy: But you will.

Alan: So it seems that with one system then there's a clearing out. In the other system you have an alternative. But, like one goes to avoid proposing an alternative. And the other one, an alternative . . .

John: . . . and the implications of which kind of thinker you're talking to in terms of how you formulate your verbal communication is critical. Take a child. Here's a little five-year-old boy carrying a glass of milk across the living room and mom says, "J.T., don't spill it." We have claimed in our work on second-attention logics called *Patterns of the Hypnotic Techniques of Milton H. Erickson, Volumes I and II* that the unconscious, what we're referring to primarily as second attention here, does not compute negation.

Judy: Don't think of blue.

John: . . . or green.

John: You know how much more powerful and smooth your relationship with your children goes if you go, "Would you go outside and see if the apples are ripe on the tree?" when they are doing something that's making you crazy in the house rather than, if you say, "Don't make noise," if you say "Don't . . ." you have offered no alternative. Or the class of alternatives you have offered are too closely allied, like visualizing the cat and the rat running in opposite directions instead of running in the same direction. There's a lot of evidence that this is one of the most important parts of the distortion of the imposition:

John: Another classic imposition of syntax on our experiences, another distorting function—a transform—which comes out of the structure of language which has nothing to do with the structure of the world although we act as if it's the world we live in.

John cut the tree down with an axe.

The linguistics tells me that there is an agent, an active principle, John, who is using an instrument, an axe, to cut a stationary, nonparticipatory object, a tree, down. Nothing could be further from the truth from other perceptual positions, from second and third descriptions. If I were a mathematician and were interested in writing equations that predict the future behavior of the tree, the axe, and the man alluded to in the sentence, "John cut the tree down with an axe," I could write an equation that made John's movements the dependent variable specified as a function of the location and depth of the notch in the tree. And it would be as precise a representation and epistemologically as sound as the sentence, "John cut the tree down." Because at every point, the axeman's movements and the movements of the axe are determined by the last cut in the tree. So you can punctuate the sequence at any point and hopefully you're beginning to understand how language is a particularly dangerous case of violating the well-formedness condition of having double descriptions. And how important it is to have alternative representations.

Judy: What's happening Consuella? Ahhhghhh!

Consuella: When you asked us to represent the sentence, "The cat didn't chase the rat," I didn't get a picture. I said "all other possibilities."

John: You said that.

Consuella: I mean, I heard that. I switched from visual to auditory.

John: Now one of the ways to make sure you get double descriptions is to switch representational systems. Now, when you say "all other possibilities" you simply have brought up a file that says, "Now, depending on any other cue in context I may go into this file which is all the other possible relationships." That is a logical level higher, like the slash, but it's in a different system—a different logical type—so you get the advantage of a separate perceptual position altogether. . . .

Judy: . . . see-feel or hear-feel, that you have to bring in the other component in the system.

Woman: I had an experience similar to Consuella's. It occurred to me that my representation of "The cat did not chase the rat" was one possibility out of many. I knew that there was a cat and a rat and that what I did not have was a relationship.

John: Right.

Woman: And my tendency would be to fill in a relationship.

John: And that's the tendency that George bought, that's the one that Marne bought, that's the one that . . . Right. Nice.

Kari: I got a dissolve.

John: So it just faded. So that's like "Anything else."

Georgine: The point about negation—I'm familiar with the fact that children will have a negative polarity if you say, "Don't do that."

John: No-no, they're just obeying the part of the instructions they hear at second attention. They don't compute the negation.

Georgine: They don't compute the negation. So, for example, if you say, "Don't do that!" . . .

John: They'll do it.

Georgine: . . . the child hears, "Do that."

John: Right.

Georgine: How would you classify the opposite pattern where for example a teacher or parent says, "Let's do this," and the child literally has the opposite experience?

John: The growth of an independent personality. It's a different logical level, I think, of functioning than the level of deciphering and decoding and digital communication. The Russians did a series of exercises with children. They created a situation where they gave a child—usually just about four years old where mastery of the verbal language was tentative—a single button to push and two lights and they said, "If this light goes on, press this button as fast as you can. And if this light goes on, don't press the button."

Judy: Well, we can all guess what the consistent results were. The reaction times were almost the same for both lights. They couldn't not push the button. Think of it in terms of physiological muscular precepts in a developing organism. It says, "A stimulation from the outside! Act!" And it didn't matter which stimulation even though they knew the difference at a cognitive level. By setting up the tension in the body—the expectation—the stimulation arrives and that was all the trigger they needed. They didn't differentiate behavior.

Woman: So, with this in mind, a sign that says, "Don't drink and drive" will not have the same effect as a picture of a car and a martini glass with a red circle and slash through it. Would the iconic representation be more powerful?

John: In terms of eliciting what?

Woman: In terms of eliciting behavior . . .

Judy: People not drinking and driving?

Woman: Right. Because a visual sign you see this is the combination, now cut the circuitry for it as opposed to the words written out.

John: I can guess but I don't have enough experience. I think it's an interesting question. In fact Benjamin Whorf was at one point in his life a safety inspector. Whorf was a linguist who had an appreciation of the class of events that we're talking about. Whorf was a salesman for a while and a safety inspector in factories and pointed out "nonflammable," "inflammable," and "flammable"—what the hell do all these representations mean? He gathered some information that indicated that accident rates in factories would vary depending on which representation was used.

The Russian child stimulation problem . . . There was a man in Charlotte Bretto's certification program in South Carolina who did a similar application. Remember the opening exercise typically conducted in certification programs to develop sensory acuity where you make subtle discriminations between different sounds, feelings, and visual inputs? This man went to a factory and taught a short-term conditioning program. They were having the following problem: there was some kind of geared machinery that they were operating. And the sound of the machine changed when something was caught in the tines. And people would have a reflex movement to try to clear the tines. Of course, they were losing fingers and hands and so forth. He went in and taught them, conditioned them, to take one step back whenever they heard a change in the whine of the engine; he got a phenomenal reduction in injuries by that simple conditioning technique he took out of the first weekend of a practitioner training. See, in the Russian experiment the child had to do something. If the child had been given two buttons or if the child had been told, "When this light goes on hit the button. When that light goes on, touch your forehead," . . .

Judy: . . . it would have probably worked.

John: So the second characteristic is humor and the third is syntax. And there are worlds upon worlds to be explored here. And I'm quite serious when I point to us as a group of people at this historical moment who, to the best of my knowledge, have more tools, and tools with more precision, to explore these mappings—mappings which involve the distortions which, according to Gregory, have in large part resulted in the ecological crises, both at the social as well as the environmental levels.

Judy: Where are the epistemological errors? And there's a whole lot of territory before you get to any boundaries, I'm sure, that have not been looked at, listened to.

Alan: I've lost the thread for a moment. Are these the three things that . . .

John: . . . distinguish our species . . .

Alan: . . . from other species?

John: Somebody touch him. Touch him. There we go. Reality strategies again. (Laughter)

Alan: Are we talking about the price you pay for dissociation?

John: No. You're talking about the price that you pay for disassociation. (Laughter and applause)

Alan: Go on, so what . . .

Judy: . . . the three things that distinguish us as a species from other species. One of those is the ability to dissociate there is a price that we pay for that dissociation. Syntax is another. Humor the third.

John: There's an interesting argument about the cost of insulating ourselves from the wisdom of our heritage. In Castaneda there is a situation where Carlos is taught to access his experience as a hunter as a boy. As Judy said he had an uncle who had a chicken farm . . .

Judy: . . . a Leghorn chicken farm . . .

John: . . . and he used to hunt hawks. Later, in this state, one of the things that don Juan noticed was, as I said, there are various forms of self-indulgence. One of the forms of self-indulgence that Carlos really was remarkably, astonishingly adept at was overidentification, or what we're calling "extending the self inappropriately." So he would indulge himself by becoming confluent with parts of his environment and could not differentiate himself. Now, that's a gift, that's a gift that an artist has to have. That's a gift that a woodsman, a hunter needs but there's a lot of professions where you can't do that for some aspects of the experience; you're not going to be successful in your movement through the world if you do. The trick of course is to know when you are indulging yourself and when you are using these tools appropriately.

John: So he has Carlos construct a trap and successfully trap a rabbit. And then he tells Carlos to kill the rabbit with his bare hands because it is obvious to don Juan that Carlos is indulging himself by overidentifying with the rabbit. There is a legitimate relationship, as we as humans have set it up, especially in the Yaqui culture, that you always take only what you can use to respect the ecology of the system that you're in, never more than you can use. The predator-prey relationship is an acceptable and wise relationship in the world. There are lots of ways to think about that. The squeamishness, because of the overidentification, the extension of self, which is inappropriate is another thing. Hunting, in a respectful fashion is very appropriate in that context.

Think of the ritual dances in cultures preparing for the hunt. Among the !Kung San, the bushmen of the Kalahari, and many other hunting tribes, the hunters do a ritual dance before they go on the hunt. What position do they occupy in the ritual dance?

Man: The prey.

John: It's called sympathetic magic by anthropologists. It's a lot deeper than that; it's the ability to access the class of representations which the hunters will need to conduct a successful hunt. They accomplish this by becoming the prey.

Judy: Carlos was a hunter as a boy. Don Juan says, "Well, what do you mean you can't kill this rabbit? You killed hawks. You killed all these other animals. Why can't you kill this rabbit?"

John: Now Ardry, and Lorenz to some degree, would also point out the cost of disassociation—the serious danger of attendant upon technology because of removal of the context and its loss of wisdom—in this case by the removal of signal systems. In a wolf pack, when a wolf bitch wants to wean a pup, and the pup comes around for lactation . . .

Judy: . . . nosh . . .

John: . . . the female, will press her head down on top of the pup's head pinning the pup to the ground. Doesn't injure the pup. But this is the signal consistently used for weaning purposes.

In the case of a wolf pack, sexual access to the females is one of the "rewards"—it depends on how you think about it, I suppose—that the dominant male in the pack has. Again and again and again it has been observed that if one of the other males is caught in intercourse with one of the female wolves in the pack and the dominant male comes along, he does not attack the wolf that is so engaged. He does not injure that wolf. He uses the same weaning motions to press that adult male's head to the ground as a signal between the two. Having gotten the reciprocal signal in return—the submission signal—that indicates the violators acceptance of the relationship, nothing further is required.

Woman: We don't need war any more.

Judy: Well, I believe that.

John: Well, if you are sitting in a silo or flying at 70,000 feet how the hell do you get the submission signals that say it's unnecessary to push that button or drop that bomb

Woman: . . . before you launch a strike.

John: I don't even know anybody over there. How could I get those signals? And that's one of the dangers resulting from breaking our link with context by insulating ourselves with technology. It removes the wisdom of thousands and thousands of generations of our heritage.

Judy: There was a real simple case when I was learning Greek, having conversations in Greek. One of the things that my Greek friends thought was really amazing was that people here don't know where their food comes from. And that was a real phenomenon for them that many urban Americans don't know where their food comes from.

John: Everybody knows it comes from the supermarket.

Judy: Right.

John: I could never understand how they grew cans on trees like that, you know.

Man: You know, if we understood how it got to the supermarket, what they did to it . . . (Laughter)

John: Packaging, right? We'll I don't know—it might be a problem for a little while. Then it wouldn't be a problem at all.

Judy: Let's take a break.

John: Ten minutes, folks.

BREAK

John: Notice, the notion of disassociation becomes a much more general function now. We can disassociate the reflexive consciousness as in the traditional V-K disassociation. You can disassociate through representational system sorts; you can dissociate from higher levels of mind to go to subcircuits in order to become a demon. So dissociation becomes a very fluid function in the system that we've created here.

An easy example: We were sitting in a Japanese dry sauna. The thermometer read 195° Fahrenheit in there . . .

Judy: . . . and we had a bucket of water, a little bucket of cold water in there . . .

John: . . . and when it got to the point that it was so hot that we were going to leave but we wanted to stay a bit longer we just put our feet, one foot each, in this cold, cold water . . .

Judy: . . . and self went there . . .

John: . . . and we lived in our feet. And we weren't hot. Now that's an example, a very physiological example, of shrinking one's first attention. That is, taking this function of first attention—dropping reflexive consciousness altogether—and then collapsing the first attention into a very limited subset of our circuitry, going down inside the subcircuits to find only the class of subcircuits which had a temperature we wanted to live at. We lived in our feet for the period of time that we wanted to stay in the sauna and we could, with ease, remain in that tremendous heat without any discomfort.

David: That's where your sole was. (Groans)

Judy: Milton would call that cheapo ambiguity.

John: No-no, he would have loved it. Actually Milton once wrote Richard Bandler and me a letter. Betty Erickson had written us asking, "Would you please explain the dedication in Volume I of *Patterns*?" and then she offered her interpretation. I only remember part of it. We dedicated it to this, to that, and thirdly, "to Mazda (the car for people who can hear)," If you drive a rotary-engine Mazda, the pitch centered in the efficient range of operation of the rotary engine (3,000 rpm more or less) is almost exactly the same pitch as you hear when people go, "Hm-mmm," as in, "Hm-mmm, let's see." So if you are sensitive to that class of sounds the sound of the engine constantly puts you in a visual access mode. Mrs. Erickson had this much more aesthetic representation about Mazda being the god of light in the pantheon of the Persian gods. And so in response we wrote her an interestingly ambiguous (laughter) letter using Ericksonian patterns. And immediately got a chastizing letter from Milton who pointed out . . .

Judy: . . . that's not the way Betty thinks . . .

John: . . . and in thinking with a linear thinker you think linearly as a respectful way of approaching them and with a nonlinear thinker you think nonlinearly a matter of respect—again, there are obvious exceptions in terms of stretching the other person in an appropriate and respectful fashion.
We were appropriately—I, at least—was appropriately chastized. I don't know if I've ever seen Richard appropriately chastized. (laughter) At any rate, Milton added this little line at the end of the letter that said, "You two boys remind me

of a loaf of bread." That's right. And so the next time we travelled to Phoenix he said, (imitating Milton's trance voice) "Did you understand what I meant by 'a loaf of bread'? A loaf of bread is made up of two heels and it's crummy all the way through." (laughter) He was right. In that particular context he was absolutely accurate.

Judy: Yeah, he was a crusty old man himself. (Laughter)

Woman: When you . . . ?

Man: He really toasted you guys. (Laughter)

John: (to woman asking question) This is going to go on for a minute or two, you might as well wait. (Laughter)

Judy: All disassociations have to be re-integrated.

John: All the circuits have to be run.

Man: Don't butter him up with that one.

2nd Man: You may need some penicillin for this.

John: That takes a double thought.

Woman: When you put your two feet in the bucket did you notice any shift in your physiology?

John: Yeah, I got real cool.

Woman: Did the sweating stop?

John: My sweating stopped. Because I was in the bucket of water. I noticed the rest of the circuits that I had left behind were sweating as profusely as ever. And it was indeed my intention not to interrupt that because that's part of the point of the sauna.

Judy: Part of the process.

2nd Woman: With your feet in the bucket, what takes care of the rest of your physiology. I mean, is there a point of risk?

John: Absolutely. Any disassociation involves risk.

Kari: I was thinking about how, when we dance here, I experience absolutely no pain and no fatigue and was aware of the disassociated state facilitating that. But when I do aerobics, just dancing to the same old popular music every time, I do experience fatigue at times and I don't enjoy that state. So I generally do shift my attention; instead of thinking about my legs which are getting tired and worn out, I think about what my hands are doing, how my fingertips are getting blood in them, and it's marvelous.

Judy: When you reassociate later are you sore?

Kari: No.

John: See, that's a phenomenon worth tracking. Those of you who are interested in finding out whether levitation occurs— How is it possible for somebody to be cataleptic for hours and experience no muscle fatigue? What's that? I don't understand that. I've done it myself, I've done it with other people and I haven't a clue what it is. The epistemology of disassociation of body parts, is astonishing in terms of its physiological effects.

Man: Is that part of "stopping the world"?

John: It certainly involves "stopping the world," yeah.

Kari: When I think about being disassociated from my body that means that I really don't have . . .

Judy: . . . feedback from your body?

Kari: Yeah, I don't have the feedback from my body. But when I'm dancing it's like I focus so that I decide to use up my conscious . . .

Judy: . . . chunks . . .

Kari: . . . chunks in a particular place. But I'm intimately in that place.

John: . . . you're associated in that particular place and you dissociate from the rest.

Kari: . . . I'm totally associated. I'm really in the dancing; I'm dancing, I don't feel pain, fatigue, whatever. And when I'm partially there I feel it. It's like . . .

John: Kari has found herself already making the passionate commitment to the artform Kongolese dance, here. When she does aerobics it's repetitive. Predictability makes a hunter the hunted. Predictability causes fatigue. Predictability, even at the physiological level, means that you are exhausting the same circuitry. Part of an artform is that it is not highly repetitious.

Judy: . . . and it is most efficient.

John: Now, she handles the fact that she is not 100% passionately committed to aerobics—as opposed to "Afrobics" (laughter)—by shifting from one part of her body to another. So she goes to her feet as we did in the sauna, she goes to her arms, she goes to her lower back, she goes to her pelvic region, she goes to her calves, as a way of staying invested, of not quitting at that point in time. Runners can tell you lots about this sort of thing. Now what you're talking about is the same class of commitment we're saying is true of any demon state. You don't know fatigue, you don't know any of those things unless you're using a comparison. Entertaining representations not only of what you are doing but also of other things you might be doing instead of what you are doing. You are partially disassociated, you are not passionately committed to that moment. As you achieve the ability to make 100% passionate commitments to demon states, which, we're saying, means that you go from the center of the sphere . . .

Judy: . . . of the sphere and operate only out of those circuits, like our example of living only in our feet in the sauna—in this case, only living in part of your body without representations of what else you could be doing, whether you are now tired, how long you've been dancing, did the drums just . . . Those are meta-comments—intrusions from a higher logical level—which take you out of the state of being passionately committed. Now, as you become better and better at those kind of commitments, it becomes more and more important that the Viola Legere contextual markers and the priority survival programs can interrupt your demon states. You could hurt yourself badly otherwise. And you wouldn't know it until the value of the variable had become damaging to your physiology.

Woman: So, in doing aerobics, if you are disassociated, the potential to harm yourself would be greater.

John: . . . unless you set up the priority programs that break your demon state. That's why good athletes have the ability, not only to disassociate, but to have priority programs that say when certain thresholds are reached they had better pay attention to them. They're not athletes long if they don't have that.

Judy: The strength and the control and the balance and the artistry . . . , the lightness that Titos has as a dancer are absolutely amazing. We put him on a trampoline once; he didn't like it. He had had no experience of moving surfaces. With all that lightness, with all that strength, with all that ability . . .

John: We took Titos down to the horses. As a boy in the Kongo he had seen lots of cowboy movies and to him the horses were really astonishing. See, none of the west African tribes that I know of have a relationship with large animals like we have with our horses. Judith Ann and I went down to the corral with him and while we were brushing the horses and putting on the bareback pads and the headstalls we started explaining to him about horses—what you do and what you don't do, real basic stuff. He listened for a couple of minutes, then he turned to Judy and said, "I have to go into a trance."

He walked away, went into this deep six- or seven-minute trance, reorganized his experience based on what we had offered him, and introduced into his personal history—I'm guessing now, but the trance was obvious—the possibilities of another kind of relationship with an animal this size. That was the first move. That got him into the game. He then watched very carefully and had this moment of enlightenment as he watched me canter my horse around in figure eights in the corral; he went, "Oh! You're dancing with the horse!" He then got on and rode bareback with a level of skill that you would anticipate would require months of practice.

Judy: Then he took the horse out and ran the horse and that's something that he'd wanted to do since he was a little boy.

John: We came to a nice, long, gentle uphill grade. I said, "You ready?" He said, "Yeah," and I led off in a canter up the hill and as I got up there I turned back to make sure he was doing all right and reined my horse in. He came up and almost fell off the horse because he was laughing so hard. He was only four years old at that point. (Laughter)

Judy: He had on his African robes and a cowboy hat. It was wonderful. (Laughter) He took pictures to send to his mama.

John: His mama thought that was pretty amazing all right.

EXERCISE: BLIND MAN EXERCISE

John: We have a little exercise; it's not a difficult exercise but it's one that has tremendous learnings available. We have the three-foot sticks, right? We have some sticks and what I want you to do is get in pairs and either using an actual blindfold, or keeping your eyes closed . . .

Judy: . . . on your honor . . .

John: . . . I want you to go explore your environment using the stick as only a blind man or a blind woman must. Now there are several points to this. One, I'd like you to discover—by requesting from first attention to second attention—that first attention can be invited down to the class of circuits necessary for you to move with safety, without visual means, substituting an extended tactile sense, through the environment. And I'd like your babysitters to set up problems for you once you've had the chance to play, that is, to take you to some part of the environment and stay close enough that you're safe . . .

Judy: . . . not the swimming pool.

John: I don't know how involved you want to get. You might discuss the constraints you are willing to operate within. And what I'd like you to do is to explore strategies for accentuating—shrinking, in one sense, yourself, by removing visual input; and extending, in a second sense, tactilely and auditorially and olfactorially—your way of mapping your environment so you can move with safety through your surroundings with this special condition available to you.

Judy: So we can find out exactly where self is on that stick.

John: How far down the stick can you get yourself? How far out, in terms of your auditory sensing, can you get? Do you understand the task? Half an hour. I'd like you each to have fifteen minutes to play with the strategies. Enjoy yourself. Get down into second attention.

Judy: Get down!

John: I hope that your experience during the exercise was far too complex for you to put it in the linear form called language. But I would like to ask you, especially at second attention now, to mark shifts of strategy, shifts of mapping . . . There were profound differences, for example, when you started with your eyes open in an area and began to explore blind from that point where you had an initial reference point,

. . . a profound difference between that situation and being disoriented, twirled about and so forth, and moved to a part of the grounds here where you didn't know the reference point that you started from. The class of maps that you constructed in one situation were profoundly different than the class of maps you constructed in the other.

Of equal importance for our purposes is the notion of the extension of self, the ability to identify with subcircuits because of a contextual shift—in this particular case, removal of one of your sensory input channels—and the attendant extension of self in other channels to make up for the classes of information which were denied by the normal channels. One of the most powerful resources available to you in your community are people who have suffered some sensory deprivation. By the nature of the situation some of them have developed strategies and sensitivities and refinements in the alternative representational systems and input channels which indicate that it is only our comfort at our past homeostatic levels that prevents us from refining our sensory apparatus to that extent.

And it gives us some idea of what our range may possibly be . . . . . . if we were to actually push it to some of the limits which none of us have ever approached anyway. Some years ago I met a fifteen-year-old boy who was blind, not congenitally, but from the age of about six. By the way, do you know how you can tell a congenitally blind person from one who is not? Have you ever noticed how congenitally blind people often wear sunglasses? It's not to protect their non-eyes from the sun.

It's because the seeing community is upset kinesthetically by the fact that there are random eye movements in congenitally blind people. There is no systematicity to their movements. In fact, it's diagnostic; you can immediately tell whether somebody is congenitally blind or not by whether they have systematic, as opposed to random, eye movements.

In the '20s or '30s reflective sunglasses were referred to as "cheaters," . . . . . . because those they rob you of a certain amount of information that you normally have access to by the systematic movement of the wearer's eyes.

John: A fifteen-year-old boy, who had been blinded in an accident at about age six, had gotten so good he could walk into a room he had never been in and (John claps his hands six times, pausing every two claps) tell you the dimensions of the room, tell you roughly the amount of furniture in the room, and sometimes tell you the types of furniture there down to within plus or minus a couple of feet of the actual dimensions. He used visual predicates. Blind people use, if anything, an excess of visual predicates. This is an adaptation to a visual world in our culture. When asked to define things like "green" he gave the most elegant olfactory, tactile, auditory, gustatory description that I've ever had the opportunity to listen to; it was pure artistry. Based on this "deficit" which he had suffered due to an accident to his sight he had come to make refinements in the distinctions he could make through his other sensory channels. The other thing that was really extraordinary about him was he rode skateboards. A lot better than I can.

John: Jerry, do you have any comments about this? Jerry happens to be working with a blind man at the moment.

Jerry: Yeah. I was asked to teach a class in music at Cabrillo College for the handicapped—so-called—and . . .

Judy: . . . it was hard to figure out who was handicapped.

Jerry: The only person who showed up for the first semester was a person who was blind from birth. He was one of those premature babies who got too much oxygen in the incubator and so his retina pulled away and then he got glaucoma in one eye and so his vision is gone.

This isn't congenital, and he has systematic eye-accessing cues—which was my first glimmer that visualization might be something other than what we think it is. And so I made a deal with him. He wanted to learn how to play the violin and I'm a violinist and so I said, "Fine. Do you have a violin?" He says, "Yeah, I bought one three months ago. I don't know what to do with it but I bought it." And so he brought it the next time. I didn't know what to do. I mean, I've been in lots of situations like that but this one was really peculiar. How are you going to . . . ? All of my teaching strategies up until that moment . . .

John: If you want to teach to your weakness, place yourself in challenging situations—this is a warrior trait. Everything that happens to you, if you take a warrior's position, is simply a challenge. It's not a good challenge, it's not a bad challenge, it's not a pleasant challenge, it's not an unpleasant challenge. Those are evaluative functions. It's simply a challenge. And if you're very good at this sort of thing you pick the challenges for maximum stretch.

Jerry: I thought, alright, he can feel things and he can hear things and he has everything else except vision. He's a little smaller than I am so I crouched down a bit and held his violin in the correct position and then I had him hang his body on my body from behind until we could tell without saying anything that he had some sense of this motion. And then I said, "Alright, when you feel like it, let me know and I'm going to stop doing it and you do it—you make me do it." So he made me do it. We did that for some minutes and then I asked him to stop, took myself away, and said, "Stand there and assume the position." He played the violin in the air more beautifully than I've seen anyone do it the first time. When I gave him the violin his position was still there. So we proceeded . . . , I mean, there's a lot more to the story obviously, . . . but the thing that got me was that that you don't need to see to play the violin. (Laughter)

John: Cognitively that's easy. But if you're a violist or a violinist and you've taught it, it becomes revelatory in practice.

Jerry: Right. So then I began to wonder what's going on inside this guy's brain? What does he see? How does he get the world organized? He does things like that fifteen-year-old boy that John described does, like sensing his surroundings by echolocation except that he'll walk into a room and do that (Jerry snaps his fingers once) and he's got it. He can tell by air pressure how far a building or any other object is from him. How big it is, whether there are plants, and so on. He can tell how far away people are from him and—I haven't explored this yet because I, again, am at a loss, but I'll find some way—he can tell about a human being by the emanations that are coming from that person. Whether he feels safe or whether he should get the hell out of there. So he's real good at all of that.

Jerry: But what was beautiful—after doing a little decoding exercise on "How do you get from here to the bus stop?"—was having him describe his "visual" systems. We tried everything. How do you get somebody who's never seen to talk about things that can be seen? I was talking with John over breakfast and he suggested, "Have him draw on your hand. That might be a way to do it." So he drew on my hand and the only way I could get access to what was going on on my hand was to render myself blind. So I had to make a trance like *that* (snapping his fingers) and say to myself, "OK, you're blind. You can't see. So now what is he drawing on your hand?" Then I understood that what I got are versions of the funny little pictures that you guys have been drawing on the blackboard for the last few days except they are geometric maps of the world. Some are loose, and some are real tight. They have to do with first and second attention. He has a big map which has little things in it. Depending on where he is on the map, he brings one up "visually"—into the focus of his field of vision (whatever that is). He pays attention to that until he has moved past that part, then the next one comes up. He's unerring.

Jerry: He comes up to my house for a violin lesson and he has to take the bus back and it's about a block and a half. We walk out the door and we're talking. He doesn't hang on to me anymore because in one trial he knows my neighborhood, right? And I said, "Whoops, there's the bus," and he's off like a shot. He grabs me by the arm. But the point is that since he had no vision he had to derive a map. That was the only way. There wasn't anything else for him to do. We have all this stuff that we have to sort out so that we can arrive at the place that he's already at.

John: Certainly the discussion of the frog visual system and the discussion of some of the transforms that occur moving back from the peripheral organ called the eye in the human visual nervous system should indicate to you that there is more than a metaphor to this blindman/blindwoman's exercise we've just done here. And I'd invite your second attention to consider habits down to and including the level of scanning. Who here scans their body internally, for example? If you take a tumble, if some accident befalls you, do you have a set of automatic scanning programs to use before you move, so you don't exacerbate the situation?—scanning internally so you know with precision, along the lines of the kinds of maps that Jerry is referring to in this man's experience, whether you may safely move without causing any further injury? There are all kinds of scanning patterns, internal as well as external that can be thought of as our blind spots at the moment because of our failure to develop alternatives to what has served us well but has nothing to do with the alternate realities that are available perceptually if we can make the shifts.

Man: I once asked a blind man whom I knew how he got across the street with the traffic and he said, "By the sound," and he said, "I've only been run over twice." That's a warrior's stance.

Georgine: At one point I had terminal cancer, so I now have a program where I scan through my body. If I have to go into surgery because I can't *not* have something checked out, I will scan through my body ahead of time. Every time—before going into surgery—I know the answer as to what I'm going to be up against.

Stephanie: I'd like to comment on something Jerry told me about the man he has been working with and get your thoughts about it. Jerry said, "If he has visited a place outdoors where there is obviously a large landscape then he makes (and he describes it in visual terms) a map, a picture of the landscape." So Jerry was exploring with him what it was he was doing. Well, it turns out that he maps it in perspective. In other words, he knows that there's this huge expanse of trees and even though his direct experience of each tree is probably "big,"—right?—when he's standing there and he's making an internal map of the landscape the trees in the front are big and the trees in the back are tiny and they get littler and littler. And I'm real curious about how, without having ever had visualization, he has perspective wired in here. Does that mean that perspective is necessarily a neurological function?

John: I don't know. There is lots of evidence that you do not learn visual phenomena without movement and the movement, in fact, has to be voluntary. So if you give someone glasses that reverse left and right and up and down and you put them on a trolley and take them through an environment they will learn it only minimally. That is, they will be unable to correct the "distortions" which are introduced on the "distortions" that they usually have—which is what the glasses do—unless they can move about voluntarily as part of the learning process, number one.

The second thing that occurred to me, Stephanie, is that I remember reading, in a book called *The World of Mathematics,* about the rediscovery of perspective during the Renaissance. They taught themselves, mechanically, to achieve the visual distortion necessary for mapping three dimensions onto two by literally tying strings between points on the distant object they wanted to paint and the corresponding points on the canvas to discover what the geometric relationships were. The geometry of mapping is something that you now are quite familiar with from this last exercise. For example, Vera found a pole with her stick; she recognized what it was as soon as she heard the sound. She verified it with her other hand and then began moving directly to the next pole; she had started to create a map. The first movements were quite tentative, but after a couple of pieces had fallen into place she could move with a lot more confidence. This suggests how a blind person might use the kinesthethics, tactile and spacial, to create maps (with distance moved being correlated with the decrease in size associated visually with the increased distance); the interesting thing is that, as in a visual perspective painting, things which are further away are represented in his or her internal representations as smaller.

Stephanie: One of the things that a friend showed me is how to shrink down as though I am a cell in my hand and follow all the parts (the blood, the muscle, or whatever) to the point where when I move my finger I can hear the bones creaking. And after being so totally into my hand my experience is that my hand becomes an incredible sensor.

John: By taking your first attention, bringing it down into the circuitry of second attention, you really do activate sensitivities that you did not have before.

Judy: It seems to be a question of flexibility and personal alternatives. One that always really interested me, studying biology, was the mammalian dive reflex. Sperm whales are good examples because they can stay forty-five minutes under water. Marine mammals that dive take a big breath of air and then submerge, they're down there forty-five minutes and their body goes through incredible somatic changes. Their heart rate slows down and the oxygen supply goes just to the places where it is needed the most, the brain, and blood flow to everything else is minimized. And so I wonder: I'm a mammal. What's my range of flexibility here? There've been some cases where people have been drunk and they've fallen into the water . . .

John: . . . especially if it's cold water . . .

Judy: . . . and they were down there for a long period of time—twenty minutes, thirty minutes—and did not suffer any permanent injury. There are some possibilities here waiting to be discovered. So that's real . . .

John: . . . flexibility. I have a question for you as a group. We started this whole process with the question and we keep returning on some cyclic, recursive pattern to the question, "What kinds of balance do we have to create for ourselves in a technical society where we can't count on a shared culture —a set of external structures to reinforce our own value systems? With that responsibility, what can we use as a model?" And we have constantly been turning back to traditional cultures where there is a wisdom to the people in relation to their context, where there is a wisdom in terms of social relations, because each coherent traditional culture is a successful adaptation on the part of our species to the environment and to each other. Essentially it constitutes a human possibility. To me, this is the point of anthropology, to take us out of our parochial understandings of what we have taken for granted and what first attention has now seized upon as reality, which has very little contact with the reality that could be if we chose to change it, and to demonstrate another human possibility—to shake us out of our epistomological slumber.

Obviously, as I said the other day, we've been offered a gesture from Titos—an offering of certain kinds of rhythm, drumming, singing, and dancing. I would like you to consider the question: Would it be of utility in furthering the models we've been creating . . .

Judy: More descriptions.

John: . . . to have some description from him of how in his culture certain classes of events (relationships, individual performance, . . .) are handled? I have in mind possibly taking a couple of hours tomorrow afternoon for this purpose if you think this is appropriate. Now, that requires some judgment, some balance. Let it sit at second attention. If you want to talk about it among yourselves during lunch that would be fine. I'll raise the question again about three o'clock. I think it would be only appropriate if we were going to do it to extend the invitation to Titos this afternoon.

Woman: I, in doing this blind exercise process, I've really always wanted to do it because when I was a kid I used to do this in the dark and try to feel the colors of walls and stuff . . .

Judy: Or when you draw on your friend's back.

John: "Draw a circle on the old man's back."

Woman: . . . and going on a drug experience I noticed how a visual memory can really . . .

John: . . . distort the map that you're trying to create.

Woman: Yeah! (laughter)

Marne: I heard someone going towards the swimming pool and I figured, "Great. I want to see what water feels like."

Judy: You mean you want to feel what water feels like.

Marne: . . . feel what water feels like. And I got up there and I noticed a couple of interesting things about what this information gave me compared to what verification-at-hand information gave to me. And how my fingers are much more finely tuned to seeing things than my eyes are. And I made a deal with myself that these sensors get blindfolded too. Fair is fair here. When you were talking about form and function and . . .

John: . . . context . . .

Marne: . . . structure, function, and context—in going to the swimming pool there was information about it that I don't necessarily pick up with my eyeballs; I found the swimming pool but I didn't know what the hell it was. And I thought, "Wow! I really get to play with that."

John: By the way, at that point, just before the "Wow" (or maybe even during it), that was "an experience without meaning."

Marne: That's when someone said, "I don't know what you're talking about."

Judy: "I don't know what you mean."

John: I hope they applauded.

Judy: Good test.

Marne: I also noticed that I'll go to my right hand for information when I feel my physical being is on the line. So I just said, "Stretch it. Go to your left hand and start." The sensations were incredibly different. And also in the sense of levels of going up and down.

John: That's one of the things I was most looking for. By the way, there's an observational task I can easily give you, two of them actually. One of them is: Can you walk like someone else? How profoundly does that change your appreciation of context? If you want insight into somebody else's reality, taking something as dynamic as the walking pattern; with your refinements at the sensory and motor levels, you will enter an alternate reality which will give you a glimpse of what it might mean to move across cultures where the differences are obvious. Within a culture, when you move across boundaries of mind from person to person the profound differences are masked by things like so-called "common language" and common external behavioral patterns. These have very little to do with the differences in the internal mapping functions which each of us carry.

Judy: I've danced with Titos for a long time and when I first started dancing with him when there would be steps that seemed really complex to me. There are steps that he does that look like they are three touches on the floor and they are really six touches but until I got to a certain level of discrimination I didn't even notice that. I'd be working so hard and it would seem so difficult—it was like they were there but not there—and he would walk up to me and he'd go, "Walk with me, Mama, just walk with me, that's all you have to do," and everything would fall into place.

John: Some of you were fortunate. I remember watching Jane do it. Alan was another example. If you dance very close to Titos suddenly you can do things . . .

Judy: . . . you get caught in this loop . . .

John: . . . that you couldn't do before. Proximity is one of the ways to enhance the extension of self; you define self to include Titos as a part of the circuitry. Suddenly you can do things that you were unable to do before.

Antonio: I was in Paris one time on the street. And there was this guy. People would walk by . . . and he would walk exactly the same—you know?—it was incredible. And the person wouldn't notice. Everybody that was there seeing it would notice . . . and he would walk . . . everybody, there was no one who would cross that street that he could not follow and walk exactly the same.

Judy: He was getting a lot of information about the world . . . whether he was doing anything interesting with it . . .

Antonio: . . . well, he was making money entertaining people, you know . . .

Judy: . . . that's interesting . . .

Antonio: . . . it was incredible. It could be a big guy or a small guy, any weight.

John: Shape changing. The second observational task is, like the left-right difference Marne noticed in the tactile information flow, people offer one ear or another depending on their attitude toward the person and the information that's being passed. I should like you to make some observations along those lines to discover what generalizations are available to you. It's as systematic as eye movement patterns. Do you understand the tasks?

Woman: No.

John: If I'm listening to you and I offer this ear as opposed to this ear that's a signal, as definitive as eye movements, about my response either to you and/or to the information you're offering me—often in terms of belief or disbelief. Alternatively, at a more sophisticated level, incorporating what we've explored in the last three and a half days, you could interpret it as an indication of how well it matches or doesn't match the perceptual filters by which we defend the homeostatic centers of our beliefs. I have a puzzle. We're getting altogether too solid here in terms of understanding and so forth. So I'd like to read you . . .

Judy: . . . an agent of entropy . . .

John: Yeah, a little entropy is in order here. I'd like to read you a rather astonishing account of a set of experiments that were done and invite you to spend some time musing over what they might represent. The original experiment was started by W. MacDougall at Harvard in 1920. The context was that this man wanted to make an experimental demonstration which would once and for all—this is one of the amusing thing about the first attention—settle the question of Lamarckian versus Darwinian inheritance.

In specific he had the hope of providing a thorough test of the possibility of Lamarckian inheritance. The experimental animals were white rats of the Weistar* strain which had been carefully inbred under laboratory conditions for many generations. Their task was to learn to escape from this specifically constructed tank of water by swimming to one of two gangways which led out of the water. The wrong gangway was brightly illuminated while the right gangway was not. If the rat left by the illuminated gangway it received an electrical shock. The two gangways were illuminated alternately, one on one occasion and the other on the next. The number of errors made by a rat before it learned to leave the tank by the nonilluminated gangway gave a measure of the rate of learning.

John: And they had very smart rats and they had really dumb rats. The dumbest rats ran around 330 or so trials before they got it.

The experimenter commented spontaneously that there was a point at which it was obvious to the experimenter that the rat had learned and from that point forward made no errors. In each generation the rats from which the next generation were to be bred were selected at random before their rate of learning was measured although mating took place only after they were tested. This procedure was adopted to avoid any possibility of conscious or unconscious selection in favor of quicker-learning rats. The experiment was continued for 15 years and 32 generations. In accordance with the Lamarckian theory there was a marked tendency for rats in successive generations to learn more quickly.This is indicated by the average number of errors made by rats in the first eight generations which was over 56 compared with 41, 29, and 20 in the second, third and fourth groups of eight generations respectively. The difference was apparent not only in the quantitative results but also in the actual behavior of the rats who became more and more cautious and tentative in later generations. MacDougall* had anticipated the criticism that in spite of his random selection of parents in each generation, some sort of selection in favor of quicker-learning rats could nevertheless have crept in. In order to test this possibility he started a new experiment with a different batch of rats in which the parents were indeed selected on the basis of their learning score. In one series only quick learners were bred in each generation and in the other series only slow learners. As expected, the progeny of the quick-learners tended to learn quickly, relatively, while the progeny of the slow learners learned relatively slowly.

John: Here's the first anomaly.

However even in the latter series, the slow learning rats, the performance of later generations improved very markedly in spite of repeated selection in favor of slow learning. One of the critics, a man by the name of F. A. E. Crew of Edinburgh, repeated MacDougall's experiments with rats derived from the same inbred strain using a tank of similar design. He included a parallel line of untrained rats some of which were tested in each generation for the rate of learning while others were not tested and served as the parents for the next generation thereby removing any training in terms of the passing of acquired characteristics. Over the next 18 generations of this experiment he found no systematic change in the rate of learning in either the trained or the untrained line. However the average scores of Crew's rats, right from the beginning were similar to those of MacDougall's after more than 30 generations of training on the same maze.

John: Do you understand?

It was as if, the commentator points out, the experiment had been continued even though there were time, space, and individual organism differences which could not be accounted for except by the usual understandings. Fortunately this is not the end of the story. The experiment was carried out once again by W. E. Aegar and his colleagues at Melbourne using methods that did not suffer from the disadvantages that Crew's did. Over a period of twenty years . . .

These people have persistence, eh?

. . . they measured the rates of learning of trained and untrained lines for 50 successive generations. In accordance with MacDougall they found there was a marked tendency for the rats of the trained line to learn more quickly in the subsequent generations.

And here comes the amazing paradox:

But exactly the same tendency was also found in the untrained line.
R. Sheldrake, *Biology: A New Science of Life.*[10]

This is not the end of the story either.

In leading up to our exercise this afternoon, a review of the primary relationships in your life, I would like to propose that your second attention assemble a cast of characters who, in its opinion, constitute your primary relations. We will give instructions on to how to use this information when we return in an hour and a half from whatever time José's watch says now.

LUNCH

Judy: (reading from Bateson[11])

Items of diet, conditions of life, temperature, entertainment, sex and so forth are never such that more of the something is always better than less of the something. Rather for all objects and experiences there is a quantity that has optimum value. Above that quantity the variable becomes toxic. To fall below that value is to be deprived. This characteristic of biological value does not hold for money. Money is always transitive value. More money is supposedly always better than less money, for example, $1,001 is to be preferred to $1,000. But this is not so for biological values. More calcium is not always better than less calcium. There is an optimum quantity of calcium that a given organism may need in its diet. Beyond this calcium becomes toxic. Similarly for oxygen that we breathe or foods or components of diet and probably all components of relationship . . .

John: "Probably all components of relationship"?

Judy: Nah!

Enough is better than a feast. We can even have too much psychotherapy. A relationship with no combat in it is dull and a relationship with too much combat is toxic. What is desirable is a relationship with a certain optimum of conflict. It is even possible that when we consider money, not by itself, but as acting upon human beings who own it, we may find that money too becomes toxic beyond a certain point. In any case the philosophy of money, the set of presuppositions by which money is supposedly better, and the better the more you have of it, is totally anti-biological. It seems nevertheless that this philosophy can be taught to living things.

John: By the way, I would claim: only living things with first attention.

George: What was that?

John: It was a series of words from which you may make meaning. Do you understand the notion that it can only be taught to living systems with first attention? George, I'm looking at *you.* (laughter)

George: I thought we were exchanging glances.

Judy: And you thought right.

John: Relationships.

EXERCISE: REVIEW OF PERSONAL RELATIONSHIPS

Judy: Did you all prepare to do a review of your primary relationships over lunch?

John: I hope you have assembled your significant others. This exercise is simplicity itself in terms of the organizational principles involved. I'm going to describe those and let them sit in your second attention while we talk about the well-formedness conditions on how you carry out those particular instructions. I would recommend, consistent with the aesthetic frame we are attempting to develop, that you choose some metaphor for yourself which has the kinds of aesthetic balance and value that you yourself find attractive. I want to emphasize the importance of the periodicity—the cyclic nature—of these reviews, of this inventory process. I remember bursting into absolutely warranted laughter in the face of a friend who, with a serious expression on his face and with genuine sincerity in his heart, was telling me that things were just all messed up in his life; and it was only six months ago he had had everything perfectly sorted out. And when I finished laughing I said, "Thank God." This is the kind of dynamism in a system which insists that you are alive and that you have not yet pushed your filters out to the extent that your loss of difference is preventing you from appreciating an ever-changing set of relationships between yourself and other people and between yourself and the context.

John: One metaphor is to walk to the edge of a cliff . . . And stand at the edge of the cliff . . . look out into the distance and see what there is to see. And after you have very carefully examined that environment for a while, you turn back and notice that assembled behind you are the group of people you've called. And you walk back and take them one by one by the hand, and hand in hand you walk to the edge of the cliff with them. You look off into the distance holding their hand. They look off into the distance, shoulder to shoulder with you. What we see out there in some sense represents possible futures for both of us. We then look at each other. There could be a verbal exchange. Typically, given my predilections, it's all nonverbal. But I then switch perceptual positions to see myself through their eyes and to see what they saw—through their eyes—when looking off into the horizon.

Judy: Double description. Use this sort of a format cyclically with each member of the group which you've called, and before you move to taking the next one by the hand and walking to the cliff with them, as in the editing function, see from the outside—from third position, the next higher logical level, meta-position—the relationship between the two of you. Here's where some of the well-formedness conditions apply. And please, first attention, this is your responsibility: to remind second attention as you go into this loop of these well-formedness conditions. One, notice we've already insisted on triple description: My position, the position of the significant others, and the position of editor from outside. I should also mention that among these significant others may be ones that you don't know, that you don't recognize, which your second attention may provide. This is a representation of the re-balancing necessary to create the kind of balanced dynamism that you're after. That's where I would invite your second attention to surprise you by presenting among your significant others people you don't immediately recognize. When you see yourself through their eyes and you see from the editor position you'll come to have an appreciation at second attention of what they represent in terms of rebalancing your life. Get some news.

John: Triple description at minimum; the first well-formedness condition. Second: From the editor position you are to answer the question of intent—that is, what is the intent in this relationship? You don't have to do the editing at this point, but some scribe in there had better keep track of where there may be a profound difference between your intent and your actual performance when you link up with this other mind in a larger unit of mind. And in particular, perhaps the most critical well-formedness condition here is that from that outside position you can observe with clarity the cases in which you have come to play an arc in their circuits in such a way that you've entered the tyrant position with respect to them; you've enslaved them, you are squeezing the world.

Judy: And the flip side of that coin.

John: In what way have you come to depend upon them to play arcs in your circuitry which would otherwise be interrupted if they weren't there to play those arcs? There is absolutely no judgment involved here in terms of good or bad. I'm saying, a well-formedness condition on you as an organism is that there be circuit integrity here so that you have the capacity to reach out and link up with another intact unit of mind; and to create a new class of information by the double description that's inherent in that relationship. But insofar as you have to serve as an arc in their circuit—or vice versa—you are enslaving one another. Some of the finest teamwork in the world, some of the most exotic, erotic, lovely, passionate, marvelous parts of your life involve playing arcs in circuits with other people. I'm pointing to the situation where disuse or atrophy of your own circuits, or somebody else's circuits, has led to a situation of dependency, in the sense of having lost your integrity.

John: I remind you of my grandmother as an example of a woman who was able to lead an interesting, balanced life—and notice that she had the healthy ability to . . .

Judy: . . . recover those arcs which her husband had played in her circuitry . . .

John: . . . when it was required; so that she met the well-formedness condition which I'm discussing—namely, that you have the capacity to play an arc in somebody else's circuitry and vice versa, and when desired or required could recover the arcs which someone is playing in your circuits and vice versa. That's a well-formedness condition on this personal relations review.

Woman: Among my significant others I have a person who fulfills two fairly distinct roles: one personal, one business. On my list, as I created it, I listed this person as two separate individuals. Is that an appropriate way to go about it?

John: Well, I mean, it's appropriate if there is at least an implicit contract between you and the other person that respects context. If, in the connection with this person in the business context, their behavior leads you to believe they are making exactly the same contextual distinction you are and you find it effective and healthy for both of you, that's a perfectly good way of organizing. Remember the distinction I was talking about between the part of the room that I use for work, my standup desk, and other parts of the house that I live in?

Judy: As you go through this review, second attention, make sure you leave time for the surprise presentation of significant others who are not immediately recognized by first attention. What other well-formedness conditions come to your mind as you consider this? First attentions, do your task.

Man: Safety lines?

John: Safety lines, absolutely. Now let's discuss the relationship between you and your witness. You're going to work in pairs. A full hour for the exercise, half an hour for each of you. Once again, it is my suggestion . . . Consuella and I were talking about this yesterday. She said, "Thursday—what I do Thursday is what counts. Not what I do Saturday, Sunday, Monday, Tuesday, Wednesday. Thursday I won't have a baby sitter; I'll be on my own." So, what I would like you to do is to make all the arrangements as if you didn't have a baby sitter. That is, either time lapse kickouts; or kickouts when there is a shift in state, for example, self-indulgent moods as you review relationships seem to me entirely inappropriate to the spirit of what you're doing. Now, you can indulge yourself if you choose . . . it's a choice. Seems to me less appropriate than other qualities such as impeccability that you might use in this area. But this is style now. As long as you're willing to accept the consequences of the decision either way, I respect that decision. As long as it is a choice . . .

Judy: . . . and as long as it has a frame of artistry and respect around it. And that becomes critical, the notion of respect, because when you're outside, in the editor position, reviewing that relationship for circuit integrity in each individual, notice that you could have a beautiful intent for this other person and vice versa; but what if you're intervening at the wrong logical level? What if you're sending aid to people in such a form that it's disrespectful—that it ensnares them? . . . or that it just continues to strengthen, to maintain that cage but makes them comfortable there? If the intent is caring, is there a congruity in the way you are entering their circuitry in the relationship? Or are you supporting self-indulgent behavior over there by making them comfortable? If they were not comforted in those particular ways would it move them to change themselves—to recapture arcs of their circuitry which you have inappropriately been playing—in such a way that they would become whole again, that they would recover their integrity?

Georgine: Now are you referring to this integrity from the position of the person that's working with you?

John: I'm saying that you need to evaluate it from at least three positions. Yours, theirs, and the outside position.

Georgine: That's within you as a subject. So are you talking about the integrity between your own editor and your . . .

John: I'm talking about the relationship you have with X. I want you to review that relationship from inside your own perceptual position; I want you to have the perceptual position of the other person, X, and get a second description; and then I want you to get a third position. You're the director in a play and you're watching this go down. From that position you have to assess the intent as well as the congruity of that intent with the actual logical level at which you've been offering support in terms of playing parts of their circuits.

Georgine: OK, I understand. I assumed you were talking from the position of our baby sitters in this exercise and describing what the baby sitter's role is.

John: No, no, no . . .

Judy: Good idea.

John: Baby sitter. The only thing the baby sitter does is that after you've made all these lifeline arrangements for yourself—a kickout if there's a certain kind of state shift; a kickout if there's a certain kind of change in context, with emergency programs to intervene; a kickout in terms of time lapse (you know how much time you have to work)—he or she arranges a signal with your second attention to pull you out, to run your lifeline for you if necessary. So that you really are operating as if the baby sitter is entirely redundant, 100% redundant.

Georgine: I was just going to ask why we would even want the baby sitter.

John: Because I want the fallback.

Judy: It's sort of like soloing.

John: David Gaster stood on the ground and watched me make my first couple of solo circuits with landings and takeoffs and it was comforting to me, even at the time when I was entirely alone in the airplane, to know that he was watching. Silly, but nevertheless comforting. I don't know whether anyone here needs it at this point, but you're going to arrange it.

Any other well-formedness conditions that you'd like to propose for discussion?

Woman: This business of time really intrigues me—you keep referring to time distortion. I'm wondering if there is some optimum element of time involved in an exercise like this. I could see where it could be self-indulgent to really get into this kind of exercise and not really get some of the same kind of critical realization from it. Is there any . . . ?

John: I would run two clocks, if I were you. I would run a clock which corresponds to external clock time. That's a requirement you have for symmetry with your partner. It's another form of balancing, right? That is, your baby sitter is going to sit there with you for half an hour; they need their half hour too. So the minimum kickout is at the end of half an hour; and baby sitters, if they are not back at the end of that half hour, you bring them back. That's your right.

Judy: You'll certainly have had enough practice by that time that you can finish in dreaming what you've begun here.

John: Now, the other clock—the internal clock—is a free variable. You can spend days and weeks and months and years in there, if you need to, in that half-hour period. So, I think that both clocks are essential. They are like two perceptual positions. And, if you've played with time distortion, subjectively you have an enormous amount of time in there if you make those arrangements.

Woman: You were talking about a cybernetic loop and what effects that information from the double and triple description has—whether or not it gets implemented and at what time.

John: Suppose that you're in a primary relationship with X and . . .

Judy: . . . you've probably discovered it by now anyway . . .

John: . . . contrary to your intent, you've been exercising what you believe to be an appropriate intention, but you've been entering at the wrong logical level. You've been supporting weakness where you want to develop strength in yourself and in the other person. Now, I said I don't think you need to do all the editing now, but you need the scribe in there to make a note: "This is incongruent, and not only that, I've lost some of my integrity and I am enslaving the other person at the same time by causing them to lose their own integrity." A note goes down. The note has two pieces: one, what logical level shift to enter at; and number two, a transition mechanism for change—to achieve congruity. There's a frame of respect here.

Judy: Yes. That's where I talked about the larger frame of respect, and the larger frame of artistry.

John: Y'all checking back? You didn't bring all your primary relationships with you. There wouldn't be enough room in this place for them.

Judy: In case you hadn't noticed, you are, and will continue to be, very different than you were when we started this thing. May it accelerate into the future. (laughter) That is, we're setting in place mechanisms that are dynamic, not static. Think ahead for a moment: in twenty-four more hours, you'll be heading back to your own personal contexts—to your close ones. There is a sense of respect that I would take in approaching people when I go back, to understand . . . Georgine gave us an example: if I hook up with another person, and I put the circuits in place, and now I get so enthusiastic that I lose feedback, I can literally "overwhelm them." The notion of "overwhelming them" has a real significant concrete realization in terms of circuitry. I just overwhelm them with the stuff. I could overwhelm them with rate of change; I could simply overwhelm them by being so different that they can't miss it even though they have the perceptual filters; or I could be graceful about the whole thing. TaTitos and the steps and the movements and the physical demands alone on you has increased each day.

John: You all knew that at second attention. My proposal is that that might be a model for how you would respectfully but thoroughly begin to shift the relationship in positive ways. So the scribe should make a note that not only is the intent and the behavior incongruent, and that the behavior has to be shifted to a different logical level, but there has to be some graceful way of doing that, respectful of the other person's circuitry as well. To withdraw suddenly from arcs of circuits you played for them, they'll fall flat on their face. They may be threatened by the move. It will seem so alien. And remember, this is a natural conservative principal of the body, in the sense of homeostasis. They've become addicted to you. Or rather, acclimated, if you prefer the metaphor. Formally, they're identical . . .

Judy: . . . And vice versa . . .

John: So now the withdrawal—in order to create an integrity within you and an integrity within them that will allow you both to meet with more joy and creativity in your interaction than ever before—is still one that has to be done carefully, with respect. It would not, for example, be wise to approach the topic with such a person through first attention. Because first attention doesn't operate with loops, it operates with arcs of loops and you could be defeated in linear arguments if you choose to approach this with first attention. But you know perfectly well at a deeper level that the logical arguments, linear in nature, are faulted by the distorting effects of language and consciousness. So surely, that much will be part of your well-formedness approach when you get back into your personal context.

Woman: Lara Amber Ewing was telling me one time that, in essence, she takes the end point of what this process is going to be, in the sense that she has a being in here that's her all day, which of course changes as her circumstances change and as she evolves, but she periodically checks in when she has to make a major decision, so that she can, in essence, sort of track backwards to see what would be the best choices, and in keeping with that end point that she wants to choose.

John: As long as the end point is constantly validated by second attention it sounds fine—very much like the strategy I use for teaching. Judy and I decide, before we walk in here, that these points probably go in this sequence so we'll head in here with roughly this much time for these points and then we both go to second attention and into a loop together with you. And it has been so uncanny that you have asked exactly the class of questions that give us the natural lead to where we want to go anyway. And that tells me that we really have been cybernetically sound in our approach, in terms of working together in a loop with you.

John: If any of you want earplugs as a counterpart to the blindfolds for this exercise, you're welcome to them. They're sitting up here. If my mouth is moving and you hear no sound you probably already have them so . . . (mouthing words without sounds) I'm happy with that set of well-formedness conditions. Check second attention.

Judy: (pointing to George.) He didn't check second attention. Go ahead.

John: (interrupting George) No, no, I agree with Judy. I'm waiting for a second-attention input. And it may simply be, "Go." And if that's true, come on back and give me a first-attention signal, so that I know that you're back. OK. Now are there any first-attention questions George? (laughter) George, do you know what an important role you're playing? I hope you understand how much I appreciate this.

George: Thank you. We decided self-indulgence wasn't really a well-formedness condition, but by the time we got finished talking about it, it almost became one. I would appreciate more of a sense of how I could know when self-indulgence is taking place. What's the test for it?

John: I take self-indulgence to be on the opposite end of the continuum from balance. An example in the world might be an artist who becomes so obsessed with one component of the world that he or she literally cannot occupy a survival position. Every demon is by definition self-indulgent. That's why you have controllers, conductors, and technical staff—so that the structure as a whole is balanced, and yet you are self-indulgent at each demonic point. I think of it in terms of both how much of your resource base is committed to that class of events and the amount of time spent at it. May you have a lovely journey. Be back in an hour, folks.

BREAK

John: There's a certain dance here between focus-focus-focus whether it's entirely at first attention or at second attention and floating. Also, when you do this kind of focused work, when you are preparing to extend yourself out to your subcircuits be sensitive to your own physiological needs. You need to float for awhile, too. The issue here is balance at the meta-level. We're about to engage in an activity which is inherently healing anyway; that part will be nicely taken care of. If the work was done with the quality I've witnessed you doing in the exercises that we've done so far, it couldn't possibly be usefully discussed with first-attention code.

Judy: Homework.

John: Living systems identification. Every living system—whether it's your cat, a plant, a flower, a tree, whatever—every one has something to teach you if you are able to safely extend yourself into it; that's your job tonight. Your job is to find and go to a living system, and extend yourself. What I want you to do is have such a thorough experience . . . that you. There are some "tricks" you can do: First of all, get validation that second attention is willing to extend itself. Get a commitment from first attention to go down in the circuitry which second attention chooses to use to envelop this living system. You can even do the referential-index shift that you were doing in this review process by seeing yourself from the other side, and thereby a change of identity over there which you can then sink into. I should like you to have the experience of such identification.

John: Those of you who have seen the movie *The Emerald Forest* remember it was not adequate for the protagonist to identify with the eagle; he actually saw from the eagle's perspective. There are certain qualities of the living systems people identify with which will surprise you—when you achieve that identification. Make sure you set your lifelines. I leave it up to you whether you take a baby sitter. It is now time for you to start exercising your own choice in this area.

Christian: Is there any special tasking for those who have done this before?

John: I have several. For you, I have the task of finding power places.

Man: What's a power place?

John: There are places around us here where you can go and you're soothed. There are places you can go and you feel protected. There are places you can go and you feel empowered; there is something there for you to draw upon in a more positive sense than just being soothed. There are places you positively avoid; you feel weakened when you spend any amount of time there. Now, I would be foolish to pretend that I could offer you adequate verbal instructions except with the cooperation of your second attention, who knows more about this than I can possibly say through first-attention code. I have some skill in some environments, especially the high desert, of being able to locate and differentiate such power spots with precision and have apprenticed with people who've taught me rituals for approaching them. It would be adequate for purposes of the way you're approaching it that you would check—do a first-attention check with second attention—once it has identified a place, before you approach . . . just a "go" or "no go" signal to the question "May I approach it safely?" We're going to talk a bit about ritual tomorrow. If some ritual, Christian, occurs to you as you approach it, use it. Please be respectful in your approach.

Judy: Fort Point.

John: If you're interested, it's a beautiful place, even for first attention . . .

Judy: . . . and it's another perspective on the bridge . . . from underneath the bridge . . .

John: Fort Point is easily reached. As you approach the Golden Gate Bridge, you notice where all the old tollbooths and stuff are on the right before you start out onto the bridge. There's also a turnout there. If you follow that turnout around to the right, it takes you to stop sign, you go left, and I think the first left after that (which is sort of a back left) takes you back down and underneath the bridge to where the fort was constructed that used to guard San Francisco harbor. And from there, you get an entirely different perspective of another experience you've already had.

Woman: Do we have to be in the presence of the other living system?

John: I think that after some practice, just like with power spots, you can reach to them from a distance. You may be able to do it on your first flight. I personally would go and be in the physical presence of the living system I was doing the identification with until I had mastered some facility in doing such identification. Then, I could go from a distance. Unless you already have a lot of experience in going across distances without moving your body in the usual sense. And, since you're frowning at me, I take it that it's not a common experience. Go there.

Judy: Can I use your example, Britt? When Britt came to the end of the last exercise she thought, "Well, I'm finished," and her guardian angel said, "Well, go check your sixth sense and make sure that's all of them." Right? And then her cats came, so she went into the perceptual position of her cats, like seeing the world through her cat's eyes. She said it was like all these little things moving in the bushes that she'd never noticed before.

John: That is one of the quality indications that you've done the class of identification you are after. You will have perceptual experiences which are not normally available to humans, but are typical of the living organism that you do the identification with.

Larry: John, to what extent is it important to know . . . ? You're talking about entering realms which other cultures have developed and explored and understand; and which, to our culture, we are, at least I am, an absolute novice.

John: First attention does not know the unknown. And a lot of the rebalancing here has been to invite you to occupy second-attention circuitry exclusively.

Larry: Is there something that . . . ? Are there any instructions regarding . . . ?—Hm, maybe that's just in the lifeline.

John: That's exactly where you're going and that's the importance of the very first exercise we did, which we've insisted be part and parcel of every move you've made in this seminar. You've got such contextual markers so you can get back out. Lifelines.

Judy: So you have the freedom, like Viola Legere does, to commit.

John: By the way, I want you to appreciate this is a really intelligent, articulate man trying to find the representations at second attention.

Larry: I got it. (applause) The turn of the century grammarian, Fowler, talks about dead metaphors. "Please examine this pen." You know the metaphor in that sentence. The word is "examine." You have a metaphor for "examine," as does everyone else in the room, even though very few people know the etymology of the word "examine," which is latin for *exima,* the point on a balance. It occurs to me that there are parts of the unknown for which the lifeline exercise that we have done may be completely inadequate. (laughter) Because there are metaphors . . . If you accept the presupposition that some of the beliefs in the world are real, then I question . . .

John: . . . the adequacy of the safety lines we've arranged.

Larry: . . . the adequacy of the safety devices that we've come up with, or at least, certainly, the ones I've come up with.

John: When I'm lead climbing I trust the rope. I also have some control over how I place the protection in the rock so that I can choose the level of risk in a strong way. But risk there will always be.

Larry: So you're saying don't be foolhardy about where I venture.

John: Yeah. This is a beginning, we've made a beginning together . . .

Judy: . . . and we're talking about the range of human possibilities . . .

John: . . . not simply personal alternatives . . .

Judy: . . . but the range of human possibilities.

John: The range of personal alternatives for me at this moment in time is a small, small subset of human possibility. And you're pointing towards areas of human possibility that you are beginning to have the technical competence to enter where you doubt that the safety-line arrangements will be adequate to protect you.

Judy: That's why you have to respect the circuitry, the context, the structure, and the function.

John: You've got to set a level of risk that's acceptable to you, since you've noticed there are areas . . .

Judy: Have you found any?

John: I've momentarily visited some.

Larry: I have a sense that they exist, but heretofore I've denied it.

John: So, with the choice of moving into these areas, comes an added responsibility for personal safety. In general, second attention won't even notice—as first attention never does—what you cannot accept, right? The filters can protect you. But as soon as you start to change perceptual filters, then you incur extra risk, and attendant upon that, you carry the extra responsibility of making arrangements. What arrangements are appropriate I'd be happy to do some dreaming about tonight; I'd invite all of you to do the same.

Judy: Let's dance!

John: This woman says, "Let's dance." I say, "Let's dance." Be back in ten minutes.

DAY FIVE

Judy: Good morning.

John: Good morning.

Francis: As a check in the ecology of this workshop I wonder if we're qualified to make the decision to invite the Kongolese to come this afternoon to offer us some alternate descriptions.

Judy: What decision?

John: What qualify?

Francis: . . . Are we qualified to make that decision?

John: No, you're not. (Laughter) But, as Judy said on day one, life is the art of drawing sufficient conclusions from insufficient data. The problem is that you are never qualified, but you're the only one who can do it.

John: There's a Nigerian man named Babatunde Olatunji who is often identified as the African who brought the traditional rhythms of West Africa, especially Ghana and Nigeria, to the United States in recent years.

Judy: He's about sixty years old, and he's been here for a long time.

John: You'll find lots of people, from Coltraine, twenty years ago, to the Chuck Davis Dance Troupe, who were inspired by Olatunji's work bringing traditional West African rhythms to jazz, to dance, to the blues, et cetera. The West Africans, brought here as slaves several hundred years ago, were responsible for so much of what we consider American music; and then comes an update, as Olatunji brings in fresh new material. He was sitting at the ranch with TaTitos and TaMalonga, and Judy and I, eating bugs—specifically, lobster. Take it easy, Consuella. (Laughter) Got to be careful about those hear-feel circuits.

Judy: All the children in the neighborhood really believe that John does eat bugs.

John: Specifically, dead flies. It's true, ask them. They all believe it.

Judy: Until we had our little goddaughter Talia who brought one and wanted to see him do it. (Laughter) Then he had to go . . .

John: (pretending to eat a fly) No problem!

Judy: . . . like that.

John: Impeccability is the order of the day, you know? (Laughter)

Babatunde Olatunji has learned a number of things about Western culture. One of them is the importance of capital. So at the table he was discussing the best-paying gig he ever did and it turned out to be up in Poughkeepsie, New York for IBM. He said, "It's really amazing, when I was up there they took me to this place where we were to stay overnight and it was the most luxurious apartment I've ever been in. It had everything. It had a bar, it had all the music and stereo equipment . . ."

Judy: ". . . everything you could ever want," he said.

John: ". . . thick carpets, whatever you want, and the man said to me, 'If you want something and it's not here, you just pick up this phone and call me; I'll be downstairs and I'll see if I can get it for you.' " And Baba asked, "Who normally lives here?" and he said, "Oh, we have employees who think for us. They come and they stay here while they're thinking." And he said that the arrangement is, they come there when they're ready to do some thinking on contract. They go in there and the man downstairs unlocks the door to one of these luxurious mini-universes, microhabitats, which has everything, as Olatunji said, that you could want, and if it's not there you just ask for it. So he goes in and the man locks the door. And Olatunji looked and he looked around and he said, "It was so beautiful, in a way it was like paradise, but *the guy downstairs has got the key.*" So he hadn't drifted that far from his African roots. (laughter)

Woman: I had a dream last night, when I first closed my eyes, that we were all doing this wonderful dance together. (laughter) It was an experience; it wasn't something that I just created.

John: Right. By the way, mark that difference! That's the difference between real metaphor, a second-attention production, and what Gregory calls "allegory," which is a first-attention construction which gets dressed up as if it came from second attention. And you all know that difference. And that's an important difference to respect. One is crass and the other one is art.

Judy: Yeah. Good point, John.

John: Thank you. (Laughter)

Judy: It really is.

Woman: Well, one of the nice things about the dream was that everyone was moving in such harmony together that they were just right-on. The rhythm was just perfect and it was right in sync the whole time. And the moves were really beautiful and everyone danced gorgeously and, ah, thank you. (laughter)

Judy: You can see beyond a situation where another person doesn't yet have the skill—the basis of any aesthetic act—to appreciate their purity of intent at the level of the spirit. There's good reason to be able to shift attention when you're in the presence of a group of people who share a common intent. You were able to occupy the subcircuits for dance even though the circuits were not yet well-trained. There's a profound difference between someone whose focus is a first-attention focus on technique—"Are my feet moving in exactly the way TaTitos's are?" (the answer is: "Never!") . . .

John: . . .—and someone who shifts to second attention and commits with the kind of passion that we've been discussing.

Christian: I had an experience last night which was real similar to ballet; it was George Balanchine's choreography, and I was able to appreciate the skill that went into doing what they do —because they *do* make it look so effortless, just like TaTitos makes it look so effortless. Every once in a while I'd see a fine muscular trembling in the dancers and I'd realize . . .

Judy: . . . what was going on there.

Christian: It was really an incredible experience.

John: We have a gift for you. There's one final piece—final only in the sense of completing your readiness to leave here with adequate preparation for your own exploration. I mentioned the other day that one of the men in the group felt disappointed when he succeeded in "stopping the world" and didn't receive direct revelatory information from God (laughter)—or the world—however you want to talk about it. I reminded you that such skills require practice.

I would like you to develop for yourself a disciplined program of shifting, from first to second attention and back, cleanly with no residue. Notice, you never have to wait again. (laughter) You never have to wait again. It would be self-indulgent for you to wait, in the traditional sense, because you are surrounded by a world that's mysterious if you have the choice of shifting attention. I remind you of the aesthetic question: How much do you change your filters . . .

John & Judy: . . . and how much do you change the world?

John: Some balance has to be achieved there. In some contexts you want to confront the world directly and in other contexts you want to shift filters. Every experience, remember, is some interactive product of those two processes.

Susan: Are arcs created by going across the circuits?

John: By "arc" I mean subsections of a complete circuit. So the conscious mind can pull into consciousness seven plus or minus two pieces of circuits. Those pieces can be called "arcs" because they are subsets of the circuit.

Judy: You're never going to have the whole circuit in consciousness.

John: In and of themselves arcs are not particularly useful. That's how we get the narrow-band, purposive kinds of first-attention behavior which have to be balanced by artistry and by wisdom, that is, context—drawing from the rest of the circuit as a minimum. That's the sense in which I mean you're using some external device for tuning your own circuitry. A fine example was when we were singing yesterday. We sang together, all of us . . .

Judy: . . . as a group, and then TaTitos said, "All the ladies, high."

John: Let's differentiate "Whoo, who-who-who-who, whoo."

Judy: "Now, the men sing low."

John: And it was beautiful, the differentiation.

Richard: Yesterday was the first time I experienced a double description of the dancing. What you said about the linkage between dance and drummer was interesting; I felt that the drum was beneath my feet and each beat was pushing them. And there was some connection, as you said, to proximity—the difference between dancing closer to Titos and dancing further away. It was uncanny.

Judy: It's the form; you got the same form. It's falling into . . .

Woman: . . . the different perspective of sitting in front of the drummers and hearing them, watching them . . .

John: . . . driving you.

Judy: TaTitos said that would happen, too, didn't he? It keeps you honest also. Sit in front of the other drummers. You can't get out of place.

John: Our topic for this morning is shifting your perceptual filters. Remember that that little diagram of reality depicting the eyes, the afferent nerve tracts, second attention, first attention, possibly reflexive consciousness on top of that, and back out down the efferent paths with connections across so that there are subsystems between the different and efferent where expectations get organized? The question becomes: What set of moves do you have to make in order to change those perceptual filters—to change the way in which you distort the inputs? It's not a question of removing distortion. It's a question of changing it. So the issue of right and wrong is not relevant to what we're doing here—except at the higher frames of aesthetics and your obligations with respect to the environment and other units of mind. We are not going to change from an unreal value on one of the variables of perception to a real one; they are all unreal. The question is: Do you have the flexibility of occupying a second and a third and a fourth perceptual position in the deep sense of changing your perceptual filters?

Antonio: I'm thinking about this shift from first to second attention. In Brazil when they have a soccer championship of the world people change from first to second attention repeatedly.

John: And they identify completely with the team. . . . there is no difference.

Antonio: Exactly. But there is an incredible change between first and second attention. The whole country. (Laughter) In every city . . .

Judy: I think that happens in Texas when the Cowboys are going to the Superbowl.

Antonio: . . . an incredible change. In Brazil you cannot work. If there is a Brazil game nobody goes to work.

Judy: Everything stops.

Antonio: So if the team loses, you know, the whole country is . . .

John: . . . depressed.

Antonio: The production . . .

John: . . . drops.

Antonio: . . . goes down, yeah. The whole country is depressed.

John: Profitability falls off.

Antonio: It's incredible.

John: The issue today is perceptual filters. First of all, reflective consciousness is going to be of little use to you in these exercises. The distinction we worked out yesterday, between the first attention and reflexive consciousness, will be critical. Reflexive attention is something on top of that. George was asking me yesterday how to think about self-indulgence.

Judy: Today you are to do some things that you've never done before. Today is the payoff, in a sense. Part of which will be for you to take your first attention and move from the center to the surface of the sphere to have some appreciation of the patterns of logic at second attention.

Rosalie: Judy gave me an assignment last night; I had asked for one. I laughed because her assignment was to begin to discover the logics of second attention—which she wanted to me emerge with. And I laughed and I said, "Judy, I can't do logic or grammar at first attention. Not only can I not do grammar, it was my job to teach grammar and I couldn't do it." And here's what came out, the rules of logics of the second attention:

It's a world of generalized deletions and specified nonsense,
Where houses have a deep down green crunchiness
And trees march whinnying through the dark.
Where the sun-bright tube of my childhood
Warmed the morning porridge.
It's a world where plowed-down obsidian shines
And blue bleak embers fall,
Gall themselves, and ah, gash gold vermillion.
It's a world where the angels' wings
Brush the darkness from one's heart
From the black terror of mid-day.
It's a world where logic has no toes
And senses are multi-fingered modalities.
Using the depths of one's being into transforming realities.
It's a world where ego functions
And the Earth springs footsteps into skies that mirror.
Ohmmmmm.

Rosalie: (applause) Second attention. I couldn't do it at the level of first attention.

John: The rules of the second-attention logics are in that production.

Judy: That's right. Whether the first attention is disciplined and clever enough to ferret it out in a first-attention format is a separate issue. You did your assignment very well indeed.

John: I'd like to read you an attempt by a master of first attention, Bateson, to examine the same issue that you addressed with such an aesthetic response: The algorithms of the heart.

> These algorithms of the heart, or, as they say, of the unconscious, are . . . coded and organized in a manner totally different from the algorithms of language. And since a great deal of conscious thought is structured in terms of the logics of language, the algorithms of the unconscious are doubly inaccessible.[1]

By the way, this last remark is simply not true of you as a group of people. This was written some twenty years ago. Consider what Bateson says in his introduction to *The Structure of Magic:*

> It is a strange pleasure to write an introduction for this book because John Grinder and Richard Bandler have done something similar to what my colleagues and I attempted fifteen years ago. . . . they have done something which, as I see it today, we were foolish to miss. . . . this discovery seems obvious when the argument starts from linguistics. . . . but, indeed, much that was so difficult to say in 1955 is strikingly easier to say in 1975.[2]

And here we are in 1986 and we have the tools required to explore the logics of the second attention—to map the transforms that occur at the 1st/2nd attention interface, to develop and purpose the corrective processes necessary to rebalance ourselves and to re-connect ourselves to one another and to our context in such a way that there is some wisdom informing our behavior. Similarly, I would claim this notion that the algorithms of the heart are "doubly inaccessible" is not a limitation on us.

> It is not only that the conscious mind has poor access to this material, but also the fact that when such access is achieved, *e.g.,* in dreams, art, poetry, religion, intoxication, and the like, there is still a formidable problem of translation.[3]

John: Rosalie's production this morning demonstrates that this class of second-attention patterns is not "doubly inaccessible." It's directly accessible if you have the discipline and the skill to shift into second attention. It's only singly inaccessible; and that's a funny kind of inaccessibility. an artistic production like Rosalie's is a demonstration that she can, in

a balance dance between first and second attention, access second-attention patterns and bring them back in words. But the language itself, in its very structure, demonstrate that it is pure second-attention material. There still remains the problem of translation. But that's only a problem for teachers and translators, not for artists. (laughter)
Bateson goes on to say that primary process, (second attention is the way we've talked about it) "is characterized as lacking negatives," and, if you think about Rosalie's production, "lacking tense, . . . ," that is, yesterday and tomorrow and today and ten years ago and the twenty-second century are present together without time markers.

It is also true that the subject matter of primary-process discourse is different from the subject matter of language and consciousness. Consciousness talks about things or persons, and attaches predicates to the specific things or persons which have been mentioned. In primary process the things or people are usually not identified, and the focus of the discourse is upon the *relationships* which are asserted to obtain between them.[4]

Judy: Nice.

John: And if you go back and listen to what Rosalie did, part of that elegance was to take a relationship and fill in the relata —the things that are being related, the substantives and nouns—with things that second attention knows those relationships are true things which first attention had never before considered.

Judy: Just like "Men are grass."

John: Syntax—two days ago in the context of developing the operations called awareness, attention, and disassociation, I asked you to "trust me!" to explain later how we got from the complex and congruent deer grazing in the meadow by the stream to McDonald's. I said that the critical step was to understand how the representation of a possible and never before experienced world entered the neurology of that beautiful, innocent deer. Mark that—the first disassociation, the first breaking of the close bonding between creature and context, the first incongruity, original sin, the tree of knowledge and the apple of disassociation—whatever you want to call it. The critical move is the one which bridges between the naive organism fully connected to context—whose internal representations contain only natural representations—ones which originated in the world and passed through the sequence of transforms neurologically specified—and a creature who has a representation which it has never experienced—where did that possible but never before experienced representation come from? Thanks for trusting me—here's my story.

I was proposing yesterday that syntax is one of the three characteristics that distinguishes our species from other species. So, one morning a long, long time ago, caveman Gork comes out of the cave. Of course, this is when everything is still second attention. So Ork comes out of the cave one morning. One of 'em. I couldn't tell 'em apart. They all look the same to me. (Laughter)

Judy: It's up to you to keep the distinction.

John: (yawning and stretching.) So Ork comes out of the cave and looks around. Sees this basin of water, catchbasin, right? And Nork comes out and stands next to him. Now, in their previous linguistic history together there have been sentences that have occurred which have been useful and repeated such as, "Water tastes good."

Judy: "I drink water." . . .

John: . . . and "I see rock" and "I see water" and "I see saber-toothed tiger; run!" Lots of things like that. That is, there are classes of sentences which they have produced which are well-formed in the syntax of the language they are using where nouns like "water" and "rock" and "saber-toothed tiger" and "George" and "Mary" and "Martha" all occur in the same syntactic slot, say, subject or direct object of the sentence. Notice what the inductive consequence of having a syntactic system—a system where position relative to other parts of the sentence contributes meaning to the entire sentence—is with respect to our internal representations. Presumably, before a syntactically based language system our internal representations were very closely tied to certain characteristics of the physical world. For example, those portions of the physical world which we had had experience of which were hot were sorted into a natural class—those portions of the physical world which had highly reflexive surfaces or, say, perhaps, portions of the world which make a sound when struck—each of these constituted a natural class. Thus the sensible physical properties of the world interacting with our genetically specified neurological filters determined the sorting principles which allowed us to group the multivaried experiences into natural classes. Note that each of these were justified epistemologically—they were a predictable result of the strong interaction of our perceptual filters and the world. Here comes the wild card—syntax. The syntax of natural language inductively establishes an entirely novel internal sorting principle. That is to say, portions of our experience are sorted into the same class with no justification either in the world or in our neurologically specified filters—the resulting internal representations establish connections and groupings of real world counterparts which are completely arbitrary connections which have never occurred in the experience of the bearer of these representations. The stage is now set. And now Ork goes, . . .

Judy: He's real tired. Ork's really tired, probably.

John: . . . probably, it was a long night. And he goes, "I drink water, water good." And Nork goes, Oh, yeah. Actually he doesn't go, Oh, yeah, that is, he doesn't have internal dialogue yet. (laughter) That's one of the ways in which consciousness emerged. So he doesn't go, Oh, yeah. Only modern humans do that, right? That external stimulus triggers a motor program, drink water. So he goes over, takes a deep drink of water and starts to say, "I drink water," but as he gets to about the "I" in the sentence, "I drink water," a saber-toothed tiger walks out from behind a convenient boulder. This is important news. This is news of difference.

Judy: Something you can notice.

John: . . . by its presence, not by its absence. So in the second attention's representational system of Nork there is triggered a move to grab a rock for obvious purposes. So there's a internal shift during the act of speech and instead of saying, "I drink water," he ends up saying "I drink rock."

At second attention, we have the sum of all the representations of real world events which reach us through the filters in our neurology. They're the sum total of our experience as distorted through the neurological filters and then stored in relatively unorganized ways at second attention. That means there's nothing in second attention that has not been in the world of experience at some point in the history of that individual phenotype, that organism, Nork. In a sense, this organism is tied to its environment too tightly. By misspeaking, a magic moment in human history has occurred, because later that evening, after the saber-toothed tiger has departed, and they're all sitting around the fire, Ork goes, "Uh, Nork said, 'I drink rock.' Haw-haw-haw!" and everybody at the campfire cracks up, right? And this is a magic moment in human evolution because in the minds of each and every one of those second attentions . . . What has happened?

. . . something has occurred in their representations of the world which never occurred in the world. And by misspeaking they have liberated themselves from the tyranny of exclusively sensory experience. It's not a problem we have, you understand. We're trying to get back. But they were trying to get out. I cannot over emphasize the importance of this strange creature-syntax. You can even catch a glimpse of the kind of distortion that amazing creature works even in modern natural languages. The process of nominalization is a case in point—any creature who can fool us into initially talking and subsequently acting as if *love, decisions* and *power* are in the same class as *bricks, water* and *Kleenex* is a wily and dangerous creature—one that's to be watched carefully.

Judy: They created a possible world . . .

John: . . . by misspeaking and I would argue that technology is our response to the discrepancy between the representations that we have created internally in second and first attention by misspeaking and what we can actually accomplish at that point. Somebody watching a bird one day might have said, "I fly."—mistake, mistake. And now we do. Good old Nork.

Judy: Good old Nork. We owe a lot to that guy.

John: Boy, I tell you.

Dr. Erickson invented a game for his grandchildren which amused both him and the children and which illustrated nicely the use of second-attention logic patterns. We were exposed to this game on the occasion of a visit to Erickson during a trip from Oklahoma back to our place in the Santa Cruz mountains. When we arrived at Erickson's home, Betty Erickson, Milton's wife and lifelong collaborator, greeted us graciously and directed us to join Milton and some visitors from Michigan in the other house. Dr. Erickson received us warmly and we were mildly surprised to recognize his visitors as some people we had sent to him. After several minutes of polite and quite pleasant conversation, Erickson handed me a typed sheet of paper, announcing that it contained a puzzle and directing Judith and me to read the clues on this sheet of paper to our children, Mike, Kathie, and Eric, and the other visitors for their consideration. At the top of the paper was an introductory statement to the Erickson grandchildren inviting them to solve the puzzle and send the solution to Grandpa Erickson with the offer of ten dollars to those who arrived at a solution which matched Grandpa's. It further stated that the grandchildren could enlist the assistance of their parents in endeavoring to arrive at a solution but that Grandpa himself suspected that such adult assistance was unlikely to be useful. Below was a list of a dozen or so clues. These clues were to be read aloud—so the instructions stated —and the listener was to think of a word which was a synonym for the clue phrase. At some point—so the instructions continued—the name of a familiar activity engaged in by humans would spontaneously emerge from the second attention processes of the attentive listener and that was the answer to the puzzle. Taking turns Judith and I read the following phrases:

(a) the last thing a society lady puts on before leaving the house for tea
(b) a group of fully mature maggots
(c) a group of males singing with deep register voices
(d) a flying mammal
(e) a kind of English cigarettes
(f) piece of carbon subjected to high pressure and temperature
(g) multiple imperfections in a woman's nylons

Certainly in such a clever group—one which respects autonomous second-attention circuits—this partial list of clues will be adequate. Yes! I see you've got it. Those of you who have an answer raise your hands and when you answer is verified, review the clues with someone who hasn't yet popped the solution into first attention—create additional clues to assist but do not be too obvious. . . . (pandemonium) . . .

OK, let me have your attention back up here.

So after having read the list of clues to our children and Erickson's visitors we talked over the guesses (none yet correct) which the clues had stimulated until the old man wisely redirected our first attention away from the puzzle to other matters. At this point, Eric, who was then seven or eight years old, became restless and asked for and got permission to leave and go over to the five-and-ten store nearby—he had been promised that he could go shopping that morning. When he returned half an hour later, several of us had solved the puzzle—imagine our delight when he proudly showed us what he had purchased—that's right—a baseball, bat, and glove. Please note the elegance of this child's solution. Presented with a second-attention puzzle, he used second-attention behavior and circuitry exclusively in reaching a solution —that's congruity.

What? Sure, here are the words which are synonyms for the phrases

(a) the last thing a society lady puts on before leaving the house for tea	(a) gloves

(b) a group of fully mature maggots	(b) flies
(c) a group of males singing with deep register voices	(c) basses
(d) a flying mammal	(d) a bat
(e) a kind of English cigarettes	(e) Players
(f) piece of carbon subjected to high pressure and temperature	(f) diamond
(g) multiple imperfections in a woman's nylons	(g) runs

The underlying second-attention pattern here is phonological ambiguity—the word *flies* can mean either the clue phrase, a group of mature maggots, or in baseball, the balls hit in the air to players. Similarly, with each of the clues. The solution, therefore, can only emerge as the second-attention, unconscious intersection of the secondary meanings of the phonologically ambiguous answers to the phrasal clues.

Francis: There's a creative strategy format called Synectics which seeks to do that.

John: That's where you identify with whatever the problem dictates? Yeah, it came out of a Boston group.

Francis: They've used it in the advertising business and in product development and so on. It seems like a codified forced second-attention strategy.

John: It is a forced second attention strategy. It's like allegory. What Francis is saying is, you get a group of engineers where you want to solve an engineering problem, for example. And so you'll ask them to identify with the mechanics of the system. That is, like Tom's visual art, like Titos' drumming, singing, and dancing, like any aesthetic act, they do second-attention identifications with the object or the system and by so doing shift attention and get a second description, a double description, which often yields rather astonishingly quick results in terms of problem-solving.

Francis: The case they cited that comes to my mind was that of a paint manufacturer who wanted to manufacture paint for a certain kind of surface, so they became climbers on the surface and they found out what they need was little stickers, like suction cups that an octopus has, in order to grab onto the surface. They used that as the metaphor to then develop a surface emulsion process that would create microscopic little stickers so the droplet of paint could stick to surfaces that otherwise would not hold paint.

Judy: Whoa! That's cool.

> In primary process the things or people are usually not identified, and the focus of the discourse is upon the *relationships* which are asserted to obtain between them. This is really only another way of saying that the discourse of primary process is metaphoric. A metaphor retains unchanged the relationship which it "illustrates" while substituting other things or persons for the relata.[5]

Judy: Do you recognize this from when you learned how to build metaphors?

John: And you recognize it from Rosalie's production.

Judy: . . . maintaining the relationship while changing the characters and context.

John: Erickson had a procedure, "Allow your arm to go down only as quickly as you dream a dream in which exactly those things which you need to consider to make the class of changes you have come here to make are illustrated for you in the dream." Honest unconscious movements, the dreaming arm goes down, time distortion, *pop!* Raises that arm again. "Dream that dream again, hold constant the relationships, change all of the cast of characters," and he would have them dream it a dozen times. What's he doing? He's activating precisely the class of circuits that need to be balanced and rearranged, again the arcs that are missing have to be put in place . . . or take Feldenkrais—a person would come to Moshe complaining of an ache in a muscle in the upper arm.

Would Moshe touch that muscle?—probably not, he would find a series of motor programs which included the indicated muscle as a component—he would activate the larger circuit, the physiological context for the muscle—the kinesthetic counterpart of Erickson's dreaming arm procedure. He's doing straight programming in the sense that we're talking about, making sure there's an integrity to the circuits, which are the most relevant ones for the situation the person has come to change.

In a simile, the fact that a metaphor is being used is marked by the insertion of the words "as if" or "like." In primary process (as in art) there are no markers to indicate to the conscious mind that the message material is metaphoric.[6]

Remember Rosalie's production this morning? There were no metamarkers on that.

The focus of "relationship" is, however, somewhat more narrow than would be indicated by merely saying that primary-process material is metaphoric and does not identify the specific relata. The subject matter of dream and other primary-process material is, in fact, relationship in the more narrow sense of relationship between self and other persons or between self and the environment.

Anglo-Saxons who are uncomfortable with the idea that feelings and emotions are outward signs of precise and complex algorithms usually have to be told that these matters, (that is,) the relationship between self and others, and the relationship between self and environment, are, in fact, the subject matter of what are called "feelings" —love, hate, fear, confidence, anxiety, hostility, etc. It is unfortunate that these abstractions . . .[7]

. . . which you now know—and Gregory didn't at the time he wrote this—as nominalizations. And there is a very specific first-attention linguistic process which reduces a predicate, with its related material, to a nominalization, where the relata are gone. And we act as if that's a thing now in first attention. And the second attention laughs at us.

It is unfortunate that these abstractions referring to *patterns* of relationship have received names (nominalizations-JD/JG), which are usually handled in ways that assume that the "feelings" are mainly characterized by quantity rather than by precise pattern.[8]

John: "How strongly do you feel about that?" Nonsense. "What pattern in second attention is activated by this class of experiences?" Yeah, now you're doing something in the dance between first and second attention that might be worth pursuing . . .

Judy: . . . at the right logical level.

This is one of the nonsensical contributions of psychology to a distorted epistemology.[9]

Judy: Anybody have any comments about that?

George: Clarify that one.

John: (laughing)

Judy: (screaming) Aaaaghhh!
This is "Evolution of Behavior." It's an article by Conrad Lorenz, written back in December of 1958.

A whale's flipper, a bat's wing, and a man's arm are as different from one another in outward appearance as they are in the functions they serve. But the bones of these structures reveal an essential similarity of design. The zoologist concludes that whale, bat and man evolved from a common ancestor. Even if there were no other evidence the comparison of the skeletons of these creatures would suffice to establish that conclusion. The similarity of skeletons shows that basic structure may persist over geological periods inspite of a wide divergence of function. Following the example of zoologists who have long exploited the comparative method, students of animal behavior have begun to ask a penetrating question. We all know how greatly the behavior of animals can vary. Especially under the influence of the learning process. Psychologists have mostly observed and experimented with the behaviors of individual animals. Few have considered the behavior of species. But is it not possible that beneath all the variations of individual behavior there lies an inner structure of inherited behavior which characterizes all the members of a given species, genus, or larger taxonomic group just as the skeleton of a primordial ancestor characterizes the form and structure of all mammals today. Yet it is possible and let me give you an example which, seemingly trivial, has a bearing on this question. Anyone who has ever watched a dog scratch its jaw or a bird preen its head feathers can attest to the fact that they do so in the same way.

John: Access your representations. Verify that for yourself. A dog scratching its head, . . .

Judy: . . . and a bird preening its head feathers.

The dog props itself on the tripod formed by its haunches and two forelegs and reaches a hind leg forward in front of its shoulder. Now the odd fact is that most birds as well as virtually all mammals and reptiles scratch with precisely the same motion. A bird also scratches with the hind limb, that is its claw, and in doing so it lowers its wing and reaches its claw forward in front of its shoulder. One might think it would be simpler for the bird to move its claw directly to its head without moving its wing which lies folded out of the way against its back. I do not see how to explain this clumsy action unless we admit that it is inborn. Before the bird can scratch it must reconstruct old spacial relationships of the limbs the four-legged common ancestor which it shared with mammals. In retrospect it seems peculiar that psychologists have been slow to pursue such clues in hereditary behavior.[10]

John: There are a number of powerful points to that passage. The one I select out is the acuity and the second-attention states that are presupposed by the observation this man was able to make. He knows how to extend self. And it involves shrinking self from reflexive consciousness and first attention to second-attention circuitry and the extension of self to the organism that he wants to come to understand. There are worlds upon worlds around us which are available if we have the ability to shift those perceptual filters which is the subject of this morning's work. I often wonder, having spoken to people who spent time with Lorenz who invariably told me stories about his extraordinary ability to identify with other species as his first step in coming to an appreciation of the significance of their behavior. I've always suspected that that old guy was activating the circuits within himself which are the homologues of the circuits of the creature he wishes to identify with . . . (pausing) . . . Your task is to explore anywhere along the afferent or efferent chain of events between you and the world. So this morning specifically you're not out to change the world, you're out to change the perceptual filters you use to interface with the world . . .

Judy: . . . at the periphery or any place along the circuit. I urge you to get out as close to the periphery as you're capable of at this moment in time and to set yourself a disciplined task of a first-/second-attention dance, over the next weeks, months, and decades, of seeing how far out on the periphery you can change the values of those filters.

Judy: Those people with glasses, take off your glasses and hand them to somebody who doesn't wear glasses . . . Oh, two people with glasses can trade.

John: Now notice when the visual value shifts, what happens to the kinesthetics and the auditory? "Distorted"/"changed"—I would prefer "changed" because it indicates difference without evaluation. Pass them around a little bit. Here, have another shot at the world.

Allen: Move your head while they're on.

John: Yeah, move your head while you have them on. Reach out for something and grab it.

Man: Wearing bifocals is a new thing for me because I can hold two images of you.

John: Double description. Pass 'em again, what the hell?

Woman: I've worn glasses since I was twelve years old and last year went to bifocals; but I didn't want the granny glasses for obvious reasons so I got just regular glasses. I got so sick to my stomach. Every time I'd go, "Oh, my God! . . ." . . . going back and forth . . . . . . up and down . . .

Judy: . . . that distortion. I've heard other people say that exact same thing.

John: (harshly) Come back to first attention! Where are you people? Come back here, come back here. Petty tyrants are in the area. Please pass the glasses back to their so-called owners who might want to think about just how many forms petty tyrants can take.

Maureen: I want to relate an experience that I had—if anyone swims. I decided to start doing more serious long-distance swimming which required the use of . . .

John: . . . goggles . . .

Maureen: . . . goggles. And I couldn't swim when I put the goggles on; I could not swim. I was running into walls . . . I had to relearn how to swim with goggles on. Now I can't swim without goggles.

Judy: Yes you can.

John: That's the importance about somatic flexibility as opposed to genetic codes. See, if Lamarck was right your baby daughter Katy would be in trouble.

Judy: Acquired characteristics would be passed on.

John: And that's why Lamarck has to be wrong. Actually, Lamarck is right at the wrong logical level. As we said the other day, Lamarckian evolution is the dynamic principle of selection in the world of mind. Darwinian evolution governs the world of biology.

> It is sometimes said that the distortions of art (say van Gogh's "Chair") are directly representative of what the artist "sees." If such statements refer to "seeing" in its simplest physical sense, (e.g., remediable with spectacles), I presume that they are nonsense. If van Gogh could only see the chair in that wild way, his eyes would not serve properly to guide him in the very accurate placing of paint on canvas.[11]

John: There's a story that Picasso was riding a train somewhere in Europe once and he got into this compartment with an older gentleman who happened to recognize who he was . . .

Judy: . . . and who didn't like his art . . .

John: . . . strictly a first-attention type . . .

Judy: . . . strictly.

John: Do you understand the ways in which people become unbalanced and ultimately one-dimensional in this way? His companion insisted on critiquing Picasso's art. Apparently Picasso was more polite than I would have been and listened to him; finally the man made the statement that the real function of art was not the crazy thing that Picasso was doing, . . .

Judy: . . . distorting . . . reality.

John: . . . the real function of art was to represent reality.

Judy: ". . . to represent reality." So what do you think Picasso said? He said, "Do you have an example of reality in art?"

John: So the man reached into his wallet and extracted a photograph of his wife.

Judy: And Picasso said, "Boy, she sure is little." (Laughter)

John: "And she's very flat."

Judy: "She doesn't have a lot of color either."

John: Remember the exchange between Larry and I yesterday? There are worlds upon worlds out there and one of the ways to find them is to shift perceptual filters—a strategy for exploration. Technical climbing has some of the elements you need for your work. When I climb there are a number of factors I have to take into consideration. My own skill levels, obviously. The larger context such as weather: Will I get caught on a wall in a snow storm?—no, thank you.

Judy: If you don't mind.

John: I have to consider who my partner is; I have to know that he or she is competent to come after me in the kinds of situations that I could possibly get myself into, that is, downside planning. I must also address the nature of the rock I will be climbing on.

Judy: . . . there's a lot of different rocks out there, too . . .

John: . . . and I have to do route planning. I have to decide what route I'm going to attempt, especially if it's never been climbed before, if it's a first ascent. And you're doing lots of first ascents these days. Somehow I have to balance the amount of risk with my ability to get off the rock. If I'm very good at route planning and I'm very good at risk taking—in terms of deciding what level of risk is acceptable for my skill levels and the partner that I'm with and the rack that I'm carrying (the material that I have to assist me in protecting me as I climb)—You set the level of risk so that in the worst case you will get out alive. But as I said to Larry yesterday there are serious dangers; in fact, I've only been glacier climbing once and I'm not sure I'll ever do it again.

Judy: Ice moves more than rock moves.

John: I could feel the creeping of the glacier when I was on this vertical wall with these crampons, these claws lashed onto my boots, with these two ice axes looped around my wrists here. I could feel the whole environment—the context that I was on—creeping. And that triggered deep, deep programs in me. (Laughter)

Judy: And that's why I go to Mexico for my vacations. (Laughter)

John: I mean everybody draws the line somewhere. There's a man named John Bacher who climbs solo. He does some of the hardest climbs in the world, routes which twenty years ago nobody could do; and he does them solo without protection. John Bacher and I don't do the same sport. What he does is a different sport. And all I am saying is that there is a difference. I do not make an evaluation except to say it's amazing to watch this man do what he does. And you won't find me there next to him. And that's a decision I've made. It's a line I've drawn. He's only allowed one mistake. Hell, my learning strategy is to go out and make as many mistakes as possible to get feedback from the world. (laughter) That's not an appropriate strategy in technical climbing when you're soloing.

There are interesting balances here. You've got to move with some rhythm. For example, I get a perceptual reality shift when I move from the flatland to the land of verticality, especially if I've slept on the rock overnight and climb straight out of an alcove in the wall the next morning and keep on going. I have departed from the flatland. In that world, when that shift occurs, horizontal lines like ledges are illformed. As ill-formed for me as they must be for the BaMbuti once I've made that shift. Not only is that true in a direct perceptual sense but "objectively" speaking it's true. Because when I move in the vertical world, if I fall I want an air fall.

Judy: You don't want to hit that ledge below.

John: If it's an air fall, and I've been impeccable in the placement of the protection—the devices that fit into cracks in the rock —and if they hold the way they're supposed to, I'll climb again. Now, how much protection do you want to put in as you move? Well, if you put something in every five feet or five yards it slows you down and then the second comes up and has to remove the protection you've placed thus slowing your progress even more.

Judy: You better have some real endurance . . .

John: . . . because you're on a vertical face and there's a certain amount of strength that's required and you better get it done. You can't stop and dally. No lolly-gagging on a vertical wall.

Judy: Let me tell you about a time John climbed to a part on the rock which he described as "smooth, round, and impossible."

John: There were no edges. And it was between 85 and 90 degrees so it was as vertical as anything you're going to climb.

Judy: So Geoffrey scurries up this section . . .

John: He didn't scurry; he worked at it.

Judy: He gets up there—John can't see him at this point—and he's singing cowboy songs and waiting for John to find his way up. And John said he tried every possible avenue that he could think of; he felt everywhere on the entire rock. It wasn't possible. But at the same time he knew it was possible because somebody had just done it. So finally he said, "Geoff, give me a hint, just a hint, you know, anything," and Geoff says, "Consider the implications of the word 'smear.' " You have to get traction with your entire body. It was a salamander type of move. It was pure second attention; there was no room . . .

John: . . . for anything except first attention collapsed into the circuits necessary—almost as though it were a phylogenetic regression to a reptilian or amphibian level—(Laughter) to get to this class of moves that I needed to move up this vertical face without any holds. It was about a fourteen-foot section.

The notion of Viola Legere lifelines is so important. You can't go to the second-attention circuit necessary to accomplish something impossible (or close to it) unless you've already assessed the larger context and made arrangements for a retreat if necessary. That's why you're roped and that's why you use protection on the rock. You're responsible for arranging the larger context within which you can make that class of commitments. And if you're unbalanced in either way, if you fail to be impeccable in doing the first-attention route-finding, risk-taking assessments in your dance with second attention, then you will not have the freedom to commit to the subcircuits of second attention necessary to do these impossible things. The other thing which is useful in the kinds of perceptual filter changes I want you to explore today is that when I'm climbing—when I'm balanced and I've done my first-attention assessment of routes and am placing my protection impeccably but not overplacing and I know, worst case, worst case, worst case, I know I've got air falls instead of ledges that I could hit—everything is right and I'm right, the world is right. There's no difference between me and the world. The rock and I are together.

I'm dancing. I am not climbing; I'm dancing and there's a rhythm to my movements. And as I look up for the next move I can see a glow on the rock in the areas where my hands and feet should go. And as I reach for a minimum hold for balance, as I shift my position, that hold enlarges for my fingers. The world affirms that I am correctly situated with respect to it by giving me more than was there when I reached for it.

Alan: In that case the world had changed. It wasn't just a perceptual change.

John: Interesting ambiguity. And this is part of the arc of what we're doing. I don't know the answer to that question in a deep epistemological way but I know the experience directly and that's the point of what we're doing this morning.

Timothy Gallway has put together a marvelously effective and simple procedure for developing perceptual filters—specifically designed to optimize certain perceptual motor skills. He has successfully used this procedure in the sports of skiing, golf and tennis. It's part of what I call the Gallway format. Any of you who have had difficulty in translating NLP patterns such as physiological states of excellence, use of personal history resources in tasks, . . . into English and very specific application areas, read Gallway. Excellent work —effective and simple—not easy, mind you, but simple. Appreciate Gallway's content—he is out to optimize someone's tennis game. (*The Inner Game of Tennis.*) He places the learner in context and has them perform. Observing closely he allows the player to continue until he detects a decrease in the quality of their game—precisely at this point he interrupts them, physically and with the question, "What are you trying to do?" Answer—"I'm trying to X." Where X could be making sure the racket is completely vertical when impacting the ball or moving the weight entirely onto the ball of the foot. Response by Mr. Gallway—"Ok, quit trying to X and simply play tennis." Gallway has correctly noted that "trying" is a label which identifies a state of heightened muscular tension and increased internal dialogue—two factors which guarantee a decrease in performance. The simple instruction to quit trying releases the player from the failure mode of "trying," clears first attention (removing informal dialogue . . .) freed of the twin despots of internal dialogue and muscular tension, many players find their game vastly improved. However, for some players, the instruction to "quit trying" is not entirely effective—thus the need for the second intervention in the hierarchy implicitly specified by the Gallway format. Suppose Gallway is working on someone's ground strokes (forehands and backhands from the baseline). His second intervention would be to pick a couple of reference points in the external world perceptually available both to the player and to him as coach, and which are important in the successful execution of the ground strokes. This is the origin of the "bounce-hit" perceptual filter. He has the player say "bounce" when he or she sees the tennis ball bounce as it approaches and "hit" at the instant when the racket's strings and the tennis ball make contact. As Gallway reports, it is often the case that the player's report of these two reference points and his personal perception do not match. That is, the player will frequently be out of synch with the actual real world event (as witnessed by Gallway). Bringing the player's perceptions and report of the real world event into synch with his perception of those same reference points invariably improves the quality of the player's game. Those of you trained in the NLP technology have, no doubt, noted how clever this intervention by Gallway is—with a single move he successfully interrupts the internal dialogue (the auditory channel is committed externally saying "bounce" and "hit"); re-directs the player from a split attention state (mixed focus between internal dialogue and external events) to a single coordinated focus (on the movement of the ball); and arranges a respectful and appropriate division of labor between 1st and 2nd attention—the *tonal* seizes the reference point, inventorying it in real time and then relaxes, releasing to the *naqual* where the strength, timing and grace necessary for a proper ground stroke are ready and waiting. The important issue here, however, for our purposes is the bounce-hit format—it's a prototype for the construction of perceptual filters.

EXERCISE: CHANGING PERCEPTUAL FILTERS

Exercise. Do you understand the purpose of this next drill? It's to arrange impeccably—in a dance between first and second attention—to make arrangements to go to a perceptual filter near the periphery and change the value of some of the filters that are deep within you. Out beyond second attention, out along those afferent or efferent nerves, so that you have a class of sensory distortions. The question of what you see and feel and hear and sense, whether it's the world changing or your perceptual filters changing—notice that that's not a disjunction you have to accept. It could be that by changing your perceptual filters you are allowing information of difference which was always there to come along those pathways. So I would at the moment say that you're not ready to answer the question that Alan has posed because you don't have an adequate experience base for exploring those possibilities. You don't have an adequate database, in terms of direct second-attention experience of changing filters, to decide whether you are changing filters in such a way that you're allowing information of difference to enter that has always been in there but has been blocked in order to maintain the stability of your standard world description—to protect your homeostatic centers—or whether, in fact, the world is changing.

Judy: Now there are a number of ways to accomplish this. I will make some suggestions to you and then invite you to make arrangements. There's a wisdom to what you've already arranged. It's time to use it. The eyeglasses could be used as an approach. I put Karen's glasses on and all values in all systems changed, as was predictable. I noticed how much effort it took me to restore my usual visual field by playing with the muscles of my eyes. It's an interesting measure of the difference between my filters and yours. There are other ways to do this.

John: Those of you who are adept at official trance work, which is, by the way, obsolete, you understand . . . (laughter) The notion of trance induction is your ability to make the first-attention safety arrangements, the Viola Legere arrangements, and then to commit to your subcircuitry—to move first attention to identify with second-attention circuitry. This makes the notion of altered state a variable you have control over. Some of you are familiar with the rituals of hypnosis. And rituals are not to be scoffed at. They can establish a state from which extraordinary things can occur.

Judy: Gregory talked about ritual in the context of play; he says that if all the moves are known by both people in the party, for example, so that there are no unknowns, then it's ritual. In the cybernetic loop, say, between Amber and I, if we go through a set of interactions and she knows what I'm going to do and say and I know what she's going to do and say . . . , and it's all known then it's called ritual.

John: The dance we'll do this afternoon, that we've practiced for the last couple of days, is approaching the level of ritual because we know exactly what steps we're going to go through. Now notice that because everything is known doesn't mean it's not useful.

Judy: Bateson says "It can be character building."

John: It can be the basis of skill. It can be direct access to altered states which are otherwise very difficult to achieve.
I was trained by Jesuits. I have great respect for their ability to think. They are impeccable at first attention. In the discussion of ritual with some Jesuit friends of ours what was fascinating was that they came to recognize that when they were being prepared to be ordained as priests, there was an older Jesuit who was in charge of their training—who was their coach. And as they went through the liturgy, specifically, a ritual called the Mass, they would practice specified physiological positions and movements in sequence and the older, more experienced Jesuit would evaluate the movements and have them do it again and again and again until he was

satisfied. And what was it he was using as his criteria for evaluation?—whether those sets of movements, those uses of voice, those postures, those breathings induced the proper state of reverence in the practitioner, the younger priest, which would then make him an appropriate model for the congregation to identify with.

John: When we all sing together or dance together, you notice what it does; the Japanese custom in certain work environments of breathing and doing calisthenics together as a beginning ritual has a powerful communal effect of coordinating the second attention of a large number of people.

Judy: And it's also interesting to think about where our rituals are in our own behavior, in our loops with other people, and evaluate whether we want more unknowns in there or not.

John: Diane was talking about the fact that there are movements that classically trained conductors are taught. They are standard. When she conducts she doesn't use any of those. My response was, "It's because you're an artist. You have found your own ritual."

Judy: She already learned the rules and now she's bending them; and she knows how to bend them in a well-formed way.

John: So if you wish to employ old rituals, such as hypnotic rituals, you could for example sit opposite each other and identify A and B. Make your first-attention arrangements, establish all your safety lines, and make a commitment. A goes to a class of experiences internal or external. I would prefer that it be external. Perhaps if Robert and I were doing this he would walk and I would shift to second attention and I would become Robert by walking like Robert. We could look into each other's eyes deeply and he could go into deep parts of his mind (second attention) and I could follow via our communication both visually and tactilely, breathing together. We might use one of those mutual nonverbal trance inductions; some of you have played with those in other seminars. I could work in a three-person group. Notice there is a lot of flexibility in this exercise. Suppose Tom wants to become Robert or vice versa. From a third perceptual position—the outside position—I can easily make comparative judgements that will allow me to adjust Tom's body until it matches Robert—some then that he might have difficulty achieving from his own perceptual position. So I might insist that they breathe together—the basis of empathy.

I've met lots of registered nurses, for example, who are psychic in the usual sense. They have developed the ability to extend self to patients. They don't always make great choices about when they do it but they can do it. And they can know things, like Erickson did, about somebody else's personal history that they have no right to know. That's content. I'm not talking about that. I'm talking about entering another person's circuitry, in the sense of learning how they process the content; and how that will change your world more profoundly than any substantive identification, that is, learning the content of their experience. As a secondary effect you might in fact know things about them that you have no right to know in the sense of information exchange. But that's not the logical level you're entering at. You're entering at the level of processing and perceptual filters because I want you to change the value of your perceptual filters as close to the periphery as you can get.

There's one intermediate place that I want some of you to visit for me and then let me know about later. And that is, if relationship—as in Rosalie's production this morning and as in my reading from Gregory's article—is the organizing principle you might use a format where you go pick some relationship, such as the relationship of "above." The relationship that's expressed by the word "above" in English; the word "above" is not the relationship, it's the word in first attention. And now you go to second-attention circuitry and begin to discover things which are possible relata of this relationship. You're holding constant the relationship, and, like in "Dream the dream and dream it again and dream it again," you are identifying some of the things which can be in this relationship. That's what Rosalie did this morning; it was art. So for "above": sky and ground. Cliff and river. Bird and snake. Your task, of course, if you're tuned into the circuit, is to notice what's similar and what's different . . .

Actually I recommend that you imitate them, that is, set up those same relationships in yourself because what your partner is doing is teaching you something about his or her second-attention organization which is indeed how he or she processes. That's like an intermediate way station on the way out to the perceptual filters at the periphery that I want you to go to. It might be interesting on your way. See you in an hour. Enjoy your journeys.

BREAK

Judy: How did it go?

John: Thank you for not answering her question. You've passed the test. You are all now certified in knowing when to apply second attention as opposed to first attention. The basis of any aesthetic art is skill. And you need to learn to extend your second attention into areas you don't even at present know exist. The only way I know you're going to get there is to make a commitment. Second attention, I'm calling you to make a commitment on some daily basis. For example, you can never wait again; you have to use that time in the most disciplined and impeccable of ways . . .

Judy: . . . in the most efficacious manner . . .

John: . . . and that's a commitment; for whatever credit the two of us have built up over these five days, you owe us that much —and I'm saying more. There are worlds upon worlds out there.

Judy: You knew that.

John: Urban areas are really strange environments, but even here there are mysterious things available if you have the appreciation and sensitivity to note them. Identification with another living system. Profound.

JUGGLING: FINAL MOVEMENT

John: Now to the juggling task for today (demonstrating the first juggling move) Day one went like this, right? Yes, Marne.

Marne: In learning to juggle there's an unpopular step that I've found valuable. It's called "the drop"—that's the first step.

John: You actually, deliberately drop . . .

Marne: . . . the ball.

John: The second day's move was this: Waiting until the last possible moment, making your throw as uniform as possible —in both directions, obviously. In these next ten minutes when you're going to secure three of these and juggle, I'd like you to review the previous days' steps. I'd like you to start with the first day and do this first day move until you're satisfied that those circuits are tuned. Then I'd like you to go to the second day to work, in both directions. When you get to the third day, if you have any trouble I want you to stop and go back to the second. If you have any trouble doing the second, go back to the first. It's only three steps. Notice the relationship; once again, your eyes should be better now. Remember, one hundred years ago this was magic because people did not have adequate visual scanning patterns to notice what was going on. Notice what I'm doing here. Your job is to make a template for this because in a moment we're going to pick up the third ball. I want you to be able to see what I'm doing when there's three of them moving. Any questions? Good. You already passed the test. (laughter) Remember the trick is "stop the world," find the state, tune the circuits, first day, second day, and make the final move. And enjoy your juggling. Be back in ten minutes, folks.

John: Notice please what your beliefs were about the possibility of juggling in the amount of time that you've had and the difference, in terms of your learning ability when you shift attention. Next comment. There are still some interesting things going on —There are still people who are making this a difficult task because they're doing this . . . (demonstrating an inappropriate state and behavior) That's hard. You've got two in the air at the same time.

Judy: Notice when he does it there's only one in the air.

John: (demonstrating) I wouldn't ever teach you anything difficult. (laughter) I'm serious. We have only taught simple things. That doesn't mean that they're easy to do, but it does mean that they are simple in the sense that they are within anybody's grasp, with the appropriate attention shifts and a certain amount of personal commitment to practice. So if you remember you want to keep the minimum number of balls in the air at a time, then look at how much time I have to make these things work. Now if you throw two at once, that's a bit more than I can do. Maybe it's something you want to stretch yourself for. Those who are interested, obviously, you can easily do tricky things—right?—like (demonstrating a over hand catch routine)

Judy: Then you can move on to other kinds of juggling like juggling with pins, bowling pins.

Antonio: What can they do with five? I knew a guy who used to sell oranges in my hometown and he would have five oranges going and he was not worried about what was going on.

Judy: He couldn't afford to be.

John: I'd like to propose that there be some parts of your circuitry that now, deliberately at second attention, come to occupy the positions that Judith occupies, I occupy, George occupies, and the others of us here occupy. Your circuit integrity is of supreme importance if this piece of work is to have any impact beyond these five days. Also, remember, as you return to your homes, to do so with some sensitivity. Satellites don't come straight in, you know, they skip off the atmosphere and slow down a little bit. If they come straight in they burn up, I mean, at the rate of speed you're presently moving at . . . Be respectful of the people with whom you about to recouple with—in the sense of the joint circuitry becoming larger aggregates of mind. If you appreciate the notion of wisdom and aesthetics which is frame around everything we've done here, then you'll appreciate how carefully you must approach recoupling with the various parts of the world that you're going back to. But never make the mistake again, and I call upon your second attention to insist upon this, of believing that what you can understand at first attention is anything more than a small fragment of your personal alternatives, which in turn are a small fragment of the human possibilities that exist within each of you.

Judy: Hear, hear!

John: The major contributors besides you, me, and Judith, are the people we've mentioned: Gregory Bateson, a fine thinker, a master of first attention, but an artist who always knew that the wisdom resided in second attention; Carlos Castaneda, who rechronicles his experiences of being induced into an alternate reality of the Yagui Indian; the Turnbull material, which is such a powerful example of traditional cultures and the importance of passionate involvement; and of course, our treat this afternoon, to be induced partially, as we have been each afternoon, into a Kongolese reality. We went to each of these major contributors for a last word, a word of advice, their suggestion about how you might proceed. And I am not speaking lightly when I say that of all the people I know who could accomplish some of the goals that Gregory set out in this meta-science of epistemology, you are the best prepared to do that.

John: Gregory Bateson—I read a piece this morning that ended with these sentences,

> It is unfortunate that these abstractions referring to *patterns* of relationship have received names (nominalizations), which are usually handled in ways that assume that the "feelings" are mainly characterized by quantity rather than by precise pattern. This is one of the nonsensical contributions of psychology to a distorted epistemology.[12]

John: He goes on.

All this indicates that primary-process thoughts and the communication of such thoughts to others are, in an evolutionary sense, more archaic (that's a difference, not a value judgment) than the more conscious operations of language, etc. This has implications for the whole economics and dynamic structure of the mind. Samuel Butler was perhaps first to point out that that which we know best is that of which we are least conscious, *i.e.,* that the process of habit formation is a sinking of knowledge down to less conscious and more archaic levels. The unconscious contains not only the painful matters which consciousness prefers not to inspect, but also many matters which are so familiar that we do not need to inspect them. Habit, therefore, is a major economy of conscious thought. We can do things without consciously thinking about them. The skill of an artist, or rather his demonstration of a skill, becomes a message about these parts of his unconsciousness. . . .

But the matter is not quite so simple. Some types (levels JD/JG) of knowledge can conveniently be sunk to unconscious levels, but other types must be kept on the surface. Broadly, we can afford to sink those sorts of knowledge which continue to be true regardless of changes in the environment, but we must maintain in an accessible place all those controls of behavior which must be modified for every instance.[13]

John: You have gone a step past that. You have sorted and structured and created functions—such as "self"—which allow you to sink into these track them with your first attention. You have choices that he didn't represent.

The lion can sink into his unconscious the proposition that zebras are his natural prey, but in dealing with any particular zebra he must be able to modify the movements of his attack to fit with the particular terrain and the particular evasive tactics of the particular zebra.

The economics of the system, in fact, pushes organisms toward sinking into the unconscious those generalities of relationship which remain permanently true and toward keeping within the conscious the pragmatics of particular instances.

The premises may, economically, be sunk, but particular conclusions must be conscious. But the "sinking," although economical, is still done at a price—[14]

according to Bateson, "the price of inaccessibility." *This* you have demonstrated is not true in the epistemology that you have arranged.

Since the level to which things are sunk is characterized by iconic algorithms and metaphor, it becomes difficult for the organism to examine the matrix out of which his conscious conclusions spring. Conversely, we may note that what is common to a particular statement and a corresponding metaphor is of a generality appropriate for sinking.[15]

John: As you heard me say before,

It is sometimes said that the distortions of art (say, van Gogh's "Chair") are directly representative of what the artist "sees." If such statements refer to "seeing" in its simplest physical sense, (e.g., remediable with spectacles), I presume that they are nonsense. If van Gogh could only see the chair in that wild way, his eyes would not serve properly to guide him in the very accurate placing of paint on canvas. And, conversely, a photographically accurate representation of the chair on the canvas would also be seen by van Gogh in the wild way. He would see no need to distort the painting (to begin with).

But suppose that we say that the artist is painting today what he saw yesterday—or that he is painting what he somehow knows that he might see. "I see as well as you do—but do you realize that this other way of seeing a chair exists as a human potentiality? And that that potentiality is always in you and in me?" Is he exhibiting symptoms which he might have, because the whole spectrum of psychopathology is possible for us all?

Intoxication by alcohol or drugs may help us to see a distorted world, and these distortions may be fascinating in that we recognize the distortions as ours. In vino pars veritatis. We can be humbled or aggrandized by realizing that this, too, is a part of the human self, a part of Truth. But intoxication does not increase skill—at best it may release skill previously acquired.

Without skill (there) is no art. . . .

It was noted above that consciousness is necessarily selective and partial, *i.e.,* that the content of consciousness is, at best, a small part of truth about the self. But if this part be selected in any systematic manner, it is certain that the partial truths of consciousness will be, in aggregate, a distortion of the truth(s) of some larger whole.

In the case of an iceberg, we may guess, from what is above surface, what sort of stuff is below; but we cannot (necessarily) make the same sort of extrapolation from the content of consciousness. . . . Such a selection . . . would only promote optimism.

What is serious is the crosscutting of the circuitry of the mind. If, as we must believe, the total mind is an integrated network (of propositions, images, processes, neural pathology, or what have you —according to what scientific language you prefer to use), and if the content of consciousness is only a sampling of different parts and localities in this network; then, inevitably, the conscious view of the network as a whole is a monstrous denial of the integration of that whole. From the cutting of consciousness, what appears above the surface is arcs of circuits instead of either the complete circuits or the larger complete circuits of circuits.[16]

John: You can do better now. That what this epistemological enterprise has been about.

What the unaided consciousness (unaided by art, dreams, and the like) can never appreciate is the systematic nature of mind.

This notion can conveniently be illustrated by an analogy: the living human body is a complex, cybernetically integrated system. This system has been studied by scientists—mostly medical men—for many years. What they now know about the body may (aptly) be compared with what the unaided consciousness knows about the mind. Being doctors, they had purposes: to cure this and that. Their research efforts were therefore focused (as attention focuses the consciousness) upon those short trains of causality which they could manipulate, by means of drugs or other intervention, to correct more or less specific and identifiable states or symptoms. Whenever they discovered an effective "cure" for something, research in that area ceased and attention was directed elsewhere. We can now prevent polio, but nobody knows much more about the systemic aspects of that fascinating disease. Research on it has ceased or is, at best, confined to improving the vaccines.

But a bag of tricks for curing or preventing a list of specified diseases provides no overall wisdom. The ecology and population dynamics of the species has been disrupted; parasites have been made immune to antibiotics; the relationship between mother and neonate has been almost destroyed; and so on.

Characteristically, errors occur wherever the altered causal chain is part of some large or small circuit structure of system. And the remainder of our technology (of which medical science is only a part) bids fair to disrupt the rest of our ecology.

The point, however, which I am trying to make in this paper is not an attack on medical science but a demonstration of an inevitable fact: that mere purposive rationality unaided by such phenomena as art, religion, dream and the like, is necessarily pathogenic and destructive of life; and that its virulence springs specifically from the circumstance that life depends upon interlocking *circuits* of contingency, while consciousness can see only such short arcs of such circuits as human purpose may direct.

In a word, the unaided consciousness must always involve man in the sort of stupidity of which evolution was guilty when she urged upon the dinosaurs the common-sense values of an armaments race. She inevitably realized her mistake a million years later and wiped them out.

Unaided consciousness must always tend toward hate; not only because it is good common sense to exterminate the other fellow, but for the more profound reason that, seeing only arcs of circuits, the individual is continually surprised and necessarily angered when his hardheaded policies return to plague the inventor.

If you use DDT to kill insects, you may succeed in reducing the insect population so far that the insectivores will starve. You will then have to use more DDT than before to kill the insects which the birds no longer eat. More probably, you will kill off the birds in the first round when they eat the poisoned insects. If the DDT kills off the dogs, you will have to have more police to keep down the burglars. The burglars will become better armed and more cunning . . . and so on.

That is the sort of world we live in—a world of circuit structures —and love can survive only if wisdom (i.e., a sense or recognition of the fact of circuitry (and context)) has an effective voice.

What has been said so far proposes questions about any particular work of art somewhat different from those which have been conventionally asked by anthropologists. The "culture and personality school," for example, has traditionally used pieces of art or ritual as samples or probes to reveal particular psychological themes or states.

The question has been: Does the art tell us about what sort of person made it? But if art, as suggested above, has a positive function in maintaining what I called "wisdom," i.e., in correcting a too purposeful view of life and making the view more systematic, then the question to be asked of the given work of art becomes: What sorts of correction in the direction of wisdom would be achieved by creating or viewing (or participation in) this work of art?

The question (then) becomes dynamic rather than static.[17]

Judy: (reading from Carlos Castaneda's *Journey to Ixtlan,* Chapter 8: "Disrupting the Routines of Life.")

We spent all morning watching some rodents that looked like fat squirrels; don Juan called them water rats. . . .

I became engrossed in observing them and I had what would have been a field day for hunters as I spotted so many of them. And finally I could predict their movements almost every time.

Don Juan then showed me how to make traps to catch them. He explained that a hunter had to take time to observe their eating or their nesting places in order to determine where to locate his traps; he would then set them during the night and all he had to do the next day was to scare them off so that they would scatter away into his catching devices.

We gathered some sticks and proceeded to build the hunting contraptions. I had mine almost finished and was excitedly wondering whether or not it would work when suddenly Don Juan stopped and looked at his left wrist, as if he was checking a watch which he never had and said that according to his timepiece it was lunchtime. I was holding a long stick, which I was trying to make into a loop by bending it into a circle. I automatically put it down with the rest of my hunting paraphernalia.

Don Juan looked at me with an expression of curiosity then he made the wailing sound of a factory siren at lunchtime. I laughed. His siren sound was perfect. I walked towards him and noticed that he was staring at me. He shook his head from side to side.

"I'll be damned," he said.

"What's wrong?" I asked.

He again made the long wailing sound of a factory whistle.

"Lunch is over," he said. "Go back to work."

I felt confused for an instant, then I thought he was joking perhaps because we really had nothing to make lunch with. I had been so engrossed with the rodents that I had forgotten we had no provisions. I picked up the stick again and tried to bend it. After a moment don Juan again blew his "whistle."

"Time to go home," he said.

He examined his imaginary watch and then he looked at me and winked.

"It's five o'clock," he said with the air of someone revealing a secret. I thought that he had suddenly become fed up with the hunting and was calling the whole thing off. I simply put everything down and began to get ready to leave. I did not look at him. I presumed that he was also preparing his gear. When I was through I looked up and saw him sitting cross-legged a few feet away.

"I'm through," I said, "We can go any time."

He got up and climbed a rock. He stood there, five or six feet from the ground, looking at me. He put his hands to either side of his mouth and made a very prolonged and piercing sound. It was like a magnified factory siren. He turned around in a complete circle making the wailing sound.

"What are you doing, don Juan?" I asked.

He said that he was giving the signal for the whole world to go home. I was completely baffled. I could not figure out whether he was joking or whether he had simply flipped his lid. I watched him intently and tried to relate what he was doing to something he may have said or done before. We had hardly talked at all during the morning and I did not remember anything of importance.

Don Juan was still standing on the top of the rock. He looked at me, smiled, and winked again. I suddenly became alarmed. Don Juan put his hands over both sides of his mouth and let out another long whistle-like sound. He said that it was eight o'clock in the morning and that I had to get my gear set up again because we had the whole day ahead of us.

I was completely confused by then. In a matter of moments my fear mounted to an irresistible desire to run away from the scene. I thought don Juan was crazy. I was about to flee when he slid down the rock and came to me smiling.

"You think I'm crazy, don't you?"

I told him that he was frightening me out of my wits with his unexpected behavior.

He said that we were even. I did not understand what he meant. I was deeply preoccupied with the thought that his act seemed thoroughly insane. He explained that he had deliberately tried to scare me out of my wits with the heaviness of his unexpected behavior because I myself was driving him up the walls with the heaviness of my expected behavior. He added that my routines were as insane as his blowing his whistle.

I was shocked and asserted that I didn't really have any routines. I told him that I believed my life was in fact a mess because of my lack of healthy routines.

Don Juan laughed and signaled me to sit down by him. The whole situation had a mysteriously changed again. My fear had vanished as soon as he had begun to talk.

"What are my routines?" I asked.

"Everything you do is a routine."

"Aren't we all that way?"

"Not all of us. I don't do things out of routine."

"What prompted all this, Don Juan? What did I do or what did I say that made you act the way you did?"

"You were worrying about lunch."

"I didn't say anything to you. How did you know I was worried about lunch?"

"You worry about eating every day around noontime and around six o'clock in the evening and around eight o'clock in the morning," he said with a malicious grin. "You worry about eating at those times even if you're not hungry.

"All I had to do to show your routine spirit was to blow my whistle. Your spirit is trained to work with a signal." He stared at me with a question in his eyes. I could not defend myself.

"Now you're getting ready to make hunting into a routine," he went on. "You have already set your pace in hunting; you talk at a certain time, you eat at a certain time, and fall asleep at a certain time."

I had nothing to say. The way don Juan had described my eating habits was the pattern I used for everything in my life. Yet I strongly felt that my life was less routine than that of most of my friends and acquaintances.

"You know a great deal about hunting now," don Juan continued. "It'll be easy for you to realize that a good hunter knows one thing above all—he knows the routines of his prey. That's what makes him a good hunter.

"If you would remember the way I have proceeded in teaching you hunting, you would perhaps understand what I mean. First I taught you how to make and set up your traps, then I taught you the routines of the game you were after, and then we tested the traps against their routines. Those parts are the outside forms of hunting.

"Now I have to teach you the final, and by for the most difficult, part. Perhaps years will pass before you can say that you understand it and that you're a hunter."

Don Juan paused as if to give me time. He took off his hat and imitated the grooming movements of the rodents we had been observing. It was very funny to me. His round head made him look like one of those rodents.

"To be a hunter is not just to trap game," he went on. "A hunter that is worth his salt does not catch game because he sets his traps, or because he knows the routines of his prey, but because he himself has no routines. This is his advantage. He is not at all like the animals he is after, fixed by heavy routines and predictable quirks; he is free, fluid, unpredictable."

What don Juan was saying sounded to me like an arbitrary and irrational idealization. I could not conceive of a life without routines.

I wanted to be very honest with him and not just agree or disagree with him. I felt that what he had in mind was not possible to accomplish by me or by anyone.

"I don't care how you feel," he said. "In order to be a hunter you must disrupt the routines of your life. You have done well in hunting. You have learned quickly and now you can see that you are like your prey, easy to predict."

I asked him to be specific and give me concrete examples.

"I am talking about hunting," he said calmly. "Therefore I am concerned with the things animals do; the places they eat; the place, the manner, the time they sleep; where they nest; how they walk. These are the routines I am pointing out to you so you can become aware of them in your own being.

"You have observed the habits of animals in the desert. They eat and drink at certain places, they nest at specific spots, they leave their tracks in specific ways; in fact, everything they do can be foreseen or reconstructed by a good hunter.

"As I told you before, in my eyes you behave like your prey. Once in my life someone pointed out the same thing to me, so you're not unique in that. All of us behave like the prey we are after. That, of course, also makes us prey for something or someone else. Now, the concern of a hunter, who knows all this, is to stop being a prey himself. Do you see what I mean?"

I again expressed the opinion that his proposition was unattainable.

"It takes time," don Juan said. "You could begin by not eating lunch every single day at twelve o'clock."

He looked at me and smiled benevolently. His expression was very funny and made me laugh.

"There are certain animals, however, that are impossible to track," he went on. "There are certain types of deer, for instance, which a fortunate hunter might be able to come across, by sheer luck, once in his lifetime."

Don Juan paused dramatically and looked at me piercingly. He seemed to be waiting for a question, but I did not have any.

"What do you think makes them so difficult to find and so unique?" he asked.

I shrugged my shoulders because I did not know what to say.

"They have no routines," he said in a tone of revelation. "That's what makes them magical."[18]

John: Some of you have the option to make this gesture. Perhaps as important as anything we've done here is a commitment, made by both first and second attention, that you will review, on some periodic basis, the arrangements which have been made here and which you have exercised to ensure the kind of fluidity and grace and freedom that differentiates the hunter from the hunted Now, if you should arrange or decide to arrange a time and a place where you could even go off by yourself, I offer you a description of a celebration of life, a success, that was achieved by Carlos after years of hard work in his training as a hunter.

John: (reading from Carlos Castaneda's *Journey to Ixtlan,* Chapter 13: "Stopping the World.")

The next day as soon as I woke up I began to ask don Juan questions. He was cutting firewood at the back of his house, but don Genaro was nowhere in sight. He said that there was nothing to talk about. I pointed out that I had succeeded in remaining aloof and had observed don Genaro's "swimming on the floor" without wanting or demanding any explanation whatsoever, but my restraint had not helped me to understand what was taking place.

"It's like a disease," I said.

"There are no diseases," don Juan replied calmly. "There is only indulging. And you indulge yourself in trying to explain everything. Explanations are no longer necessary in your case."

I insisted I could function only under conditions of order and understanding. I reminded him that I had drastically changed my personality during the time of our association, and that the condition that had made that possible was that I had been able to explain to myself the reasons for that change.

Don Juan laughed softly. He did not speak for a long time.

"You are very clever," he finally said. "You go back to where you have always been. This time you are finished though. You have no place to go back to.

Don Juan's tone was friendly but unusually detached and that made me feel an overwhelming loneliness. I expressed my feelings of sadness. He smiled. His fingers gently clasped the top of my hand.

"We both are beings who are going to die," he said softly. "There is no more time for what we used to do. Now you must employ all the *not-doing* I have taught you and *stop the world.*"

Don Juan was alone in the house when I arrived the next morning. I asked him about don Genaro and he said that he was somewhere in the vicinity, running an errand. I immediately began to narrate to him the extraordinary experiences I had had. He listened with obvious interest.

"You have simply *stopped the world,*" he commented after I had finished my account.

We remained silent for a moment.

"What stopped inside you yesterday was what people have been telling you the world is like. You see, people tell us from the time we are born that the world is such and such and so and so, and naturally we have no choice but to see the world the way people have been telling us it is."

We looked at each other.

"Yesterday the world became as sorcerers tell you it is," he went on. "In that world coyotes talk and so do deer, as I once told you, and so do rattlesnakes and trees and all other living beings. But what I want you to learn is *seeing.* Perhaps you know how that *seeing* happens only when one sneaks between the worlds, the world of ordinary people and the world of sorcerers. You are now smack in the middle point between the two. Yesterday you believed the coyote talked to you. Any sorcerer who doesn't *see* would believe the same, but one who *sees* knows that to believe that is to be pinned down in the realm of sorcerers. By the same token, not to believe that coyotes talk is to be pinned down in the realm of ordinary men."

"Do you mean, don Juan, that neither the world of ordinary men nor the world of sorcerers is real?"

"They are real worlds. They could act upon you. For example, you could have asked that coyote about anything you wanted to know and it would have been compelled to give you an answer. The only sad part is that coyotes are not reliable. They are tricksters. It is your fate not to have a dependable animal companion."

"If I were you," he added, "I would never trust a coyote. But you are different. . . .[19]

Judy: From *The Forest People:*

> One night in particular will always live for me, because that night I think I learned just how far away we civilized human beings have drifted from reality. The moon was full, so the dancing had gone on for longer than usual. Just before going to sleep I was standing outside my hut when I heard a curious noise from the nearby children's bopi. This surprised me, because at nighttime the Pygmies generally never set foot outside the main camp. I wandered over to see what it was.
>
> There, in the tiny clearing, splashed with silver, was the sophisticated Kenge, clad in bark cloth, adorned with leaves, with a flower stuck in his hair. He was all alone, dancing around and singing softly to himself as he gazed up at the treetops.
>
> Now Kenge was the biggest flirt for miles, so, after watching

a while, I came into the clearing and asked, jokingly, why he was dancing alone. He stopped, turned slowly around and looked at me as though I was the biggest fool he had ever seen; and he was plainly surprised by my stupidity.

"But I'm *not* dancing alone," he said. "I am dancing with the forest, dancing with the moon." Then, with the utmost unconcern, he ignored me and continued his dance of love .[20]

AFTERWORD

This man of the early race . . . dearly loved his black and white cattle. He always took them out into the veld himself, chose the best possible grazing for them, and watched over them like a mother over her children, seeing that no wild animals came near to hurt or disturb them. In the evening he would bring them back to his kraal, seal the entrance carefully with branches of the toughest thorn, and watching them contentedly chewing the cud, think, "In the morning I shall have a wonderful lot of milk to draw from them." One morning, however, when he went into his kraal expecting to find the udders of the cows full and sleek with milk, he was amazed to see they were slack, wrinkled and empty. He thought with immediate self-reproach he had chosen their grazing badly, and took them to better grass. He brought them home in the evening and again thought, "Tomorrow for a certainty I shall get more milk than ever before." But again in the morning the udders were slack and dry. For the second time he changed their grazing, and yet again the cows had no milk. Disturbed and suspicious, he decided to keep a watch on the cattle throughout the dark.

In the middle of the night he was astonished to see a cord of finely-woven fibre descending from the stars; and down this cord, hand over hand, one after another came some young women of the people of the sky. He saw them, beautiful and gay, whispering and laughing softly among themselves, steal into the kraal and milk his cattle dry with calabashes. Indignant, he jumped out to catch them but they scattered cleverly so that he did not know which way to run. In the end he did manage to catch one; but while he was chasing her the rest, calabashes and all, fled up the sky, withdrawing the cord after the last of them so that he could not follow. However, he was content because the young women he had caught was the loveliest of them all. He made her his

wife and from that moment he had no more trouble from the women of the people of the sky.
His new wife now went daily to work in the fields for him while he tended his cattle. They were happy and they prospered. There was only one thing that worried him. When he caught his wife she had a basket with her. It was skillfully woven, so tight that he could not see through it, and was always closed firmly on top with a lid that fitted exactly into the opening. Before she would marry him, his wife had made him promise that he would never lift the lid of the basket and look inside until she gave him permission to do so. If he did a great disaster might overtake them both. But as the months went by, the man began to forget his promise. He became steadily more curious, seeing the basket so near day after day, with the lid always firmly shut. One day when he was alone he went into his wife's hut, saw the basket standing there in the shadows, and could bear it no longer. Snatching off the lid, he looked inside. For a moment he stood there unbelieving, then burst out laughing.
When his wife came back in the evening she knew at once what had happened. She put her hand to her heart, and looking at him with tears in her eyes, she said, "You've looked in the basket."
He admitted it with a laugh, saying, "You silly woman. You silly, silly creature. Why have you made such a fuss about this basket? There's nothing in it at all."
"Nothing?" she said, hardly finding the strength to speak.
"Yes, nothing," he answered emphatically.
At that she turned her back on him, walked away straight into the sunset and vanished. She was never seen on earth again.

The Heart Is The Hunter

FOOTNOTES

Preface

1. We have heard several variations on this story. The only written reference we found occurs in John R. Ross' thesis published under the title *Infinite Syntax* (Ablex Publishing Co., Norwood, NJ, 1986), where a version appears as the Fragestellung. As Ross comments, it may be apocryphal.

Day One

1. Gregory Bateson, *Steps to an Ecology of Mind* (New York: Ballantine Books, 1972), p. 128.
2. William Shakespeare, *Macbeth,* Act II, Scene I.
3. Richard Lewontin, "Adaptation," *Genetics*; introduction by Cedric I. Davern, W. H. Freeman and Co., San Francisco, 1981, pp. 253-255.
4. Ibid., p. 257.
5. Derek Blickerton, "Creole Dialects," *Scientific American* 249: 116-22, January 1983.
6. Tepilix Ore Saitoti, *The Worlds of a Masai Warriors* (New York: Random House, 1985).
7. Colin Turnbull, *The Forest People* (New York: Simon and Schuster, 1961), pp. 252-53.
8. Ibid., pp. 132-33.
9. The material offered here regarding the ! Kung San comes from a number of sources, primarily *The ! Kung San* by Richard Borshay Lee, Cambridge University Press, London, 1979, and the series of books by Laurens Van Der Post on the ! Kung San.
10. Robert A. Heinlein, *Stranger In A Strange Land*, New York, 1968.
11. H. Storm, *Seven Arrows* (New York: Ballantine Books, 1973).
12. Roger Fisher (personal communication).
13. Claudia J. Carr, *Patoralism in Crisis: The Dasanetch and Their Ethiopian Lands* (Chicago: University of Chicago Press, 1977).
14. Jay Haley, ed., *Advanced Techniques of Hypnosis and Psychotherapy* (New York: Grune and Stratton, 1967).
15. Gregory Bateson, *Steps to an Ecology of Mind* (New York: Ballantine Books, 1972).
16. The material in this discussion is drawn from Chapter 4 of *Variations In Human*

Physiology, edited by R. M. Case, Manchester University Press, Manchester, England, 1985.
17. E. Boring, *History of Experimental Psychology* (New York: Appleton-Croft, New York, 1957).
18. E. Tolman, *Purposive Behavior in Animals and Men* (New York: Appleton-Century, 1932).
19. J. B. Watson, *Behavior: An Introduction To Comparative Psychology* (New York: H. Holt, 1915).
20. H. Gleitman, "Place Learning," *Psychobiology: The Biological Basis of Behavior*, edited by McGaugh, Weinberger and Whalen (San Francisco and London: W. H. Freeman and Co., 1966).

Day Two

1. Carlos Castaneda, *The Fire From Within* (New York: Simon and Schuster, 1984), p. 25.
2. Gregory Bateson, *Steps To An Ecology of Mind* (New York: Ballantine Books, 1972), p. 73.
3. Carlos Castenada, *Tales of Power* (New York: Simon and Schuster, 1974), pp. 231-33, 245, 247-48, 265.
4. W. R. A. Muntz, "Vision in Frogs," *Psychobiology: The Biological Basis of Behavior*, edited by McGaugh, Weinberger and Whalen (San Francisco and London: W. H. Freeman and Co., 1966).
5. Carlos Castenada, *Journey To Ixtlan* (New York: Simon and Schuster, 1972), p. 71.
6. Carlos Castaneda, *The Fire From Within* (New York: Simon and Schuster, 1984), p. 29.
7. Gregory Bateson, *Steps to an Ecology of Mind* (New York: Ballantine Books, 1972), p. 434.
8. Robert Heizer and Albert Eisasser, *The Natural World of California Indians* (Berkeley, CA: University of California Press, 1980).
   B. J. LeBoeuf and Stephanie Kaza, eds., *The Natural History of Ano Nuevo* (Pacific Grove, CA: The Boxwood Press, 1981).
9. "Capoeira: A Martine Art From The Streets and Jungles of Brazil Comes North," *Co-Evolution Quarterly*, Summer 1983, p. 122.
10. George Polya, *Patterns of Plausible Inference* (Princeton: Princeton University Press, 1960).
   George Polya, *Induction and Analogy in Mathematics* (Princeton: Princeton University Press, 1954).
11. Roger Fisher and Willian Ury, *Getting To Yes* (Middlesex, England: Penguin Books, Ltd., 1981).
12. Polya, ibid.

Day Three

1. Carlos Castenada, *Tales of Power* (New York: Simon and Schuster, 1974), p. 126.

2. Gregory Bateson, *Steps to an Ecology of Mind* (New York: Ballantine Books, 1972), p. 445.
3. Carlos Castaneda, *The Fire From Within* (New York: Simon and Schuster, 1984), p. 75.
4. George A. Miller, *The Magic Number Seven Plus or Minus Two, American Psychologist,* 1956.
5. H. Gleitman, edited by McGaugh, Weinberger and Whalen, *Place Learning in Psycho Biology* (San Francisco and London: W. H. Freeman and Co., 1966).
6. T. Taber, *The Santa Cruz Mountain Trail Book* (San Mateo, CA: Oak Valley Press, 1985), p. 10.

Day Four

1. Gregory Bateson, *Steps to an Ecology of Mind* (New York: Ballantine Books, 1972), p. 128.
2. Konrad Lorenz, *Studies in Animal and Human Behavior, Volume I & II* (Cambridge: Harvard University Press, 1970),.
3. Rupert Sheldrake, *Biology: A New Science of Life* (Los Angeles: J. P. Tarcher, Inc., 1981), p. 186.
4. Wolfgang Kohler, *The Mentality of Apes* (New York: Harcourt, Brace and Co., 1927).
5. Konrad Lorenz, *Studies in Animal and Human Behavior, Volume I & II* (Cambridge, Mass: Harvard University Press, 1970).
6. Wolfgang Kohler, *The Mentality of Apes* (New York: Harcourt, Brace and Co., 1927).
7. Schmidt-Nielsen and Schmidt-Nielsen, *The Desert Rat.* Introduction by Norman Wessells (San Francisco: W. H. Freeman and Co.), p. 30.
8. M. Hilderbrand, "How Animals Run," *Vertebrate Adaptations*. Introduction by Norman Wessells (San Francisco: W. H. Freeman and Co.), p. 30.
9. Ferdinand de Saussure, *Course in General Linguistics* (London: Duckworth, 1983).
10. Rupert Sheldrake, *Biology: A New Science of Life* (Los Angeles: J. P. Tarcher, Inc., 1981).
11. Gregory Bateson, *Mind and Nature* (New York: E. P. Dutton, 1979), p. 54.

Day Five

1. Gregory Bateson, *Steps to an Ecology of Mind* (New York: Ballantine Books, 1972), p. 139.
2. Richard Bandler and John Grinder, *The Structure of Magic* (Palo Alto, CA: Science and Behavior Books, 1975), introduction.
3. Gregory Bateson, *Steps to an Ecology of Mind* (New York: Ballantine Books, 1972), p. 139.
4. Ibid.
5. Ibid.
6. Ibid.
7. Ibid., p. 140.
8. Ibid.
9. Ibid.

10. Konrad Lorenz, "The Evolution of Behavior," *Psychobiology: The Biological Basis of Behavior*, edited by McGaugh, Weinberger and Whalen (San Francisco and London: W. H. Freeman and Co., 1966), p. 33.
11. Gregory Bateson, *Steps to an Ecology of Mind* (New York: Ballantine Books, 1972), p. 139.
12. Ibid., p. 143.
13. Ibid., p. 140.
14. Ibid., p. 141.
15. Ibid., p. 142.
16. Ibid.
17. Ibid., p. 143-44.
18. Carlos Castenada, *Journey to Ixtlan* (New York: Pocket Books, 1972), pp. 71-76.
19. Ibid., pp. 246-47.
20. Colin Turnbull, *The Forest People* (New York: Simon and Schuster, 1961), p. 272.

BIBLIOGRAPHY

Bandler, Richard and John Grinder. *Reframing*. Moab, Utah: Real People Press, 1982.

Bandler, Richard and John Grinder. *Frogs Into Princes*. Moab, Utah: Real People Press, 1979.

Bandler, Richard and John Grinder. *The Structure of Magic, Vol. I.* Palo Alto, CA: Science and Behavior Books, 1975.

Bandler, Richard and John Grinder. *The Structure of Magic, Vol. II.* Palo Alto, CA: Science and Behavior Books, 1976.

Bandler, Richard and John Grinder. *Patterns of the Hypnotic Techniques of Milton H. Erickson, M.D., Vol. I.* Cupertino, CA: Meta Publications, Inc., 1977.

Bandler, Richard and John Grinder. *Patterns of the Hypnotic Techniques of Milton H. Erickson, M.D., Vol. II.* Cupertino, CA: Meta Publications, Inc., 1978.

Bandler, Richard, John Grinder, and Virginia Satir. *Changing With Families.* Palo Alto, CA: Science and Behavior Books, Inc., 1978.

Bateson, Gregory. *Mind and Nature.* New York: E. P. Dutton, 1979.

Bateson, Gregory. *Steps To An Ecology of Mind.* New York: Ballantine Books, 1972.

Castenada, Carlos. *The Eagle's Gift.* New York: Simon and Schuster, 1981.

Castenada, Carlos. *The Fire From Within.* New York: Simon and Schuster, 1984.

Castenada, Carlos. *Journey to Ixtlan.* New York: Simon and Schuster, 1978.

Castenada, Carlos. *Tales of Power.* New York: Simon and Schuster, 1974.

Davern, Cedric I. *Genetics*—Reading from *Scientific American.* San Francisco and London: W. H. Freeman and Co., 1981.

Dilts, Robert, John Grinder, Richard Bandler, Judith DeLozier, and Leslie Bandler. *Neuro Linguistic Programming.* Cupertino, CA: Meta Publications, Inc., 1979.

Fisher, Roger and William Ury. *Getting To Yes.* Middlesex, England: Penguin Books, 1981.

Fundamentals of Neurophysiology. Ed. Robert F. Schmidt. New York, Heidelburg, Berlin: Springer-Vertig, 1975.

Gallway, W. Timothy. *The Inner Game of Golf.* New York: Randon House, 1979.

Grinder, John and Michael McMaster. *Precision: A New Approach To Communication.* Bonny Doon, CA: Precision Models, 1980.

Grinder, John and Richard Bandler. *Trance-Formations.* Moab, Utah: Real People Press, 1981.

Jaynes, Julian. *The Origin of Consciousness in the Breakdown of the Bicaminal Mind.* Boston: Houghton Mifflin Company, 1974.

Kohler, Wolfgang. *The Mentality of Apes.* New York: Harcourt, Brace and Co., 1927.

Lee, Richard Borshay. *The ! Kung San.* London: Cambridge University Press, 1979.

Lorenz, Konrad. *Studies in Animal and Human Behavior, Vol. I & II.* Cambridge, Mass: Harvard University Press, 1970.

Psychobiology: The Biological Basis of Behavior. Eds. James L. McGaugh, Norman Weinberger and Richard Whalen. San Francisco and London: W. H. Freeman and Co., 1966.

Sheldrake, Rupert. *A New Science of Life.* Los Angeles: J. P. Tarcher, Inc., 1981.

Turnbull, Colin M. *The Forest People.* New York: Simon and Schuster, 1962.

Van der Post, Laurens. *The Heart is The Hunter.* New York: Harcourt, Brace and Co., 1960.

Variations in Human Physiology. Ed. R. M. Case. England: Manchester Press, 1985.

Vertebrate Adaptations—Reading from *Scientific American.* Ed. Norman K. Wessells. San Francisco and London: W. H. Freeman and Co., 1968.

Grinder & Associates
• Books

A Framework For Excellence: A Resource Manual For NLP
Charlotte Bretto
ISBN 0-929514-03-3 PB

Leaves Before The Wind
Edited by Charlotte Bretto, Judith DeLozier, John Grinder & Sylvia Topel
ISBN 1-55552-051-0 PB

Making The Message Clear: How To Master The Business Communication Tools That Direct Productivity, Excellence And Power
James Eicher
ISBN 1-55552-048-0 PB

Patterns of the Hypnotic Techniques of Milton H. Erickson, M.D. Vol. I
Richard Bandler & John Grinder
ISBN 1-55552-052-9 PB

Patterns of the Hypnotic Techniques of Milton H. Erickson, M.D. Vol. II
John Grinder, Judith DeLozier & Richard Bandler
ISBN 1-55552-053-7 PB

Practical Magic
Stephen R. Lankton, ACSW
ISBN 0-916990-08-7 PB

Precision: A New Approach To Communication
Michael McMaster & John Grinder
ISBN 1-55552-049-9 PB

Turtles All The Way Down: Prerequisites For Personal Genius
John Grinder & Judith DeLozier
ISBN 1-55552-022-7 PB